P9-AFE-228

Without God, Without Creed

New Studies in American Intellectual and Cultural History
Thomas Bender, Consulting Editor

Without God, Without Creed

The Origins of Unbelief in America

James Turner

THE JOHNS HOPKINS UNIVERSITY PRESS
Baltimore and London

Originally published, 1985
Johns Hopkins Paperbacks edition, 1986
Third printing, 1991

The Johns Hopkins University Press
701 West 40th Street
Baltimore, Maryland 21211
The Johns Hopkins Press Ltd, London

Library of Congress Cataloging in Publication Data

Turner, James, 1946–
Without God, without creed.
(New studies in American intellectual and cultural history)
Bibliography: p.
Includes index.
1. Irreligion—History. 2. Irreligion—United States—History. I. Title. II. Series.
BL2757.T87 1985 211′.8′0973 84–15397
ISBN 0–8018–2494–X
ISBN 0–8018–3407–4 (pbk.)

∞ The paper used in this publication meets the minimum requirements of American National Standard for Information Sciences—Permanence of Paper for Printed Library Materials, ANSI Z39.48-1984.

For My Mother

The event illuminates its own past,
but it can never be deduced from it.

HANNAH ARENDT

Contents

Preface

On an autumnal day in 1869, Charles Eliot Norton sat down in his Swiss resort to write to his friend and confidant John Ruskin. Norton moved with ease among the most eminent writers of England and America. Son of the distinguished Unitarian theologian Andrews Norton, he had helped to found the *Nation* and had recently retired as editor of the *North American Review*. He counted among his intimates James Russell Lowell, Thomas Carlyle, John Ruskin, Henry Wadsworth Longfellow, and Frederick Law Olmsted and shared friendships as well with such men as Charles Darwin, John Stuart Mill, Charles Dickens, Louis Agassiz, and Oliver Wendell Holmes. Few men were as well positioned to register the early tremors of any slippage in the primordial strata of Anglo-American culture.

"There is a matter on which I have been thinking much of late," he confessed to Ruskin. "It does not seem to me that the evidence concerning the being of a God, and concerning immortality, is such as to enable us to assert anything in regard to either of these topics." As he tried to sort out the implications of his loss of faith, Norton wondered, "What education in these matters ought I to give my children? . . . It is in some respects a new experiment."[1]

It was in many respects a new experiment. For over a thousand years Europeans had assumed the existence of God. Their faith might be orthodox or heretical, simple or complex, easy or troubled—and for serious, thoughtful people, it was very often troubled, complex, even heretical. Yet failing to believe somehow in some sort of deity was not merely rare; it was a bizarre aberration. Then, in Norton's generation, thousands, eventually millions of Europeans and Americans began to abandon their belief in God. Before about the middle of the nineteenth century, atheism or agnosticism seemed almost palpably absurd; shortly afterward unbelief emerged as an option fully available within the general contours of Western culture, a plausible alternative to the still dominant theism.[2]

The shock waves still reverberate. Since the end of classical antiquity, God had provided the axiom from which followed all comprehension of man, nature, and cosmos. Then His existence itself became debatable, and the center fell out of Western intellectual life. If divine purpose did not undergird the cosmos, then whole structures of meaning collapsed and new ones had to be built up, brick by precarious brick. Most Americans—probably most Western Europeans—continue to believe in God; for these individuals belief can matter a great deal. But for the common life of our culture, it matters very much less. The option of not believing has eradicated God as a shared basis of thought and experience and retired him to a private or at best subcultural role. The bulk of modern thought has simply dispensed with God. If we wish to understand our own thinking, our public intellectual life, we must know how unbelief became possible.

We do not. The origins of unbelief still lack a full and systematic explanation, although I hasten to add that utter bafflement hardly prevails. Much solid research has explored aspects of the problem: Renaissance and Enlightenment scepticism, the effects of Biblical criticism, the impact of Darwinism on theology, the rise of scientific naturalism, the implications of post-Cartesian philosophy, and more. And out of this work arises a vague but compelling impression that the rise of science, and the spread of critical ways of thinking associated with science, undermined belief in God. This view in fact dates back to the Victorians who first collectively wrestled with and wrote about the crisis of faith. More recent historians have called attention also to the effects of industrialization, urbanization, and technological change, as well as to the less easily defined social change labeled secularization. Other corrosive forces occasionally attract attention, but scholars usually identify science and socioeconomic change as the sources of God's problems.

Yet no one has put the whole story together. We still await a comprehensive answer to that fundamental question: Why did it become possible not to believe in God? Thus, this book: a first approximation to such an answer.

As I began to trace the origins of unbelief, it slowly dawned on me that the pattern I was seeing did not fit conventional expectations, including my own. The individual elements (mostly well known to specialists) conformed to anticipated contours, but the contours together produced a surprising picture, almost a photographic negative of what I had expected to see. Though both science and social transformation loom large in the picture, neither caused unbelief. To believe that either did, I now think, is to stand the problem of unbelief on its head, to give credit to the blueprint but ignore the architect who drafted it, and ultimately to distort the history of Western religion from the sixteenth century through the nineteenth. Put briefly, unbelief was not something that "happened *to*" religion.

On the contrary, religion caused unbelief. In trying to adapt their religious beliefs to socioeconomic change, to new moral challenges, to novel problems of knowledge, to the tightening standards of science, the defenders of God slowly strangled Him. If anyone is to be arraigned for deicide, it is not Charles Darwin but his adversary Bishop Samuel Wilberforce, not the godless Robert Ingersoll but the godly Beecher family.

This story, as I soon discovered, gets complicated; and the book necessarily partakes of its complexity. So I want to make very clear at the outset exactly what my subject is. The best way to begin doing that is to explain what it is not. First, I am *not* talking about secularization: the shrinking influence of religion on other aspects of social and intellectual life. Second, I am not concerned with changes in church-going nor the waxing and waning of piety. Nor, third, do I focus on the fate of any particular theologies or conceptions of God, not even Christianity in general. And, fourth, I am not in any basic way interested in the world views (or "religions") eventually developed by unbelievers; still less do I wish to estimate the numbers of unbelievers or analyze their social distribution. Disavowal of present interest implies no deprecation of importance. All of these issues illuminate modern culture and society. Good books have been written, and remain to be written, about each. Moreover, each does in fact play into my own concern. But each remains subordinate to the question I *am* asking: How did the practically universal assumption of God disappear?

Put otherwise, this book, despite all the theologians and ministers who populate its pages, is not really about religious history.

It does not ask about religious experience, much less the personal authenticity of faith. The book is, rather, a work of intellectual history and, more precisely, a study of the fate of one idea: the belief that God exists. I care (in these pages) not what personal resonances the idea of God set off, not what forms it took, not even whether people bothered to worship the God they believed to exist. I care about a very different kind of question: how the *available ideas* in the culture changed so as to make unbelief viable. A religiously oriented reader might well complain that my impoverished definition of "belief" leaves out most of what really matters about belief in God: its personal depth and meaning. An intellectual historian might complain that my blinkered approach scants the many varieties of belief. And both complaints would be justified, from their respective points of view, but they would also be irrelevant. For, completely aside from its personal spiritual import, and without respect to its many varieties, the mere assumption of God's existence—that simple, universal axiom—had tremendous intellectual importance. The unadorned fact that it became optional is more than worthy of attention—it demands explanation. But perhaps I have conceded too much. Even speaking religiously, does it matter not a whit that today a lot of people do not believe in God at all? In any case, the purpose of this book is simply to explain how it became possible for many people to say, "I do not believe in God." No more—and no less.

Immediately a question arises. What does it mean "not to believe in God"? "God" has never enjoyed a single straightforward definition. Indeed, one can scarcely penetrate the thicket of formulations that have proliferated around "belief in God." Within the Jewish and Christian traditions alone, God has assumed every guise from pure Light to superintendent of village affairs; belief has encompassed the longings for both mystical union and more rain. In medieval and early modern Europe, belief in God among ordinary folk seemed to express primarily two needs: a search for personal salvation and a structure of social bonds.[3] But this by no means exhausted the meanings of belief, which ranged from the Scholastic quiddities of Thomas Aquinas to the unsettling mysticism of Meister Eckhart to the legalistic system-building of John Calvin. No single statement could possibly incorporate the bewildering richness of belief at every stage of the European tradition.

Yet, for the purposes of this book, a workable definition of belief is feasible. What requires explanation, after all, is not the waning of particular faiths but the questioning of a reigning assumption common to all of them. Until little more than a century ago, virtually everyone within the orbit of European culture agreed that a superhuman power was somehow responsible for the universe and that this fact determined the purpose of life. Other sorts of divinities, with different relations to the cosmos and its inhabitants, can be conceived; but these alternatives never figured as God for Europeans and their American descendants. When I write of "unbelief," therefore, I mean simply the continuing absence of a conviction that any such superhuman power exists.[4]

Even in this strictly limited sense, the origins of unbelief can present labyrinthine confusions. "European civilization" includes not one but a multitude of intellectual heritages and social histories. Since widespread unbelief appeared throughout the West in the same century, one suspects that the same general causes produced it. Nevertheless, cultural differences altered its tone and timing from country to country, even region to region. In Germany, for example, unbelievers commonly spoke the language of the physiological laboratory, while in Italy they marched under political banners. Unbelief flourished in the northeastern United States when the South still scarcely knew it. To reduce such complications and to manage the vast bulk of evidence, I have concentrated on Anglo-American culture, progressively narrowing my lens, as the story grows more detailed after 1800, to focus on the United States. No compelling reason dictates this choice (or any other). But America does offer me familiar terrain, and it also lacks the strong anticlerical traditions that complicate the history of unbelief in most European countries. I would not pretend that the emergence of unbelief in the United States replicated its appearance in European or other American nations, but I do hope that what happened here will provide clues to a better understanding of its evolution throughout the Western world.

Practicality has compelled a similar limitation in tracing the religious lineage of unbelief. I have usually kept my eye on Protestantism and, within Protestantism, most often on the American Reformed tradition, very broadly defined: Congregationalists, Presbyterians, Quakers, Unitarians, the more liberal Methodists and Baptists, and inheritors who departed from this background, such as Transcendentalists and radical abolitionists. To an American historian this orientation seems almost predestined. Reformed Protestantism and its offshoots dominated the American religious scene, at least intellectually, through all the years covered by this book. Forced to single out a religious tradition as the American mainstream, one could point only to this one. Moreover, insofar as one can calculate, most of the first generation of unbelievers—and their unbelief—grew up in this background. But I should not wish to be taken as claiming some kind of exclusivity for Reformed Protestantism as a breeder of unbelief. There were other roads to unbelief; these proliferated once the option of unbelief was established. I do, however, think that the Reformed tradition played, in America, a vanguard role in the initial breakthrough from belief to unbelief.

The book divides naturally into two parts. The first, ranging from the sixteenth century to the middle of the nineteenth, sketches (in increasing detail, but still only sketches) the changes in religion that laid the foundation of unbelief. Readers who know religious history will find that this section neglects many important features of the landscape, and a writer with different intentions would certainly have seen another pattern. For I have picked out elements significant for the rise of unbelief and let the rest fall by the wayside.

The second section, covering roughly the years from 1865 to 1890, traces the actual emergence of unbelief. These dates mark off the period in which unbelief achieved its mature form; I trust that readers will understand them as approximate guides, not sharp boundaries. In this latter section most of the evidence comes from a small but diverse (and I think representative) assortment of articulate unbelievers. In part this limitation reflects the difficulty of finding, not unbelievers, but unbelievers who discussed at length their objections to belief and their sense of the superiority of unbelief. But this tight focus results more from a conscious decision to recur frequently to the same figures in different contexts. I hope that readers might thereby get a richer, more nuanced feeling for the subtle interworkings of the ideas and attitudes that led to unbelief.

And now I must ask the readers of this essay in unbelief to suspend their own beliefs. We all tend to project our own convictions about the existence of God onto the canvas of history. If believers, we often view agnostics and atheists as misguided and look for the missteps that led them into error. If unbelievers, we regard God as a delusion and His abandonment as a natural stage of man's maturation. Both perspectives paralyze the disinterested yet sympathetic curiosity with which the historian, neither believer nor unbeliever, hopes to find human truth. And we need all the open-mindedness we can muster, for that truth, never fully attainable, is often elusive indeed. If at times I seem to revel in involutions or delight in wandering through backwaters, I ask patience. There is no expressway through the human consciousness.

Acknowledgments

Any writer who attempts a work of this scope soon acquires a salutary awareness of his dependence on the help of others—the generations of scholars, the critical audiences, the librarians, the secretaries, the colleagues and friends. Only the work itself can repay these debts; but the personal ones can at least be acknowledged.

Donald Fleming continues the exemplary guide; I have pillaged his erudition, taken advantage of his sharp eye for writing, and in general exploited his generosity more shamelessly than I care to admit. Several other friends read an early draft. Russell Blake and Barbara McGowan pointed out many obscure passages; Francis Broderick ruthlessly disciplined my prose; Jack Censer refused to despair of me as a social historian; and Jane Turner Censer, associate editor of the Frederick Law Olmsted Papers, supplied not only her own surgical criticisms but also the many quotations from that cautious agnostic's letters. Harvey Graff's mark rests indelibly on chapter 4, Robert Greene's on chapter 1. William Hutchison's critique clarified the treatment of Evangelicalism, while Martin Marty offered sage advice about the book's structure. Comments on earlier work by Thomas Brown and Reneé Watkins influenced what is at once elusive and determinative: the tone and temper of approach.

I owe a great deal to four research assistants, Peter Hinks, Katharine Powers, Wu Jie, and especially Thomas Proctor, and to the staff of the Charles Warren Center at Harvard during my year there, Patricia Denault, Sally Sweet, and Mary Anne Causino. The History Department of the College of Charleston in a sense began the project by a reduced teaching load in 1977; during 1979–80 the University of Massachusetts-Boston provided leave, and the Charles Warren Center for Studies in American History a congenial home. The generous assistance of the National Endowment for the Humanities also helped to bring this book into existence. I have many reasons to be grateful to librarians and archivists at Widener Library and Houghton Library of Harvard University, the College of Charleston library, the Library of Congress, and the Southern Historical Collection of the University of North Carolina at Chapel Hill. I owe a special debt to Walter Grossman and the librarians at the University of Massachusetts-Boston, especially the energetic Jeri Vargo and her staff. At the Johns Hopkins University Press, Henry Tom remains a sharp and encouraging editor, while Carol Ehrlich's meticulous attention and fine literary touch saved the author from many embarrassments, the reader from many puzzles.

Without God, Without Creed

Prologue

By chance, a bundle of cracked and yellowed manuscripts has survived centuries of fire, flood, war, and revolution to allow a remarkable glimpse into daily life in a French mountain village around the turn of the fourteenth century. The village was called Montaillou, and its local drama centered on the village priest. This tireless servant of the Lord appears to have construed his calling chiefly as ministering to the sexual needs of his female parishioners. Less literally carnal but equally worldly concerns preoccupied his flock. One thing strikes modern eyes as remarkable about this collection of rogues (or perhaps run-of-the-mill human beings). Although they habitually flouted God's laws, wallowed in heresy, and thumbed their noses at God's Church, it never occurred to them to doubt His reality. The villagers faithfully performed the exercises of salvation, invoked Christ, the Virgin, and the saints, and sought absolution for their sins.[1] By no stretch of the imagination did God obsess them, yet He framed their world.

In their ingrained belief the folk of Montaillou typified the religious life of medieval Europe, up until at least the sixteenth century. The religion of the common folk appears often to have been more a kind of collective habit than personally felt belief, their beliefs perhaps closer to folklore than Christianity. Ordinary people often knew nothing of the most fundamental doctrines. Nor was irreligion rare at higher and better informed social levels. But belief in God seems to have remained all but universal.[2]

This universal assumption of Deity did not restrain radical questioning of every other religious belief, nor did it necessarily mean that belief in God Himself came easily. All manner of scepticism and infidelity flourished among both the literate elite and the common folk. The long train of heresies that bedeviled the medieval Church is well known, and Christians more than occasionally slipped over the border into Islam. The court of the astonishing Holy Roman Emperor Frederick II (1194–1250) won notoriety, at least in papal circles, for a deeper scepticism.

Amid these diverse scepticisms, a more fundamental doubt probably intruded on occasion. An individual can question his own existence, at least momentarily; it would have been miraculous had doubts about God's existence never crossed anyone's mind. Even in a culture infused with the axiom of God, feelings of despair, aloneness, and futility could evoke a sense of the unreality of all that could not be seen or touched. Some such gnawing uncertainty seems to have formed part of the spiritual anguish that the Spanish mystic St. John of the Cross (1542–1591) later called "the dark night of the soul."[3] We know little about the inner lives of medieval men and women, but we cannot assume that they never underwent this trauma.

However, such questioning could sustain itself and grow into lasting disbelief only if nourished by social and intellectual sustenance. Food for unbelief did not suffice in medieval culture. So passing doubts withered, the desert was crossed, belief in Deity endured. The absence of atheism has never discouraged defenders of orthodoxy from accusing people of it. But there is no clear evidence that any permanent state of unbelief, genuine atheism or agnosticism, ever actually existed in the Middle Ages.

Indeed, it is a difficult question whether unbelief could have existed. The distinguished French historian Lucien Febvre argued that, as late as the sixteenth century, disbelief in God was literally a cultural impossibility.[4] At least as regards the sixteenth century, Febvre probably overstated his case—but not by much. Even to reject Christianity was difficult in a culture permeated by it: difficult, but not impossible, for other living religious traditions implicitly challenged Christianity. But all serious alternatives assumed some sort of God. Little, if anything, existed to support real doubt about God Himself. So interwoven was God with daily life and with the workings of nature that virtual extraction from one's surroundings would have been necessary to make unbelief plausible.

The social environment played a large part in securing God

from questioning. Although religious practice was often spasmodic and at times as nearly pagan as Christian, religious observance in some form or another remained integral to the social fabric. For the individual, swathed in communal ritual, birth meant baptism; adulthood brought marriage by the priest; and life's journey ended in the churchyard but in a sense continued amid the chanting of masses for the dead. These rites of passage stood out against a daily backdrop of routinely mumbled prayer, wayside shrines, and special invocations (by priest or wise woman) when the rain failed or a child sickened, the church spires looming over city and village alike. Much of social life centered on religious confraternities. Holidays—note the etymology of the word—saw festive processions, a saint's statue parading the streets. Guilds, towns, royal courts marked their triumphs and sorrows by hearing mass collectively. Sacred anointment bestowed legitimacy on the king himself. In this atmosphere the existence of God became as natural and almost as inevitable as breathing.[5]

The patterns of medieval thought also forestalled doubt about God's reality. One could not satisfactorily explain the world without Him. Intellectual activity depended on God for coherence. Why did plants grow and the sun rise? What held the stars and planets in their orbits round the earth? Why did the cosmos exist? How did life—vegetable, animal, and human—come to exist? Why did folk think, and think as they did? Why was it wrong to kill another, and why was it sometimes right? Why must the rich succor the lowly, and the mean submit to the mighty? How did kings come to exist, and whence arose their authority? Through tangled labyrinths of explanation, through folk beliefs and philosophies, the answer to all of these questions, elaborated in a thousand tales, sermons, treatises, and summas, led back ultimately to God. Without some sort of God, the world disintegrated into incomprehensibility. In a medieval mentality, giving up God meant abandoning any coherent world picture. Unbelief therefore came close to being, in the primal meaning of the word, unthinkable.

To a postmedieval religious sensibility, these social rituals and intellectual presuppositions have little to do with authentic belief. And the complaint is well lodged. Belief, in the limited sense intended here, did not necessarily inspire devotion nor even interest in God. Whoring, murdering, and grinding the faces of the poor went happily along with unquestioned acceptance of God's existence. Indeed, believers may have grown more *concerned* about God when He became less certain. Moreover, apart from the issue of devoutness, a vast gap divided the religion of Thomas Aquinas or that of Francis of Assisi from the magic of the village wise woman or the half-Christian practices of her clients.

The point is not that God's pervasiveness in the culture made for a uniform type of belief, much less that it made saints, but rather that it made God's existence extremely difficult to question seriously for any length of time. However shallow or varied the *effect* of belief on different groups and individuals, the *assumed reality* of God twined inextricably through all their lives. Indeed, so basic was God to medieval man that belief in Him often seems not so much a formal tenet as an apperception hovering around the edges of consciousness. Belief, whatever else it became, almost verged on a felt sense of the structure of things, in the way that one "believes" in the change of the seasons or the rising of the sun.[6] Unbelief in God thus required so extreme an estrangement from "obvious reality" as to be, if not strictly impossible, practically so for medieval men and women.

Yet by the late nineteenth century unbelief had become a fully available option. How this happened is a formidable and complex question. If God permeated the world, how could normal people cease to believe in Him? How could a culture dispense with one of its most deeply rooted, most essential axioms? Modern unbelief burst into full blossom in American culture rather suddenly, in a few decades after 1850. But no great cataclysm then made it possible. Rather, many changes in belief, some rapid and striking, some so glacially slow as almost to escape detection, gradually accumulated and interacted over hundreds of years. Only at the end of this road did many erstwhile believers find God no longer there. In fact, the story begins long before serious doubts of His existence arose, as the world of Montaillou began to fade.

I

Modern Belief, 1500–1865

1

A New Age

One fine summer Sunday in 1667, Samuel Pepys strolled toward Whitehall. "Being weary," his diary relates, he stepped into St. Dunstan's Church to listen to the sermon. The sermon was "able" but did not distract Pepys from "a pretty, modest maid" whom he "did labour to take by the hand and the body." Pepys sidled toward her; the modest maid edged away, until "at last I could perceive her to take pins out of her pocket to prick me if I shall touch her again." Undaunted, Pepys rounded on "another pretty maid in a pew close to me." More complaisant or less well armed, she let Pepys hold her hand, "which she suffered a little and then withdrew. So the sermon ended, and the church broke up, and my amours ended also."[1]

This scene smacks of Montaillou, with its casual mingling of the sacred and profane, its snubbing of God in a setting predicated on His unquestioned reality. Yet Samuel Pepys (1633–1703) walked in a world as far removed from Montaillou as his own London is from us. Even his immorality (and he always regretted his philandering as wrong) diverged subtly but unmistakably from that of the folk of Montaillou. A few months after evading the pins of St. Dunstan's, Pepys was leafing through his bookseller's wares when he chanced upon "the most bawdy, lewd book that ever I saw," a French production so obscene "that I was ashamed of reading in it." Three weeks later he came back to buy it—but in plain binding "because I resolve, as soon as I have read it, to burn it." The next morning (a Sunday) Pepys slipped away to his office with his purchase; that evening, as soon as he could hurry away some dinner guests, he repaired to his chamber to finish reading. Thereupon he did burn the offensive volume. He could not dispatch his conscience so easily. Pepys, needing to justify himself to himself, assured his diary that the book "doth me no wrong to read for information sake."[2]

What makes this little episode revealing is not Pepys's almost routine lapse from grace but his characteristic wrestling with his conscience. This sense of struggle less often stirred the typically more casual moral climate of the Middle Ages. Driven by some confused impulse to suppress his unruly desires, Pepys cloaked all diary references to sexual activity (even with his wife) in a weird jumble of Spanish, French, and Latin. Throughout the diary, the dominant moral note is the need—and frequent guilty failure—"to command myself."[3] Although Pepys had left his Puritan antecedents far behind him, a moral intensity uncommon a few centuries earlier still discomfited his inner life.

Indeed, the dawn of a new and in some ways more troubled age suffused the religious background of Pepys's life: the "business of religion doth disquiet everybody." Europe had for over a century suffered discord and warfare as the medieval church split asunder. Less clamorous but perhaps even more radical disturbances had also shaken Christendom. In July 1666, Pepys heard a sermon (a bad one, he reported) on a topic not uncommon in pulpits of his day: "the great point of proving the truth of the Christian religion."[4] The need of addressing that great point would scarcely have crossed the mind of a medieval preacher.

What was this new environment of religious belief? How did God stand in it?

The Church in Retreat

The religious "disquiet" of which Pepys wrote sprang from a number of disruptions—political, social, and intellectual. Of these, the most publicly jarring was the Protestant Reformation. The leaders of the medieval church often had, of necessity, exercised their supposed primacy very loosely. The "unity" of Christendom covered some quite divergent beliefs and practices. Nevertheless, ecumenical councils did agree on anathemas; papal jurisdiction did eventually compel compromise if not submission; a more or less common liturgy and a more or less shared creed held Europe more or less together. Heresy existed, but so did an ecclesiastical institution and belief system with enough power and legitimacy eventually to crush or absorb heresy. The universal church amounted to less than its own ideal but a good deal more than fiction.

The Reformation shattered this unity, much against the wishes of the leading reformers. Instead of the universal church, churches emerged, spelled out their differences, and competed with each other—often violently, always vocally. Protestant was set against Catholic, then Protestant against Protestant. Religion and politics swirled together in fratricidal wars that ravaged France, the Low Countries, Germany, and England in the century after Luther posted his theses. The peace settlements, cobbled together when all sides had grown too exhausted to kill their countrymen any longer, usually involved a de facto neutralization of key social and political institutions so that citizens of the major sects could adhere to them.

This pattern unfolded erratically, as the inclinations of monarchs and pressures of circumstance dictated. The Dutch, driven to the wall in their struggle to throw off the Spanish yoke, agreed out of desperation to tolerate each other's beliefs even before the sixteenth century ended. The English meanwhile teetered on the verge of a century of internecine strife that subsided only after the Glorious Revolution of 1688 opened politics to all Trinitarian Protestants and granted grudging concessions even to Catholics. Three years earlier, however, Louis XIV had revoked the limited toleration granted Huguenots by Henri IV in 1598; and the French state sporadically persecuted Protestants, though with flagging zeal, until the eve of the Revolution.

This rise of religious competition affected in two ways the future of belief in God. First, open religious debate, sometimes about the most fundamental Christian doctrines, occasionally raised questions that probed even deeper (more about this later). Second, squabbles among churches, and the toleration eventually imposed to reestablish civil peace, compromised church authority and accelerated a process of secularization already under way for other reasons.

During the Middle Ages, no clear line separated the religious from the secular. To be sure, popes and emperors clashed over their respective powers, but both claimed spiritual as well as temporal jurisdiction; and this overlap was typical in all areas of life. The church and the world blended. Parishes provided local government, and holy days seasonal celebrations. Universities were as fully church institutions as monasteries, and the clerks who struggled to bring order to the king's chaotic finances were, as the word suggests, clerics. And why not? Many bishops felt more at home in royal councils than ecclesiastical ones. A man might hate the church, but he could avoid it no more than the rising and setting of the sun. The church was as inevitable as death and taxes, one of which it presided over and the other of which it collected.

Temporal rulers seldom rejoiced at the church's power. They needed the church and its functionaries, but they also resented it as a barrier to their own ambitions. Toward the end of the Middle Ages, the increasing cohesion and efficiency of central governments began to weld fragmented feudal kingdoms into modern nation-states. The enhancement of the state put more power into the hands of princes and enabled rulers like Henry VII of England (reigned 1485–1509) and Francis I of France (reigned 1515–1547) to chip away at the church's independent influence, to subordinate more of its activity to their own political purposes. The church remained very much a force to be reckoned with, but its grip over politics and society began to loosen somewhat as the state's grip tightened.

The Reformation speeded this tendency. As the price of maintaining civil peace and the necessary minimum of popular allegiance, governments had to put some distance between themselves and the quarreling churches. State churches remained the rule, but with a much diminished range of influence. The churches found themselves increasingly confined to religious, charitable, and educational functions, increasingly excluded from legal and political power. Separation of church and state proceeded slowly and haphazardly. Catholics did not gain full political rights in England, for example, until 1829; Jews not until 1858. Religious tests for Oxford and Cambridge degrees were eliminated only in 1871. But the civil power of the churches had centuries before begun substantially to diminish, the extent of their influence palpably to contract.

At the same time as state power and religious toleration undermined ecclesiastical sway, economic innovations were also weakening the churches' leverage on the populace.[5] The fecund marriage between capitalism and technology made it more difficult for the churches to exercise effectively whatever legal authority they retained.

The most celebrated offspring of this union was printing. Before printing, the church, standing at the center of both intellectual and village life, had considerable power to organize the flow of ideas, even to some extent of everyday news. The village pulpit served as a conduit for royal commands as well as a local bulletin board. The church's universities performed a similar function in the more rarefied world of ideas. Control was, however, anything but absolute: suspect manuscripts circulated, and folk traditions flourished that flouted Christian orthodoxy. The official church itself showed notable suppleness over the centuries in accommodating new perspectives. Nevertheless, the church's control over crucial switching-points in the circuits of intellectual communication placed large obstacles to the development and spread of dissenting ideas.

The printing press dynamited these barriers. From the mid-fifteenth century onward, the proliferation of books and pamphlets multiplied the sources of ideas and information and multiplied the readers of each source. And the authorities found it harder to suppress hundreds of copies of a printed book than a few copies of a manuscript. The printing press effectively ended church regulation of learning. Nor was its effect limited to scholars. In the tiny Italian village where a miller called Menocchio lived in the sixteenth century, a network of humble readers flourished, eking out their coins by sharing books. Books filled Menocchio's head with strange news: knowledge that inspired even stranger speculations when he tried to fit it with his own oral culture. These unorthodox ideas led him into the hands of the Inquisition, and only for that reason does any trace of Menocchio survive. But there surely were others for whom the printing press made absurd "the pretension of priests to maintain their monopoly over a knowledge that could be bought for '2 soldi' on Venetian book sellers' stalls."[6] Ecclesiastical censorship could in the long run no more regulate this tide than Canute could hold back the waves.

Other children of early capitalism also contributed to curbing the church's influence over people's minds. Expansion of trade increased the number of travelers and, more spectacularly, the distances traveled; new worlds opened to Europeans, filled with exotic plants, exotic peoples, and exotic religions. The creation of joint-stock companies, banks, and stock exchanges swelled the number of institutions over which churches exercised little or no authority yet which absorbed the energies of more and more men. This proliferation of secular experiences and organizations hardly constituted a rebellion against the church, any more than did Gutenberg's Bible. But the number of secular voices was growing.

As secular voices displaced clerical ones, the church's influence diminished bit by bit. These small, even imperceptible, abridgments accumulated, the abrasion of religious dissension, political autonomy, and economic change each wearing away ecclesiastical power year by year. From decade to decade no noticeable difference appeared. But from 1500 to 1700 the relationship of many people to the church changed dramatically.

Look again at Samuel Pepys—hardly a typical Englishman but, as secretary of the Admiralty and president of the Royal Society, one of considerable stature. His affairs make clear how much the church's authority had diminished. Pepys always maintained a politic conformity to the Church of England, even seemed fond of it in a mild way (though clerical influence often left a bad taste in his mouth). He despised atheism, conventionally enough. But that was about as specific as his loyalty to religion became, and the church no longer wielded the power to regulate his wanderings. Pepys comfortably attended Roman Catholic mass at the queen's chapel and indulged his curiosity with a visit to a synagogue. He carried on an active intellectual life—but wholly within secular institutions like the Royal Society. He contributed to the improvement of education—but by encouraging secular training in subjects like navigation. In earlier centuries so prudent a careerist as Pepys would have indulged these interests within the church, would have avoided heretical worship, and would have quelled his unguarded speculations on religion. But by his generation the English church had lost much of its hold over inquiring yet conventional men.[7]

The effect should not be exaggerated. The church in Pepys's day still, for example, retained a firm grip on formal education, and outward conformity remained the high road to worldly success. More important, the shrinking role of the *church* did not make Europe less *religious.* Indeed, disturbers of the church often appeared more devout than its defenders. Nor did secularization significantly undermine Christianity: the reverse may have occurred. Perhaps on the average believers actually developed a firmer and more comprehending faith as a result of freer religious discussion combined with the advent of printing. Of the books published in Paris just before the mid-seventeenth century, 48 percent concerned Christianity; fifty years later the figure was still 49 percent. Not until the eighteenth century do publishers, in France at least, appear to have redirected their lists toward the modern predominance of secular writings.[8] A strong argument could be made that, with worldly ambitions curtailed and legal powers shorn, the churches exercised deeper spiritual influence.

Yet the stunting of church authority and the weakening of church influence did have important consequences for belief. Secularization stripped away one sort of built-in protection of religious belief. When the church formed a pervasive part of the social and cultural background, questions about its assertions were less likely to arise; when secularization put the church at a greater distance, gave more perspective on it, people became more likely to wonder about its claims, perhaps even its axiomatic principles. More concretely, the church's words, though still formidable, competed with a widening range of alluring voices that (while rarely anti-Christian) did not have the church's vested commitment to defend Christianity. Not dishonesty but training and personal situation made a clerical scholar less likely than a secular inquirer to turn up uncomfortable religious questions; not self-interest alone but a sense of its mission made the church more likely than the Royal Society to discourage investigations that challenged orthodox beliefs. And, to unsettle matters further, ecclesiastical authority tottered just when an unprecedented wave of geographic and scientific discoveries poured a flood of new information into European minds.

The door opened to all sorts of religious questioning. When John Bunyan wrestled with the devil in the 1650s, the Old Deceiver asked him how he could "tell but that the Turks had as good Scriptures to prove their *Mahomet* the Saviour, as we have to prove our *Jesus* is."[9] Granted, Bunyan's grasp of Islamic theology seemed shaky, but two hundred years earlier how many Englishmen of Bunyan's limited education would have known that Islamic scriptures existed? How many would have thought to compare the authority for Jesus' teachings with that for Mohammed's? Most relevant, would an account of such a temptation have been heard of or read by the thousands who read Bunyan? What the devil hinted to Bunyan he elaborated far more dangerously in the writings of a sceptic like Thomas Hobbes. But the point is not that explicitly sceptical writings circulated widely in the seventeenth century (though some did). The point is that even devoutly orthodox Christians encountered questions that earlier would never have achieved public notoriety. A new structure for intellectual life had taken shape, a secularized structure less subject to churchly restraints, more open to conflicting ideas, less apt to stultify or freeze out questioning about God and His ways.

New Knowledge of a New World

Construction of this secularized mental framework had only begun when, between the middle of the sixteenth century and the end of the seventeenth, there exploded a burst of new ideas.

These demolished the familiar medieval picture of nature and of human society. They implied, in fact, a new approach to knowing both physical and human reality. As men struggled to piece together with this new method a new cosmos, they had also to puzzle out how God fit into it. For any conception of the Creator must come to terms with how one conceives of His creation.

The Scientific Revolution makes up the best-known part of this story. The basically Aristotelian cosmology of the late Middle Ages had depicted a hierarchical universe of concentric spheres. These centered on the mutable earth and rose through realms of changeless splendor to the sphere of the fixed stars. Beyond the sphere of the stars lay the abode of God, His angels, and His saints. God Himself imparted motion to the several spheres, which wheeled eternally in perfect circles.[10]

This finite, bounded cosmos, vast in dimension but compact in conception, fell comfortably enough within human comprehension. Its hierarchical structure even lent it, by analogy with human societies, a certain familiarity. Man himself, though living in sublunar squalor on a tiny sphere at the lowest point of the cosmos, nevertheless stood at the center of things, acting out his petty deeds and misdeeds directly under the watchful eye of God.

Copernicus and his successors shattered this world. Between the publication of his treatise *On the Revolutions of the Heavenly Spheres* in 1543 and the appearance in 1687 of Isaac Newton's *Mathematical Principles of Natural Philosophy,* a radically different universe unfolded. Gone were the hierarchically ascending spheres, replaced by a less clearly ordered cosmos of infinite extent, in which the earth had lost its central spot.[11] Gone, too, were the ancient four elements (earth, air, fire, and water) that had composed all the stuff of the world man knew, gone with the old Aristotelian principles that had for almost two millennia explained motion and chemical change.

For a long while confusion reigned. New world pictures were devised; but none won general acceptance until the Newtonian system took shape near the end of the seventeenth century, finally to achieve consensus in the eighteenth. The seventeenth century was thus a time of immense excitement but even greater unsettlement. When in 1611 John Donne confronted the work of Copernicus, Kepler, Gilbert, and Galileo, he could make no sense of it all. The implications of magnetism and the telescope set his subtle head spinning. Aristotle was as dead as a stone, but only confusion survived him.

. . . new Philosophy cals all in doubt,
The Element of fire is quite put out;
The Sun is lost, and th'earth, and no mans wit
Can well direct him, where to looke for it.
And freely men confesse, that this world's spent,
When in the Planets, and the Firmament
They seeke so many new; they see that this
Is crumbled out againe to'his Atomis.
'Tis all in pieces, all cohaerence gone . . . .[12]

Many others were shaken by Donne's bafflement, his fear that man's grasp of the world had utterly slipped.

Amid confusion one thing was clear: the new universe dealt a blow to old familiar pictures of God. And the punch hit more of the psyche than the intellect, which made it all the harder to defend against. The universe, now less analogous in structure to human institutions, seemed less familiar, less likely to have been designed with human beings in mind. Its Creator grew more distant; an absolute monarch ruling over an infinite realm, He seemed less certain to be particularly concerned with man's fate. As the new cosmos pushed God farther away, so it shrank His creatures into profounder negligibility. Human beings now tenanted only an insignificant grain of sand floating in some indeterminate corner of an incomprehensibly vast congeries of worlds. Queen Christina of Sweden (1626–1689) feared the consequences, now that astronomy had banished man from the center of creation where God, so the church taught, had placed him.[13]

The first new cosmologies would not have justified the queen's fears. If anything, the earliest founders of modern astronomy intended to narrow the gap between God and man. A Neoplatonic mysticism probably encouraged Copernicus to place the sun, "the Visible God," at the center of his new system; at any rate, he invoked Neoplatonism in its defense. Such mysticism even more powerfully influenced Johannes Kepler's search for the laws of planetary motion and Giordano Bruno's assertion of the infinity of the universe.[14] In their view a seeker could, if enlightened through mathematical, Hermetic, astrological, or Cabbalistic studies, tune in directly to the mystic, divine life-currents behind the shadows of physical reality. The cosmos provided, potentially at least, a more direct channel of communication between God and man.

Yet Queen Christina's uneasiness was not misplaced. As the seventeenth century proceeded, a more mundane view of the universe challenged both the old Aristotelian and the new Neoplatonic cosmologies. It incorporated the sun-centered universe evolved under Neoplatonic influence. But in this version God set the cosmos in motion and sustained it without benefit of any mysterious spiritual forces through which one could commune with the divine. Instead, according to such earthbound natural philosophers as Galileo and Descartes, the universe constituted a kind of cosmic mechanism, cranking along according to regular natural rules that were expressed mathematically but shorn of mystical overtones.[15]

Mechanism did not drive mysticism from natural philosophy without a prolonged struggle. Isaac Newton himself, whose *Principia* was seized upon as the summation of the mechanical philosophy, strove mightily to keep science a sacred study and sought God through the mathematical laws of motion. The more thorough-going mechanist Leibniz assailed Newton's laws for needing occasional divine corrections of planetary motion. "God Almighty," he snorted, " wants to *wind up* his Watch from Time to Time." But Newton characteristically replied that these interventions, far from implying imperfection, evinced God's personal care for His creation. Newton believed in Pythagorean numerology and Cabbalistic mysticism and never deemed his pursuit of alchemy as in any way at odds with his *Principia*.[16]

The mystical side of Newton, however, represented a style of science beginning visibly to date by the last years of the seventeenth century. The victory of mechanism was far from complete around 1690, but the tide was clearly running in its direction. A new conception of the universe's operation formed. Although God's constant attention sustained the whole cosmos, He no longer took personal charge, as it were, of every detail. Instead, He commanded His creation to obey regular rules. Scientists interpreted physical events as nature's response to these divine commands; natural "laws," they said, "governed" the universe.[17]

This idea of natural law put a greater distance between a more impersonal God and His creation. A clearer distinction now separated the realm of law from the realm of grace, "natural" from "supernatural." This division mirrored the growing gap between the church and the secular world; secularization may even at some subliminal level have nurtured the scientists' new conception of divine action. In any case, this kind of thinking about God's relation to the world did not halt at the boundaries of natural philosophy. Students of history and society were simultaneously reassessing God's rule and coming to similar conclusions. There, too, in a desacralized understanding of the workings of human societies, God's actions acquired greater regularity and impersonality as He began to operate through secondary causes akin to natural laws.

Medieval chroniclers (when bothering at all to put their annals in a broader frame) had typically set human affairs within a supernatural scheme of salvation, progressing from the Fall through the Incarnation to the looked-for Second Coming and the end of time. But they hardly qualified as historians, for they lacked any sharp distinction between past and present. It was the Italian humanists, inspired by admiration for antiquity and contempt for the intervening centuries, who discovered that the outlook and customs of the past differed, sometimes radically, from their own.

Thus, roughly speaking, the modern study of history saw the light. The ultimate result, slowly accomplished, was to wrench history writing out of a theological framework and install it in a secular one. Less often did writers interpolate human events into God's eternal plan of salvation. More often did they view the vicissitudes of kingdoms and republics, ancient and modern, as the timebound outcome of human ambition and scheming and eventually of cultural, social, and economic forces as well.[18]

This new approach matured spasmodically, mostly outside of the chronicles themselves. Secular historiography germinated in the philology of Lorenzo Valla (1407–1458), and early in the next century Machiavelli ruthlessly expelled God from politics in *The Prince* (1513). In Tudor England, controversies over church, law, and language began to engender a consciousness of history as a product of human experience, a viewpoint distinct from (though not opposed to) theological interpretations of history. In the seventeenth century, these new attitudes shaped formal works of history such as the Earl of Clarendon's great *History of the Rebellion,* completed in the 1670s. Yet an unabashedly providential history like Cotton Mather's *Magnalia Christi Americana* appeared in 1702, and came from a man in many ways a figure of the Enlightenment.[19] Obviously no consensus existed.

Yet a sort of history very different from Mather's was on its way to becoming the norm. Robert Viscount Molesworth's *Account of Denmark* (1693), for example, though a heavy-handed morality tale, displayed no trace of the finger of God and even groped toward a socioeconomic explanation of political change.[20] Molesworth's *Account* and similar histories did not attempt to thrust God out of human affairs, but they removed Him from direct interference. They foreshadowed an emerging mode of understanding human society which assumed that God directed human action only through secondary causes.

This same point of view infiltrated inquiries into contemporary society. The Englishman Thomas Mun hypothesized in the 1620s a set of general principles that, he claimed, regulated economic activity. By the later seventeenth century, many others had come to believe that "commerce followed its own laws."[21] This novel assumption did not push God out of the picture. Morality still mattered; and Who, after all, had ordained these economic laws in the first place? But, like the natural laws of the scientific mechanists, they did make of God an impersonal distant force, regulating human affairs only at second hand.

A new mental world struggled to be born. These novel approaches to natural philosophy and social studies both fostered and reflected its emergence. So did a host of other intellectual changes: growing scepticism about magic, doubts about witchcraft, increasing fascination with machines.[22] All of these manifestations pointed toward a new cast of mind: more insistent on the regularity and orderliness of phenomena; more comfortable with tangible, measurable realities than with the unseen and mysterious; more dubious about traditional explanations and more inclined to experiment with new ones. This intellectual transformation was so amorphous that it defies specification, yet so crucial that it demands an effort at definition.

Roughly speaking, metaphorical and mythical explanations of reality gave way to formally rational ones couched in a linear logic of cause and effect. Medieval writers commonly imposed order on reality by fitting it into patterns of similar items. Explanations of the king's relation to the people he governed, for instance, drew analogies to God's relation with His creatures, the head's with the body, or a father's with his family. This analogical approach gradually yielded to the modern inclination to define relations of influence and causation—to fit reality into lines of cause and effect. Kingship thus came to be explained in terms of society's need for law and order. It was from precisely this standpoint that John Locke's two *Treatises on Civil Government* attacked Sir Robert Filmer's traditional analogical defense of the divine right of kings, *Patriarcha*, near the close of the seventeenth century.

The relevant question became less often, What is this like? and more frequently, Why does this happen? Renaissance figures like Johannes Kepler and Giordano Bruno had explained nature by analogies between macrocosm and microcosm. Their approach battled in the seventeenth century with the linear mechanistic philosophy. Galileo, Torricelli, and Newton's *Principia* explained nature by developing laws describing how a given phenomenon invariably followed from an antecedent one. Kepler asked, What moves the planets? and came up with a mystic emanation from the sun, analogous to the action of divine grace on the human soul. Newton's *Principia* asked, What moves the planets? and set forth a mathematical description of the force of gravity acting between heavenly bodies. Patterns of analogy faded before lines of cause and effect.

At the same time—and equally important in the new mental outlook—concreteness and precision became more valued attributes of knowledge. The taste for empirical testing increased (as in Galileo's urge for experiment), and people began to worry more about exactitude (as in the mathematizing of Newton's laws). Quantitative descriptions came to seem more certain than qualitative assessments. (Thomas Sprat, in his *History of the Royal Society* [1667], urged that words themselves be reduced "as near the mathematical plainness as possible.") Tradition lost some of its authority to experimentalism and personal experience, as people tended more to think out new solutions to particular problems rather than to rely on customary answers. Though best exemplified in science, this new approach was by no means confined to natural philosophers.[23]

Indeed, all of these traits shaped the enormously influential logical system of the French educational reformer Petrus Ramus (1515–1572). Ramus devised a system of dichotomies into which each bit of knowledge could be slotted. All knowledge became specifiable, definable data; each datum had its precisely ordered place. (It was no surprise that Ramus urged teachers to stress mathematics.) The voraciousness with which educators devoured Ramist method bespoke the tremendous popularity of this new approach to knowledge. Ramus's works (together with those of his collaborator Omer Talon) went through 1100 separate printings between 1550 and 1650. His logic became standard fare in school texts for generations. In far-away New England, Harvard College students droned over his system; even on Sundays they listened to sermons hewn by his method.[24]

Mental revolutions do not slip in overnight. This new cast of mind expanded certain intellectual habits that had been slowly gathering strength for centuries, then accelerated around the beginning of the sixteenth century. Medieval scholastic philosophers, for example, had displayed much more concern for "fixity and exactitude" than classical writers. Medieval logic, with its prominent use of quasi-arithmetical terms like "all," "every," and "no," was notably more quantitative than Aristotelian logic. And the scholastic concentration on Aristotelian physics and cosmology helped to orient thought "toward the observable, physical world more than had been usual before."[25]

The burgeoning of these new ways of thinking probably owed something to technological and economic changes. Communication by printing, as opposed to communication through personal contact, by its very nature espoused a less fluid, a more fixed and exact, form of knowledge. The printed page encourages authors to formulate their experiences and ideas as rigidly defined intellectual structures—units of meaning that a reader who does not share the author's experience and cannot cross-question him can readily grasp. The printed page indeed delivers an image of exactitude even when its content is lamentably different.

Likewise, rapid economic changes in this period of nascent capitalism may possibly have fostered the new mentality. Caution must, however, hedge any such speculation—after all, an early-modern merchant could easily cherish a very traditional world view, while a very noncommercial aristocrat could dabble enthusiastically in mathematical studies and chemical retorts. Nevertheless, certain specific economic situations may have inclined their occupants toward this modern style of thinking. A merchant trying to survive the fluctuations of distant little-known markets, a lens-grinder alert to changing techniques and uses of his trade, a bureaucrat struggling to bring order to the chaos of personal government in the new nation-states—all had powerful incentives to put aside tradition and apply their intellects to their problems in a more systematic, precise, concrete fashion than had their medieval ancestors.[26]

Samuel Pepys for instance: what Galileo did for natural philosophy, what Ramus did for education, what merchants were doing for commerce, Pepys did for the Royal Navy. "Method" was all. Pepys regularized purchasing arrangements, demanded strict accounting, inquired the exact dimensions and quality of ship lumber, instituted examinations for the lieutenant's commission, introduced rules regulating the flow of information, standardized the stationery at Woolwich Dockyard, even devised an analytic table for judging prospective chaplains! He also pioneered the impersonal style of communication that has since become the stamp of bureaucracy: each dispassionate letter of rebuke or pleading argued its case by reference to a supposedly objective set of "facts"; subjectivity and personal feeling had lost their place so far as Secretary Pepys was concerned. Off the job, Pepys became another story, yet even in private hours he took almost as much pleasure in casting his accounts or cataloguing his books as in chasing Mrs. Bagwell.

Impelled by this itch to rationalize the world and by his insatiable curiosity, Pepys pursued the new science with perhaps even more avidity than he did his wenches. At the Royal Society he heard Robert Hooke discourse on the periodicity of comets, observed the first efforts to transfuse blood, watched physiological experiments on dogs—these things fascinated him. He peered at Jupiter through his own telescope, acquired binoculars, a magic lantern, a microscope. More impressively, for a man who had to learn simple arithmetic after landing his Admiralty job, Pepys grew very interested in mathematics and apparently fairly accomplished. He was no virtuoso; more than once he confessed himself baffled by experiments he observed. Yet in the great naval crisis of 1667, with the Dutch in the mouth of the Thames and Pepys scurrying between London, Deptford, and Gravesend, he still took pleasure "as long as it was light reading Mr. Boyles book of *Hydrostatickes,* which is a most excellent book as ever I read."[27] The rationality of the man of business blended in Pepys with the rationality of the man of science. It was apt that Newton's great *Principia* bore on its title page, as imprimatur of the Royal Society, the name of Samuel Pepys.

Yet Pepys can give the wrong impression of his period. His new cast of mind had by no means routed more traditional ways of thinking. Indeed, there is real danger of exaggerating the speed and pervasiveness of change, since the seventeenth-century figures who still attract interest are the ultimate winners, like John Locke, and not the losers, like his antagonist Robert Filmer. The seventeenth-century mind remained very tradition-bound when compared, say, to Victorian culture reeling under the impact of factory and metropolis. Until late in the century, Filmer's brand of political theory exerted wider appeal than Locke's. Even Pepys's scientific rationality involved a more generous conception of what "reasonable" included than later generations might entertain. He regarded ghosts with a certain scepticism yet never denied their possibility, even considered them a fit subject for scientific investigation. Against all this, the new outlook continued to edge forward. One benchmark was the first appearance of the word "statistics," in a book published in 1672, just ten years after John Graunt's *Observations on the Bills of Mortality* had ushered in the analysis of social statistics.[28] But statistics did not stop highly educated men from relying on Biblical prophecies to calculate the welfare of England.

Challenges to Belief

Belief had to adapt. Or, to put the matter less abstractly, the guardians and interpreters of belief in God—priests, ministers, theologians, lay writers—had to come to terms with a radically changing social and intellectual environment. With the church's influence shrinking in an increasingly pluralistic and secularized society, conventional religious beliefs were less taken for granted, more exposed to questioning. With the old cosmology disintegrating, old understandings of God's relationship to man and nature were falling apart. With new approaches to knowledge gaining prestige, the old assumptions about how man knew God faced scepticism. The rules of the game shifted constantly; no one could predict the next hand.

No wonder the guardians of belief proved often skittish. No wonder they began to see atheists under the bed, especially after 1600. Their position was not enviable; they could no more predict the new world a-borning than they could cement Christendom together again. Yet they had to guide believers through these stormy waters—and without tacking to every fickle breeze. Their decisions called for extraordinary shrewdness and promised heavy consequences, for their choices would set the course for believers for centuries to come.

In its rawest form, the problem came down to the new cast of mind. It was already clear on the eve of the Reformation that linear, empirical, precise ways of thinking enjoyed increasing application. It was not clear even at the end of the seventeenth century how far and to what matters this modern approach to knowledge ought to extend. Church leaders, in effect, had continually to judge during that span of time how, if at all, this new mentality bore on religious beliefs. Should the church conclude that rationalization provided a solid approach to God as well as physical reality, build on the intellectualist heritage of medieval theology, expand the role of logic in religion, and weld belief securely to the new outlook? Or should theologians decide that the kind of concrete, precise thinking appropriate to natural philosophy and mercantile life did *not* suit thinking about God, reject it as misleading in religion, and bend their efforts to strengthening autonomous foundations for belief?

There was no easy answer, certainly no consensus. The sixteenth and seventeenth centuries witnessed, among other things, one of the greatest flowerings of mysticism in Christian history. Teresa of Avila, John of the Cross, Jakob Boehme, and George Fox all achieved their mystical illuminations between 1550 and 1650. This upwelling of spirituality was in no sense peripheral to the mainstream of Protestant or Catholic Reformations. SS. Teresa and John spearheaded the regeneration of the Carmelite order; George Fox founded the Quakers. Ignatius of Loyola is chiefly remembered as the activist creator of the Jesuits. But he passed through an inner conversion much like Martin Luther's (and only a few years later) and inscribed its effect in the *Spiritual Exercises,* probably the most widely employed manual of spirituality in the Christian tradition. Logic-chopping or scientific analysis this was not.

Yet an unmistakable current flowed also in the other direction. By the late seventeenth century, church leaders had gone a long way toward revising belief to fit the new intellectual style. Indeed, religious writers added notably to its spread, since the doctrinal controversies following the Reformation were commonly cast in the new mold. True, church leaders often seem to have moved toward rationalization without quite realizing what they were doing. Precisely because the new orientation affected so basic a level of thought, it was easy to slip into it without reflection.

The very meanings of "religion" and "belief" began subtly to change. Theology bulks large in church history, masking the fact that during the Middle Ages religion involved not so much assent to doctrines (though this formed part of it) as participation in devotion, particularly communal ritual. Religion was more a collective than an individual affair; and collectively it came closer to a system of practice than a parcel of tenets, while individually it meant more a person's devoutness than his adherence to a creed. In the earliest stages of the Reformation, this perception still dominated. Luther indeed scarcely used the word "religion"; his concern he called "faith." Calvin and Zwingli did write on "religion" but meant by it something roughly equivalent to piety.[29]

The Reformation, however, brought to the fore doctrinal disputes, first with Rome, then among the Reformers themselves. By so doing it put greater stress on doctrine. The ensuing orgy of creed making probably owed something to the advent of printing, which provided an ideal growth medium for theological polemics. But it owed much more to the Protestant spokesmen and Catholic apologists who chose to use the press (and councils and synods) to draw lines of division along ever-finer points of creedal logic. Protestantism began with the flourish of Luther's theses in 1517 and quickly radiated into a bewildering profusion of creeds. Earlier heretics had equaled Calvin's devoutness, but their zeal had never emanated anything like the elaborate logical architecture of his *Institutes of the Christian Religion* (1536, 1539). Rome's theologians measured up to the Protestant challenge, producing a flood of doctrinal definitions at the Council of Trent (1545–1563). By its educational and parochial reforms the Council also helped to ensure (as the Protestants did with their schools and preaching) that its conception of religion, and the intellectual style it reflected, would spread among the laity.[30]

This does not mean that creeds came to outweigh worship in religious life. The balance of the two defies calculation, but probably doctrine never overshadowed ritual or piety for the typical believer. Yet emphasis did shift toward doctrine. Fairly early in the Reformation, Protestants apparently began to conceive of religion as belief in the articles of a specific creed, at a time when Catholics still clung to the notion of religion as practice. Catholics soon drifted in the same direction, though perhaps never as far as the Reformed churches.[31]

What it meant specifically to "believe in God" also began to shift along a similar trajectory. Religious belief has always implied not only intellectual assent but approval and trust. To "believe in Christ," for instance, suggested both intellectual assent to the proposition that Christ is the Son of God and personal reliance on Christ as one's own hope. Historically the dominant sense of "believe" has been confidence in a person, not credence in a statement.[32] Yet if "belief in God" continued to include both connotations of the word, their relative weight did not remain constant. Theological warfare during the sixteenth and seventeenth centuries fostered an obsession with doctrinal distinctions, often drawn so finely as almost to disappear before a modern eye. This ingenuity of church leaders magnified the intellectual aspects of "believing," pushed belief closer to the new objectifying, logical, demonstrating cast of mind.

Belief in God by no means lost its footing in personal trust, but it came to depend more heavily on cognition and intellectual assent. It gravitated slowly from the subjective toward the objective mode. And this was hardly surprising: with a forest of doctrines enveloping thinking about God, the role of ratiocination in belief imperceptibly but steadily expanded. In the mid-seventeenth century, Lord Herbert of Cherbury expounded a method for weighing the truth of a religion. Herbert thought he could assay the validity of a faith simply by examining the propositions of its creed. No one before had ever proposed quite this. Yet subsequent writers (while often horrified at Herbert's conclusions) seldom found anything remarkable in his approach. Therein lay the magnitude of the revolution in "belief." Just as religion had become more a matter of creedal assent, so belief had become more an intellectual proposition subject to logical proof—like the propositions of natural philosophy.[33]

There was, emphatically, another side to the story. For Luther, Calvin, and the other Protestant reformers, religious belief was anything but a purely intellectual exercise; and, while the Tridentine reformers may have drummed doctrinal distinctions into the laity, above all they demanded regular religious practice in order to instill real interior devotion into folk whose religion previously had amounted mostly to external observance. The stress on belief as doctrinal assent in the sixteenth and seventeenth centuries formed part of a complex (sometimes even a balanced) whole. Cultivation of piety, personal faith, and mystical seekings flourished alongside it.

Church leaders did not turn belief into a baldly intellectual proposition; however, they did greatly expand the role of creed and doctrine in belief—and generally made doctrines more concrete and precise. By so doing they realigned belief more toward the realm of specifiable logical judgments and thus brought it closer to the new cast of mind displayed so well in natural philosophy. No wonder that Ramist schema proved a wholly congenial framework for thinking about God; by the seventeenth century the rationalization of belief had gone rather far.

And on this rationalized belief churchmen relied as they faced a threat that terrified some of them: the specter of atheism. Since antiquity the guardians of orthodoxy had occasionally cried atheist at heretics, but genuine fear of atheism seemed markedly to increase toward the end of the sixteenth century. An overwrought Bishop of Exeter complained in 1600 that his flock carried on a running dispute "whether there be a God or not." Treatises defending belief and assailing atheists began to appear in the decades before 1600 and multiplied thereafter. The number of such tracts mushroomed in the second half of the century as did their sophistication and coherence, beginning most notably with *An Antidote Against Atheisme* from the pen of the Cambridge Platonist Henry More in 1652; from then onward the presses fairly teemed with jumpy refutations of "the abounding atheism of this age."[34] There is no question that atheists authentically alarmed many religious leaders.

It is not so clear that any atheists actually existed. Searching for full-fledged deniers of God before the eighteenth century sometimes resembles hunting the unicorn. Part of the problem is that, lacking a tradition of open unbelief, contemporaries also lacked the vocabulary to describe it. Thus the word "atheism" could apply to everything from denial of the Trinity to gross immorality—and did. One Essex vicar prophesied that digging on the Sabbath would issue in "flat atheism." As Francis Bacon cannily observed, "All that impugn a received religion or superstition are by the adverse part branded with the name of atheists."[35]

If one unimaginatively takes the word "atheist" to mean someone who denied that any God exists, then the number of atheists before 1690 shrinks almost to the vanishing point. A Pyrrhonist scepticism derived from classical antiquity engaged a number of intellectuals of the sixteenth and seventeenth centuries (Montaigne, for example); these writers, sometimes labeled atheistic, questioned all *knowledge* of God (among other things) but finally left open a fideist path to *assurance* of His existence. The most feared "atheist" of the age was Thomas Hobbes. His materialism rightly sent shivers down Christian spines, but Hobbes left a place for a not very attractive God; few would now call him an atheist. It is not impossible that a few genuine atheists appeared among alehouse scoffers, but no convincing evidence supports the speculation. One could go on—Christopher Marlowe, for instance, may indeed have been an atheist—but the situation ought to be clear enough. Just possibly a few atheists lived between the Reformation and 1690; but their number, if greater than zero, must have been exceedingly tiny.[36]

Nor is their rarity surprising. The shattering of the medieval cosmology did not make God any less vital to a plausible picture of reality. For one thing, the unsettling new ideas changed even educated thinking slowly and incompletely. When Milton wrote *Paradise Lost,* well over a century after Copernicus, he laid out opposing arguments for both the Copernican and ancient Ptolemaic universes, then figuratively threw up his hands and refused to decide between them. Privately Milton probably inclined to Copernicanism, but he chose to frame the action of *Paradise Lost* in the Ptolemaic system, more familiar to his readers and more suited to the cosmic drama of the Fall.[37] The universities more often than not looked suspiciously on the upstart assertions of the new science; and secular historical consciousness, erratic even in a Molesworth, penetrated the culture even more spasmodically than did the implications of natural philosophy. Cotton Mather's *Magnalia* demonstrated that even an enthusiast of the new science could continue to conceive God as busily superintending human society.

More important, the new philosophy itself in no way curtailed the necessity of God. No clear distinction severed the connection between "natural" and "supernatural." And, while God might regulate the wheeling of the planets and the affairs of nations by predictable law, few doubted that He still kept His hand in everyday reality. Faith in God's regular laws seldom seemed at odds with faith in His irregular providential interventions. The Essex vicar Ralph Josselin (1617–1683) was, as a village youth around 1630, "much delighted with Cosmography," which suggests a more than ordinary attention to the new science. Certainly as he grew older Josselin thought of God as normally governing the world through regular natural laws. Yet to the end of his life he habitually regarded sickness, accident, and the weather as direct interventions by a personal God "present in every puff of wind." As the modern scholar Walter Ong has pointed out, the seventeenth-century mind did "not feel the exterior, objective world and the interior, personal world as distinct from one another quite to the extent that we do. Objects retain[ed] a more personal, or at least animistic, glow." Fellows of the Royal Society were prepared to accept ghosts and second sight. Yet it was not merely lingering habits that protected belief. Even those few minds who had entirely given the universe over to orderly natural law still needed to assume God's existence. For natural laws themselves presupposed a divine Lawgiver.[38]

Because unbelievers had no solid ground to stand on, it is no wonder that temptations to atheism (presumably present in all ages) brought undeniable anguish of spirit but very rare or no enduring unbelief.[39] Of course, to say that a mechanistic philosopher like Robert Boyle and a Quaker mystic like George Fox both believed in God is not to say very much—and even less if one adds the sceptical materialist Thomas Hobbes, who in important respects may have stood closer to atheism than to any live religious belief. The point here has nothing to do with authentic faith but only with available ideas. The existence of God remained so interwoven with understandings of man and nature as to be close to indubitable.

Were the antiatheist writers then paranoids and dimwits? Decidedly not. Sensible men might well take alarm, for both the church itself and the old pictures of God had certainly fallen into a crisis of confusion. John Donne was not the only one who suspected all coherence gone. With the church disunited and each sect denouncing the others, might not sceptics begin to doubt the validity of any belief whatsoever? Apologists pegged ecclesiastical disarray as a prolific source of atheism. Disturbing questions arose from other quarters to tug at the back of the mind—and, more upsetting, sometimes to appear in print. Did the remote impersonal Deity hinted at in science and social thought care about one's own fate? Could He—or It—indeed care about the human race, when the infinite universe might harbor countless intelligent species? Could the human mites in such a cosmos really have secure knowledge of God? Would concentration by the learned on secondary causes eventually obscure the First Cause? Worse, might mechanistic natural laws actually suffice to explain the world? Might God prove a needless hypothesis? And there perhaps lurked behind these worries a deeper, unarticulated question: did the new insistence on precise logical specification—the "clarity" that Descartes demanded—leave room for knowledge of an indefinable God?

When Blaise Pascal, on the night of 23 November 1654, gave up the God of the philosophers for the God of Abraham and Isaac, he personified the key religious problem of his age. Belief in God might still be virtually universal. But on what should belief rest in order to secure it in the new world taking form?

A Faith Reasonable and Moral

For the historian, the atheist controversy acts as a lens to bring into sharper focus certain tendencies and tensions beginning to shape belief in God. These particular developments were by no means the only ones of significance for religion. In truth, other changes mattered more for most sixteenth- and seventeenth-century Christians: strains and choices forced by church divisions; refinement and codification of traditional doctrines; exploration of mysticism and the "inner light"; growing regularity and frequency of religious practice; and, above all, that Christianizing of Europe in which all of the foregoing played a part and by which religion became for growing numbers of people no longer merely an external communal bond but an inward and personal experience. All this constituted the forcing-ground of new attitudes toward

God. Yet one must dig in other soil to learn why God Himself ultimately became less plausible.

As the intellectual environment altered in these centuries, people responded in four ways to the problems created for belief. One, probably typical of ordinary folk, was simple ignorance that anything much had changed. Another was to stand firm upon old ideas and reject any disconcerting novelties; the Inquisition taught Galileo how dangerous it could be to underestimate this impulse. The third was more accommodating: it maintained the autonomous bases of religious belief but accepted the new understandings of the natural and social worlds—and assumed that somehow no inconsistency spoiled the compromise. A good guess (nothing more is possible) is that most educated people were coming to something like this position by the end of the seventeenth century.

The fourth response threw caution to the winds—or perhaps calculated most cautiously of all. It asserted the universality and sovereignty of modern approaches to knowledge of reality. Perhaps man could know God through inner light and divine revelation as well as empirical rationality. But he could learn of nature and history in only one thoroughly reliable way: the new way. Since this cosmos and its human inhabitants had, after all, come from the hand of God, man must be able to understand the Creator in the same way as he understood the creation. And that way indeed provided the surest and safest road to knowledge of God, for reason and observation gave always the most certain knowledge of any reality that lay outside our own minds. Belief for its own good must therefore be fitted to the new cast of mind. This became the task of a growing number of writers, especially and self-consciously after 1650. A reasonable faith, they hoped, would stand secure against any onslaughts.

This posture dictated the strategy of most of the antiatheist polemicists. They fought, therefore, a war on two fronts. They attacked of course the elusive, perhaps even mythical, atheists. But they also battled the antirational mysticism and "enthusiasm" embodied in groups like the Quakers, who seemed to feel that belief in God fundamentally eluded rationality (not the same as saying that belief was irrational!) and therefore had to spring from some kind of intuitive perception rather than from analysis.[40] On the contrary, the rationalizers insisted, belief in God was entirely reasonable and plausible. And they trimmed it accordingly where its reasonableness seemed shaky. They played down creeds in general and mysterious doctrines in particular. Truth could not be obscure. They repudiated the metaphysical flights of scholasticism, both Catholic and Protestant, in favor of common-sense arguments grounded in palpable reality. Truth must be plain to see.

The new science offered an especially appealing field on which to vindicate the reasonableness of belief and throw atheists into confusion. The revolution in the heavens seemed to the great scientist Robert Boyle, for example, to demand a revolution in theology. Boyle, one of the most influential advocates of a mechanistic world view, described nature as "a matchless engine" and habitually spoke of God as its Engineer, operating the world-machine according to invariable rules. And in his *Christian Virtuoso* (1690) Boyle tried to show how the mechanistic universe proved to any rational inquirer the existence of a similarly rational Deity. The "exquisite wisdom, which the omniscient Maker has expressed" in both "the peculiar fabrics of bodies" and their "skilfully regulated motions" produce (claimed Boyle) "in the mind of an intelligent contemplator a strong conviction of the being of a divine Opificer, and a just acknowledgement of His admirable wisdom."[41] There is a degree of irony here. Theology was subjected to the Newtonian revolution long before many branches of science. This use of science soon became a phenomenally popular apologetic tool. On the preliminary constructions of a few men like Boyle there arose after 1690 an elaborate architecture of scientific natural theology.

The rationalizing temper typical of antiatheist writers hardly made them unique. Their vision of a reasonable Christianity touched a sympathetic nerve in many church leaders—and in a good many characters not strongly attached to any church. As well it might: the obsession with doctrinal disputes in the wake of the Reformation, while its stress on creeds disturbed "reasonable Christians," nevertheless displayed an intellectualizing impulse that pushed religion more into the realm of logic and evidence. And a simple, plain religion—a faith on which almost all Christians could agree—gave some hope, however illusory it finally proved, of reuniting the fragmented shards of the church. More generally, the new cast of mind described earlier put a premium on palpable, common-sense "reasonableness." As the poet Abraham Cowley wrote, "Our Reasoning Faculty as well as Fancy, does but Dream, when it is not guided by sensible Objects."[42] The popularity and evident success of the new science attested Cowley's point.

Rationalization offered anxious Christians a temptation hard to resist. Reasonable Christianity was the touchstone of the widely-read Anglican Latitudinarian theologians of the late seventeenth century. But it appealed equally to men with no ecclesiastical ax to grind, and they were the ones that churchmen most wanted to reach. Samuel Pepys believed that an honest man had to approach the questions of divinity, as all else, with a sceptical, inquiring mind. Only by following a road such as that blazed by the Royal Society—the path of investigation, precise experimentation, and cool logic—could one ever arrive at reliable knowledge. "When all is done," wrote Pepys, "reason must govern all since our very faith must be a reasonable faith."[43]

By no means all Christians shared a Pepysian faith in reason and science, but most did stand on the other main plank in the rationalizers' platform. This was morality. To say that all Christians believed in morality (if they did not always practice it) seems to push truism to its outer limit, but the point is actually not quite so obvious nor so trivial.

As the Middle Ages drew to a close, moral standards began to stiffen. At least as early as the sixteenth century, churches showed more concern for moral behavior and applied stricter moral principles (especially to sins of the flesh). The scant evidence available suggests greater popular effort to live up to these stricter precepts. God seemed to demand more from the burghers of Amsterdam in 1600 than the villagers of Montaillou in 1300. Calvinism in particular required exemplary behavior of even the unregenerate as a way of glorifying God. A blameless life indeed came to be regarded among Calvinists, despite protests by theologians, as evidence of saving grace. But, though Calvin's Geneva and Cromwell's England loom in historical memory as peculiarly grim and godly commonwealths, Calvinists did not alone drive "the Harrow of discipline." Other Protestants, and Catholics as well, preached a new moral rigor.[44]

Whether capitalism nourished or fed on this moral athleticism has been much debated. Probably it did both in a dialectical interplay with moralistic religion; and moralism does seem to have had a bourgeois tilt. Perhaps competition between the churches in the Reformation era also fostered stricter morality, although moral fervor was cause as well as consequence of church reform. And as secularization (adding its pressures to those produced by church conflict and reform) pushed religion toward the private sphere, emphasis fell increasingly on inner religiousness rather than externalities of ritual. Cultivation of a clean conscience, then, seems to have become a more common test of inward sanctity, a measure of how close one stood to God.

Whatever its roots, heightened moralism percolated through Europe and crossed the Atlantic on the *Mayflower* and *Arbella*. Occasionally it fired a pastoral revolution, as occurred in Geneva when Calvin's Bolsheviks established the dictatorship of the elect or at the Council of Trent from which a stream of decrees pushed the Catholic clergy toward the straight and narrow. To be sure, Old Nick survived. Cursing, drunkenness, murdering, and fornicating seem not to have gone entirely out of style, especially among the aristocracy and the poor. But there was no mistaking the shift in moral tone and pumping up of moral intensity. Religion had grown much more preoccupied with behavior in everyday life.

This held true even for folk not outstanding examples of morality. Samuel Pepys never managed to shake off his Puritan watchdog. It barked every time his wayward flesh inclined "to run to its old wont of pleasures": "it is high time to betake myself to my late vows, which I will tomorrow, God willing, perfect and bind myself to." Pepys was forever making vows to do better—and then, when temptation beckoned, calculating nicely just how he could squeak by his promises without actually breaking them. These were not the quasi-magical vows common in traditional religion, oaths to perform some ritual act in order to invoke supernatural assistance. They were resolutions to control Pepys's own behavior, solemnified by calling God to witness. They provided a major weapon in Pepys's lifelong battle to bring himself under firmer moral control. Not that his morality exhibited any elevated intent; his major reason for wanting to whip himself into shape was "to grow rich."[45] Pepys also wished, more vaguely, to please God; but it would be hard to imagine a worldlier morality without utterly divorcing it from God. Yet his moral struggles formed the liveliest element in Pepys's personal religion.

For morality bulked large in even the most barebones Christianity, and this constituted its great appeal for "reasonable" apologists. A stress on morality allowed escape from both the divisive welter of doctrinal disputes and the uncertainties spawned by new philosophies. Moreover, the growing concern with morality in virtually all religious camps since the Reformation offered hope of bringing warring sects together on a broad platform of unity. Above all, the fact of moral obligation seemed so clear, so universal, so plain on its face that only the most perverse could fail to recognize it. Just as the workings of natural laws revealed God's rational wisdom, so did the lineaments of human nature and the consciences of all men show forth His moral law. Ethics as well as physics confuted the atheist and confirmed the reasonableness of Christianity.[46] The rational man demonstrated God and everything essential to religion (including, generally, the veracity of Christian revelation) through the marks that Deity had left in this world, ready for reason and observation to discover. Only the fool stumbled into the pit of atheism or the mumbo-jumbo of mystery. Good morals and a small clutch of plain, rational beliefs kept the Christian safe from unbelief and guided him to eternal reward.

Not every Christian confessed this sensible creed. On the contrary, most stuck obstinately with their mysteries. (Indeed, with few exceptions even the most reasonable Christians did not abandon the Trinity, though they found it best not to dwell on this unquestionably mysterious doctrine.) To be sure, moral fervor gave Christians something to agree on—but not something to unite on. After all, the Carmelite reformer Teresa of Avila and the Quaker founder George Fox were moral rigorists, but also great mystics. Morality meant different things to different Christians. For Teresa it was a preparation of the soul for an ineffable union with an ungraspable God. For John Tillotson, the Latitudinarian Archbishop of Canterbury, morality was more like a commonsensical set of rules that God had laid down to guide men in the paths that led them to rational satisfaction on earth and a due happiness in heaven.

This distinction was no small one. True, few Christians exhibited it so starkly as St. Teresa and John Tillotson. But to lean very far in one direction or the other involved more than a mode of piety; it affected one's conception of God and thus the nature of belief. Mysticism tilted toward a God divorced from the everyday world and inaccessible to human rationality. The moralism of reasonable Christians assumed a God more focused on the earthly behavior of His creatures and Whose purposes were mirrored more clearly in the palpable, comprehensible world. Tillotson and Teresa both reflected the Reformation-era upsurge in moralism, but there was very little ineffable about John Tillotson. In a sense, that strength was his weakness. The apologists of reasonable Christianity, intelligent men all, entertained such deluded optimism about uniting Christians around their program because, believing a taste for mysticism a habit of foolishness, they never understood the enduring appeal of mystery in religion.

Yet their effort hardly went to naught. They invented, shepherded, and strengthened a powerful constellation of ideas. Their viewpoint shaped the thinking of subsequent generations even more than their contemporaries'; transformed and attenuated, it is still felt today. And who can say that they did not, in fact, accomplish what many of them regarded as their most urgent task: to stave off the threat of atheism? Certainly their strategy seemed to be working in 1690. "Reasonable religion" would not achieve its full development until the eighteenth century. But already at the end of the seventeenth a new, firmer, more enlightened basis for belief seemed to be taking on an enduring shape and wider appeal. These believers, at least, had come to terms with modernity and had refitted belief to sail in its waters. With much of the incomprehensible and mysterious taken out of it, belief in God was now based more solidly in morality and rationality; that is, in tangible human experience and demonstrable human knowledge. Confusion and uncertainty, apologists might rationally hope, would now give way to a new confidence in a reasonable and moral religion.

2

Enlightenment and Belief, 1690–1790

Ideas about God that still seemed strange and risky at the end of the seventeenth century settled into a kind of orthodoxy as the eighteenth wore on. Lineaments of change barely visible earlier grew more pronounced as thoughtful people in larger numbers struggled to bridge the widening gulf between natural and supernatural, to reconcile rational conviction with intuitive faith, to fit natural law into divine providence, to balance moralism and spirituality—in short, to adapt their belief in God to modern ideas. Many Christians went about their business altogether untroubled by these questions; others pushed their rational religion completely beyond the bounds of Christianity. To estimate the average is impossible. Despite the perils supposed to beset belief, unbelief in fact remained unthinkable to all but a tiny handful. But if belief were to remain secure, it needed footings solid enough to endure the buffetings of changing times. Thus, by the 1790s its underpinnings had altered drastically, at least for the educated, as believers sought to anchor God firmly in the modern world.

The Problem: Nature's God

A willful personal God jarred many sensibilities in the eighteenth century. Neither the majestic minuet of the Newtonian heavens nor the orderly habits of the counting house comfortably accommodated a Father Who arbitrarily and unpredictably tinkered with His creation. The mechanistic strain in seventeenth-century science had suggested instead a more impersonal Deity ruling through invariable natural laws, and glimpses of a similar Being had peeped through the pages of the period's histories. Now, in the eighteenth century, the spread of science and commerce tempted many more people with this new image of God: an abstract Supreme Being Who dealt with His cosmos and His creatures through impersonal secondary causes.

This divine Engineer prospered most where He had always been most at home, in natural science. So complete was the victory of mechanism that even much of Newton's work sank out of sight. Newton the mechanist suppressed in public consciousness the complexities of the real Newton. The great philosopher's excursions into esoteric realms of alchemy and prophecy were forgotten by a people who found it embarrassing to recall that their scientific hero had believed physical appearances only a veil over a deeper spiritual reality. Science inclined increasingly toward God the Watchmaker. And as improved observations eliminated apparent anomalies in Newton's laws—suggested that God did not have to wind His watch after all—the universe more and more seemed given over by its Maker to impersonal natural laws.

The New Learning spread quickly, even in Britain's American provinces. In Boston as early as 1683 the Reverend Increase Mather, later a friend of Robert Boyle, had organized a short-lived scientific society. Mather's son Cotton kept furiously abreast of European learning. "There were scarcely any books written," marveled his fellow minister Charles Chauncy, but Mather "had somehow or other got the sight of them." He peered through a microscope at "little eels" in a water droplet and bombarded English correspondents with curiosities of American natural history, finally winning his reward with election to the Royal Society in 1714. Mather's later sermons, laced with Newtonianism, fed the growing scientific appetite of another Bostonian, young Benjamin Franklin.[1]

Franklin proved more fortunate in his instructor than his wealthier contemporaries who endured a Harvard education, for, however quickly the New Learning spread, it advanced very erratically. True, Harvard kept pace with the more advanced European universities, even taught Copernicanism before 1660. But Newton entered the curriculm only in the late 1720s. Yale students were worse off: until about 1717 they learned that the earth sat still at the center of the universe and that the four elements (earth, air, fire, and water) composed all matter—a physics drawn undiluted from that "Muddy-headed Pagan" Aristotle.[2] New Haven had also apparently not yet heard of John Locke. Princeton, however, gave the new science a prominent place in its curriculum from its founding in 1746. Farther south, the Enlightenment made slower progress. Locke, however, was quickly and hospitably received there—but as a political rather than philosophical writer. Locke's southern reception typified the usual situation: one or another congenial portion of the New Learning nestled cheek-by-jowl with notions inherited from the Schoolmen. Nevertheless, by mid-century "the *Principles* of our *Perpetual Dictator*, the Incomparable Sr. Isaac Newton" commanded general admiration among the educated of America.[3]

And science continued to whittle away at the need for divine interventions. Lavoisier's theories provided the infrastructure for a chemistry built on regular natural laws—an achievement aptly symbolized when he and others published in 1787 a universal logical system of chemical nomenclature. Experimenters with electricity, most notably Benjamin Franklin, were beginning to articulate rudimentary laws of what would become known as electromagnetism. At the century's end Laplace's nebular hypothesis subjected even the creation of the solar system to regular natural processes. In sum, God's hand was withdrawn ever further from nature, as nature came to be understood—not only in conception but in accumulating detail—as governed by God through secondary causes. The great French naturalist Buffon indeed defined nature as a system of laws established by the Creator.[4]

This extension of secondary causes was, if anything, even bolder in the science of man. The transformation appeared everywhere. Montesquieu explained the development of institutions and national character as resulting from climate. Adam Smith expounded laws of political economy governing the wealth of nations. Gibbon, disinclined to sweeping general laws, nevertheless refined a historiography of purely natural causes, from which all trace of divine purpose vanished. Voltaire speculated on the social origins of morality. The greatest audacity was reserved for David Hume, whose "Natural History of Religion" calmly put religious belief on a par with other natural phenomena and traced its genesis to human efforts to quell fear of the unknown and allay anxieties over the uncertainties of life.

In the writings of scientists and social theorists, God had not disappeared (except perhaps for Hume), but He had adopted a new mode of operation. Where once His finger had immediately guided His creation and creatures, He now appeared to have left the running of the world to impersonal laws. In the elite circles where these ideas prevailed, the natural had become more sharply separated from the supernatural. The modern conception of the natural world, understood as clearly distinguished from and even opposed to an impalpable spiritual world, was being invented. The process was comparable to (and perhaps encouraged by) the differentiation of religious from secular aspects of personal and social life, which was also picking up speed in the eighteenth century. In the medieval world view, the supernatural had blurred into the natural. The rationalizing tendencies of the sixteenth and seventeenth centuries, incarnated most clearly in the Scientific Revolution, had begun to pry apart the two orders of being; yet, as the beliefs of Isaac Newton and even Samuel Pepys showed, interpenetration was still considerable.

The divorce became almost complete in Enlightenment science and social thought. In the supernatural realm God often remained, even for those receptive to natural philosophy, a mysterious but loving Father Who watched each sparrow's fall, bent His ear to each child's prayer, and (depending on one's theology) extended His grace to every sinner. But in the natural order He pulled a quick about-face. There an abstract Supreme Being made the universe, laid down its rules, and sustained it, but in effect stepped back and let the mechanism run with little if any direct intervention.[5]

Nowhere was this extrusion of the supernatural from the natural clearer—nor its hesitancy, awkwardness, and complexity more obvious—than in the transformation of providence in the eighteenth century. Both Christians and Jews had traditionally conceived God as exercising supervisory care for His creatures in two modes: first, by ordering the course of events in general so as to achieve His broad purposes; second, by intervening specially in the lives of particular individuals and groups (sometimes miraculously, sometimes through natural causes, the distinction seldom being entirely clear). This latter doctrine of "particular providences" had lately achieved a furious apotheosis in Anglo-American Puritanism, the literature of which teems with divine intrusions.[6] Any stray bolt of lightning was apt to carry a very personal message from on high.

Then, in the space of a few decades, special providences came to seem awkward, faintly archaic, to modern-minded believers. A revealing note, for example, crept into a letter from a family friend to the young James Boswell in 1767. The friend encouraged Boswell in those virtues that older men conventionally urge on young men:

> I have the superstition to believe that whilst you go on in this train (I mean sobriety, diligence in your business, and attentions to the best of parents) God will bless you, not only with conferring on you his imperceptible favours, but will even condescend to gratify you with reputation and other worldly enjoyments, which we may desire but never set our hearts upon.[7]

The writer clearly believed in particular providences. He just as clearly knew that an up-to-date young man might be inclined to snicker at his "superstition."

People could hardly study a cosmology of immutable mathematical laws and a history devoid of divine activity yet, without pausing for breath, still expect God to step in personally to chastise sinners and rescue the righteous. The obstacle was less a problem of logic than of consistency. The Divine Engineer could presumably twist His contrivances to His own ends, but such pettiness began to seem out of character for the lofty Lawmaker of the infinite universe. Young Boswell himself, pondering the "providential" chance that preserved his sight when a tree limb struck his eye, followed a line of reasoning wholly characteristic of his century:

> Should I now have said that Providence preserved my eye? But, I pray you, why did Providence permit the branch to strike me? Oh, that was a natural event. Very well, and the degree of force was natural too; so that very naturally I have not lost my right eye. For shame, divines, how dare you bring in Providence on every trifling occasion? . . . Yes, the universal eye perceives everything in the universe. But surely, the grand and extensive system employs the attention of God, and the minutiae are not to be considered as part of his care; at least, we are not to presume that he interests himself in every little accident.[8]

Boswell, to be sure, was an advanced thinker if not a particularly profound one. Even so liberal a clergyman as Charles Chauncy of Boston still cherished particular providences. When an earthquake shattered the predawn quiet on 18 November 1755, Chauncy hastened to improve on the catastrophe with a wholeheartedly traditional sermon: *Earthquakes a Token of the Righteous Anger of God*. Bostonians, it turned out, had lapsed from righteousness again—drunkenness, uncleanness, Sabbath-breaking—and God had shaken them with His displeasure. Yet a new note sounded in Chauncy's discourse. A law-breaking God was too much for him. He felt obliged to expound in some detail that earthquakes had natural causes; God had not violated these secondary causes, only arranged them by His foreknowledge to remind Bostonians of their sins.[9] Chauncy's compromise (an amplification of an older view) provided a common way out of an increasingly obvious conflict of beliefs. Those writers who clung to special providences often displaced their operation into the general system of nature; God then did not tamper with the machinery but simply foresaw when He constructed it how the regular workings of His laws would affect individuals.

More thoroughgoing moderns took Boswell's route to its end. Providence came to mean solely God's beneficence in constructing the world so that it conduced to good. "Many theists, even the most zealous and refined," observed Hume, "have denied a *particular* Providence, and have asserted, that the Sovereign mind, or first principle of all things, having fixed general laws, by which nature is governed, gives free and uninterrupted course to these laws, and disturbs not, at every turn, the settled order of events by particular volitions." Calvin's divine governance faded before Leibniz's law-regulated cosmos that, however imperfect, was the best of all possible worlds.[10]

By no stretch of the imagination had providence disappeared. But even in Chauncy and much more in Boswell, it had edged toward a more abstract, regular character. In the extreme (and unusual) case of Hume's zealous and refined theist, providence was subsumed entirely under constant laws of nature and society. Thus, it became not only an automatic product of natural laws but also, practically speaking, bound within the physical world. The distinction between providence and the ordinary course of nature lost meaning. As far as physical reality was concerned, God tended to retire into the role of an abstract, impersonal First Cause and Sustainer. Did this mean that a personal God survived only in a segregated and intangible supernatural sphere?

Divine providence appeared naturalized in any number of forms: the laws that held planets in their orbits, the drives that induced men to buy and sell, the love of parent for child. Occasionally it also assumed a novel guise that invested all of human history with a new meaning and sense of direction. Providence expressed itself as progress.[11]

Progress, in the sense of the indefinite continuance of human development, was not a familiar idea to ancient and medieval writers, who tended to view history as cyclical rather than cumulative. Christianity imposed a progressive salvation history, moving from the Fall through the Incarnation to the Second Coming; but this was a supernatural story, bursting into the understanding of temporal history only in chiliastic movements, and then as a proclamation of the millennium rather than theory of progress. Bits and pieces of a theory of secular progress surfaced in the Renaissance, notably in the writings of Francis Bacon and Jean Bodin, reflecting the growing consciousness of social and technological change over time. Many early members of the Royal Society nurtured a vision of science as contributing to social improvement. But these hints often went unregarded and never added up to a clear idea of permanent human progress.

In 1688 Bernard de Fontenelle, pinning his argument on the assumption that "a good cultivated mind is composed, so to speak, of all the minds of preceding centuries," declared flatly that "men will never degenerate" and knowledge will grow indefinitely. His conviction gained a certain currency among French philosophes in the eighteenth century, though often hedged by scepticism and uncertainty. Such progress in knowledge did not necessarily imply any corresponding social improvement. But something—possibly the pronounced tendency to link science with social utility—encouraged an embryonic notion that prosperity and manners would advance hand-in-hand with enlightenment. Thus, as Turgot assured the Sorbonne in 1750, "The whole mass of humankind, through alternations of calm and tumult, of well-being and adversity, progresses always, although slowly, toward greater perfection."[12] Condorcet lurked just around the corner.

Ideas of progress were most at home on French soil and often met a cool reception even there. British and American writers seem to have been not so much hostile as unconcerned; one has to dredge quite deeply to bring up any assumptions about progress, pro or con. Hume, characteristically, was sceptical. Gibbon, in contrast, allowed himself to "acquiesce in the pleasing conclusion" that every age had seen progress, though this statement amounted to little more than an obiter dictum thrown off in the course of a longer argument confuting the possibility of a total relapse into barbarism.[13] No one in England had much to say; in America even less.

Still, hazy expectations about progress slowly drifted across the horizon of consciousness. The British and Americans, after all, believed even more deeply than the French that science promoted social improvement, a tradition running from Bacon through the founders of the Royal Society right down to Franklin's American Philosophical Society "held at Philadelphia for promoting useful knowledge." Add to this the belief in the indefinite advance of knowledge, and a theory of progress lay ready to hand. Franklin foresaw vistas of magnificent material improvements born of science (which made him regret "that I was born so soon"), though doubting any equivalent moral progress. John Adams detected in history an erratic trend toward "Amelioration in human Affairs." A vision of moral as well as material progress struggled to emerge from the ideology of the American Revolution, which vaguely tied together enlightenment, political liberation, and social betterment. The mixture bubbled up in a political song of the late 1780s:

> Each town and county's wealth and peace,
> Its trade and all connections,
> Science, arts must all increase,
> Upheld by free elections.

This ditty hardly amounted to a coherent faith in progress, but it evidenced an idea taking shape.[14]

Near the end of the century, hope for progress began to feed heavily on religious beliefs, especially in America, where Protestantism harbored a pronounced streak of millennial expectation. This hope gradually took a form among some believers that dovetailed with the idea of steady human improvement culminating in a perfected society. Belief in the kingdom of God tottered as one approached the philosophes, but something of it may have survived in rational religion's recasting of providence as an agency for the gradual perfecting of man. Given the intimacy of religion and science, religion could inoculate secular culture with, not exactly the conviction that Christ would descend with Newton on one hand and Locke on the other, but at least an unfocused sense that, in God's plan, science would gradually cleanse humanity of error and injustice.[15]

By the 1790s, both sacred and profane impulses (insofar as the two can be separated) pushed people toward a belief in continuing human progress, with science as God's most likely agency for effecting it. This infant conviction was none too sturdy, often barely whimpering in its cradle. But it gathered strength. The stage was being set for faith in progress to sweep through the next century and star as perhaps the leading motif of that age.

What, meanwhile, had happened to providence? It was still there, lurking within the universal laws of human development that made for progress. The whole engine ran by God's design, was continually powered by His hand. But it also ran without His personal intervention. This abstract providence was a far cry from the divine care that had once upon a time stayed the course of nature to pluck a single sinner from the jaws of impersonal fate.

Now God's care expressed itself in ordinary natural processes and in human beings working to improve their lot. The concept of progress made it possible to understand the operation of providence, including the translation of humankind to a higher plane of existence, within the scope of everyday life. It minimized the transcendent mystery within the divine design.

This reinterpretation of providence thus manifested the new habits of mind that had become influential in the two centuries previous. An orderly, natural-law God, using physical nature and ordinary human action to accomplish His ends, fitted the taste for regularity and linear cause-and-effect logic, for clarity and plainness rather than mystery, for down-to-earth, tangibly experienced hard fact rather than impalpable transcendence.

A new picture of man and nature, long in the making, had fully emerged. Innovators in earlier centuries had patched their insights onto old world views: the political naturalism of Machiavelli, the mechanism of Galileo, the cosmic laws of Newton, the consciousness of historical process of a hundred scribblers, lawyers, and pamphleteers. New understandings of this or that portion of reality gradually accumulated. In the Enlightenment this conglomeration achieved coherence in a unified comprehension of the cosmos and its human inhabitants. Indeed, this may provide the best definition of the Enlightenment. The result was not a system, such as Spencer or Hegel would later squeeze reality into, but rather a consistent approach to explaining all aspects of the world. True, this point of view remained the property of a small elite (not, incidentally, limited to the socially elite), which was even something of an avant-garde. Most ordinary folk still found astrology more to the point than astronomy, and divination more congenial than experiment.[16] But for a significant minority the functioning of nature, the workings of the individual and of society, even the promise of man's future were all explained through the regularities of natural processes, which were accessible to reason.

The Problem: God's Nature?

Belief in God had to be reconciled to this world view. Old conceptions of God no longer made sense, and old foundations of belief crumbled when thoughtful people took the Enlightenment seriously. The guardians of belief thus faced the same kind of problem that had confronted the writers who tried to adjust belief to seventeenth-century science and rationalism, only now belief needed deeper and more extensive realignments.

And, again, fear of unbelief prodded apologists to action, except that the fear grew in the eighteenth century, and grew more realistic. Nervousness about atheism peaked during the Deist controversy early in the century and then again near its end in consequence of the radical ideologies that swirled around the French Revolution. But even during the relatively quiet interim, an undercurrent of anxiety about unbelief marked many religious writers. And there were now real atheists to substantiate these fears, at least in the last decades of the century. The greatest ogre, Baron d'Holbach, and his circle epitomized the wickedness of Paris. There in the heady 1790s even the American radical poet Joel Barlow lost his New World innocence and slipped temporarily into atheism. At about the same time, the London Corresponding Society, a haven for anticlerical radicals, was rumored to have divided its membership into atheist and Deist sections, though this report may have owed more to the fevered imagination of the Tory reporter than to reality.[17]

In fact, the danger was in general much exaggerated. What the orthodox called "atheism" usually amounted to nothing but a Deistic denial of revealed religion. (The term "Deist" neither had nor has any consistent definition. I shall adopt one of its usages, somewhat arbitrarily, and refer by it to believers in natural religion who rejected any divine revelation.) If one disregards the expatriate Barlow just before 1800, America does not seem to have harbored a single individual before the nineteenth century who disbelieved in God. The archsceptic David Hume averred that he had never laid eyes on an atheist, and he was probably correct until he dined with the Baron d'Holbach. Even the infamous *coterie holbachique,* vilified in later years as the citadel of Enlightenment atheism, included among its fifteen regulars only three committed unbelievers and possibly three others who privately flirted with atheism. And that was in France, where hostility to the Church in enlightened circles sometimes ran high enough to spill over onto God.[18] Some historians speculate that atheism flourished silently underground, and this guess cannot be disproved any more than the existence of millions of quiet disbelievers in the law of gravity. But the known unbelievers of Europe and America before the French Revolution numbered fewer than a dozen or two.

For disbelief in God remained scarcely more plausible than disbelief in gravity. Even radical thinkers almost universally regarded an afterlife in which God punished the wicked as a necessary sanction for morality. True, sometimes they meant only that hell was a useful fiction to keep the *ignobile vulgus* in line. (This fear of social anarchy accounted for Voltaire's notorious warning to his loose-lipped friends speculating on religion: Not in front of the servants!)[19] But more than the social consequences appalled. Godlessness violated in the moral realm the regularity that enlightened men and women expected in nature. No Deists ever fully articulated this problem, but the basic assumption underlay all their thinking about man in society. Human beings were part of nature. Therefore, laws like the orderly ordinances of the cosmos governed human behavior. These social laws must somehow dictate morality, else human societies would never have risen above the jungle. But since the world does not always reward virtue and punish vice, there must be a future existence and a God to right the balance. Otherwise the human condition seemed hopelessly disordered, out of tune with the rest of the universe. This line of thinking could hardly stand up to logical criticism. But that small flaw did not reduce its persuasiveness, so powerful were the habit of God and the example of the orderly Newtonian universe.

This universe taught the incredibility of unbelief not only by analogy but directly. In Linnaeus's *Systema naturae* (1735), the century's commanding work of natural history, the Enlightenment had a forceful proof that the order that Newton had shown in the physical world also pervaded the biological. Thomas Jefferson deemed it literally "impossible for the human mind not to perceive and feel a conviction of design, consummate skill, and indefinite power in every atom of [the universe's] composition." This persuasion sprang as much from a sense of the ongoing process of the world as from its present structure. Extinct races of animals and the death and birth of stars all argued to Jefferson "the necessity of a superintending power, to maintain the universe in its course and order."[20]

Philosophy reinforced this almost intuitive perception. In the Newtonian system, matter was dead; it required a Power to set it in motion. The very conception of natural laws (as distinct from the modern scientific conception of statistical regularities anachronistically called "laws") presupposed a Lawgiver, and the continuance of lawful processes from day to day assumed a Sustainer. How could regularity in nature exist and continue without a Regulator above nature? To reject God, one had first to abandon not merely the best but the only really coherent scientific explanation of the world. Even the handful of radical pantheists, John Toland the best known, could not quite wrench loose from the idea of God. Whether they merited their frequent denunciation as atheists is perhaps a matter of definition. These writers, as much scientific as religious heretics, regarded nature as the only reality, eternal and self-moving. Yet, rather than dispensing with the idea of God and promulgating a thoroughgoing naturalism (as would nineteenth-century believers in the self-sufficiency of nature), they identified nature with God! Thus the otherwise puzzling dictum of the French materialist La Mettrie, who if not an atheist passed for an excellent facsimile: "I do not call into question the existence of a Supreme Being; on the contrary it seems to me that the balance of probability is in its favour."[21]

The Enlightenment spawned much religious doubt and some atheistic speculation, but even in its radical variants, eighteenth-century culture could scarcely support unbelief as a really viable option. If Deists and the rare atheists sometimes allied with each other (as happened in France), it was because they faced the same enemy: intolerant Christians. The common inclination among later historians to see rejection of the Christian God as a halfway house to unbelief in any God misunderstands both Deism and the Enlightenment. The "natural religion" favored by the more adventurous Enlightenment thinkers constituted a legitimate if thin-blooded form of theism, not a road to unbelief. Only much later, in indirect ways and under very different circumstances, did it—could it—contribute to the eventual emergence of a widespread and enduring disbelief in God. Unbelief required too great a divorce from reality, as understood during the Enlightenment, to be either palatable or plausible.

Why, then, such a hue and cry from Christian apologists? In part, the answer is that rejection of Christianity alarmed them (and understandably so) almost as much as real atheism. Indeed, Christians commonly regarded Deism as certainly leading to atheism and scarcely different from it; so "atheists" they often called the disciples of natural religion. This confusion of terms reflected also the continuing lack of a graduated nomenclature to describe the increasing degrees of scepticism, a deficiency not to be remedied until unbelief came into its own in the later nineteenth century, at which point more exactitude became urgently needed. Besides, "atheist" provided such a convenient term of abuse.

Yet Christians—and indeed other believers—had more than semantic reasons for voicing concern about atheism. For the Enlightenment had brought that possibility closer to reality than at any time since the end of classical antiquity. Some versions of the law-abiding universe so distanced God from the actual workings of nature as to make conceivable His extrusion from the machinery altogether. Might natural laws not really require a Lawmaker? Was that assumption too an unnecessary hypothesis, like the occult forces of medieval physics? Might nature be self-contained and self-sustaining? And if, as Deists proposed, Christianity had a purely naturalistic origin—granted, a large "if"—might not, as the outrageous and elegant Mr. Hume suggested, belief in God also have?[22] Almost any level head would answer, no, absurd! to all of these questions. Still the worry would not down. Cultural change had stirred up enough turmoil in religious belief to make anxious souls legitimately nervous.

All the more so as such speculation took place in a social environment less protective of religious belief. In part, this was just a matter of secular concerns jostling out religious interests, a continuation of the secularization already well begun in the seventeenth century. At Rouen, for example, the proportion of books published on religious topics declined from 35 percent in the first decade of the eighteenth century to 12 percent in the decade preceding the Revolution.[23] Yet a more specific transformation was also afoot. The way in which a figure like Voltaire made a sport of shocking the bourgeosie disguises the new phenomenon that he represented.

Traditionally, the patronage of church, state, or powerful individuals supported almost all writers. Under this circumstance, naturally, a conservative bias guided cultural activity. But the spread of printing made it easier to propagate heterodox ideas, and by the eighteenth century presses had become ubiquitous. As a New England minister noticed early in the century, "The Mechanick, yea, the Ladies, as well as the Scholar, the Philosopher, the Christian and the Divine are furnished with agreeable libraries." Few mechanicks, even fewer farmers, were as well equipped as the reverend gentleman suggested, but his remarks contained more than a kernel of truth. Had he survived into the last quarter of the century, however, he would have found a number of American libraries considerably less agreeable, crowded as they were with the works of heretics and Deists.[24]

For, as presses became commoner and the audience for printed matter larger and more various, the old patronage system was undercut. Newspapers and other periodicals did particularly severe damage. Hatched in the seventeenth century, they took wing in the eighteenth. Such journals eventually provided the margin that allowed a few writers to eke out a living without patronage. Samuel Johnson's famous rebuke to the Earl of Chesterfield in 1754 constituted a declaration of independence not only for Johnson but for unborn generations of intellectuals: "I hope it is no very cynical asperity not to confess obligations where no benefit has been received, or to be unwilling that the Publick should consider me as owing that to a Patron, which Providence has enabled me to do for myself."[25]

The significance of such writers lay not in any inherent unorthodoxy—Johnson was safer than the Archbishop of Canterbury—but in their independence. They represented a further stage in the slow contraction of churchly influence since the Reformation, the loosening of the churches' hold over intellectual life. To put the matter in its crudest terms, writers did not have to appear to subscribe to Christian doctrine in order to put food on their tables. Their increasing autonomy made them both more likely to suspect old truths and less hesitant to broadcast their doubts. Granted, authors who outraged prevailing beliefs did not always eat well, as Thomas Paine learned in the later stages of his career, but neither did they starve. And more temperate criticism, if decked out to sell, was by no means incompatible with a hearty appetite. Among Americans, Benjamin Franklin stood out as the archetype of the self-made and self-sufficient intellectual, a prolific scribbler whose journalism had won him independence from powerful patrons. Not that Franklin ever turned up his nose when the governor opened his purse (that was part of the trick); but, when so inclined, he could afford to say what he thought. It was perhaps no accident that this printer's apprentice grew up to become America's best-known Deist. The number of individuals who lived on writing or editing was still minute (London's Grub Street housed a remarkably high proportion). But it was growing, and with it grew the society's potential for questioning, even radical questioning.

No wonder, then, that religious apologists worried about what lay in store for belief. With divine providence transmuted into impersonal law, with little check on what some scribbler might publish, there was no telling where the ideas of the Enlightenment might lead. If defenders of the faith perhaps too readily saw atheists where only a handful existed, they might be forgiven, for they had a right to be nervous.

Yet more than self-interest or defensiveness forced church leaders to rethink the nature of God and the justifications for belief in Him. Anxiety only prodded them to a task essential anyway;

honesty even more urgently than expediency required a fresh look at belief. The Enlightenment's new ways of thinking demanded a correlative reassessment of thinking about God—one more far-reaching than, though continuous with, that begun between the Reformation and about 1690. What implications did the rule of law in nature and of secondary causes in human affairs have for the understanding of God? How far and in what ways should the Enlightenment's approach to the study of man and nature apply also to God and belief? Could these methods of knowing also comprehend God? Was there more than one road to knowledge? What relation did knowledge have to belief? From the end of the seventeenth century, religious thinkers struggled to answer these questions in an ongoing dialectic of adaptation and resistance.

An Answer: Belief Rationalized

To call the eighteenth century by its traditional title, the Age of Reason, ignores most of the period's reality. But it also captures a fundamental truth about the aspirations of most educated people during those years. Alexander Pope gauged this temper when he deified Newton as a demiurge of rational clarity:

> Nature and Nature's Laws lay hid in Night.
> God said, *Let Newton be!* and All was Light.[26]

That Pope repressed Newton's lifelong pursuit of decidedly unrational mysteries only testified more strongly to the rationalizing urge of his own audience.

As Newton was deified, so the temptation was great to Newtonify the Deity. If science and rationalism had raised questions about God and unsettled belief, then what more logical response than to shore up religion by remodeling it in the image of science and rationality? Accordingly, many spokesmen of the church—theologians, ministers, lay writers—enthusiastically magnified the rationalizing tendencies already apparent within belief, increasingly conceived assurance of God as a matter of the intellect and the grounds of belief as rationally demonstrable. So easy was it to slip into this way of thinking that many of the rationalizers of belief only half-realized that they had in fact made a choice—and never really stopped to consider its implications.

This was not for lack of warning. Early America's most eminent theologian, Jonathan Edwards, though deeply impressed by Locke and Newton, still insisted that belief involved something much deeper than intellection. The "word 'confess,' as it is often used in the New Testament," he wrote, implies not only "establishing and confirming a thing by testimony" but also "declaring it with manifestation of esteem and affection." And, drawing on Calvin, he went beyond him to try to articulate a new, extrarational road to knowledge of God consonant with the New Learning. Real belief flowed from profound personal involvement with God, a consequence of divine grace, not simply from weighing the evidence.[27]

Yet "confirming a thing by testimony" seemed to more and more writers the kernel of belief. As early as the 1660s the Anglican Latitudinarian theologians, notably sympathetic to the new science, had exalted reason at the expense of revelation. The most eminent of them, Archbishop John Tillotson, was very widely read in the eighteenth century; indeed, novelists and poets aside, was probably the well-read American colonists' most popular author. Without denying the authority of Scripture, Tillotson treated nature as a more basic divine revelation and turned reason loose to find the grounds of belief in the natural world. In a similar spirit, divines increasingly treated Scripture itself as a kind of historical data, analogous to the facts of nature, rather than as the living voice of God. The Bible in such hands imparted proofs rather than personal faith, words rather than the Word. Less popular but perhaps more deeply influential than Tillotson (though not indiscriminately admired) was Newton's disciple the Reverend Samuel Clarke. In his Boyle Lectures of 1704–5, "On the Being and Attributes of God," Clarke stressed the "clearness, immutability, and universality of the law of nature," along with the need for a First Cause, as the foundation of belief. Revelation provided only a requisite supplement to this evidence, additional proofs of certain facts about God.[28]

Jonathan Mayhew, pastor of Boston's fashionable West Church from 1747 to 1766, was a great admirer of Samuel Clarke. For him, "confirming a thing by testimony" constituted the really crucial element in belief. He warned his congregation not to believe "that there is, or that there is not a God; that the Christian religion is from God, or an imposture" until "we have impartially examined the matter, and see the evidence on one side or the other." After presumably impartial examination, Mayhew concluded that Christianity comprised three theorems:

> I. THAT there is a natural difference between truth and falshood [*sic*], right and wrong.
> II. THAT men are naturally endowed with faculties proper for the discerning of these differences.

> III. THAT men are under obligation to exert these faculties; and to judge for themselves in things of a religious concern.

Mayhew could hardly have made clearer his agreement with Jefferson's contempt for "Platonic mysticisms" and his definition of belief as "the assent of the mind to an intelligible proposition."[29]

Yet, for all this reliance on natural faculties and rational judgment, Mayhew did not transform religion entirely into a celebration of reason. He preached a hellfire as warmly traditional as any Puritan's, and he sought to nourish personal spiritual intimacy between the soul and its Maker. Mayhew's religion typified the Enlightenment far better than Voltaire's, for the forgotten majority of the Enlightened stayed in closer touch with traditional Christianity than the more famous radicals did. But even the Voltaire who subscribed *Ecrasez l'infâme* to his letters may well have felt genuinely moved by religious emotion for his philosophical God.[30]

Rationalization, even in the rationalists' camp, hardly swallowed religion whole. What was happening was both more limited and more complex. As part of their attempt to modernize belief, church leaders and religious writers were splitting the old conception of "belief." They were, in effect, dividing the conviction of God's reality from the trust and love that He inspired. The former became increasingly an intellectual question; the latter remained a more complex matter involving other areas of the psyche. This conceptual shift took place subtly, generally eluding observation, so that language did not always keep pace with thinking. Nevertheless, "belief" and "faith," previously interchangeable, were in practice increasingly employed in different contexts—the one pointing to intellectual conviction of definable propositions, the other to personal trust.[31] Jonathan Edwards, as in so many other affairs, ended on the losing side. Belief in God, for many Christians, now meant primarily a rationally verifiable proposition: a conclusion at which the individual must arrive prior to entertaining questions of any relation to God involving more than the intellect.

It was hard, however, to purge Christianity of all mystery. Mayhew's three theorems omitted too much. So the rationalizing impulse could carry beyond Christianity. Samuel Clarke teetered on the brink—the reason the orthodox suspected him—and a good many actually fell over into Deism. Deism professed to be a religion founded on reason alone, composed solely of truths about God evident in the order of nature, subjecting all beliefs to the tests of reason and experience.[32] In fact, it usually amounted to a severely stripped down version of Christianity, with all that smacked of mystery and superstition pared away. The issue that ultimately divided Deists from rationalizing Christians was the Christian claim, to Deists absurd, that a rational and benevolent God had revealed to one backward tribe mysteries not accessible to any reasonable person. The aboriginal Deist is conventionally taken to be Lord Herbert of Cherbury (1583–1648). Though Herbert's philosophical underpinnings differed from his eighteenth-century progeny's, his tract *De Veritate* (1624) did lay down what remained the fundamental tenets of most Deists: that a Supreme Being exists and requires worship, that a moral life is the best worship, and that God will reward virtue and punish vice in an afterlife.[33]

A disciple of Herbert, Charles Blount, was insinuating in print the absurdity of revelation as early as 1680. But the most influential progenitor of eighteenth-century Deism was John Toland's *Christianity Not Mysterious,* published in 1696 on the heels of Locke's more conservative *Reasonableness of Christianity* (1695). Though prudent enough to tiptoe around the Trinity and in general to maintain a veneer of orthodoxy—a young man was burned at Edinburgh in 1697 for ridiculing the Bible—Toland argued from Lockean principles that only reason offered certitude and that revelation itself must submit to reason's judgment.[34] This assertion, however discreetly draped, was strong stuff. Toland and his less-inhibited followers in the next century—Thomas Woolston, Anthony Collins, Matthew Tindal, to list a few of the more notorious—provoked a nearly universal throwing up of hands among the orthodox, at least the orthodox who had access to a printer.

Deism chimed too nicely with the Christian advocacy of reasonable religion to be silenced by Christian polemics. It flourished in England and Holland during the first decades of the eighteenth century and was carried thence to France, most famously by Voltaire in 1728. A few years earlier and a few thousand miles farther west, in Puritan Boston, the teenaged Benjamin Franklin pored over Collins in his brother's printing shop and emerged a Deist of the most disputatious sort. He outgrew his contentiousness but never his Deism.[35]

Not until the last decades of the century did Deism really come into its own in America. It then ranged from the strident anticlericalism of Thomas Paine and Ethan Allen through the quiet, socially conservative moralism of Franklin and Jefferson until it merged imperceptibly with the vaguely sceptical Christianity of Washington and the waveringly Deistic speculations of John Adams. Deism reached its zenith in the 1790s, when, as Lyman Beecher remembered, farm boys "read Tom Paine and believed him" and Yale students "called each other Voltaire, Rousseau, D'Alembert, etc., etc." Enthusiasm for French radicalism even encouraged some feeble efforts to institutionalize Paine's variety of Deism. But the result never amounted to much.[36]

For Deism was less a positive religion than a critical movement. It formed the extreme wing of the campaign to adapt Christianity to a Newtonian universe of regular natural laws. "Reasonable" religionists of all stripes insisted (like the Latitudinarians) on the rationality of belief in God and the primacy of moralism within religion. They confirmed these principles by appealing to natural religion and the orderliness of nature. Necessarily the rationalizers denigrated mystery, made reason the standard by which to judge revelation, and diluted the particularity of Christianity. When diluted to homeopathic proportions, Christianity turned into Deism. Thoroughgoing Deists expunged everything unsuited to a clockwork God: anything irregular (miracles, special providences, divine revelations), anything inaccessible to reason (the Trinity, the divinity of the man Jesus, the Resurrection). Deists took rational religion with full seriousness.

Granted, Deism had its irreligious side. The "young and gay" in particular delighted in shocking conventional pieties. As early as 1741 a Charleston lady lamented that "pretending to a disbelief of and ridiculeing [*sic*] of religion" had become a "fashionable but shameful vice" of young men feeling their oats.[37] So young men thumbed their noses at their fathers, flaunting modish beliefs in the face of dowdier convictions; and some, like Franklin and Voltaire, never outgrew their delight in poking fun. At times snickering verged toward anticlericalism and impiety. Neither should be taken too seriously nor exaggerated into disbelief in the Deity. Although a few French Deists passed into atheism, Deism did not fundamentally tend in that direction; it rested squarely on the rational necessity of a God. No one could imagine Franklin as devout, but his faith in "the Supreme" was no less sincere for that reason.

Nor should the quarrels between Deists and "reasonable" Christians obscure their family ties. True, rational Christians like Jonathan Mayhew could hardly have satisfied their residual but genuine need for piety with the philosophical God of Deism; as Franklin kept finding, the rarefied and immovable Supreme made an unsatisfactory party to converse with. Yet among reasonable Christians, too, those aspects of God that utterly transcended human knowing were beginning to recede in importance. In theory, God remained incomprehensible. In practice, He became more and more bound within the limits of reason, confined within cognitive categories suited to this world rather than apprehended through spiritual capacities supposed to open doors into another world. Hence Deism, for all its shock to orthodox sensibilities, did not basically stand at odds with enlightened Christianity but only carried to offensive lengths a tendency within all reasonable religion.

A religion prudently rationalized offered too sharp a weapon against the ever-threatening atheists to pass up. And, not incidentally, its comforting assurance of one's own belief was almost too tempting to turn down. Antiatheist writers in the previous century had exploited the theological possibilities of the new science, but it was a burst of ingenuity in the 1690s that really initiated the astonishing exfoliation of the so-called argument from design—what William Derham named in 1713 "physico-theology." So solid a proof of God's existence did this argument provide that it dominated the arsenal of philosophic theologians for the next century and a half. The enlightened Puritan Cotton Mather enunciated in 1721 the animating strategy of this natural theology: "If Men so much admire Philosophers [i.e., scientists], because they *discover* a small Part of the *Wisdom* that made all things; they must be stark blind, who do not admire that *Wisdom* itself."[38]

More precisely, the argument from design professed to demonstrate the existence, power, wisdom, and benevolence of the Deity from the appearance of planned order in nature. This claim was itself nothing new. The idea that the structure of nature evinces intelligent purpose behind it goes back at least to Diogenes of Apollonia in the fifth century B.C.; and Diogenes's younger contemporary Xenophon, in his *Memorabilia,* attributed a full-blown version of the argument to Socrates. The argument thereafter surfaced occasionally throughout classical antiquity and the Middle Ages, but it spawned no sizable body of literature.[39]

Fear of atheism prompted apologists to look again at natural theology. At the same time, ironically, a prime disturber of belief, the new science, provided a rich lode for theologians to mine. A range of options existed. Apologists might have contented themselves with simply pointing out the intelligibility of the universe (as manifested in the regularity of scientific laws) and arguing thence to an intelligent Creator. But this modest demonstration would take less than full advantage of science's persuasive appeal.

The temptation was great to go further in the direction of integrating science's work with theology's.

Thus, the first generation of Newtonians in England had appropriated the machinery of science to construct buttresses for Christianity. Newton himself seems never to have doubted that his laws demonstrated God, and his disciple, the classicist Richard Bentley, became the first to elaborate at full length the details of the connection. In the last three of his 1692 Boyle Lectures, *A Confutation of Atheism,* Bentley (with Newton behind the scenes helping him over the hard spots) argued directly from the Newtonian cosmos to the necessary existence of a Designer of such efficient machinery, and thence to the power and beneficence of this celestial Engineer.[40] The trouble was that the very simplicity of this elegant world-machine meant that the examples of design it provided, however stunning, were relatively few.

The work of natural historians provided richer evidence of God's hand. The profusely varied and intricate structures in organic nature formed a bottomless reservoir of nature's proof-texts; an apologist could let down his bucket and lift it up brimming over with gems of divine engineering. Natural theologians soon succumbed to this lure and made natural history their favored resource. The early master was the great naturalist John Ray, who published in 1691 the most distinguished work in the canon of physico-theology, *The Wisdom of God Manifested in the Works of the Creation.* Ray pioneered the classic examples of divine design—the eye, the hand—that were to be impressed upon generations of undergraduates even unto his grandchildren's grandchildren.[41] And, as befitted so eminent a scholar, he was mercilessly plagiarized for almost two centuries.

Ray was only the most highly evolved member of a proliferating species. Whether looking toward the heavens or the meadows, theologians throughout Europe and America seized upon the careful design and regularity now found everywhere in nature to manufacture ammunition against atheists. Eighteenth-century science, given to relentless classifying, offered an endless stock of raw material. At times the arguments grew excruciatingly convoluted; both an Insecto-Theology and a Water-Theology appeared. When Herder in 1774 asserted that fifty different physico-theologies existed, he may have exaggerated, but not by much.[42] Thus was enthroned in theology scientific rationality and its Designer God.

The argument from design had less overwhelming force than

apologists assumed. It did not prove *one* God, an *infinite* God, or a *perfect* God, but at best only a Creator proportioned to the creation's observed degree of perfection—which, given dread diseases, famine, and carnivorous beasts, fell somewhat short of absolute, as David Hume pointed out. Yet Hume's critique seems to have convinced almost no one at the time, even among his fellow philosophes, with the considerable exception of Immanuel Kant. Despite its power, Hume's scepticism proved unpersuasive because he carried it too far. He rejected one of the most fundamental Enlightenment axioms: that the universe was ordered rationally and was thus ultimately intelligible to the human mind. Without this assumption, the scientific enterprise seemed crippled. Hume's denial of causation as normally understood threatened not only to destroy scientific laws (as then conceived) but to invalidate all knowledge. No wonder that the Scottish philosophers who refuted Hume called their answer "common sense." If eighteenth-century science could not tolerate Hume, it was hardly surprising that natural theologians regarded his *Dialogues concerning Natural Religion* as diabolical logic-juggling rather than a plausible conundrum. Only in a later age, which had discarded the argument from design on other grounds, reconceived the scope of science, and already opened itself to doubt about God's reality, would a significant number of thinkers take Hume with full seriousness. For the time being he remained only a somewhat alarming curiosity.

Disregard of Hume, however, did not account for the persuasiveness of the design argument. Why should it have been widely taken to prove so much more than it could have? Part of the answer is that the argument did not operate in a vacuum. Apologists, after all, were looking to prove not just any god, but the Christian God; if a God existed, they implicitly assumed, it must be that sort of God. Therefore, evidence of intelligent and benevolent design was treated as manifesting the hand of, not merely a smart, kind, and powerful Being, but the one, omniscient, infinitely loving, and omnipotent God.

Physico-theology also drew strength from the intimate relationship of God and science. Natural philosophers and natural historians did not regard God as external to their work but rather incorporated Him into their systems and hypotheses. God was not, from a scientific point of view, an extrascientific issue on which scientific evidence happened to bear; He was in the fullest sense a strictly scientific cause, essential to explanations of nature.

The laws of motion, the division of flora and fauna into distinct genera and species, the adaptation of dentition in ruminants to feeding on grasses—all were referred to divine agency. The great naturalist Linnaeus, whose *Systema naturae* laid the foundations of modern botany and zoology, explained his work by saying that "God had suffered him to peep into His secret cabinet."[43] To be sure, day-to-day scientific work dealt with more mundane business: fitting facts into a classificatory framework or explicating fine details of natural laws. Scientists had no need continually to invoke the hand of God. Astronomy in particular showed by the late eighteenth century a practical tendency (as distinct from a philosophical one) to treat God as a passive First Cause now retired from the scene—a posture that chemistry and geology began to emulate.

But no science could ultimately explain its own findings without resort to the Deity. God therefore remained as much a scientific as a theological necessity. So preachers did not distort science in voicing the design argument; in fact, from Boyle down to Priestley scientists threw themselves into theological polemics with the zeal of missionaries. Among noteworthy scientists of the century, apparently only Henry Cavendish failed to appreciate properly the divine design in nature; he did not deny it but "was simply indifferent."[44]

Natural theologians were not inclined to check the teeth of this gift horse any too carefully. Given its scientific backing, they generally overlooked the logical lacunae of the argument from design, overlooked its hidden assumptions, overlooked too the way in which it made assurance of God depend on the current structure of science. Why question so appealingly modern, so powerful a bulwark against unbelief? By enlisting the best science in support of God, physico-theology appeared to make His existence irrefutable. "A BEING that must be *superior* to *Matter*, even the *Creator* and *Governor* of all *Matter*, is every where so conspicuous," trumpeted Cotton Mather, that "*Atheism* is now for ever chased and hissed out of the World."[45]

By linking belief in God with the methods and discoveries of science, the argument from design simply carried to a natural conclusion the tendency to rationalize the foundations of belief. This linkage was consciously forged in the conviction that faith would be strengthened by making it clear and rational. When Richard Bentley was publishing his celebrated Boyle Lectures on natural theology, Newton phrased the intention this way:

> The human race is prone to mystery, and holds nothing quite so holy and perfect as what cannot be understood. Yet in the conception of God this is dangerous, and conduces to the rejection of his existence. It is of concern to theologians that the conception be made as easy and as agreeable to reason as possible, so as not to be exposed to cavils and thereby called into question.[46]

To say that the mysteriousness of God conduced to disbelief in His existence—which, to put it mildly, ran against the available evidence—showed a faith in rationality so deep that it hardly noticed reality. Even Newton, for whom both science and religion blended into occult mysteries, had imbibed a very large dose of the rationalizing impulse. Still more had his theological admirers, who, if aware of his secret pursuits, disdained them. By the end of the eighteenth century the lesson was well learned. Educated Christians commonly assumed that the existence of God could and should be deduced logically from tangible evidence. Reason and experiment seemed the high road to certainty.

Not everyone thought so. Long ago Calvin had warned against overreliance on natural theology for evidence of God. To be sure, nature manifested God. But man's corrupted faculties could derive from nature only confused and distorted ideas of Him unless guided by grace and enlightened by revelation. Calvin encouraged the study of nature but as an aid to piety rather than a proof of God to the benighted.[47] Something of this suspicion persisted. Jonathan Edwards preferred to delight in Nature's God instead of nailing Him down with scientific proofs. Joseph Butler's *Analogy of Religion* (1736), though distinctly a rationalist work, sought to make the paradoxes of Christianity more acceptable by pointing out the puzzles and mysteries in natural religion. Neither stopped the clerical rush to embrace John Ray, but both showed that caution was possible.

In general, reasonable religion progressed less steadily and uniformly than this compressed summary has suggested. Fitting religious beliefs to the New Learning sometimes proved troubling even to zealots, often produced a good deal of wobbling. Samuel Johnson of Connecticut graduated from Yale College in 1714 into an Aristotelian-Ptolemaic universe still unprofaned by Copernicus. Within weeks of his commencement, a shipment of some seven hundred volumes rounded up in London by the colony's agent Jeremiah Dummer arrived at Yale. Newton, Locke, Boyle, Descartes burst into Johnson's world. Within a year he announced himself "wholly changed to the New Learning." By the 1720s Johnson, like Voltaire strongly affected by Samuel Clarke, was drifting toward a mild Deism. In 1727, shocked by the extreme heterodoxy of English Deists, he pulled up short. By the 1750s he had moved so far in the opposite direction as to regret his youthful ardor for modern learning and repudiate the chimera of a religion founded on reason. Yet Johnson had not buried his head in the sands of the past. His God, though ultimately inscrutable, remained a distant spirit who worked through regular natural laws and dealt predictably with His creatures.[48]

Johnson's wanderings illustrate well the considerable range of Enlightenment Christianity as well as its pitfalls for the orthodox. Ezra Stiles, Yale's president from 1778 to 1795, followed a very similar course from orthodoxy to Deism and back to a much modified orthodoxy. Even strays who never looked back did not invariably regard the universe with Samuel Clarke's cheerful faith in the power of reason to dispel its mysteries. Old John Adams told Jefferson, "When we say God is Spirit, we know what we mean as well as we do when we say that the Pyramids of Egypt are Matter." That was to say, "we know nothing." "It has been long, very long a settled opinion in my Mind," he wrote, "that there is now, never will be, and never was but one being who can Understand the Universe. And that it is not only vain but wicked for insects to pretend to comprehend it."[49] So much for the Boyle Lecturers.

Moreover, the God of rational religion had His weaknesses. True, He was benign, wise, powerful, and pleasantly straightforward. But He had the habit of working through mathematical laws and secondary causes; He kept His majestic distance from His creatures; He lacked, in short, the personal touch. The Designer God did not satisfy hunger for communion with the Almighty, counsel in perplexity, reassurance in dejection, inspiration to carry on. Some of the enlightened, Franklin for instance, seem not to have missed this paternal side of the Deity. Most, though, did not want to surrender their old personal God to this abstract Deity. At the same time, neither did they want to sacrifice their modern reasonable God. They resolved the dilemma, more or less, by yielding physical reality and intellectual belief principally to the Designer God while leaving spiritual matters and religious emotion in the warmer clutch of a divine Person.

The outcome was a schizophrenic conception of God. Intellectual assurance came from the Divine Engineer; personal religious experience assumed the Heavenly Father. European religion had perhaps always latently harbored this dissociation, for God straddled the distinct roles of Creator and Savior. But Deism, rational

Christianity, physico-theology magnified the differences and pushed the two personalities toward divorce. In strict logic the two were compatible, but psychologically they now stood light-years apart. The personal God retreated into an impalpable spiritual world. The everyday world was left to the Designer God, drifting ever closer to identity with the anonymous forces of nature.

Most Christians did not have to work out this kind of compromise because they never subscribed to reasonable religion. Samuel Clarke's God would have felt decidedly out of place at a Methodist revival. Granted, most people never had the chance to agree with Clarke because they never heard of him. Yet many writers alert to the religious Enlightenment chose to reject it. Few intellectuals had as firm a grasp of Locke and Newton as Jonathan Edwards, and few as staunchly resisted accommodating God to human reason and hopes. Not all resisters, however, measured up to Edwards's standard of competence. Notwithstanding its author's reputation for wit, Robert South's "Christianity Mysterious," a turn-of-the-century assault on those like Toland who asserted *Christianity Not Mysterious*, seems likely to have convinced only the converted. In contrast, Henry Dodwell the Younger's *Christianity not Founded on Argument* (1742) appeared persuasive enough to provoke some distinguished retorts—possibly not from the quarters he expected, for it is unclear to this day whether Dodwell wrote from Christian faith or Deist irony, to support or to undermine Christianity.[50]

The confusion says volumes about the intellectual climate. Even Edwards's immediate disciples did not always seem to know in what direction they were headed. The so-called New Divinity men never flinched from shocking modern sensibilities with undiluted Calvinist predestination and hellfire; yet (unlike Edwards) they sought to justify Calvinism rationally in terms of human happiness, as if they were a pack of Deists who had somehow got off on the wrong scent. Edwards himself had no taste for an arbitrary and unpredictable God (he denied, for example, the efficacy of petitionary prayer); yet unlike his followers he refused to bind God to human standards, to confine Him within human interests and expectations.[51]

Reasonable religion provoked a widespread and increasingly self-conscious opposition. A kind of ill-focused, often untutored reaction had grown up along with the rationalization of belief, and the counterrevolution gained strength and cogency as the eighteenth century progressed. This pietistic resistance first emerged with real power and coherence toward the end of the seventeenth century in the teachings of the German Lutheran Philipp Jakob Spener. Spener rebelled against his church's stress on dogma and intellectual religion and demanded instead a faith founded on the Bible and personal spiritual experience. Like reasonable Christianity, German *Pietismus* was on the intellectual level a response to the cosmological and metaphysical puzzles and to the proliferation of doctrinal distinctions that troubled the seventeenth century.[52] But pietists reacted in the opposite direction. The pietistic current tapped by Spener soon swelled far beyond the borders of Germany. (Pietism is an amorphous word. It is used here as a very general label for those who denied the primacy of reason in religion.) Pietism burst forth during the eighteenth century in Methodism in England, the Great Awakening in America, even Hasidism in the Jewish communities of Eastern Europe. Its voices ranged from the prayers of unlettered laborers to the erudite elegance of Jonathan Edwards's treatises. Behind these diverse forms, pietism everywhere engendered suspicion of overly intellectualized belief and encouraged an affective, spiritual, or mystical road to God.

Pietism in whatever form represented a sharp dissent from the strategy of the rationalizers of belief. Pietists seldom bothered to challenge directly scientific natural theology, for their concern was less how to show that God did exist than what constituted saving faith in Him. Nevertheless, no one as dubious as pietists could find the argument from design very appealing. Their whole effort insisted that mere reason gave at best a scanty, lifeless knowledge of God. The believer must seek for deeper wells of faith, in whose dim, still waters the soul felt God's touch. Pietists held open a door to knowledge of God not rooted in the sensible world. This is not to make them out as anti-intellectual. No one could levy that charge against Edwards, and the German pietist Nicolaus von Zinzendorf's favorite book after the Bible was Pierre Bayle's sceptical *Dictionnaire historique et critique*. Yet they refused to make intellectual assent the criterion of belief. "We do not lay the main stress of our religion on any opinions, right or wrong," wrote the Methodists' founder John Wesley; "orthodoxy, or right opinions, is at best but a very slender part of religion, if it can be allowed to be any part of it at all." Pietism was more a tendency than a consensus. Edwards, for example, would have blanched at Wesley's cavalier dismissal of the right creed; but he shared the thrust of Wesley's reliance on a spiritual sense rather than on logical demonstration for true knowledge of God.[53] Against the prophets of reasonable Christianity, the pietists protested that the heart has its truths.

It would be wrong to draw a sharp division between rationalism and pietism in eighteenth-century religion. Direct confrontations did sometimes occur, but most people who wanted to rationalize belief were also convinced that knowledge of God lurked within the human mind at a level more primordial than reason. A notion of something like Calvin's *sensus divinitatis* remained common. Cotton Mather, a popularizer of the argument from design, spoke also of the "way of Intuition" as "a more *Immediate* way" of access to Christian truths.[54] Mather implied no denigration of rational belief, only a rather vague companion to it. Indeed, intuitionism could even be worked into an intellectualized system of belief, if the writer were not distracted by the grinding of pietists' teeth.

The Scottish "common sense" philosophers based their epistemology on just such a rational intuitionism, developed most ably in the writings of Thomas Reid. Reacting against Hume's scepticism, these philosophers appealed to certain permanent principles of the human mind—"necessary" or "self-evident" truths—supposed to be recognized intuitively. On the basis of such intuitive judgments, knowledge could be securely founded, knowledge of God in particular. Even morality Reid conceived (following Francis Hutcheson) as flowing from an innate moral sense: a faculty of perception independent of, and equal in status to, other powers of the mind.[55]

The Scottish philosophers, having supposedly done to death the infidel Hume and rescued human knowledge from sceptical carping, enjoyed an influence outweighing their philosophic merits. Americans especially celebrated them. Reid's words, embalmed in the "self-evident truths" of the Declaration of Independence, rang second-hand through thousands of college courses. Americans continued to reverence him and his fellow Scots through most of the nineteenth century. The Scottish philosophers were anything but irrationalists, yet their version of rationalism—and hence their belief in God—rested on prerational intuitions. They owed much of their appeal to the ingenious way in which they preserved and updated a nonrational path to God within the secure, modern structure of Enlightenment rationalism. One could apparently have one's cake and eat it, too.

In this intuitionism, despite its dressing of rationality, there whispered a very old theme that sounded much more loudly in

Edwards, Wesley, and others: a stress on religion as a matter of the affections, the heart. This note could harmonize as well as clash with rational religion. Some Deists, for instance, began to find reason alone too flimsy a platform for their religion. Rousseau, who derived his Deism largely from the archrationalist Samuel Clarke, gave reason a less tyrannical role than did Clarke. Rousseau found the basis of belief in personal spiritual experience, the impulses of the heart. Reason served an essential but subsidiary function: to clarify and test the material provided by feeling. Reason transformed intuitions into a coherent set of beliefs and verified these by rational demonstration, but inner feeling and personal conviction remained always primary.[56]

Neither Reid nor Rousseau wished to break with rational religion; neither divorced the validity of belief from the standards of knowledge that animated science and physico-theology. For Rousseau the intellect remained the ultimate court of appeal; a belief that failed to satisfy reason simply failed. For the common-sense philosophers reason made understandable and accurate beliefs that were ultimately founded on intuition; without shaping and testing in the forge of reason, belief remained chaotic and unreliable. Neither point of view broke with, but rather modified, the religion of reasonable men.

One small side-current in Rousseau's life tells as well as any volume by Samuel Clarke the story of the intellectualizing of belief. Around 1764 Rousseau discovered an interest in botany. Trees and flowers revealed to him "nature's astonishing complexity and 'prodigious variety.'" Rousseau being Rousseau, botanic intricacies inspired emotional effusions. But he could not fend off another, less characteristic train of thought. Faced with nature, Rousseau—this Isaiah of the heart, this Newton of the emotions—could not help rehearsing to himself the well-worn cadences of the argument from design, those austerely logical progressions that led from a rational creation to a rational belief in the power and wisdom of a rational Creator. The reflex would have gratified John Ray.[57]

Leaders of religious opinion had gone a long way toward turning belief in God into a rational assent. The existence of their God was known in the same ways that one confirmed the facts of this tangible world. So solid, clear, and concrete a belief they hoped would send atheists flying into oblivion. Whether they would succeed in this, or even in winning over believers who doubted that God fit so easily into a rational, graspable world, remained uncertain. But then, so did the wisdom of their strategy.

An Answer: Belief Moralized

Rational religion needed an agenda as plain and reasonable as its credenda. Traditional goals lost their obviousness. Praying for divine aid seemed a trifle odd if the Supreme never budged from the course set by regular laws, and ritual worship sometimes began to give off a faint aroma of superstition or, worse, of the ridiculous. Not that the enlightened suffered embarrassment when caught at these primitive mysteries. Franklin himself from time to time frequented public worship (though he apparently thought it more for the public good than his own), even at some periods indulged in regular private prayer.[58] But trying to win the Deity's favor or to commune with Him or to sing His glory—these traditional religious purposes no longer struck reasonable believers as adequate. There was (most agreed) nothing *wrong* with prayer and praising. But they failed to satisfy the appetite for a really substantial religion. They belonged more properly with the incomprehensible, arbitrary God of benighted Hebrews and gothic ignorance than the businesslike, plain-dealing Monarch of Newton's cosmos. These otherworldly enthusiasms might be fine in their place; but a Christianity really *centered* on them looked weak: old-fashioned and faintly silly, an easy target for scoffers and atheists.

To put the case so baldly overstates it considerably, but also points to a real and important tendency. Apologists feared that, without a clear and universally acceptable purpose, religion might easily fall prey to scepticism. And, apologetics aside, many church leaders felt uncomfortable with a belief still oriented toward some ungraspable unfamiliar . . . something, rather than realigned toward the comprehensible and rational world of modernity. They did not want belief to evaporate into wispy pieties, and they were anxious to make their religious beliefs congruent with their principles in other matters: they sought consistency and wholeness.

For these reasons a thoroughly down-to-earth moralism became as important as rationality in reasonable religion. This judgment may ring strange to one who recalls Voltaire's mistresses, Franklin's affairs, or even the timid worldliness of eighteenth-century Boston, woefully fallen away from its Puritan mission. But in fact morality was the business of rational religion, in both its Deist and Christian variants.[59]

This approach hardly set the enlightened apart as a peculiar people, for the same moralistic streak ran through pietism. The Methodists in England bent their efforts (with remarkable success) toward the moral reform of the laboring classes. What struck contemporary observers most forcefully about the American revivals of the 1740s—aside from nasty tempers and bizarre behavior—was a notable elevation in the moral standards of the converted. Even Jonathan Edwards, a man with more taste for mysticism than moralism, began his defense of the Connecticut Valley revivals by heralding the moral cleansing that had left his town of Northampton unprecedentedly "free of vice." The local youths had given up their "reveling, frolicking, profane and unclean conversation, and lewd songs"; and there had "also been a great alteration amongst both old and young with respect to tavern-haunting."[60] Probably in the worst of times the citizens of Northampton had seldom been much assailed with tavern-haunters' lewd songs rending the night. So when Edwards called attention prominently to the general straightening up, he revealed how deep now ran concern for moral behavior. The difference between an Edwards and a Wesley, on the one hand, and a Samuel Clarke or Jonathan Mayhew, on the other, was not moral intensity but the context and purpose of morality.

The moralism that dominated reasonable religion—and struggled for ascendancy even in pietism—needs to be understood in a broader context than the Enlightenment. Religion is Janus-faced. With one countenance it looks at everyday life and provides rules to regulate conduct; with the other it peers beyond earthly confines and claims to offer glimpses into a transcendent life. These two spheres are rarely, if ever, divorced. Moral behavior has usually been regarded as in some way connected with, as cause or effect of, the path to the transcendent. And some form of supernatural grace has appeared the indispensable aid to a moral life. Nevertheless, there is tension, even competition, between morality and (for want of a more precise word) holiness. The result can be that one dominates so heavily that the other fades into insignificance. Or morality and holiness can drift apart, so as to seem almost irrelevant to each other. Some religions (Hinduism, for example) concentrate their energies on what transcends this world; others (such as Islam) stress action in this world. Religion in the Christian West has historically struggled to resolve the tension, to hold moralism and spirituality together yet to strike a balance between them. The balance was now shifting toward morality: a perennial religious concern for morality was turning into moralism.

Moralism had not burst suddenly onto the religious scene in 1700. Ever since the pre-Reformation period, a higher premium on right behavior had begun to alter the balance within Western religion between this mundane world and the world of the spirit.

But, for most of the religious leaders of the sixteenth and seventeenth centuries, morality remained tightly yoked to a sense of the mystery and majesty of a God Who transcended worldly categories. This perception survived into the eighteenth century in, for example, Jonathan Edwards, in direct descent from John Calvin. In such a union, morality was only one facet of humanity's seamless relationship to the universe and the mystery of being. Concern for upright behavior was shaped by a feeling of man's utter dependence on a fathomless power. Morality became, potentially, a way of directing human activity toward the transcendent divine. The average preacher perhaps lacked Teresa of Avila's feeling for this point; but the structure of, say, Calvin's theology or Ignatius's *Spiritual Exercises* did not allow him to forget it.

The apologists of reasonable religion wanted to forget it. From their point of view, Teresa's feeling was just the problem. Directing human activity toward an unfathomable transcendent sent it in precisely the wrong direction. It was *this* world, not some other, for which morality mattered. Deists and enlightened Christians alike divorced morality from spirituality, played down the latter, and made of religion mainly a moral guide.

The Deists' reduction of religion to morality is well known. Jefferson managed the astonishing trick of distilling Jesus' teachings into nothing more than a set of moral maxims: all else smacked of priestcraft and superstition. Franklin (who appreciated a lively preacher) found sermons "very dry, uninteresting, and unedifying" when "not a single moral Principle was inculcated or enforc'd." The most famous section of Franklin's famous autobiography is the elaborate chart that he prepared for his daily examination of conscience. For morality was the alpha and omega of his religion: "The most acceptable Service of God was the doing Good to Man." And morality itself he defined in purely human terms: "Vicious Actions are not hurtful because they are forbidden, but forbidden because they are hurtful, the Nature of Man alone consider'd." Franklin was not aberrant. To Deists generally a moral life was the worship that God demanded. Morality was, as Rivarol put it, "a universal religion."[61]

Even the Deist who brushed closest to mysticism, Jean Jacques Rousseau, held morality to be the essence of religion. True, religion had to satisfy emotionally, but its substance was purity and innocence. Worship and doctrines signified little. "What matters to man," declared Rousseau, "is the fulfilling of his duties on earth."[62] For other Deists emotion also figured, but their reverence and awe were fuzzy responses to the sublimity of nature rather than longings for union with God. Voltaire was capable of revering his clockmaker Deity, but to call the man otherworldly would be ludicrous. Behavior in this world was what religion was all about.

Christians who combined their rationalism with revelation did not lag far behind. Jonathan Mayhew described Christianity as "principally an institution of life and manners, designed to teach us how to be good men, and to show us the necessity of becoming so."[63] Not every enlightened Christian steered so near to Deism, but all tacked to the same breeze. Cotton Mather, a much more orthodox Puritan, would never have thought instruction in "life and manners" the principal purpose of Christianity. But the moralistic impulse that underlay both the reforming societies he founded and his "essay upon the good," *Bonifacius* (1710), leaned somewhat in Mayhew's direction. It is ironic that Mather's essay is best remembered through Franklin's parody, the Silence Dogood Papers. For despite Franklin's jabs, those two preachers stood shoulder to shoulder in the conviction that God's will is the improvement of this world. What separated Mather, Mayhew, and Franklin was that the erratically enlightened Puritan still felt the transcendent mystery of God, while the rational Christian had pared away most of it, and the Deist had discarded virtually all.

As with the Enlightenment generally, only a minority fully embraced the moralism of reasonable religion. After all, Calvinists rather substantially outbalanced the Franklins and the Mayhews in America, even in 1790. But minorities sometimes exert influence out of proportion to their numbers. By the end of the century, even Edwards's heirs were stumbling into an awkward accommodation with the moralist stance of enlightened Christianity. The so-called New Divinity men could not altogether resist the appealing down-to-earth sensibility that Edwards had rejected. Their moral teaching lost some of the deeper resonance that morality had had in Calvin's Geneva and Pascal's Port-Royal and Winthrop's Boston. It came closer to an insistence simply on molding behavior into prescribed norms. To be sure, the norms were still held to be divinely prescribed, and behavior was still linked with personal salvation and, at least rhetorically, with the inhuman purposes of God. But the mystical strain was perceptibly fading; moralism was looming larger—and more and more becoming valued as an end in itself. The change is difficult to define precisely, more a matter of attitudes than of ideas. But certainly the meaning and end of morality had come to be conceived more narrowly, and moralism itself had come to bulk larger in religion, as the mystery of the divine receded from attention.[64] Here lay, as many commentators have pointed out, the final tragedy of Edwards's career. Where he, beneath all his rigorous logic, had still understood morality as one reverberation of man's encounter with the terrible sweetness of divinity, his disciples increasingly conceived it as a rational weighing of merit and demerit by a rational Judge. By doing so they eventually undercut the whole Calvinist scheme, but that is another story.

Even in these unlikely hands, then, the moral eagerness of the Reformation was being transformed into something new. Moralism increasingly stood on its own, understood as almost an end in itself (though one specified by God), more and more often divorced from spirituality, rent out of the seamless web of love and salvation and dependence that in an older view had bound God and man together. This was not an accident but the result of a deeply held and far from contemptible conviction that belief in God needed to be demystified and shaken loose from an antiquated world view in order to appeal to the best minds of this new age.

And this moral transformation of religion involved more than the simple ascendency of moralism. In an effort to reconcile older beliefs with the Enlightenment's new world, the very conception of morality was being changed: both its sources and its basic dictates. These new views remained the property mostly of Deists and rational Christians. But from that strategically placed elite they would later ramify through Anglo-American culture.

Enlightenment writers, accustomed to causation through regular laws and convinced that natural laws governed human nature itself, grew restless with the idea of a morality handed down directly from on high. Resentment of authority, an active principle in men like Voltaire and Franklin and Adams, sometimes gave an added twitch to their unease. They sought the origins of morality instead in human nature and social life, bypassing or at least supplementing the dictates of the Almighty. This did not entail a repudiation of the past. Stoicism had imparted to Christianity in its cradle an enduring confidence that morality was rooted in the law of nature as expressed in human nature.

Still, the change was real. Its less significant aspect involved more frequent allusions to natural morality, fewer to divine commandments. More specific and important was the conviction that natural moral principles could be extracted from study of the collective vicissitudes of human lives. Moralists here took a large step away from the medieval and Renaissance approach to natural law, which proceeded from God as a first postulate. They thought themselves to be staking out a new science of man, like political economy or psychology. It would preserve traditional religious values—and particularly the axiom that morality derived ultimately from God's will—by justifying them in modern secularized terms.[65]

Although moral philosophy strictly defined was more a psychological than historical science, morality was thought to be revealed in the study of history and civilizations. Morality did not become precisely a product of history, for its principles remained timeless and universal, as originally cast into law by the Author of the code. But history was a mine from which the ore of human behavior could be dug out, the obscuring dross washed away, and the lineaments of moral law clearly seen in human nature. Never mind that the natural morality thus excavated bore a family resemblance to Christian canons of behavior; that was only to be expected. What mattered was the root assumption. And in that respect enlightened moralists moved, as one of their late-Victorian heirs, the psychologist G. Stanley Hall, once wrote, "from the view that morality was a code of laws which God revealed in Scripture, to the view that his code was best studied in the innate intuitions and sentiments of man."[66] Moral law still came from God, but finding it out became a matter of observation and reason.

In this climate, any moral precept resting solely on divine decree, especially one useless in common-sense living, could appear suspect if not palpably fraudulent. Benjamin Franklin was prepared to toss aside traditional commandments as readily as the leavings from yesterday's dinner unless they showed themselves fitted to human needs. He reinstated humility in his list of virtues only when friends warned him that his arrogance impeded his social climbing. Franklin was an extreme case, but any enlightened preacher who wished to vindicate Biblical morality felt obliged to justify its usefulness to man. Though its umbilical cord still tied it to God, morality showed an inclination to migrate toward self-consciously human standards.

Writers of this mind leaned more heavily on those moral principles that carried obvious human import. Montesquieu conceded in 1721 that the "first aim of a religious man must surely be to please the divinity who established the religion he professes." But what Montesquieu gave with one hand he took away with the other: "The most certain way to achieve this end is without any doubt to observe the rules of society and the duties of humanity."[67] A disarmingly bland statement until one stopped to think about it.

Most of the "duties of humanity" needed no specification; the ancients had inculcated them. But some were new in the eighteenth century, at least in the prominence they were gaining. The greatest novelty was humanitarianism. Those broadly tolerant Anglican preachers called Latitudinarian, in the latter part of the seventeenth century, were among the first to enjoin firmly the duty of compassion. Their writings built a broad circulation in America during the next hundred years. Sympathy for suffering remained fitful and cramped but did burst forth at times. Compassion (among other motives) inspired the coeval desires both to drown in tears the readers of English novels and, more substantially, to abolish slavery. Not, however, until after 1800 would humanitarianism fully flower.

Already in the eighteenth century compassion began to realign moral principles. Suffering, even of strangers or animals, provoked unexampled revulsion; the infliction of it stank of grave sin—among the relatively few who cared much. "We may pretend to what RELIGION we please," exploded an Anglican divine in 1776, "but Cruelty is ATHEISM." (The habit of attributing atheism to any unpleasant person had not yet petered out.) The invention of sadism, after all, required not only the divine Marquis but also a sensibility shocked by his taste. A man more widely acquainted with actual suffering than de Sade, John Wesley, observed that "benevolence and compassion toward all forms of human woe have increased in a manner not known before, from the earliest ages of the world."[68] As compassion infused moral sensibilities, it grounded morality more solidly in earthly concerns. Did cruelty seem sinful because it offended God or because it hurt man?

The idea of progress also contained the germ of a new moral principle. The gradual betterment of human society, the relief of suffering, the spread of enlightenment, all the benefits of progress implied a moral purpose incarnated in the actual course of human history. Conceivably the struggle for progress could thus itself become a moral imperative. Already at century's end the more up-to-date millennialist Christians were preaching a hybrid kind of secular progress toward the Kingdom of God: ultimately mapped by God but immediately powered by human effort exerted within the confines of human history. Even outside the millennialist camp, progress radiated beneficence. Whether these moral implications would ever amount to much remained uncertain. Only a few brash optimists like Turgot invested more than a flickering hope in the continuance of progress. Still, to the limited extent that progress was congealing into a moral goal, it, like humanitarianism, pulled morality into closer identification with the course of events on this earth.

This change in the moral center of gravity tugged God along in the same direction. Such a secondary effect was easily overlooked but none the less real. The dominance of moralism over enlightened religion induced devotees to regard God Himself as concerned first and foremost with morality. A person who believed that the best worship of God was doing good to man—as Franklin and Jefferson and Mayhew believed—naturally attributed the same sentiment to God. When Mayhew declared that "the whole tenor of our Lord's preaching was *moral*," he assumed that the Son spoke for the Father.[69] The moral warmth of the climate wilted other aspects of the divine nature, less protected by their relevance to human life. Man's existential dependency and God's ultimate mystery still usually got a nod, but often only that, and occasionally even less. This did not always reflect active hostility on the part of the enlightened, sometimes just neglect, the unintended consequence of a decision to cultivate other gardens. In reasonable religion God, like His human creatures, began to seem essentially a moral agent.

His morals, moreover, bore remarkable resemblance to human moral ideals. This coincidence did not strike the enlightened as odd: it was indeed the whole point, for religion was to be made easy and open to human understanding. A rational God would scarcely display a morality befogged in mystery, incomprehensible to the poor creatures commanded to obey it. Therefore, the morality that reached perfection in God (and bound Him, for God could not contradict His own nature) seemed necessarily the same as the natural morality evident imperfectly but substantially to human beings.

Thus, for example, God had to be a humanitarian. His creation, perplexingly, did not always give that impression. And the Enlightenment's obsession with the theodicy problem—how could a good God create evil?—reflected a puzzled insistence that God measure up to human standards. Eternal damnation and original sin in particular jarred humane sensibilities and stumped rational minds. In 1710 Daniel Whitby, rector of Salisbury Cathedral, attacked original sin on the ground that imputing Adam's malfeasance to his descendants was "exceedingly cruel, and plainly inconsistent with the Justice, Wisdom, and Goodness of our gracious God." The dilemma so exercised that humane and enlightened man Charles Chauncy that in 1782, to the scandal of Boston's other ministers, he publicly denied the eternal sufferings of hell and pronounced in favor of universal salvation.[70] Such heresies did not spread like wildfire: Chauncy brooded his unorthodoxy secretly for a quarter century before working up the nerve to unveil it. But those who believed in the new-model Deity could hardly help raising such questions. As the archetype of human morality, God expressed the most elevated human ethics. He thus above all had to be—perhaps the favorite adjective of enlightened divines—*benevolent:* disinterestedly willing the happiness of all His creatures.

A sharper repudiation of the God Whose ways passeth all understanding is hard to imagine; nevertheless, Jehovah had scarcely vanished altogether. Methodists, Baptists—most people, in fact—clung to a pretty unenlightened idea of God. Such tenacity did not spring sheerly from ignorance (though neither should its role be underestimated). John Wesley was nobody's fool, and very few of the enlightened had as firm a grip on Newton and Locke as Jonathan Edwards. These dissenters judged reasonable religion to misrepresent God and therefore repudiated it. And even among the most enlightened Christians, like Charles Chauncy, the infinite wrath and dreadful mystery of God obtruded on occasion. On the whole, though, the inhuman face of God receded before His reliable rationality and benevolence, His comforting congruence with human sensibilities.

In their moralism, as in other respects, enlightened believers chose to adapt their belief to the rationalizing temper of secular thought. Otherwise, their apologists feared, belief in God might succumb to the growing threat (if still minute reality) of unbelief. Yet reasonable religion added up to more than an apologetic strategy. It was the latest chapter in the perpetual struggle of believers to reconcile their belief in God with the persistent realities and changing human understandings of the world about them. A rationalized and moralized belief was not the only option for adaptation, but it was the most self-consciously and appealingly modern. And to many, perhaps most, educated people it seemed far and away the most promising. Where it would lead in the next century remained to be seen.

3

A God of Mind and Heart, 1790–1850

In the 1790s the enlightened believer, drowsing in his cozy rationalism, was startled awake. The Reverend Jedidiah Morse rose up, terrible as an army with banners, and from the rude outreaches of Charlestown, Massachusetts, swept down upon the cities of the plain—that is, Boston—to smite the infidel Deist and the rationalizing Unitarian. Hundreds of his brethren from pulpits throughout the land roared their own counterattacks against what Yale's president Timothy Dwight called the "Triumph of Infidelity."[1] Evangelical heart-religion, nurtured in numberless revivals, penetrated the very citadels of Enlightenment. Devastation fell upon reasonable religion. So successful proved the assault that by the 1830s the last crippled Deists had been driven into that outer darkness where dwelt only disreputable radicals. A new and very different tone inspired American religion.

Few victories have concealed so much irony. Even while damning Deists, church leaders swallowed the Deist conception of a natural-law God. Even while lauding the converted heart, they absorbed the maxim that belief in God rests on intellectual assent to a demonstrable proposition. Even while preaching the blood of the Lamb, they devoured the Enlightenment's moralism and its God bound by human morality. Ritual cannibalism purports to transfer the life-force of a slain enemy to the voracious victor. In this case it worked. The Enlightenment's animating principle in religion was to tie belief in God securely to the kind of clear, rational, tangible realities evident in the world as observed. What could not be so rooted (grace, spiritual communion, mysterious doctrines) either faded away or drifted into supernatural dissociation from ordinary reality. This same impulse inspired the leading nineteenth-century spokesmen of Anglo-American religion.

Yet unchecked contemplation of the Enlightenment's persistence distorts the picture as gravely as forgetfulness of it. Coleridge begins to appear a philosophe. Even in its heyday, the Enlightenment hardly seized every mind and certainly not every soul. Most American church members belonged to denominations professedly Calvinist until well after 1800. Outside of the seaboard centers of culture, many still lived in a pre-Newtonian world where indifference, not Deism, threatened Christianity. More to the point, even in circles where the Enlightenment prospered, a reaction set in during the 1790s. The religious landscape began to change. A new religious sensibility, warmer, more devout, more inward, suffused the principles inherited from the Age of Locke and Newton. This new temper opened new dimensions in modern belief and spread it to far wider ranges of the populace. How church leaders handled this opportunity would shape the prevailing conception of God and the foundation of belief.

Evangelicalism

Of all nineteenth-century modes of belief, none was more influential than Evangelicalism, and few more contemptuous of "reasonable" religion. Its influence gives Evangelicalism a claim to prime importance. Its suspicion of Enlightenment religion makes it a critical test of the continuing strength of rationalized and moralized belief. If ardent Evangelicals followed the example of Jonathan Mayhew, one hardly needs to point out that, for example, the Unitarians directly descended from Mayhew did also. Moreover, Evangelicalism was the primary source of the "heart-religion" that potentially challenged the long effort to make belief plain and palpable. For all of these reasons, Evangelicalism is the best window onto nineteenth-century belief—and hence onto the immediate background of unbelief.

Knowing the circumstances under which Evangelicalism grew up clarifies its mature attitudes. To conservative folk, the French Revolution seemed rationalism run wild: the nightmarish consequence of scepticism unleashed upon the restraining ordinances of religion and civil society. In 1794 Thomas Paine's Deist Bible, *The Age of Reason*, shocked the orthodox. While blood dripped from the guillotines of Paris, Paine, this rabid beast of Jacobin radicalism, unaccountably speaking English, sank his fangs into all that was good and true. He flayed the churches, mocked God's Word. Even the equable merchants of Boston panicked; tutors inoculated every Harvard student against the virus with a copy of Richard Watson's *Apology for the Bible.*[2] Rational religion had dipped its hands in gore.

These fears superheated a reaction already brewing against overrationalized religion. In both England and America, revulsion spoke loudest in the rising voices of Evangelicalism. Evangelicalism grew from the pietistic movements that had thrived during the eighteenth century among Protestants resistant to the Enlightenment: Methodism in England, the Great Awakening in America. As their name implies, Evangelicals called for a return to the authority of the Bible. They demanded conversion and personal commitment to Jesus. They insisted on moral purification of both the individual and society. They preached that religion flows from the heart; doctrines mattered, but only if infused with deep personal feeling. In the wellsprings of the heart, the child found his Father.

In the heart, Evangelicals also tapped the power that gave them triumph. Revival meetings, pioneered by Awakening preachers in America, pitched their appeal to emotion rather than reason—and swept in sinners by the bushel. During the so-called Second Great Awakening, from about 1800 to 1835, revivals peppered the country from raw Kentucky to the old coastal cities. The plea to the heart helped Evangelicalism to overcome its intellectually unfashionable origins and emerge as the greatest single force in the history of American religion.

Stress on the heart puts in question the role of the head, and Evangelicals differed on this. The movement divided roughly into two wings. One, strongest in the Southern states, typified by Methodists, Baptists, and the groups that would congeal as Disciples of Christ, played down doctrine and all matters of the intellect. Their preachers became celebrated but not their professors. A second wing, centered in the Northeast and Old Northwest but not insignificant in the Southeast, included most notably Presbyterians and Congregationalists as well as Evangelical Episcopalians and (insofar as the term can apply) Unitarians. This branch joined to heart-religion the traditional strengths of these denominations in theology and moral philosophy. Known for both preachers and professors, these Evangelicals became the most powerful shaping influence on the moral and spiritual side of Victorian culture in America (as their English brethren did across the Atlantic). It was they who had greater importance in the background of unbelief and who will principally be meant when Evangelicals are referred to.

To single out Evangelicalism for special attention is not to ignore the larger character of American religion. For Evangelicalism expressed pervasive tendencies in early nineteenth-century religion—inclinations by no means confined to denominations strictly Evangelical like Presbyterians and Methodists. Such churches indeed embraced the majority of American Protestants. But Evangelicalism exemplified a religious temper widespread beyond the boundaries of its own denominations and even those of Anglo-American culture. Moreover, educated Evangelicals invoked the same Scottish common-sense philosophy, the same arguments from design as other educated Anglo-American Protestants. Evangelicalism was a concentrated solution of active elements widely present in more dilute form.

The family resemblance between Evangelicals and, say, many Unitarians was too obvious to be interesting.[3] Consider a more extreme example. No Christian church seemed more remote from Protestant Evangelicalism, less susceptible to Evangelical influence, than Roman Catholicism. Adherents of each feared, often hated, the other. Yet American Catholicism came to display, veiled in its own traditions, many of the defining motifs of Evangelicalism. A vigorous moralism, directed especially against drink and sex; emphasis on personal religious experience; elevation of the heart over the head; talk of an imminent "spiritual revolution" in the United States—these Catholic themes uncannily echoed Evangelicals. The parish mission movement even mimicked the techniques of Protestant revivalists. The cult of the Sacred Heart of Jesus excelled in imaginative appeal any symbol of heart-religion Protestants devised. Yet these Catholic practices, though possibly encouraged by Evangelical example, did not derive from it. They sprang from the devotional revival then sweeping Catholic Europe. For the forces that powered Evangelicalism surged up throughout Western Europe and America.[4]

This was why Evangelicalism exerted such extraordinary influence. And this is also why it merits special attention from anyone trying to decipher the unique mode of believing in God that evolved during the first half of the nineteenth century: the religious culture that spawned unbelief. Evangelicalism neither rejected nor simply perpetuated the legacy of the Enlightenment. Like Anglo-American religion in general, it involved both continuity and innovation.

Continuities: God Divided

There was no escaping the fact, however much tactful words disguised it, that the God of Abraham and Isaac, of Augustine and Aquinas, of Luther and Calvin could hardly any more command credence from an alert twelve-year-old. Well before 1790, the idea had fully formed that God acted in two distinct modes. Although His spiritual governance remained immediate, personal, and except in broad principles unpredictable, He managed His visible world through impersonal natural laws. Fuzzy edges remained, but in general the supernatural had hived off from nature. At first confined mostly to Deists and liberal Christians, this image of a divided God became hard for others to elude in the early nineteenth century.

The difficulty of evasion resulted in large part from scientific advance. Natural-law explanations of events replaced classification of data as the basic method of all except the life sciences. "Science," intoned the American physicist Joseph Henry, "does not consist in a knowledge of facts but of laws." Pierre Simon Laplace's nebular hypothesis plausibly accounted for the origin of the solar system. Charles Lyell's "uniformitarian" geology explained the history and structure of the earth's surface by invoking action of wind and water. John Dalton's reformulation of the ancient atomic hypothesis provided a key for decoding chemical reactions. All of this had taken place by the 1830s, when Michael Faraday began the experiments that would lead in the end to field theory. Scientists, with the large exception of biologists, needed God now only as a First Cause, the Author of natural laws. The laws themselves explained what actually happened. Implications of this conception of God's work ramified quickly beyond science; what place, if any, remained for miracles became a hot topic in the 1830s.[5]

Evangelicals had good reason to resist this natural-law Deity. Most of them were orthodox in theology and suspicious of anything that smacked even remotely of Deism and its abstract Designer God. Their stress on heart-religion, conversion, and the sinner's personal bond with his Savior required a warm, active, personal God. One could hardly pour one's soul out to a natural law.

Yet they did not resist, for not even Evangelicals needed to fight off science to keep their personal God. The bifurcation of God's role allowed them to accept God's impersonal action in all things natural while preserving His personality and immediate loving care in all things spiritual. This divine schizophrenia did not always sit easily. But neither did it dim Evangelical fervor nor in any obvious way threaten Christianity.

Most church leaders, including Evangelicals, in fact took the opposite view. They not only yielded to this natural-law God but welcomed Him as an ally. They conceived natural laws as the agency and expression of God's loving care, natural law functioning for them much as particular providences had for their Puritan ancestors. The predictability of natural law indeed gave it advantages over a more arbitrary providence, for it lent "*great certainty*" to many human transactions with God. And yet this almost mechanical reliability entailed no lessening of divine concern for humankind. The revivalist maestro Charles Grandison Finney staunchly denied that creation was "a vast machine," going "on alone without [God's] further care." Every "natural event" displayed in its very obedience to law "a universal superintendence and control."[6] Finney was not about to put a Deist gloss on natural law.

Yet he had moved closer to the Deists than he wanted to imagine. Like them, Finney "preferred to think of God simply as the Creator and Governor of the universe, the God of nature, who works according to the fixed laws of physics and of psychology that he has made known to man." Even revivals, Finney claimed, resulted not from the mysterious workings of divine grace but were "a purely philosophical [i.e., scientific] result of the right use of constituted means"—just like the production of a crop of grain, to borrow Finney's own analogy. God, using His ministers, worked on sinners through the natural laws of human psychology; even grace obeyed natural law. Contrast this with Jonathan Edwards's description of his Northampton revival as "a very extraordinary dispensation of Providence: God has in many respects gone out of and much beyond his usual and ordinary way."[7] Finney shocked some conservatives, who accused him of heresy. But it turned out to be Finney, not his critics, who shaped the theory and practice of revivalism. And even his critics complained only that he drew the line between natural and supernatural in the wrong place. They, too, admitted that in physical events divine providence tracked natural law—agreeing in this not only with Finney but with the bogeyman of Evangelicals, Thomas Jefferson.

Jefferson's rather chilly Divine Architect, however, acquired a warmer personality in Evangelical imaginations. This was not just wooly romanticism. Evangelicals insisted that God did more than build cosmic steam-engines; He touched souls directly in a spiritual realm above the merely physical. This side of Evangelicalism is not to be underestimated; yet neither is its other side. Evangelicals, in common with virtually all educated Americans, accepted the divided God of the Enlightenment.

Indeed, they more than accepted Him: they helped to diffuse this bifurcated idea of God throughout American culture. The Enlightenment's rational religion, though influential, was no mass movement; it was a side current flowing along the edge of the religious mainstream. Evangelicalism *was* the mainstream. Evangelicals strove to shape the minds of their fellow citizens—to "Christianize America," as they said. And through revivals, moral-reform organizations, juvenile literature, Sunday schools, tract societies, public schools, and sheer persistence, they succeeded to an impressive extent. Inevitably there filtered down, especially into the growing middle classes, not only the doctrine of the Atonement and the fear of strong drink but also the views of natural-law providence common among Evangelical preachers and writers. These latter ideas penetrated even more widely than the moral reforms, perhaps because a belief in natural law put fewer strains on human frailty than a belief in total abstinence.

Thus, conviction of a natural-law God, once confined to advanced thinkers, became common property of educated Christians. The old "steady sellers" of the eighteenth-century book trade—devotional volumes featuring a mysterious, unpredictable Jehovah—expired by about 1820. They were replaced by a new religious literature with a new, reliable Deity. In the characteristic Peter Parley books of Samuel Griswold Goodrich (juvenile best-sellers from the 1830s through 1850s), thunderstorms became meteorological phenomena rather than divine tokens.[8] Few tolerably well-read people believed any longer that God interrupted the course of nature to punish or reward His creatures. A terrific storm might still in 1850 evoke thoughts of divine providence; the death of a loved one almost surely would. But providence no longer broke natural law; they moved in tandem.

Swallowing this novelty put some strain on orthodox Christians, even on some fairly unorthodox ones. After all, such division of divine labor, if it did not divorce God from tangible reality, obviously did distance Him. It was precious little comfort to know that God watched every sparrow fall if He refused to do anything about it. The intimacy, security, and immediacy of God's presence in everyday life were compromised, psychologically if not logically. Omnipotence was not reduced, for God had chosen to create natural law, but was somehow cheapened by this self-imposed obedience to law, this almost bourgeois self-restraint. Knowing that God might still swoop down upon the unsuspecting sinner in a stricken conscience or an impalpable spiritual confrontation did not entirely console. One wanted more from God.

So the division of God met some stiff resistance. The most intransigent rebels were the American Transcendentalists. Emerson ran up the flag in *Nature* (1836), where he insisted that one *could* see God "face to face" in the physical world. Natural regularities only veiled God's immediate presence. Immersed in nature, Emerson became "a transparent eyeball"; "the currents of the Universal Being circulate through me; I am part or parcel of God."[9] This was too much. Transcendentalism verged on pantheism when not collapsing into it. And if God became nature, nature could replace God: the orthodox sniffed incipient atheism here. Too, the Transcendentalists set themselves too sharply at odds with prevailing conceptions of nature for many people to swallow their ideas straight. Nevertheless, Emerson did very well as a popular lecturer on the lyceum circuit. Listeners evidently liked at least to toy with his visions. The brisk sales of Wordsworth's poetry and the vogue of the mystic Swedenborg (who taught that each natural object corresponds to a spiritual reality) also testified to a widespread longing to sustain the divine presence in nature.

Such longing usually assumed less exotic forms. Commonest was bland assertion with an apodictic air that the living God indeed dwelt in every breeze—a claim by no means intended to contradict the proposition that His presence never disturbed the regular operations of meteorology. The apparent conflict could be at least partly reconciled (though preachers seldom bothered to). As the eminent Presbyterian theologian James McCosh explained the matter, the complexity in natural events, arising from interaction of different natural laws, allows the laws to affect each individual differently. With omniscient fine-tuning, God originally constructed the machinery so that it would ultimately pressure every person in precisely the way He desired. McCosh adopted an oddly medieval simile: "While the fixed nature of the laws gives to providence its firmness, the immense number and nice adaptation of these laws, like the innumerable rings of a coat-of-mail, give to it its flexibility, whereby it fits in to the shape and posture of every individual man." God had no need to tamper with "the original dispositions and interpositions which he hath instituted." And "piously disposed minds" had no need to "be jealous of the discovery of law in the universe," for natural law implied no slackening of God's providential care.[10]

Yet McCosh's compromise, though very popular, did not really bridge the distance between God's two roles. McCosh refused to abandon God's personal control over natural events, but neither could he save it. All that he could salvage was an oddly impersonal vestige of personality, as if the running of a Model T somehow incarnated Henry Ford. For McCosh, as for others who did not wish to fling themselves athwart conventional wisdom, there was really no way out. One might devise convoluted explanations of how natural laws effected specific divine purposes; one might perceive a divine presence lurking behind impersonal nature; one might repeat over and over that every day in every way every flower manifested God. But, after all, the irreducible fact remained that God touched man directly only in the spirit. In the flesh, only God's laws touched man. At the end of the day, God remained divided. As the young Emerson shrewdly observed about the Designer God of William Paley's popular *Natural Theology*, "Paley's deity and Calvin's deity are plainly two beings."[11] Even the radical strategy of Transcendentalism could not heal what had been sundered. Insisting on God's immanence in nature did not make Him any more essential to explanations of physical events but only added a stuffing of metaphysical down, comforting but not curative. The wall between natural and supernatural might be wished away in Emerson's essays and McCosh's dialectic, but if God had changed the course of nature a whit, it would have floored both men.

One striking bit of social ideology mirrored this sharper distinction between natural and supernatural. For a long time, women had attended church in greater numbers than men. But nineteenth-century writers began to attribute this proclivity to woman's nature; "religion," said a Presbyterian minister in 1837, "seems almost to have been entrusted by its author to her particular custody." The same romantic "cult of true womanhood" that defined women as inherently more religious than men also denoted them as unfitted by nature for the crass realities of business life, or indeed almost any life outside the tender sanctuary of the home.[12] This ideology hardly matched either woman's nature or most women's lives. But the linkage of womanhood and religion (especially the intuitive, etiolated religion attributed to women) said as much about ideas of religion as of women. Just as women were perceived as separated from "real life," so on an unarticulated level religion came to be felt as disjoined from the tangible realities of everyday life.

The alienation of spiritual life from tangible realities, manifest in the Enlightenment, was spreading. Physical reality had clarity and solidity: one could touch, measure, grasp the results of natural law. Spiritual matters—no longer given flesh in earthquakes and epidemics, visions and witchcraft—by contrast often seemed unfocused, elusive, less compellingly *there*. The guardians of belief had to decide how to restore immediacy. One might try to rethink the meaning of spirit for human beings, seek somehow a reconceived grounding for spirituality, cut loose from science and objectively observed nature. Or one might move in another direction: turn attention away from compromised spirituality, seek to solidify belief in God by stressing elements of religion that seemed more solidly within human grasp. The choice was crucial, lest belief slip its moorings and float into evanescence. When Evangelical leaders launched their crusade to Christianize America, their keynote was not mystical contemplation or spiritual search. It was action in the observable world: moral reform.

Continuities: Belief Moralized

In 1797 the president of Yale College, the Reverend Timothy Dwight, mounted a counterattack against Deist encroachments on Christianity among his young charges. In the fervent revival that followed, his students' instinctive first response was to charter a Moral Society.[13] They had struck the chord that would resonate in Anglo-American religion through most of the next century.

They had also projected forward their inheritance from the Enlightenment. Morality formed the backbone of enlightened religion, and at least in this respect Evangelicalism replicated the anatomy of Deism. Far from rejecting the moralism of Jefferson and Paine, Evangelicals Christianized it, charged it with new eagerness, and diffused it throughout the American middle classes. By the 1820s and 1830s, morality had become central in most denominations and surged with an urgency lacking even in the self-improving drive of Benjamin Franklin. No longer the fairly restrained concern of an often cautious elite, moral improvement became the ebullient commitment of millions.

Evangelical morality insisted firmly on personal self-control. Behavior widely tolerated in the eighteenth century became immoral in the nineteenth. Convivial inebriation gave way to temperance, even abstinence. Bawdy tongues were hushed. Sexual peccadilloes once only reprimanded became positively scandalous. Had Lord Byron lived fifty years earlier, he would have raised eyebrows, but fewer mouths would have dropped open. Purity, temperance, duty, diligence, and that archetypically Victorian virtue, earnestness, all were taken with new seriousness.

Evangelicalism also awakened a livelier social conscience. Rational religion had urged people to make themselves benevolent and useful to their fellow creatures. But benevolence and utility are more passive notions than reform, and reform became the watchword of Evangelicalism: reform of oneself, reform of one's neighbors, the reformation of the world! Antislavery, temperance societies, prison reform, public schools—all registered the Evangelical amplification of Enlightenment moralism.

But Evangelicals had no monopoly on enlivened moralism. Unitarians, Episcopalians, Catholics, and Jews felt the impulse. Child-rearing, perhaps the most fundamental social activity, responded to pervasive moralism. Protestant child-rearing literature before 1800 commonly urged a stern regimen to make the child realize early his depravity, bring him face-to-face with the awful prospect of damnation, and prepare him for the critical moment of conversion. In the nineteenth century, child-rearing advice (and, so far as one can judge, practice) instead came to stress a tenderer, more gradual molding of moral capacities. The end in view was less preparation for conversion and more formation of character. Even clergymen writing tracts for youth subordinated saving souls to building character.[14]

It seems ironic that Evangelicals would move away from conversion (a religious concept) toward character (potentially a secular one). Their child-rearing advice suggested the same secularizing direction as Benjamin Franklin. The irony, though, was more apparent than real. Secularization here did not imply any divorce between religion and society. To the contrary, it involved infusing religion into social concerns over which churches as institutions had largely lost authority.

The American Constitution separated church and state. Yet the founding ideology of the republic, forged in the Revolution, proclaimed liberty to depend on a virtuous people; American purity, measured against European luxury and moral declension, confirmed that God had favored the patriots' undertakings. This conviction remained vital in the nineteenth century—and gave Evangelical ministers a convenient lever for thrusting their moral reforms into the center of politics. One of the greatest of those preachers, Lyman Beecher, warned his listeners in 1835, "If you wish to be free indeed, you must be virtuous, temperate, well instructed." This civil religion made traditional religious concerns, chiefly morality, critical in the secular arena, where they naturally lost their transcendental reference.[15] Not man's eternal fate, but the nation's political future, was at stake. This limitation seldom worried Evangelicals, if only because they conflated the nation's future with the coming Kingdom of God.

Nowhere was morality more closely identified with social concerns than in the public school systems that began to take shape in the 1830s. Lyman Beecher's admonition that the republic's survival depended on "well instructed" citizens echoed in Horace Mann, Henry Barnard, and scores of other school reformers, especially after the influx of Irish immigrants began in the 1840s. These educators never thought reading, writing, and arithmetic nearly as important as self-restraint, diligence, and duty.[16] Public schools consequently received wide support from Protestant ministers—and bitter resistance from Catholic clergy, resentful of Protestant flavoring of school curricula. Both sides knew what the schools were about.

To multiply instances would be supererogatory. In republican ideology, public schools, temperance societies, and city missions, an ever-louder stress on social morality resounded. This morality, rooted in Protestantism, was in some sense properly "religious"; but it no longer feared the Lord as much as social disorder. Thus, it became a common platform for religious revivalists and secular reformers, rejuvenators of Christianity as well as repairers of the social fabric. Indeed, the two impulses were often inseparable; so it would be mistaken to regard secularization and religious fervor as inherently at odds. Evangelical devotion actually advanced secularization, as ministers, zealous to bolster Christian authority in American society, imputed sacredness to secular agenda.[17]

Moralism thus served as a bridge to link church and society after the two, like separating islands, began to drift apart. Ministers expected much of moral reform. It not only gave hope of rounding up millions of strayed souls. It provided, more significantly, the strongest tie remaining between ordinary human life and an increasingly remote God. As spiritual realities thinned, the temptation thickened to seize on something as solid as morality.

In truth, many Protestant writers veered close to identifying morality and religion. Most of them would have stood aghast if told so, even more appalled if accused of thereby perpetuating the work of Franklin and Jefferson. Yet Lyman Beecher unwittingly aped Jefferson when he called the Bible "a Code of Laws" and claimed that its "real meaning" lay in the "laws of a moral government" contained in it. A few years later, the Reverend Francis Wayland, president of Brown University and author of America's best-selling textbook of moral philosophy, reduced what the Bible called faith to "a disposition to universal obedience [to God's moral law] pervaded by the spirit of supreme and grateful affection."[18] Whether affectionate morality captures precisely what the Bible meant by faith may be open to question, but Wayland stumbled into this trap only because he was walking in the right direction. Jonathan Edwards would have winced.

Probably most of Wayland's colleagues also winced at so blunt a statement. Orthodox theology would have compelled them to deny that morality was the essence of religion; and both Beecher and Wayland would have denied it, the question being squarely put. And, even beyond formal theological considerations, James McCosh dimly wondered whether modern moralism did not miss "the deepest properties of human nature": "man's feelings of want, his sense of sin, and his longing after God and immortality." But neither official theology nor occasional hesitancy really dimmed the moralism at the heart of Evangelicalism. Most Evangelicals would not have gone as far as Wayland when he declared that "in Religion our only business is to understand and obey the laws to which He has subjected the moral universe."[19] But the whole troop traveled by the same compass.

Nor were Evangelicals unique in gravitating toward identification of religion with morality. This pervasive drift showed up, for example, in the religious novels that proliferated from the 1830s, books where "earthly misbehavior and ethical redemption" eclipsed other religious strivings. Not a Methodist but the Unitarian president of Harvard, the Reverend James Walker, declared that "a man is not a Christian in proportion to the amount of truth he puts into *creed*, but in proportion to the amount of truth he puts into his *life*." Years later, when Henry Adams looked back on his mid-century youth, he recalled that "the score of Unitarian clergymen about Boston, who controlled society and Harvard College" had "proclaimed as their merit that they insisted on no doctrine, but taught, or tried to teach, the means of leading a virtuous, useful, unselfish life, which they held to be sufficient for salvation." Those Unitarians were the direct heirs of the Enlightenment. But in this respect so were the Evangelicals. And so was Frederick Law Olmsted, who owed no loyalty to any denomination, when in 1853 he tried to put his finger on the essence of religion—"the quality which God must have himself"—and pinned it down as "a fundamental sense of right."[20] And, as religion became increasingly a matter of morality, it tightened its grip on the here-and-now.

Moreover, morality itself increasingly stressed the kinds of good that had palpable value within the scope of human life. Though by definition concerned with human behavior, morality need not orient itself toward earthly human good. It can instead face toward a God Whose purposes do not correspond with human purposes, Whose will man obeys without regard to earthly consequence. In such a scheme, morality becomes a means by which man glorifies God and submits to Him; it serves as a supposed path to the transcendent, not to social or self-improvement. This was Calvin's morality and, in the final analysis, Aquinas's, too: the morality of the great theological traditions of both Protestantism and Catholicism. Evangelicals could hardly discard it. We obey the moral law, Wayland insisted, not because moral behavior leads to happiness but because it is the will of God.[21]

Yet according to most church leaders, at least outside the South, human good delightfully coincided with divine will. We recognize God's will, according to Wayland, precisely because obedience *does* maximize happiness.[22] Defenders of the faith had turned into orthodoxy the Enlightenment heresy that morality aimed at the good of humankind, and in so doing they codified a reshuffling of the hierarchy of moral principles.

The ascendancy of two particular moral ideals confirmed this realignment: the doctrine of progress and the humanitarian revulsion from suffering. The Enlightenment's circumscribed and shaky hope for progress bloomed into a confident consensus. It comes as no surprise that a radical reformer like the abolitionist and pacifist Gerritt Smith would declare, "I believe, sir, in the progress of the human race." But so conservative a man as John Calhoun thought that he stood in 1846 at "the dawn of the world's great jubilee"; this emphasizes how deeply embedded the assumption of progress had become.[23] And progress implied not merely material betterment but intellectual and spiritual elevation. It meant, above all, moral progress.

Reservations and doubts hedged these hopes. Samuel Miller's celebrated *Retrospect of the Eighteenth Century* (1804) spoke of limits, yet unknown, to the power of human intellect and warned that morality and knowledge did not advance hand in hand. Fifty years later another Presbyterian, James McCosh, repeated the admonition; material improvements could be turned to good or evil.[24] Above all, progress did not permit complacency: it demanded human striving. Yet progress *would* come, so most educated Americans believed, for it was God's will.

What connected God most directly with progress was the ancient tradition of millennialism, refurbished in Evangelicalism. The Book of Revelation vaguely prophesied (the key passage being Revelation 20:1–6) that the Second Coming of Christ would bring a golden age of a thousand years: the millennium. More or less metaphorically interpreted, the idea had periodically fascinated, occasionally obsessed, Christians. Revived in the eighteenth century, by the early nineteenth it had seized the imaginations of Evangelicals of all stripes. Among the commonest problems of the Methodist backwoods preacher Peter Cartwright was the irrepressible proclivity of the saved to fall into trances, prophesy, "and predict the time of the end of the world, and the ushering in of the great millennium."[25]

By the 1790s, millennial expectations had begun to diverge into two streams. One, called premillennialism by historians, predicted the advent of the millennium after the Second Coming: a sudden irruption of the divine into an increasingly desperate human condition. The other, labeled postmillennialism, expected the Second Coming after the millennium; the golden age, in this view, would prepare the world for the return of Christ and the final establishment of the Kingdom of God. The millennium itself would emerge, not all of a sudden, but as a gradual perfecting of earthly life through human effort, inspired by divine grace.

This latter, postmillennialism, became an article of faith for middle-class Evangelicals. (Premillennialism seems to have spoken more persuasively to the lower orders.)[26] Lyman Beecher, whenever projecting a new moral reform, was apt to wonder, would his latest endeavor form "a part of that great and new system of things by which God is preparing to bless the world and fill it with His glory?" "If we endure a little longer," he exhorted his congregation, "the resources of the millennial day will come to our aid." Charles Finney, more sanguine if possible than Beecher, believed that, if the church did her duty, "the millennium may come to this country in three years."[27] Most Evangelicals kept a lookout.

Postmillennialism steeled confidence in progress, and specifically it reinforced the secular version of progress inherited from the Enlightenment. Men like Jefferson had rested their usually tentative hope for progress on the chance that human reason would control irrational passions. Evangelicalism, looking instead to God's plan, transformed this rational hope into the divine juggernaut of history.[28] Yet the readying of the earth for God's reign, reduced to details, looked very like the thoroughly secular progress predicted by such ungodly reformers as Robert Dale Owen and Frances Wright. A typical scenario appeared in the *Treatise on the Millennium* (1793) of the eminent Congregationalist theologian Samuel Hopkins: an end to wars and lawsuits; universal good health as a result of temperance and "prudent and wise use of the body"; reduction of labor to two or three hours a day, with the time saved given to mental and moral uplift; "a sufficiency and fulness of every thing needed for the body, and for the comfort and convenience of every one"; and the New England farmer's pathetic hope that "ways will yet be found out by men, to cut rocks and stones into any shape they please; and to remove them from place to place, with as little labour, as that with which they now cut and remove the softest and lightest wood." Hopkins did expect that the happy folk of the future would especially savor "religious enjoyment" and devote themselves to "the knowledge of divinity." Otherwise, any secular prophet of progress might have ventured his prognostications.[29]

Moreover, Evangelicals expected that progress toward the millennial day would come through the same technical and scientific advances on which secular reformers pinned their hopes. Hopkins spoke of improvements in "the art of husbandry" and the "mechanic arts" as the engines of progress. By breaking the chains of drudgery, poverty, and ill health, "inventions and arts . . . beyond our present conception" would remove the obstacles to mental and moral elevation.[30] To be sure, material gains mattered only because of moral results, so Evangelicals always made scientific advance instrumental to moral reform. But so did secular reformers.

With passing decades, Evangelical millennialism merged imperceptibly into a more secular idea of progress. Evangelicals never lost the distinctively divine note: their version of progress displayed divine grace and finally led to the kingdom of God. Yet, even while Christianizing the idea of progress, they came perilously close to secularizing their divine progressivism. At times they almost identified growing prosperity, increasing knowledge, and improving social organization with the perfecting of the earth supposed to presage the millennium. In short, they read man's wishes into God's purposes. "Hand in hand with [the Spirit's] work," complacently declared the Rev. R. H. Beattie, "the conveniences of the present life have ever gone"; and he thought it "quite inconceivable" that the millennium "could ever be reached, without carrying along with it the reduction of the miseries of our earthly lot to their minimum."[31]

In this refrain there sounded also the second key theme in the eighteenth century's moral legacy to the nineteenth: humanitarianism. From a fitful and limited impulse, humanitarianism grew after 1800 into a leading ideal (if, like most, often honored in the breach). Evangelicalism in particular inspired antislavery, concern for the insane, prison reform, kindness to animals, and much else. Granted, other motives also impelled these crusades: the sexual degeneracy of slaveholders outraged some Evangelicals more than the suffering of their slaves. Motives are always mixed. This does not alter the salient fact that suffering now appeared a great evil, cruelty among the vilest of sins—and not only to Evangelicals. The notoriously maudlin Victorian sentimentalism was the treacly surface of an unprecedented commitment to ease human suffering. The new style of child rearing, with its heightened tenderness, accent on mildness and affection, and revulsion from too frequent use of the rod, offers but one example. To compare school-discipline in 1800 with what it had become by 1900 is to move from one world into another.

In its compassion, "heart-religion" took on a profoundly human meaning—and that is just the point. Moral progress and diminution of suffering each pointed to the other, and both embodied a moral principle defined in terms of human wants and needs. Both reflected human self-improvement, self-creation, cast in terms of the finite but solidly real world that human beings inhabited, although this was not the whole story. Even secular-minded believers seldom forgot that morality embodied God's will; Evangelicals undertook their crusades specifically to glorify God. Devout men and women sincerely and often at much sacrifice spurned human pleasures to devote themselves to God's work. Their rejection of the world and commitment to the spirit should not be made light of. The irony is that God's work, as conceived, often led them deeper into the world. The *content* of moral ideals projected by church leaders increasingly mirrored the knowable human world—the concrete side of the divided God—not any mysterious world beyond human knowing. The will of God became the good of man.

Conceptions of God Himself adapted to the ascendancy of moralism. Calvinism, which was the creed of most American church members in 1800, illustrated the consequences during the ensuing fifty years. In the hands of its founder, John Calvin, and his early adherents, Calvinism attempted to adumbrate in theological terms the ineffable relationship between human beings and a God so totally "other" (to borrow Karl Barth's phrase) that He lay beyond human comprehension and human standards of judgment. Calvinism's central dogma, predestination, or "election," symbolized this relationship. Human effort availed for nought; the most moral of men stood utterly depraved in God's sight; only free, apparently arbitrary, baffling grace bridged the infinite chasm between God and man. This was the vision of God that Jonathan Edwards had insistently pressed upon New England. And it was a vision increasingly dissonant with modern moralism.

Edwards failed; even New England orthodoxy preferred to accommodate the rigors of Calvinism to human agency and human moral standards. Faith in progress clashed with Calvinist devaluation of human potential; humanitarianism sat uneasily with a God Who tossed souls into eternal fire without regard for human merit or demerit. So puzzling and transcendent a God fitted awkwardly into a religion that more and more highlighted the betterment of man and his world. A few warned that God was *supposed* to be a stumbling block. The Reverend Nathanael Emmons defended original sin by simply pointing out that God transcended human notions of justice.[32] But the compromised versions of Calvinism common after 1800 could scarcely comprehend an ineffable God. Thus, the doctrine of election degenerated into a mechanistic trap, a theological roulette wheel, a caricature of Calvin's intention, with very little to recommend it but its aptitude for terrifying congregations at revival time. Or else its half-hearted proponents papered over the dogma with revisions designed to marry it to more comfortable notions of free will and human agency.

For even Calvinism's defenders knew how appalling it sounded in modern ears. Ask any of its opponents what Calvinism is, observed Lyman Beecher,

> and the response will be, Calvinism is that horrible system which teaches that God has foreordained and fixed, by irresistible omnipotence, whatsoever comes to pass; that he has made a very small number of mankind on purpose to be saved and all the rest on purpose to damn them; that an atonment [*sic*] by weight and measure has been made for the elect only, but which is offered to the non-elect on conditions impossible to be complied with, and they are damned for not accepting what did not belong to them and could not have saved them if they had received it, and that infants as well as adults are included in the decree of reprobation, and that hell no doubt is paved with their bones.[33]

Beecher should have measured the enemy right, since he spent a career soft-pedaling Calvinism to assuage their complaints.

Beecher was certainly on the mark in judging infant damnation the soft underbelly of Calvinism. The Victorian imagination, caught up in adoration of childhood, was peculiarly revolted by the idea of sending a helpless, innocent baby into eternal fire; and infant damnation became the pivot point for humanitarian assaults on Calvinism. A desperate Beecher went so far as to claim never to have "seen or heard of any book which contained such a sentiment, nor a man, minister or layman, who believed or taught it." He had missed a sermon published by his colleague, the aptly named Rev. David Harrowar of upstate New York, who assured readers that "the infants of pious people" who die without saving grace "must be consigned to eternal ruin." No matter that Calvin had repudiated the belief.[34] It seemed to follow from his teachings, and there were enough Harrowars around to color the accusation plausible. Nineteenth-century Calvinists never managed to wriggle out of it.

Yet infant damnation was only the most obviously shaky timber in a structure crumbling throughout, like the deacon's one-hoss shay in Oliver Wendell Holmes's poetic jab at Calvinism (1858). The Beecher family's history displayed in individual lives the gradual humanizing of Calvin's God. Lyman himself never deserted predestination, but he scrambled to get around its hard sayings. God, he felt sure, "will do no injustice," will condemn none but those who sin "knowingly, deliberately, and with wilful obstinancy": in the end most of the race would escape hell. Beecher's footwork looked too nimble by half to more orthodox Calvinists, who tried him for heresy in 1835. He escaped. But uneasiness with an apparently cruel God, disregardful of human striving, had driven him close to the rail.[35]

His children jumped ship. Respect for their father dampened the vehemence of mutiny but altered its outcome not a whit. Harsh mysteries that Lyman could abide, if not applaud, his children could not tolerate. The eldest child, Catharine, lost her fiance in shipwreck in 1822. Although a devout young man, he had not experienced the crucial conversion, which would have given evidence of saving grace (though no one could be certain he died without it). Without grace he died unregenerate and damned. The thought of him cast into eternal flames tormented Catharine, for she, too, had sought conversion and found only a blank wall. Her twistings and turnings drove her finally to exclaim that "a merciful Savior has not left him to perish." She did not argue the point; she simply "resolved" not to "*believe any thing* that obscured" divine justice and mercy. She would not let God be arbitrary and cruel. So much for Calvin.[36]

Catharine's brother Henry Ward Beecher, a preacher more renowned even than his father, likewise did not debate election. He only neglected to mention old doctrines until they faded away. Another sister, Harriet Beecher Stowe, turned out less politic. When her eldest son, Henry, died unconverted in 1857, her father's teaching loomed up as a work of the devil, a "slander . . . against my Lord and my God!" So she sat down at her writing desk and two years later published the literary *coup de grâce* of American Calvinism: *The Minister's Wooing,* a novel that excoriated the alleged cruelty of Calvinism by recreating her sister's horror of 1822.[37]

The Beechers recapitulated the experience of many Evangelicals. To Charles Finney, for example, the incomprehensible God of Calvin made no sense. This was, of course, precisely the point. But Finney expected Him to, expected Him to reward moral effort (as faith in progress demanded), expected Him not to inflict pain arbitrarily (as revulsion from cruelty dictated). Torn between Calvin's God and modern moralism, many born Calvinists looked for a quick exit. The Methodist circuit rider Peter Cartwright, who always enjoyed seeing a good Calvinist go under, told of a Baptist preacher, a "rigid Calvinist" on the not notably tender-hearted frontier, whose "good sense" so rebelled at the *"horrid idea"* of predestination that he plunged headfirst into "universal redemption."[38]

Calvinism did not succumb to argument alone. Criticism of Calvinism had a long history; foes had always accused it of smearing on "the Gospel the Stain of Cruelty and Injustice." Polemics could be parried; obsolescence was another matter. Not the weight of logic but the ever-heavier burden of moralism crushed Calvinism. There was no answer to emotional revulsion. In 1865 the heirs of the Puritans, the Congregationalists, adopted a new Declaration of Faith. Predestination, even Calvin's name, were conspicuously absent.[39]

God was now expected to measure up to human standards. Charles Finney wrote, *"Religion is the work of man.* . . . It consists in obeying God. It is man's duty." In such religion, God's chief emotional significance (though usually not formally His chief role in theology) often came to be that of the source, guarantor, and enforcer of morality. And no distinction in kind made human moral standards inapplicable to divinity; in fact, divine morality came to be identified with, judged by, human morality. We know God's "moral qualities," according to James McCosh, "by the analogy of man's moral sentiments."[40]

Nor did this view of the Deity flourish only among Evangelicals;

if anything, it grew sturdier in soil theologically more liberal. "We consider," said the Unitarian sage William Ellery Channing, "no part of theology so important as that which treats of God's moral character; and we value our views of Christianity chiefly as they assert his amiable and venerable attributes." Indeed, moralization of God provided a founding principle of Unitarianism. In his manifesto, *Unitarian Christianity* (1819), Channing conceded that all Christians "ascribe to the Supreme Being infinite justice, goodness, and holiness." But the orthodox tended "to speak of God magnificently, and to think of him meanly; to apply to his person high-sounding epithets, and to his government, principles which make him odious." Specifically, the orthodox felt "as if he were raised, by his greatness and sovereignty, above the principles of morality . . . to which all other beings are subjected." Channing was right, though most Calvinists were busy trying to deny it: traditionally, Christians had not confined God to the usual human rules of the game. Only now this was ground for complaint: "We cannot bow before a being, however great and powerful, who governs tyrannically. . . . We venerate not the loftiness of God's throne, but the equity and goodness in which it is established."[41] Most Evangelicals could not bring themselves to say out loud the name of the rock on which Unitarians founded their church, but the Unitarians had really gone only one step farther.

By no means everyone succumbed to this temptation, and of those who did, not all fell mortally. The sense that God's ways transcended human scrutiny remained embedded, of course, in theological formulae, and few could fail to be reminded of it at points in their lives by the inexplicable personal losses part of the human lot. But conviction of God's mystery also stubbornly persisted in the personal religion of many, sometimes the most unexpected. Abraham Lincoln, a religious man only by generous definition, saw human beings as driven by mysterious Necessity: "The Almighty has His own purposes." Lincoln was a southerner, and southerners generally retained a stronger feeling for the mystery of God when northerners were losing theirs. So did Catholics as compared with Protestants. But even Ralph Waldo Emerson, who would have shuddered at the idea of being either Catholic or southern, contemplated the "awful calamities" of the Lisbon earthquake with equanimity: "I bow to this hint, this expression of Omnipotence."[42] It is worth noting that Emerson was mystically inclined. Perhaps such a sensibility stiffened his resistance to equating divine intention with human morality. Few leading ministers or theologians evinced much of one.

Moralism thus reshaped conceptions of God's nature and purposes along lines much more recognizably human. He became an underwriter of progress (His grace leading on to the millennium), a model of compassion (Whose "intire [*sic*] moral nature" consisted of "the love . . . of communicating and perpetuating enjoyment").[43] This moralistic God did not hover faintly across some mysterious horizon but participated in the palpable realities of life. He belonged to the naturalistic, not the transcendent, side of the divided God bequeathed by the Enlightenment.

In fact, His morality fitted with apt neatness into the workings of natural laws. Some common antebellum ideas about the causes of disease exemplified this. In 1832 and again in 1849, cholera epidemics devastated the United States. Preachers in every city rushed to drive home the lessons: Cholera was the avenging hand of God, striking at the moral failures of Americans, singling out drunkards, prostitutes, and those who wallowed in slothful filth. Yet few in 1832, even fewer in 1849, claimed that cholera sprang directly from God's hand. Rather, they said, the sinful habits of victims violated the natural laws of health and disease, laid down by God to reinforce morals; and punishment flowed directly from immoral contravention of these laws, only indirectly (though no less surely) from divine action.[44]

The New York public health reformer John H. Griscom, an Evangelical Quaker, generalized the point to all illness: "Indulgence in a vicious or immoral course of life is sure to prove destructive to health." But Griscom struck a hopeful note, for God "has also given us a knowledge of the laws which regulate our growth, and our lives, so that by attending to them, and living purely and uprightly, we may avoid those diseases, in a great degree." Given what Griscom called "the parallelism of moral degradation and physical disease," how could one doubt that natural law both exhibited the rules of morality and rigorously enforced them?[45]

Few educated people did. On a philosophical level, a good deal of confusion prevailed as to just what distinguished a moral law from a natural law (at times, it seemed, nothing). But consensus held that moral law and natural law ran together: that is, the ordinary workings of physical nature and human psychology conduced to morality. The laws of political economy, for example, demanded diligence, thrift, and self-restraint. Violate them, and your punishment was poverty. Intemperance brought in its wake degradation, delirium, and often a criminal's death. Sexual immorality led to disease, loneliness, and shriveling of natural affections. James McCosh put it this way:

> As there are harmonies pre-established between one natural law and another, so there may be, so there are, harmonies between the moral law and the physical laws. God has so ordered his physical government, that it is made in various ways to support his moral government, both in the way of encouraging that which is good and beneficent, and arresting and punishing that which is evil.

And, on the other end of the religious scale, an echo in a different octave: "What a searching preacher of self-command," wrote Emerson, "is the varying phenomenon of Health."[46]

The idea that natural law embodied and enforced morality was a potent secularizing principle. For science, by studying natural law, revealed and inculcated morality—perhaps more effectively than the pulpit. In this respect, as in its contribution to progress, science became the instrument of God's purpose. The father of John H. Griscom thought it "an axiomatic truth that sound learning and science do, by a natural law, gravitate toward virtue"; and an eminent geologist, the Reverend Edward Hitchcock, found in science "a means of personal sanctification." One of the most perceptive students of this linkage between science and morality, the historian Charles E. Rosenberg, has concluded that "the similarity rather than the difference between scientific and religious values . . . made it natural for many [nineteenth-century] Americans to move fluidly from one intellectual realm to another."[47]

It is important to understand, however, that secularization (whatever its ultimate effect) was not in this case at odds with religion; to the contrary, it sprang from the desire to root religious morality in the palpable realities of the physical world. Morality still depended on God (as indeed did science), for God had ordained the natural laws that enforced morals. And these laws manifested, not chance concatenation of forces nor mere consequences of the constitution of matter, but the will of the Most High. True, in the moralism at the core of Victorian religion—in humanitarianism, progress, and the linking of natural law and morality—God Himself had been transformed: moralized, humanized, naturalized. But church leaders did not separate this moralism, however intensely human, from God. Neither, however, did the most prominent ministers and theologians often now separate God from human moralism.

Continuities: Belief Rationalized

At times, the Evangelical God seems to fit human expectations so well that one almost hears Lyman Beecher very respectfully inviting Him to the parsonage, not for a drink, certainly, but perhaps for tea. Moralism produced this sense of congruency, but so—perhaps more strongly—did arguments advanced to demonstrate God's existence. The great wave of rationalizing that had gathered theological force since Newton's day found ardent disciples among nineteenth-century churchmen. The most striking religious minds of the century—such as Schleiermacher in Germany, Coleridge in England, Emerson in America—distinguished themselves by swimming against this tide. But more representative theologians dove into quasi-scientific natural theology with zeal that would have done credit to any Enlightenment rationalizer. These once-advanced strategems became common currency of pulpit and especially classroom. And belief in God became embedded still more securely in knowledge of the world as observed.

The century opened with the classic elaboration of the argument from design: William Paley's *Natural Theology*, published in 1802. Paley cribbed shamelessly from John Ray, but he hung the material on the skeleton of his own lucid logic and meticulous appreciation of evidence. Nature led to God as surely as the shinbone led to the anklebone. The complex pattern in which the 446 known muscles overlap, enclose, and perforate each other could hardly have appeared by chance: such exquisite design pointed to a high order of "meditation and counsel." As Leslie Stephen remarked, Paley's God put James Watt to shame.[48]

So impressive was Paley's demonstration of God that *Natural Theology* became a set text in colleges throughout the English-speaking world. Lyman Beecher thought it the best antidote to scepticism, "unrivalled as a neat, copious, conclusive argument, of the existence and operation of the omniscient design, almighty power, and unmingled benevolence of an eternal mind." Charles Darwin later revenged generations of collegians by deploying Paley's evidences of design to subvert the argument itself; but he nevertheless maintained to the end of his days that Paley's logic was a model and his books the only prescribed texts "of the least use to me in the education of my mind."[49]

Natural Theology inspired a swarm of junior Paleys. It became standard practice for orthodox theologians to trot out the argument from design somewhere in their pages. James McCosh, one of the most thoughtful, not only set forth the Paleyite reasoning from the "order and adaptation exhibited in the separate material works of God," but he then proceeded, in pursuing moral arguments for the existence of Deity, to structure them also along the lines of the design argument. Lyman Beecher was admittedly a cocky man, but in this case his self-assurance was typical when he asserted that "the evidence of the being of a supreme intelligent mind, from universal design, is not the result of multiplied probabilities; but is a strict demonstration of the being of God." To catalog examples would be idle, except as a tribute to the fecundity of authorial imaginations in inventing new titles for the same book. Suffice it to say that by the 1820s no American college student could escape drilling in the rhythmic cadences of the argument from design. Rage for design peaked in the 1850s. Excursions into physico-theology were then undertaken by such luminaries as the prominent geologist the Reverend Edward Hitchcock and the nation's most celebrated scientist, Louis Agassiz.[50]

Agassiz's name calls attention to another important aspect of nineteenth-century design arguments: their diversification from the eighteenth-century originals. Agassiz was a philosophic idealist, injected in youth with a stiff dose of German Romantic *Naturphilosophie*. The utilitarian obsession of most Anglo-American natural theology left him cold. Maybe the usefulness of the hand to human beings did prove God's skill and love, as Paley said; but Agassiz's mind soared above petty adaptations that helped individual creatures to cope with their own little environments. He looked instead to the grand structure of the whole, to the patterns repeated in the skeleton of every vertebrate, even if—especially if!—those patterns had no practical use. In such numinous forms shone evidence of a Divine Mind at work, its stamp on the very architecture of life, on the magnificent symmetry of nature. "Any manifestation of thought" constituted for Agassiz "evidence of the existence of a thinking being as the author of such thought." An "intelligent and intelligible connection between the facts of nature must be looked upon as a direct proof of the existence of a thinking God."[51] Nature led to God, not because of its complex adaptations, but because it enfleshed the ideas of God, their grandeur in their pervasive simplicity.

Agassiz's idealist version of design, though a minority report, bears noting, for it shows how easily a thoroughly rationalized belief could mesh with a romantic view of nature as the living flesh of God. Romantic religion sometimes stood at odds with the rationally founded belief of the Enlightenment. Celebrated individual cases (Emerson's, for example) attest the antagonism. But as a general proposition, nothing could be further from the truth. Belief during the first two-thirds of the nineteenth century did not rest on rationalism repudiated but on rationalism romanticized.[52]

Doubtless, the God proved by scientific evidence in 1850 often differed from the Deity that nature revealed in 1790.[53] The Great Engineer gave way to a mistier Mind. For some, the whole question lay beyond the reach of the crassly material tools of science. Only direct spiritual insight could penetrate to the noumenal reality behind phenomena: one cannot imagine Theodore Parker or Ralph Waldo Emerson intoning Paley. But this response was eccentric, as the alternately bemused and outraged reactions to Transcendentalism made clear. Most theologians preserved design but brushed it with an emotional reverence for nature that was dimmer in Paley and his predecessors. God frequently now resembled Watt less than Beethoven. But belief in Him seemed more than ever securely founded on the solid physical realities of scientific natural theology.

Whether in Paley's multifarious detail or Agassiz's magnificent unities, the argument from design exhibited the same confidence: God's existence could be demonstrated with surety and logic equal to any other form of natural knowledge. The "theological department is just as accessible to study" as any other "department of the kingdom of God": "Facts and evidence are the material of knowledge, and the elementary truths of revelation are just as plain, and their results just as easily attained, and just as satisfactory and certain, as on any other subject. On the same condition that knowledge can be obtained in natural philosophy, it can be obtained in theology."[54]

It was more than happenstance that the "department of the kingdom of God" which Lyman Beecher compared here to theology was natural science. The design argument assumed continuity of knowledge between theology and science. From its seventeenth-century origins, the driving ambition of modern natural theology was to enlist science in support of God, to adapt the intellectual bases of belief to the world view of natural philosophy. Only for a few Americans did science surpass religion in authority before mid-century; nevertheless, its prestige soared in the antebellum years. Even Evangelical writers seldom resisted its temptations; more often they chose to connect belief in God to scientific knowledge as firmly as possible. For science undeniably fortified belief. Only a Cassandra would beware the bearers of such a magnificent gift.

Tensions did exist. The emergence of modern geology in the

early years of the century, capped by Charles Lyell's *Principles of Geology* (1830–1833), wreaked havoc on prevailing literal readings of the Bible. Scripture suggested that the world was about six thousand years old; geology said millions. Moses described creation in some detail in the first chapters of Genesis; the geological record told a different story. Great turmoil ensued, and many sermons. But the furor proved temporary: prudent retreat from extreme literalism (never universally practiced in any case) saved the authenticity of Scripture. By 1850, few regarded geology as a serious threat to Christianity, much less to God.

In vaguer ways, science sometimes appeared to threaten specifically the religion of the heart. The Unitarian clergyman, later Harvard professor, Andrew Preston Peabody complained in 1847 that science's "world of stiff, stubborn, angular facts" had driven imagination "from her last earthly covert." Peabody groped to find words for a change in the nature of science and its relation to religion that he only remotely glimpsed. Since the seventeenth century, science had persistently grown more empirical, more insistent that its propositions meet the test of ever-stricter empirical verification. The tendency was to restrict knowledge to what fitted within the confines of observable reality measurable by all qualified observers. Kepler's assumptions as to what constituted scientific knowledge were more generous than Newton's, Newton's more ecumenical than Faraday's. The trend notably accelerated after 1800, when the familiarity between science and metaphysics began turning to estrangement. Early nineteenth-century scientists regarded theological questions as utterly distinct from (though still related to) scientific ones. Yet, as Peabody pointed out, the "fundamental truth of theology," belief in one God, still survived as equally "an axiom of science."[55]

Peabody's consoling observation underlined the reason why an alliance between science and religion endured. As late as the 1850s, scientists commonly invoked God in scientific explanation. The Yale geologist James Dwight Dana, for example, conceived the "true notion" of species not as itself a physical reality but as an "idea or potential element" radiating from the mind of the Creator and embodied in a physical group of creatures. By no means every scientist, certainly not many geologists, steered as near the empyrean as Dana; even fewer appealed to God in their day-to-day work. But Dana was neither fool nor fossil, and most of his colleagues also deemed God ultimately indispensable to science's task of explaining nature. Without God the existence of the universe, the origin of life, the operation of natural law all became inexplicable. Hence, as the astronomer Sir John Herschel expressed the standard view in his *Preliminary Discourse on the Study of Natural Philosophy* (1830), the "natural effect" of science is to shore up religious belief.[56]

In turn, despite effusions of heartfulness, belief still seemed intellectually continuous with science. The nexus involved more than the ubiquity of design arguments. Theology did differ from science in its problems and its usual techniques, but no epistemological barrier disjoined scientific from religious knowledge. Theologians went out of their way to emphasize this; and early Victorian science exhibited remarkable flexibility, if not downright confusion, in this regard. Science required empirical evidence. But what qualified? Revelations of the Bible might constitute data; so might intuitions of the mind; and some theologians did not hesitate to say so. True, not many did: Bible verses and intuitions strained the hospitality of even the most latitudinarian scientist. Yet no consensus definitively excluded this sort of evidence in principle.

The majority of scientists and theologians were reasonably fastidious in their intellectual housekeeping, but even they separated science from theology only on something like a rule of division of labor. Natural philosophy, according to Herschel's edition of the consensus, did not concern itself with questions about the origin of things or the nature of Deity. But nothing in his definition of natural science suggested that natural theology was not the same *kind* of science, probing the same order of truths with the same basic method. He left James McCosh free to declare:

> Natural theology is the science which, from an investigation of the works of nature, would rise to a discovery of the character and will of God, and of the relation in which man stands to him. In prosecuting this science, the inquirer proceeds . . . in the same way as he does in every other branch of investigation. He sets out in search of facts; he arranges and co-ordinates them, and rising from the phenomena which present themselves to their cause, he discovers, by the ordinary laws of evidence, a cause of all subordinate causes.[57]

Educated Evangelicals, no less than the eighteenth-century "infidels" they abhorred, hitched their wagon to the rising star of science. When inducted into his chair in 1824, the first professor of theology at Virginia's Hampden-Sidney Presbyterian Seminary was officially reminded that "as the cavils and objections of infidels have been more readily answered as *natural science* has been enlarged, that branch of knowledge should form a part of that fund of general information, which every minister of the Gospel should possess." Even Lyman Beecher—the Joshua of heart-religion, apt to test the validity of his beliefs by taking his emotional temperature, still shivering at youthful memories of Deism, devoting much of his adulthood to waging jihad against those latter-day carriers of the Enlightenment virus, the Unitarians—defended his Evangelicalism by appeal to reason. "It is," he declared in 1829 in a sermon carefully groomed for the public eye, "eminently a rational system." And he meant nothing more nor less than the rationality of science.[58]

The appeal to science through natural theology was calculated to dispel the prejudice that belief involved ungraspable mystery. This antique notion made uneasy many ministers and theologians, who, anxious to bring their faith into respectable congruence with modernity, smelled hocus-pocus in things mystical. Modernity could carry too high a price tag: Evangelicals at least were not about to follow the Unitarians in abandoning mysteries central to Christianity. But even they could plant belief firmly in the sensible side of God: His manifestation in tangible, material evidence, analyzed by the mental tools employed in the most concrete and reliable forms of human knowledge. Church leaders by no means denied access to the impalpable side of the divided God. But they did teach that God can be securely known in the human world of science, and they successfully exploited that assumption to make God's reality more solid perhaps than ever.

Disbelief indeed seemed preposterous beyond words. Even scepticism about Christianity, fashionable in 1790, fell into disrepute. The Virginia Episcopal leader William Meade recalled that in the early 1800s, "in every educated young man of Virginia whom I met, I expected to find a sceptic, if not an avowed unbeliever": in short, a Deist. Deist ideas had ornamented the best parlors of Virginia and Massachusetts in 1790; by 1830 they belonged only to aging relics and shrill outcasts. The president of the College of William and Mary, Thomas R. Dew, sniffed in 1836 that "he who now obtrudes on the social circle his infidel notions, manifests the arrogance of a literary coxcomb, or the want of that refinement which distinguishes the polished gentlemen."[59] Such a climate chilled doubts about fine points of the Nicene Creed, much less God. Yet not only social disapprobation discouraged disbelief in God; the position was more difficult to sustain intellectually than socially.

Scepticism had not evaporated; a few outposts of Deism lingered on. In the 1830s, the aspiring botanist Asa Gray fell in with a clique of village infidels in Bridgewater, New York, who scoffed at Christianity and indulged materialist heresies. The publisher Henry Holt recalled a "radical tinker" who "made me a thoroughgoing skeptic in my boyhood" in Baltimore around 1850. Indeed, by that time public apostasy from Christianity was again on the rise, and throughout the antebellum period there seems to have been a fair number of quiet disbelievers in Christianity. A handful of better-publicized political and social radicals, Frances Wright and Robert Dale Owen the best known, professed freethinking. A few of them apparently strayed at least temporarily into outright atheism.[60]

Yet there were only a very few. Loose use of epithets like "infidel" and "unbeliever" obscures the freakishness of out-and-out disbelief in God before the 1860s. Even the much-execrated Thomas Cooper, who nursed Enlightenment "infidelity" from eighteenth-century Manchester to Calhoun's South Carolina, put a God at the center of his materialism. When Ralph Waldo Emerson actually met a real, live atheist (an exiled Frenchman, naturally), he could hardly contain his excitement at the unique chance to dissect the exotic specimen.[61]

That atheism seemed finally ridiculous did not mean that doubt was unusual. Nearing his death in 1852, Daniel Webster confessed that his faith had been "sometimes shaken" by "philosophical argument, especially that drawn from the vastness of the universe in comparison with the apparent insignificance of this Globe" (and Webster was not a man to underrate his place in the cosmos). James Marsh, later a distinguished minister and educator, went through a spell in college when "all my faith in things invisible seemed to vanish, and I almost doubted the reality of my own existence."[62]

Yet however fiercely doubt might stab, it could hardly mature into sustained disbelief in God. That position involved too much apparent absurdity, had too little to support it. Toward the end of the 1820s, a young tutor at Yale, Horace Bushnell, went through a religious crisis which, forty or fifty years later, might very well have ended in agnosticism. Bushnell recorded that he "nearly lost the conviction of God," found himself incapable of saying "with any emphasis of conviction that God exists." Yet, although examples of religious indifference abounded and memories of Deism still lived at Yale, there was no foundation for anything further, for outright unbelief—and there was a very persuasive one for belief. Instead of fading into agnosticism, Bushnell's faith flamed up higher than ever in the revival of 1831.[63] He ended as a minister and his generation's most seminal theologian.

For thoughtful people, faith was anything but simple and free of doubt. One suspects that it never has been. Bushnell, more pessimistic on this score than most, thought a state of doubt normal.[64] Yet amid questions endured an axiom not long questionable. God seemed unshakable, and not merely because graven in the bedrock of the culture. Ultimate doubt could hardly stand up to the rock-solid and up-to-date alliance of religion and science.

This rational, empirical defense not only secured belief but influenced its character. Evangelicals and others, at least in natural theology, had chosen to objectify God, make Him an object of natural knowledge, and minimize the traditional piety that God eluded human grasp. The effect was to pump the Enlightenment's reasonable religion into the heart of American theology. This view of his efforts would have revolted Lyman Beecher. Yet Beecher's God notably lacked any mystery. Beecher spoke contemptuously of "mysticism," sneered at those who "love to dream [about divinity] amid the repetition of beautiful uncertain sounds, and glittering undefined images."[65]

"Belief" gravitated toward the connotation it had for Deists: intellectual assent to a definable proposition. Leonard Woods of Andover Seminary once remarked that Jonathan Edwards's doctrine of necessity was "as demonstrable, as any proposition in Geometry." Woods believed that Christian doctrines could be expressed "in language which shall carry them to the mind of every enlightened Christian and philosopher with perfect clearness." To be sure, Evangelicals usually attached less importance to doctrine than moral action; but when they spoke of doctrine, they aimed for scientific precision. Lyman Beecher's most famous sermon was "The Faith Once Delivered to the Saints," a ringing defense of orthodoxy against liberalism. The sermon began: "By the faith once delivered to the saints is to be understood the *doctrines* of the Gospel"; and Beecher elaborated with a string of doctrinal statements that sounded like nothing so much as an attempt to transform religion entirely into a set of intellectual propositions honed to exactness.[66]

A propositional approach to doctrine was nothing new: read parts of the Westminster Confession or, for that matter, the Nicene Creed. What was new, at least among solidly orthodox Christians, was Beecher's equation of Christian faith with these logical propositions. If asked point-blank, Beecher would surely have corrected himself, for he did believe that faith involved more than assent to doctrine. Yet that he could slip unconsciously into this heresy told volumes. It showed how close even some unlikely Evangelicals had come to transforming faith into reason. And it points out that, while "saving faith" still required more than intellectual assent, belief had shifted substantially in the direction of a rational proposition.

Purely intellectual belief did not satisfy the hunger of even the most rational Unitarian. *A fortiori,* single-minded stress on the rationality of their belief does not do justice to the range and variety of Evangelicals. A southern Presbyterian, John Holt Rice, grumbled in 1829 that religion "is becoming cold calculating" and prophesied that this would leave the church "in a deplorably desolate and barren condition."[67] But neither the weepiness of Evangelical hymns nor the fiery emotional pitch of revival meetings should deceive. Through heart-religion ran an iron seam of conviction that knowledge of God flowed from the same rational means that ensured knowledge of physical reality.

Innovation: Intuition as Knowledge

Rational investigation was not the only source of knowledge of the divine. In truth, some Evangelicals—as well as some unorthodox writers—looked upon the whole enterprise of scientific natural theology as dangerously wrong-headed. And even its devotees often agreed that knowledge of God sprang aboriginally from deeper reaches of the mind. Belief was attested by intuition as well as empirical investigation, by the heart as well as the senses.

There was nothing novel about the idea that intuition provided knowledge of God. The claim in some form dates to the earliest reflections on belief in gods, was proclaimed anew by Fathers of the Church, and had been continuously reasserted since the Reformation. Calvin espoused it; so did Cotton Mather; so did Jonathan Edwards. Evangelical intuitionism grew, loosely speaking, from pietist movements of the late seventeenth and eighteenth centuries. Its intellectual structure owed most to the common-sense philosophers of the Scottish Enlightenment, for whom a "moral sense" and "self-evident" prerational intuitions provided weapons against Hume's scepticism.

Scottish reliance on intuition became second nature among American theologians ranging from Evangelicals to Unitarians. The forging of the Evangelical mind on the anvil of the French

Revolution stamped it, in particular, with an indelible suspicion of unaided rationalism. That prime example of Evangelical conformity, President Francis Wayland of Brown, instructed youth that the existence of "an intelligent and universal First Cause" is, in the Scot Thomas Reid's trademark phrase, "self-evident." A writer less finicky about wording simply asserted, "All knowledge and belief rests, of course, upon intuition, as its first and necessary foundation."[68] And not only Evangelicals aped the Scots; their rites were celebrated in classrooms throughout the land.

Nor did intuitionism allow itself to be pruned by the cautious Scottish gardeners. It exfoliated into all sorts of romantic blossoms: Bronson Alcott's orphic utterances, George Bancroft's faith in inward "emanations from the infinite fountain of knowledge," Henry Ward Beecher's bourgeois rhapsodies of God shining through the hollyhocks. Seldom in Western Christianity had intuitionist claims loomed so large in belief. "It is the heart which governs the intellect," according to Lyman Beecher, "not the intellect which governs the heart."[69]

Intuitionism chimed with the broader romantic cult of the heart, which throbbed ceaselessly in Evangelicalism. Just as Evangelicalism may be seen as a religious expression of romantic sensibility, so may intuitionism be understood as a mode of that romantic "interiorization of consciousness" which forms so notable an element in nineteenth-century literature: a stronger accent on the private and interior as distinct from the public and external side of life. With regard to religion in particular, inwardness may have advanced in step with God's retreat from the external world, the diminution of His exterior presence (as physical nature fell under natural law) evoking in compensation a correspondingly heightened sense of His inward presence. If this is true, intuitionism climaxed changes in consciousness long in the making.[70]

In any case, intuitionism represented a kind of "private" knowledge of God, as distinguished from the "public" knowledge provided by scientific natural theology (and, of course, revelation). This distinction should not be pushed too far, since theologians usually treated intuitions as objective facts of consciousness, common to the whole human race, rather than as subjective experiences of divinity. Nevertheless, since the seventeenth century intuitionism had come to seem increasingly different from other ways of knowing God. This growing distinctness mostly reflected the changing character of other roads to knowledge, especially the rising influence and tightening empirical focus of science. A redefinition of knowledge was in process, a separating out and clarifying of previously intermingled modes of knowing, each according to its own specific gravity, like the separation of cells in a laboratory centrifuge. Copernicus, Brahe, and Kepler had mixed empirical observation, logical deduction, and mystic apperception indiscriminately. It is by no means clear that even Newton always neatly distinguished empiricism and intuitionism. But Locke did, and so did virtually all scientists after Newton. By 1800, intuition stood radically apart from empirical modes of knowledge as a potentially quite different way of grasping reality—on this difference pivoted, for example, much romantic poetry. Theological attempts to weld the split together have, in retrospect, a rather hollow ring.

A minority of religious writers were more than willing to admit that man knew God in a radically different way in his heart than through God's world. Some indeed insisted that intuition (along, usually, with revelation) offered the only valid approach to God. God existed on a different plane from man, and man could not hope to penetrate spiritual reality with the tools of material knowledge.

The most formidable American critics of rational-empirical paths to God were disciples, more or less, of Samuel Taylor Coleridge. His influence flowed mostly from his *Aids to Reflection* (1825), the conduit being James Marsh, president and professor of philosophy at the University of Vermont and in his own right an unjustly neglected figure in American intellectual history. Marsh in 1829 published an American edition of the *Aids,* filled out with extensive notes and a long introduction putting his own gloss on Coleridge. Marsh's Coleridge became a small-scale underground best-seller, the first edition of 1,500 copies gone within a year. It shaped the thinking of many of the livelier religious minds of a generation. Moncure Conway carried Marsh's edition in his saddlebags as he rode the Ohio backwoods preaching for the Methodists, and in the early 1840s students at orthodox Andover Seminary bought "whole shelvesful" of the *Aids*.[71]

Coleridge's message to Americans, as interpreted by Marsh, was devastatingly straightforward: "The ultimate truths of Christianity and indeed all properly spiritual truths are not within the compass of speculative [i.e., reasoned] knowledge but are the objects of faith alone." Led by Coleridge to Kant, Marsh early decided that the "senses furnish us with nothing but the phenomenal aspects of being," mere appearances behind which spiritual reality lay impervious to the probing intellect. He shuddered at the vogue of the "miscalled Baconian philosophy" and the

"Scotch writers" who championed it; down that road of psuedo-scientific "proofs" of God scepticism awaited. "How can it be otherwise indeed when thinking young men are led to believe that Paley's arguments are the strong ground of our conviction of theism?"[72]

From Marsh the influence of Coleridge flowed in two major streams. One led to Emerson, Parker, and other American Transcendentalists; indeed, Marsh is today chiefly remembered by students of that movement. Theodore Parker thought the "foundation of religion" to be "laid in human nature itself," in "the instinctive intuition of the immortal."[73] Parker imagined himself a disciple of Kant; Jacobi and Schleiermacher would have been closer to the mark. In any case, lured on by Coleridge, he had leapt beyond the cautiously rational intuitionism of Scottish philosophy. He had also leapt too far doctrinally; only a few religious radicals cared to follow him or other Transcendentalists.

The other stream, more deeply influential if less brilliant, flowed principally through Horace Bushnell into the main currents of American Protestantism. *Aids to Reflection* apparently overwhelmed Bushnell, in any case indelibly marked his thought.[74] Like Coleridge, Bushnell tried to penetrate behind the dry words of creeds to grasp the indefinable but living truth that theological formulae inadequately pointed to. Bushnell did not deny that the argument from design proved a First Cause, but he shrugged it off as almost irrelevant. Belief in God was not a matter of logic but of life. How could words convey what the heart intoned? Inevitably he landed in hot water. *God in Christ* provoked accusations of heresy and eventually the secession of Bushnell's parish from its Congregationalist ties. Yet younger men thought they heard the accents of truth in Bushnell's writings, and his influence amplified as the years passed.

Marsh, Parker, and Bushnell in different octaves all registered sharp dissent from the prevailing conviction that reason and observation furnished objective and secure knowledge of God. For these men and their followers, enduring knowledge of the divine came only inwardly, through a person's own religious experience. Perhaps God ought not even be described as an object of knowledge, only of subjective faith. Certainly God existed so far beyond the familiar physical world that blasphemous efforts to reduce Him to human logic could lead only to ruin. Faith would lie shattered in the wreckage of hubris. God was not a creature of this world, but the Creator of it; the world could not contain Him. The divided God must be reunited in faith.

These prophets were not exactly without honor, but neither did they lead American Protestantism away from the fleshpots of Paley. Most theologians suspected the destination would turn out to be not the Promised Land but an orgy of the unfathomable. They inclined instead to adopt the safer Scottish technique of plugging their intuitionism into rational-empirical proofs of God. The strategy was to point to certain "self-evident truths," supposedly perceived upon introspection by all normal human beings, and to argue from these universal intuitions that a God must exist to have implanted them. The nature of the intuitions also revealed something of the character of their Author. The train of thought proceeded in the logical style of the argument from design, with observed intuitions replacing observed facts of nature.

The favorite intuition was conscience or, in Scottish terms, the "moral sense." Universal, nonrational feelings of right and wrong proved a Divine Legislator Who had laid down moral law. The "very fact of the existence of conscience" provided, according to James McCosh, "an independent argument in favour of the being of God. The existence of the law in the heart seems to imply the existence of a lawgiver." In fact, McCosh believed that conscience, not observation of nature, suggested the idea of God to the mind in the first instance.[75]

This brand of argument did not repudiate quasi-scientific rationalism in favor of intuition; to the contrary, it tried to rationalize intuitionism. It gave reason the job of judging the meaning and significance of prerational intuitions. McCosh emphatically did not assert that belief in God was somehow "innate in, or connate with, the human soul." Instead, rational reflection upon the existence of intuitions produced belief—exactly as did reflection upon design in nature. The Unitarian moralists at Harvard indeed valued moral-sense arguments for God precisely because these seemed "even more direct, logical, and convincing" than the argument from design.[76]

Despite the cult of the heart in their religion, not even Evangelicals had the heart to cut loose from empirical rationality. They shied away from claiming plainly that knowledge extended beyond a scientific style of reasoning, or from admitting that conviction of God might have to rest on human experience more subjective than knowledge of nature. They did not want to confess that belief might lie outside the purview of logical analysis and empirical observation, for to do so would have meant sacrificing the prestige of science and the comforting assurance that hardheaded men could establish God as surely as they could tote up the day's receipts in their counting houses. Hindsight suggests that church leaders were strolling on thin ice, given the slowly constricting range of acceptably scientific knowledge. But before the 1860s, warnings came from a distinct minority.

A second pillar of belief had arisen alongside the argument from design, an edifice built on inner feelings rather than the observed world. Neither, of course, rivaled God's direct self-revelation in the Bible. But these natural evidences provided proofs that were supposed to overwhelm even those blind to the light of Scripture, that were indeed logically and temporally prior to revelation. "God, whose being, perfections, and government are partially made known to us through the testimony of his works [the design argument] and of conscience [intuition Scottish-style], has made a further revelation of himself in the Scriptures of the Old and New Testaments," as Congregationalist leaders put it.[77]

If anything, the appeal to feeling woke more real enthusiasm than scientific natural theology. Preachers were far more likely to sing the glowing heart than the wonders of field and pond. Intuitionist arguments, however, usually lacked the weighty sense of solidity of design arguments. McCosh, for instance, advanced moral-sense claims more tentatively than proofs from design; and it was the invulnerable Paley whom college presidents chose to drum into the senior class. The reluctance of most theologians to stray far from the paths of science prevented them from developing intuitionism with much subtlety or real independence. Only an unruly minority looked for God outside the bounds of natural knowledge and regarded intuition as fully an alternative to reason. For the rest, intuition blended with rational belief. God remained rooted in the reality that human beings could see and touch.

Innovation: Religion as Emotional Response

Nevertheless, as mid-century approached, a decidedly warmer, less calculating treatment of intuition and feeling became first popular and then dominant in the sermons and inspirational writings of Evangelicals. Scottish philosophy remained lord of the classroom, but elsewhere its cool intellectualism faded into romantic shadings of the heart. Harriet Beecher Stowe spoke of "Divine interposition" carrying "the soul far above the region of the Intellect, into that of direct spiritual intuition." Her brother Henry Ward Beecher abandoned their father's "rational system" of belief for invocations of flowers and sunbeams.[78]

Evangelicals, for all their rationalism, always insisted that man found really crucial awareness of God primarily in the depths of the heart. This distinctive note provided the chief identifying mark of Victorian religious sensibility. Sometimes the rhetoric referred to intuitive knowledge of God; more often it essayed a less specific appeal to feeling as the well of living faith. Such writings were not so often apologetic in intent as enlivening. (Henry Ward Beecher's 1868 novel, *Norwood,* however, intended both: indeed, to persuade by enlivening.) Here the Christian left behind the issue of intuitive *knowledge* of God and crossed the border into heartfelt *feeling* about God. And yet this, too, was viewed, though vaguely, as powerful support for belief.

Emotional fervor, stoked by revivals, had always burned bright in Evangelicalism. Even the etiolated sentimentalism of the Victorian parlor faintly reflected the fires of the camp meeting. A generation that sniffled over Byron and *David Copperfield* could hardly be expected to preserve its theology from any twinge of feeling. No wonder that Evangelicals went beyond Francis Hutcheson's moral sense to seek God in "spiritual experience" more resistant to definition. And this impulse had precedents on both the orthodox and liberal sides of eighteenth-century religion: in, for example, Jonathan Edwards's doctrine of "religious affections" and Jonathan Mayhew's "affectionate religion." But few Victorian Evangelicals were willing to let go the idea of belief as concrete rational knowledge. This brake on imagination generally left the notion of personal religious experience as diffuse emotionalism rather than as a sturdy, full-blooded intuitionism such as James Marsh adumbrated or Horace Bushnell approached.

Amorphous sentimentalism found its natural home, not in treatises, but in poems and hymns and preaching. What set belief in God apart from most other knowledge—what made it living—was, in Evangelical conception, the emotional upheaval it stirred in the human breast. Sermonizing played a greater role than theological writing in coloring most people's conception of belief (even many who read theological writing); what went on in church seemed, after all, to be religion if anything was. Evangelicalism in this way turned attention to emotions and moral impulses, but it failed to explore the problematic relationship of merely human feelings to supposed ultimate meaning. Many ministers by 1850 preached as if emotion itself verified God. It took a second thought to remember that belief could hardly rest on a rush of warm feeling alone.

Sometimes it took a third or fourth. Lyman Beecher welcomed his son Charles into the ministry in 1844 with a characteristic piece of epistemological advice: "Take heed to thy heart. . . . The power of the heart set on fire by love is the greatest created power in the universe—more powerful than electricity, for that can only rend and melt matter; but LOVE can, by God's appointment, carry the truth quick and powerful through the soul."[79] When Victorian Evangelicals talked of true religion springing from inner spiritual experience, they often had in mind this sort of emotive response.

Even the writings of so penetrating a theologian as Horace Bushnell led into uncertain terrain between faith and emotion. God's "purity, goodness, beauty, and gentleness," wrote Bushnell, "can never be sufficiently apprehended by mere intellect. It requires a heart, a good, right-feeling heart, to receive so much of heart as God opens to us in the Gospel of Christ." And the human heart found God, resonated as it were with His heart, through not intellect but an "aesthetic talent, viz., the talent of love, or a sensibility exalted and purified by love."[80]

The reference to love as an "aesthetic talent" signaled a relocation of religious belief in the mental geography of romantic Evangelicals. Affairs of the heart were not matters of hard fact; they belonged to the realm of imagination. Religion, if regarded solely from this point of view (which it seldom was), had more in common with poetry, art, and music than with fact-grubbing science. James Russell Lowell learned at the knee of his clergyman father that the "faith of the *heart* is the only essential faith," and the son as adult carried the lesson to the point of scarcely distinguishing poetry from religion.[81] Both really amounted to aesthetic endeavors, poets functioning for Lowell as priests, special bearers of divine revelation.

Leanings in this direction alarmed orthodox church leaders. When Bushnell enunciated a symbolic, almost poetic, interpretation of religious language in *God in Christ*, the Evangelical establishment swiftly slapped him down. And rightly so, given the epistemological commitments of most Evangelicals. They embraced, though ambivalently and inconsistently, an unstated axiom that fostered their zeal for scientific natural theology, corralled intuitionism within rationality, and kept religious experience from seeming much more than emotion. The axiom was that all reliable knowledge could be reduced to rationally definable propositions. This principle made Lowell and even Bushnell shoals for believers, threatening to smash religion into fragments of poetry, to dissolve the solidity of belief into emotional fog.

Orthodox resistance did not curb the drift, but it did reinforce the distinction between knowledge of God and religious feelings.

Particularly after 1850, in the hands of preachers like Henry Ward Beecher, romantic Evangelicalism continued to gravitate toward an undefined kinship with art and poetry. Yet outside the pulpit theologians seldom reconsidered their determination to ground belief firmly in rational-empirical arguments. The aesthetic note sounded more loudly but remained intellectually muted—an attempt at inspiration rather than apologetics. Despite a few men like Bushnell, romantic Evangelicalism usually produced oratory rather than theology. To the extent that one could analyze a preacher's words, they seemed to suggest that faith in God equaled emotional response—that a believer found God, not through insight into any reality transcending the temporal world, but in human emotions themselves. What connection, if any, obtained between all this and the rational foundations of belief would have eluded the most incisive analyst.

No one could confuse Evangelicalism with the cooler reasonable religion of the Enlightenment. Where reasonable religion scanted Christian tradition, Evangelicalism insisted on a return to orthodoxy; where the Enlightenment worshipped an impersonal Designer, Evangelicals preached a personal relationship with the living Jesus. Above all, Evangelicals felt the tension, not troubling as many Enlightened believers, between worldliness and spirituality, between desire to secure belief in a world comprehensible to human beings and an uneasy sense that God would not fit in any such world—that He exploded the rationally understood categories bequeathed by the Enlightenment. This strain generated heart-religion. But to say that Evangelicals felt the tension is more defensible than to claim that they understood it. Heart-religion commonly dissolved into misty insistence that reason alone would not support living faith. Conceived as stoking belief more than as grounding it, it seldom opened a plausible alternative path to God. Perfervid emotion only obscured the choice already made and now confirmed between a worldly God comprehensible to man and a transcendent, inhuman God.

Thus, to chart the progress of rationalized and moralized belief from the Enlightenment into the heart of Victorian America, one need not scrutinize "advanced" theists or even Unitarians. An Evangelical like Lyman Beecher stood at the apex of the long modernization of belief, summed up choices made and strategies devised over the span of three centuries. Small wonder Beecher took such pride in his orthodoxy. Just as his benevolent reforms guaranteed the relevance of religion in an increasingly secular society, so his religion promised the happiness of humankind.

And this eminently "rational system" managed also to satisfy the heart's hunger. It is hard to conceive of a religion more up-to-date, more finely tuned to changing social realities. Naturally, baffling and offensive antiquities like predestination had to be softened or cast away. For it is difficult also to imagine a religion plunged more deeply into the needs and wishes of human beings—or a God sculpted more closely to the image of man.

4

Belief and Social Change

Not even theologians execute their mental pirouettes in pristine freedom from earth's gravity; the business of making a living, slaking appetites, hating enemies, and loving friends entangles every mind. Life is a pas de deux. Grubby realities make the partners for our most high-flown ideas. And the twinned movements must glide to the same rhythm, or we stumble painfully over our own feet; ideas will not guide us satisfactorily through life unless in tune with it. Changing patterns of religious belief reflected this ineluctable limitation. Nor did the social influences on religion escape contemporaries. Opponents of early Evangelical reformers, for example, accused the saints of trying to impose their strait-laced morality on the lower classes only in order to make more docile hands for the new mills.

Yet the connection was rarely so straightforward. Social change forces questions on people but no particular answers. And their responses are usually complex, ambiguous, ambivalent, even contradictory, for human beings instinctively cling to the familiar while wrestling with the unaccustomed.

Social change made numerous demands on religious leaders: three of particular relevance. Secularization not only stripped away much of the institutional armor that protected belief; it also intensified the question of how belief in the supernatural related to observable reality, both physical and social. A second difficulty arose from social changes that, in effect, brought to the fore a related question: what is religion good for? How, specifically, does it help the believer to cope with social reality? The moralization of belief provided one answer to this query. The third arose from social transformations that fostered new conceptions of knowledge; these forced attention to the problem of how belief is verified. Does one know that God exists in the same way that one knows about, say, commercial transactions or chemistry? None of these questions was really new; indeed, all are perennial. But social changes twisted them into different and more pressing forms.

The most visible driver of social change was capitalist economic development. From its origins in medieval mercantile enterprises, capitalism had mutated into an evermore elaborate, powerful, and widespread way of organizing production and distribution. Ideas as well as economic behavior reflected capitalist methods: capitalism comprised ways people thought as well as worked, and new attitudes and values ramified far beyond workplace and marketplace.[1]

Change invaded the lives of different people at varying times and with diverse effects. Commercial capitalism engaged the urban populations of the Low Countries in the age of Rembrandt, when most Frenchmen still regarded coins as precious oddities. An agricultural revolution began in England at the end of the seventeenth century, but Bavarian peasants cultivated their fields with basically medieval methods until the nineteenth. Massachusetts had half its manufacturing workers in factories when South Carolina scarcely had a factory.

The American colonies, founded in capitalist ventures, never lacked a complement of merchants. But through most of the seventeenth and eighteenth centuries, the great bulk of the population remained independent farmers only partially tied to any market, and that usually a local one. Even in commercial centers capitalist attitudes emerged erratically. The artisan milieu in which Paul Revere moved already pulsed with the characteristic drive of a capitalist outlook, but ropemakers in Revere's Boston regarded their work with more traditional insouciance. Only during the nineteenth century did capitalism transform profoundly the lives and world views of a majority of Americans.

After about 1780, the pace of economic change in the United States accelerated rapidly. In roughly the next half century, commercial capitalism took command. Farm productivity increased, transportation costs dropped, communication speeded up, and the size of the market grew. Inventors and mechanics added new technologies. All of this fostered greater division of labor and specialization of economic function. Self-sufficiency declined and production for market swelled, as more Americans became more thoroughly enmeshed in the commercial networks of a market economy. The class of wage-earners and the mirror-class of employers expanded enormously. Rationalized and impersonal business methods spread. Commercial and manufacturing activities concentrated in fewer locations, and towns swelled into cities, their populations multiplying to unprecedented numbers. Proportionally the most rapid urbanization in American history occurred between the end of the eighteenth century and the Civil War.

The pace of change did not lag. By mid-century industrial capitalism, prospering though still relatively in its infancy, had in some regions added greater speed and new dimensions to economic transformation. Mass communications and popular education inoculated even people on the periphery of change with new habits of mind. An entire culture absorbed ideas and attitudes that went along with capitalism, technology, and urban life. It was this torrent of new relationships and new problems with which people, religious leaders included, had to grapple. No wonder Evangelicals at times seemed almost frantic with anxiety and energy. A greater challenge than the French Revolution faced the churches.

Social Change and Secularization

Secularization implies the separation of religious from worldly concerns and, therefore, of God's realm from the everyday world that man inhabits. It is hard, perhaps impossible, to drop a bucket to the bottom of this well, to fathom, far beneath the surface of consciousness, the depths of the psyche. Nevertheless, religious beliefs grow organically from the life of a culture, and that life depends heavily on how the society deals with nature. Disruption of a culture's relationship with nature will send shock waves through its religion. Such happened in Neolithic times when hunter-gatherers settled into farming, though our historical instruments are too crude to detect more than the grossest reverberations. A similar earthquake shook religious belief in the nineteenth century when a complex commercial-urban, then urban-industrial, society transformed the landscape. Technology and science greatly amplified the sense of human control over nature. At the same time, urban living and commercial and factory work insulated people from nature in the raw.

Mastery over nature appeared to advance almost daily. The

growth of cities and commerce heightened at least an illusion of control: a farmer lived at the whim of nature, rain or drought, frost or sun; but a merchant's or shopkeeper's success seemed to hinge on other men, not nature. Increasingly the whirring of looms, pounding of triphammers, hiss of steam assailed the ear. The "scream of the locomotive and the electric flash" of the telegraph gripped the imagination. Especially after mid-century, engineers, scientists, industrialists multiplied their strengths, applying machinery and chemistry to farming, harnessing natural resources like petroleum, driving iron ships by steam across the seas. Anesthesia subdued pain, an astonishing feat now so taken for granted that we forget how it seized the minds of our ancestors. A passenger caught on a sailing ship in a North Atlantic gale, as the rigging "moaned and groaned," the ship tossed "mad with fury," and the "waves came toppling down" on it, might well tremble like "a straw" in the grip of nature's "dreadful power."[2] Yet the dreadful power paled somewhat when large screw-driven liners secured travelers against most of its perils.

Technological as well as economic changes thus reinforced the sense of control over nature provided by science's growing and better-organized knowledge of nature. Mastery may have been illusory—after all, we still suffer, die, and grope to understand. But the feeling was real, though always hedged by a countervailing sense of helplessness before nature's power. Awe and bafflement at nature had hardly disappeared; Niagara still inspired wonder. But the rising inclination was to treat nature's mysteries as problems to be solved, its powers as resources to be controlled.

The consequences should not be overestimated, for they were erratic and limited by persisting older feelings. Yet the impulse to turn from nature to God seems to have grown less immediate for many people. In the previous century David Hume, impressed in his own day by growing knowledge of nature, had speculated that belief in God arose primordially from lack of such mastery. Hanging "in perpetual suspense between life and death, health and sickness, plenty and want," yet unable to penetrate the "secret and unknown causes" of their misfortunes, primitive people (and, for that matter, the vulgar of his own age) were driven by fear and anxiety to imagine "invisible powers, who dispose of their happiness and misery."[3] Hume's theory owed more to anticlerical bias than anthropological evidence, yet it contained an element of psychological truth. God traditionally had served to explain storms and plague, to allay terrors and unwitch mysteries, to reassure people about the ungovernable, impenetrable natural world that surrounded them. Firmer control and comprehension reduced this need. The response to nature became less often to invoke God, more often to get down to work oneself.

Socioeconomic change also distanced people from nature. Work moved indoors, broke free from nature's cycles. A farmer's daily round immersed him in nature—sun, rain, dirt, manure, plants, animals—to a degree increasingly foreign to city dwellers. Objects of human manufacture enveloped people, separating them from the nature attributed to God's hand. Even God's time gave way to manmade time. Guttering candles and whale-oil lamps only feebly resisted the night; their meager light permitted little freedom from the seasonally shifting rhythms of the sun. In 1806 the steady glow of gas for the first time lighted a factory; it appeared in the United States by 1817 and in decades transformed time in every city.[4] Early factories and offices kept to the farmer's clock, with longer hours in summer, shorter in winter. But soon natural time sank into servitude: stretched, squeezed, even (as in the great steel mills after 1870) ignored altogether by artificial time.

As divinely created nature receded before the work of human hands, God's daily presence did not disappear, but it became somewhat less tangible. The effect came mostly below the level of consciousness, where poets speak more clearly than historians:

> The world is charged with the grandeur of God.
> It will flame out, like shining from shook foil
> It gathers to a greatness, like the ooze of oil
> Crushed. Why do men then now not reck his rod?
> Generations have trod, have trod, have trod;
> And all is smeared with trade; bleared, smeared with toil;
> And wears man's smudge and shares man's smell: the soil
> Is bare now, nor can foot feel, being shod.[5]

Which incidentally brings to mind that the crafting of boots and shoes moved from the cobbler's bench (outdoors in good weather) to the factory during the 1850s.

The effects on belief were as pervasive as they are difficult to trace. A tide of red brick, grey stone, and macadam spilled out over the countryside. How could the impact be measured? Before the eighteenth century (the mid-nineteenth in most places), virtually the only structures that overtopped the trees were church steeples. The terrain filled the eye with God's presumed handiwork, and churches alone of man's creations towered over nature. Did this make divine presence more manifest? Did God then more naturally flow into the background of consciousness? And did blocking out the panorama of divine creation with commercial buildings and factories diminish God's pervasion of the mental image of the world that undergirded conscious thought?

What of the language that made religious beliefs palpable? As the nation grew more urban, Bible stories, built from the metaphors and folkways of a pastoral and agrarian people, lost their immediate emotional resonance, became a touch alien. The Lord as Shepherd did not directly chime with the experience of a commercial lawyer or mercantile clerk. Response could still be evoked (as it is today), but only by special conditioning, as provided by upbringing in the church. The sometimes traumatic experience of social change may actually have caused some people to cling more tightly to the Bible's archaic phrases (as they resurrected medieval liturgies and Gothic architecture). The point is not that response to traditional religious language weakened; no evidence suggests that. But the impulse became, not unnatural, but a step removed from unthinking reaction, a step closer to conscious reflection, and a step further from everyday reality.

The effect cannot possibly be demonstrated, much less measured, but it needs to be pointed to. Insulation from nature ultimately had much the same consequence as the growing sense of control over nature. And both reinforced the encroachment, at more articulated levels of thought, of natural causes on divine activity, pushing God's direct presence farther from everyday experience into an intangible spiritual realm. Perhaps, indeed, these social changes made the notion of a natural-law God easier to swallow. In no way did social change erode the cognitive plausibility of belief in God. But this belief, like all, was to some extent a captive of the life that it grew from and the language that expressed it. Capitalist organization, technological change, and urbanization had subtly dissociated God from ordinary verities. And this subliminal disjunction more often pushed belief in God up from the dim layer of unexamined assumptions that form the background of thought into the full light of consciousness. There God lay exposed to reflection and questioning.

Meanwhile, diminished authority of the church and its ministers similarly eroded traditional protections that held questioning at bay. This transformation, occurring, as it were, above ground, is clearer to see than subliminal psychic shifts. Clerical control over ideas and information had declined fitfully but persistently since the Reformation. Clerical influence had shrunk less consistently. In some respects, post-Reformation efforts at Christianizing the lives of nominal Christians and, more recently, revivalism had increased it. On the whole, however, the grip of the churches on nonreligious aspects of life had weakened, and nowhere more than in America.

Ministerial power remained much more than vestigial after 1790. Even state-supported churches, rather enfeebled to be sure, survived in New England. More important, local ministers often still served as primary conduits of ideas, sometimes as the dominant local authority. Lyman Beecher recalled reading his first newspaper, as a boy of sixteen or seventeen in the 1790s, at the parsonage in the Connecticut village of North Guilford. The abolitionist Lucy Colman pictured the parson of the town where she grew up around 1830 as "an arrogant, tyrannical man," who told townsfolk how to vote and "was both judge and jury" in every dispute. The minister of Lyman Abbott's Maine boyhood was more benevolent, but as late as the 1840s local folk still relied on his Sunday morning prayer for "all the purposes of a local newspaper."[6] A certain nostalgic glow—in Colman's case, bitter coals—distorts these reminiscences. But a high degree of clerical influence, the result of the minister's central role in village life, shows through.

In larger towns and cities, however, other voices increasingly dampened the minister's. Colman recalled that, when a Methodist preacher arrived, the competition squelched her local tyrant, gave people a sense of choice and consequently independence. Multiplication of secular oracles widened further this kind of latitude. Newspapers, in fact, eventually penetrated even Maine; places like Boston, New York, Philadelphia, and Charleston had got their news from a printer for a long while. As the communications system became more sophisticated, in tandem with commercial links, the typical minister's influence grew more tenuous. Moreover, habits of deference were eroding throughout society, and mobility was increasing. Both tended to reduce the minister's authority and expand alternative points of view.

Capitalism in fact had much to do with all these developments. Expansion of a market economy and its transportation network increased mobility; in more complex ways, an individualistic urban and commercial society undercut traditional deference. Rises in disposable money income were as important as the spread of literacy in creating an audience for printed matter; and commercial organization and marketing by publishers were equally critical. The power-driven press, in use by 1810, greatly cheapened books and periodicals, speeding and broadening the restless flow of ideas. Urbanization concentrated specialized audiences, making it easier for relatively unpopular points of view to sustain existence. Coupled with the proliferation of sources of information and discussion—books, magazines, lyceums, mechanics' institutes, common schools, newspapers—city life diminished the influence that ministers had once enjoyed, simply by virtue of their office, over even secular matters.

This street, however, ran two ways. A high proportion of books and magazines propagated religion, championing rather than grinding down the occupant of the pulpit. And enterprising clergymen were among the earliest and most ingenious in exploiting new communications media, commercial publishing, and organizing techniques to advance their cause.

Nevertheless, the social, commercial, and technological changes of the nineteenth century completed the infrastructure of a truly secular culture. The floodgates had opened. Clergymen contributed prolifically to public discussion, but they lost their privileged rostrum. Too many competitors now jammed the marketplace of ideas: an apt metaphor, considering its origins. The clerical vocation itself moved from the status of community official to that of specialist serving a self-selected clientele—from office to profession, as one historian has put it. Even the churches' grip over education, a particularly crucial seat of influence, finally loosened. In 1855 the Reverend James Walker, president of Harvard, recalled nostalgically, "It is within the memory of some of us when professors and tutors were taken, almost as a matter of course, from among clergymen and students in divinity; now, as a general rule, a professor is as much a layman as a lawyer or a physician is."[7] Fourteen years later a chemist, Charles W. Eliot, occupied Walker's chair; a minister never again led Harvard. Clerical presidents and professors held on longer at other colleges, but as a dying race.

After mid-century the rising universities, in particular, nurtured a powerful new cultural elite, beginning to command prestige and influence rivaling the clergy's. Science, traditionally the pursuit mostly of amateurs, acquired professional status in the nineteenth century. Its full-time, nationally- and internationally-oriented practitioners carefully distinguished themselves from part-time enthusiasts centered in local clubs. The reasons why this new profession became entrenched in public respect were complex, but the technological advances fostered by capitalism ranked high among them. Technology contributed to science, if only because the demand for engineers pulled science in its wake. A pioneering manufacturer, Abbott Lawrence, endowed at Harvard in 1847 a scientific school intended to stress engineering; the zoologist Louis Agassiz took charge and twisted the Lawrence School into a seminary of pure science.[8] M.I.T., chartered in 1861, remained true to its engineers but could hardly help loading the curriculum with a stiff dose of science—and hence the faculty with scientists. And science contributed increasingly to technology, getting in return support for scientists, especially as the chemical and electrical industries and agricultural science evolved after the Civil War.

Even when science gave nothing to technology, the nonscientific public tended to conflate the two. In 1862 Henry Adams leapt from marveling at improvements in naval warfare to the conclusion that "man has mounted science, and is now run away with." The railway system, chlorine bleach, the telegraph, lunatic asylums, discoveries in physiology, cheap mail, Avogadro's law, rifled guns, armored ships, and census reports all somehow got jumbled together in admiring minds as contributions of science.[9] Wonder at technological marvels devolved often, rightly or no, into enthusiasm for science.

Waxing enthusiasm, in turn, supported the multiplication of scientists and creation of institutional niches for them. Between the late 1840s and 1870, over thirty-five colleges opened scientific departments. Scientific offices began to dot the federal bureaucracy after the Civil War, as demand for scientific counsel overcame Congress's inertia and parsimony. The proliferation of professional scientific associations started around mid-century, most notably with the American Association for the Advancement of Science. Scientific publicists created their own institutions of popular education in the form of magazines like *Scientific American* (1848) and *Popular Science Monthly* (1872). These reached a surprisingly wide audience. An aging planter named Ethelred Philips, isolated on his Florida plantation amid the upheavals of Reconstruction, took solace in the *Scientific American,* which he declared "by far the most valuable paper published."[10]

New schools and new departments meant jobs—full-time jobs, many with the chance for research. New publications meant wider audiences—the popular increasingly distinct from the specialized. Scientists hardly approached the clout they would wield in the twentieth century. But they had achieved professional solidity: an entrenched, autonomous position within the institutions of American society.

From thence they worked to secure their social and intellectual turf. Professional careers in science (and, soon, quasi sciences like economics) created a cultural elite self-consciously distinct from the older clerical and literary body of opinion molders. To establish their independence and make good their draft on resources and prestige, these professional scientists had to pry loose the prior claims of traditional literary and religious intellectuals, of whom ministers still constituted the majority. This need bred a tendency on the part of a vociferous minority of scientists to snap at the clergy and denigrate their pretensions. The most celebrated snarling occurred in the polemics that flared in the last three decades of the century over the alleged historic "warfare" between science and theology. The Reverend Charles Hodge hit the mark in 1874 when he observed among men of science "who avow or manifest their hostility to religion" an irritating "assumption of superiority, and often a manifestation of contempt."[11] By no means all scientists sneered at ministers, as Hodge freely admitted. But professionalization of science and eventually social science created competitors out to best the clergy in the struggle for public resources and respect. Social change had thus armed a new cultural elite with all the ambition that drives people advancing their livelihood, their professional status, and their own image of themselves.

The unique importance of scientists after about 1860, as compared with other secular intellectuals, was that they presented what often seemed a clear cultural alternative to the religious way of dealing with the world. And their way appealed to a growing number of educated Americans. True, enthusiasm was neither universal nor unhesitant. Yale at first made students of its Sheffield Scientific School huddle at the rear of the college chapel, quarantined from other undergraduates. Between the 1870s and 1890s, antivivisectionist attacks on science in medicine won wide sympathy, even from many doctors. A vaguer suspicion nagged that science threatened to dry up the softer emotions, imperiling art and poetry and love—an uneasiness congealed in James Russell Lowell's poem "The Cathedral" (1869) and felt even by Darwin.[12] Yet the irritations science induced did not obstruct its general welcome. By the 1860s, science had won remarkable esteem. Many Americans regarded it as the avatar of modern knowledge, modern methods, modern goals.

In one sense, shouldering aside of ministers by scientists was only another stage in the emergence of autonomous intellectuals unbeholden to the churches—a long development, going back to the Enlightenment and earlier. But the situation was more complex. After mid-century, the social structure of cultural life fragmented. Secular intellectuals did not simply break away from clerical tutelage; the clergy themselves were headed toward becoming only one professional group among many, the members of each tending to identify more closely with their peers than their communities. Yet professional science had more sweeping implications, for in a sense it rose above this disintegration. It actually erected a counterpart to the old clerical and literary cultural establishment, certainly not so influential in the whole culture but at least equally coherent in world view and self-identity.

As such, science faced the clergy with a severe challenge. The problem was less a frontal assault than a usually unintended flanking action. It was not hard to sustain both religious beliefs and scientific interests. Most scientists remained Christians and had no more interest than ministers in promoting science as an alternative to the church. Most clergymen sustained sympathy, even admiration, for science. Relatively few on either side *confronted* the other; rather, science all too easily *displaced* religion as an object of interest. Science offered an appealingly modern alternative set of commitments, leaving religion to fade from attention. Moreover, unlike the prewar period, when ministers (like the geologist Edward Hitchcock or the naturalist John Bachman) could also do important scientific work, the new professional structure virtually forced a choice between careers in religion and science; this heightened the impression of alternatives. Talented and dedicated young people, who in the antebellum years might have given their lives to the church, chose science instead. Henry A. Rowland, descended from a line of New England ministers, rejected this heritage in favor of science, becoming the first professor of physics at the Johns Hopkins University and ultimately a world figure in that field. The noted economist Henry Carter Adams intended as a young man to dedicate himself to the ministry but abandoned religion for the lure of social science. Science brought to a head the strains that secularization placed on the church at levels ranging from the unarticulated depths of belief to penny newspapers to research laboratories.[13]

Church leaders had no choice but to confront these secularizing effects in some way. The question was the right way. Should they concede primacy and set religion athwart society, in the world but not of it? Should they plunge into social change and fight to regain their traditional sway? Most of the guardians of belief, especially the energetic northern Evangelicals, chose to fight. Thus, clergymen (echoed by many scientists) chanted loudly, frequently, and nervously throughout the century the harmony of science and religion. This denial of conflict (and the zeal for scientific natural theology before 1859) was not only an effort to bridge an intellectual gap. It was also, to a degree, a half-conscious attempt to repress the pretensions of scientists to autonomy in the social structure of knowledge—before the 1850s, to keep science from appearing independent of ministerial leadership and, after the 1850s, to prevent the now undeniably autonomous elite from seeming an alternative to the church.

Ministers also initiated much more deliberate efforts to sustain the church's faltering leadership. The problem of making the flock heed the shepherd was, of course, ancient. Now, however, the obstacle was not traditional indifference and obstinacy but structural social change that undermined authority once belonging to the church by virtue of its institutional position. In response, ministers turned the disruptive techniques of capitalist organization to their own advantage. Commercial publishers found no class of writers shrewder and more profitable than ministers like Henry Ward Beecher and their female allies, like his sister Harriet Beecher Stowe.[14] Religious authors, particularly those with a weakness for novels, could not always be relied on for doctrinal orthodoxy; but they invariably stood firm for Evangelical morality and a caring God.

The press, however, probably served the church less well than did voluntary associations—and that is a large claim. Evangelicalism in particular spawned an army of moral reform organizations: societies for temperance, tract-distribution, Bible-promotion, sabbatarianism, missions foreign and domestic; antislavery, antiduelling, antiprostitution, anti-Catholic, anticruelty associations; even Maternal Associations in which mothers helped each other to rear their children for salvation. Indeed, women played a substantial, rising to dominant, role in many of these organizations; for ministers were by no means alone in their concern for the church's moral influence. Such associations represented one of the earliest and most successful efforts to put to noneconomic purposes the organizing drive and bureaucratic techniques fostered by capitalism. It was no coincidence that the most impressive Evangelical organizers, Lewis and Arthur Tappan of New York, could afford to make a career of reform only because they had first made a bundle in commerce. Lewis also founded the nation's first commercial-credit rating agency.

In voluntary associations, ministers and lay leaders moved outside the institutional church in order to open a new channel for churchly influence on society. This amounted to a kind of end-run around secularization, and it worked. No one familiar with nineteenth-century America can miss the impress of Evangelical moralism, whether in detail on movements like temperance and antislavery or on the Victorian sensibility at large.

Yet voluntarism concealed both irony and danger, as, for that matter, did the appeal to science. In order to make themselves heard in secular affairs, church leaders urged their followers to put on secular attire. But precisely because their work clothes were secular, those followers might eventually come to regard the work itself as disjoined from God. Similarly, enthusiasm for science as defender of the faith might keep reins on science; but it might also encourage some listeners to pay more attention to the new scientific elite than to the ministers who invoked it.

Deeper issues than the status of the clergy lurked here. Religious leaders were trying to protect the church against social change with the same strategy that they used to defend belief from intellectual change. Faced with a situation in which belief in God lay more exposed to questioning, they needed to secure it against doubt. Confronted with a widening gap between God and the world—or the church and society—they had to act somehow to guarantee the relevance of religion. They chose to ensure both by embracing the world, in this instance by tying the church to secular culture and temporal concerns. This plan of defense was in many respects shrewd and successful, but it held its risks. And these perils deepened when religious leaders considered the other questions raised by social change. These problems, like the challenge of secularization, pitted an impalpable God against the all-too-solid world.

Social Change and Moralization

Long ago, in *The Protestant Ethic and the Spirit of Capitalism,* Max Weber argued that the moralism of early Protestants gave birth to habits of accumulation and diligence that produced capitalism. Few scholars today would deny that Weber oversimplified the connection; even fewer would deny that he was on to something. Weber was hardly the first to suspect the congeniality of capitalism and a certain type of moralism; indeed, early Victorian merchants and industrialists on both sides of the Atlantic cherished a picture of their class as the most virtuous part of the community. This self-image may well have been accurate; it all depended on what virtues one specified. The Victorian merchants' list may have been somewhat self-serving; certainly their Puritan ancestors took a grimmer view, more than suspecting that commercial self-seeking tended to corrupt.

Clearly, capitalism had something to do with morality; equally clearly, the relationship was anything but simple. One might argue, at a highly general level, that the merchant's need to focus on the fast-changing exigencies of the market, as well as the need specifically to cultivate seriousness, frugality, and industry, engendered a more obsessive concern with behavior, particularly self-control, as key to commercial success. Either this ethic would promote capitalism, or capitalism this ethic, or both; in any case, capitalism and this down-to-earth moralism would develop hand-in-hand. The "general Practice and Habit of the Virtues" would leave the aspiring capitalist "free from the Dominion of Vice; and particularly by the Practice of Industry and Frugality, free from Debt."[15] So Benjamin Franklin wrote, and he should have known. Unfortunately, such plausible and probably accurate generalities do not get the historian very far.

American development from the late eighteenth century provides a little more specificity. As commercial capitalism accelerated its spread, farmers and artisans alike needed to pay more attention to the buy-and-sell pressures of the market. Those who did not prosper became wage-earning employees; those who prospered extraordinarily might become grain merchants or manufacturers; meanwhile, the economic role of their wives often shrank into child raising and housekeeping. Men and women, particularly young men and women, and most particularly young men, moved in large numbers out of small farming villages into more anonymous, more fluid towns and cities; quite a few small farming villages themselves became towns or cities.

All this not only transformed the economic world but the moral world as well. Manufacturers and merchants, for example, could no longer tolerate in their millhands and clerks the irregular work habits that had been typical and sufficiently functional in agrarian and artisan cultures. Employees who exhibited an outmoded looseness in matters chronological, or an excessive fondness for the bottle, threatened to clog economic mechanisms that depended on the intricate and orderly interaction of many individuals. And young men on the make, clerks or millhands or journeymen, knew this without being told; sobriety, thrift, and self-discipline made it possible for a man to climb the ladder.[16]

This was not the whole story; anxiety mingled with ambition. Rapid change unsettles anyone. The young men and women who migrated from farming communities to the new mills and mercantile establishments faced a confusing and uncertain future; religious commitments and especially clear moral guidance imparted a sense of stability. It was no accident that Evangelical revivals burned with special intensity in places caught in the throes of such change.[17] And booming commercial and manufacturing towns looked, if anything, even more threatening to securely established guardians of mores than to folk directly caught up in the confusion. Disruption of traditional ways, the temptations of life with the controls loosened, forecast moral dislocation, if not collapse. Lyman Beecher warned that "the unformed population of our cities, and mechanical and manufacturing establishments, as well as . . . our sparse frontier settlements" faced disturbing religious perils.[18]

If the Rochesters and Uticas seemed worrisome, the "Great City"—places like New York and Philadelphia, swelling into the hundreds of thousands, even millions—positively alarmed. In some ways the metropolis inspired awed admiration, but at the same time it was feared as a sink of moral degeneracy—and not always unjustly, especially if one regarded New York's notorious Five Points district from the viewpoint of, say, Litchfield, Connecticut. Whole classes of the anonymous poor, particularly their young, were tarred indiscriminately with the brush of criminality and vice: they became the "dangerous classes."[19] And their chronic criminality seemed to spring directly from the moral feebleness of their upbringing. The influx of masses of poor, Papist Irish starting in the 1840s only made the scene more nervewracking.

Church leaders could hardly ignore the moral challenge. After all, if social change had unsettled morality, the churches had the duty to light the path to righteousness. So much was indisputable. Moreover, the last century or two had infused ministers with especially intense moral sensitivity. The net thrust of religious development since the Reformation, and especially in the eighteenth century, had been toward deeper moral concern. And the yearning to reassert the churches' leadership in a secularizing society nagged at the back of the mind, if not the front: clear duty now spread before church leaders a golden opportunity. No committed Christian in any age could in good conscience have backed away from such a moral crisis. A nineteenth-century Evangelical was virtually immune to the temptation.

It is wrong to freeze the actors in such distinct categories, however, for this moral change in large measure created nineteenth-century Evangelicalism. Evangelicals did not so much respond from a fixed position to upheaval as develop their distinctive character in response to it. The moral uncertainty resulting from these social and economic changes established the context in which church leaders set the moralistic course described in the previous chapter. Picking their way through these disturbances, ministers and theologians had to decide what they meant for the church, what role moralism was to play in religion. The answer was not unambiguous; but the general impulse was to push morality nearer the center of religion, to make it the really living core of belief.

More precisely, a growing number of ministers made moral guidance through the shoals of social change the vital principle of religion. Lay activists, particularly Evangelicals, commonly did the same. The primacy of moral formation was sometimes obscured by enthusiasm for revivals, stress on individual conversion, and the rhetorical conventions of heart-religion. Nevertheless, it increasingly seemed the church's main task to help the Christian pick his way through the ethical dilemmas and personal problems of modern life. The Evangelical commitment to social reform—antislavery, temperance, and so forth—applied this inclination to the sins of society at large.

Child rearing and advice to youth, as one would expect, exhibited the change most strikingly. After the first quarter of the century, the stress in Christian child raising (at least to judge by manuals and the Maternal Associations gathered under church auspices) fell less heavily on traditional Calvinist preparation for conversion, much more decisively on the development of "character." Indeed, in Victorian notions of womanhood not only the mother's role but that of women in general came to center on moral formation of children and moral elevation of males of all ages. And the "character" that mothers were supposed to nurture increasingly meant the congeries of regular habits, reliability, and good reputation that would help a boy or girl to live successfully in the adult world. Heaven was not forgotten: getting there, after all, was the main point. True, the ticket to heaven, it was hoped, would carry a boy to commercial reward, a girl to marital bliss, on the way. So pleasant a result, however, was also too crass a goal to form the major conscious purpose of many mothers or ministers. Not just the economic but the moral aspects of life had grown too labile and confusing for people to rely on community standards and traditional signposts for guidance. If they were not to stray off the path, they needed both an interior roadmap and internal pressure to stick to its routes. "Character" provided this, and the main thrust of Evangelical child rearing became to instill character.

For those not lucky enough to have Evangelical mothers, and for those who had grown beyond their superintendence, alternative instructors strove to shape or reinforce character—or at least to mitigate the moral corruption of modern life. The Sunday School movement, achieving national organization in the American Sunday School Union in 1824, originated in worries about moral breakdown in the burgeoning cities, while the mid-century city-mission movement tried to bring the moral benefits of religion to the dangerous classes. The Young Men's Christian Association, founded in England, was introduced into the United States in 1851 to provide a moral haven—a home away from home and a church away from church—for young clerks and the like who had come alone, without family and pastoral guidance, to the perils of the big city. Authors, mostly clergymen, spun a new genre of advice literature directed to urban youth facing such uncertainty. Its obsessive stress was on character development "to bridge the gap between traditional values and new conditions": "an internal gyroscope" to guide young men among the shifting pitfalls of a disrupted society.[20]

While no one objected to morality—at least not publicly—many did resent the rigorous moral policing common among Evangelicals. Campaigns by voluntary associations to put down drinking or sabbath breaking split communities, setting neighbor against neighbor, spilling over into bitter political strife, even riots. Local churches sometimes had to abandon the traditional superintendence of their members' behavior because congregations could no longer agree on the moral standards to apply. Moral disagreement often reflected socioeconomic difference. The manufacturers of Lynn, Massachusetts, for example, were hot in the cause of temperance; the neighboring merchants in Salem, in contrast, felt no compulsion to give up their rum toddies.[21] To oversimplify yet indicate a pattern: just as capitalist development in general fostered a broad concern for morality, so specific types of capitalist development brought particular moral problems to the fore; likewise, faster or slower rates of development made for greater or less sense of urgency. No such neat correlations existed in actuality; nevertheless, one can gather how social change encouraged both moralization and resistance to it.

The humanitarianism and commitment to progress that increasingly shaped Victorian morality also owed something to the effects of social and economic change. Indeed, the prevailing faith in progress is hardly conceivable without the dramatic improvements wrought by technology and applied by capitalist business organization. Glorying in railroad, steamship, and telegraph, most Victorians explicitly rested their confidence in progress on future achievements of science and industry. Moral and intellectual advances, the ones really valued, were supposed to flow from these material improvements in the human condition. A rapidly changing society seemed to be opening on to a happier, higher future (or so the middle classes usually told themselves, in a mixture of honesty and anxiety). This vision held out a sore temptation to place progress at the apex of moral ideals, and the millennial idea of a coming Kingdom of God helped Protestants to reconcile exaltation of human progress with divine sovereignty.

In a more backhanded way, capitalist development probably also fostered humanitarianism. Amid all its wonders and perils, the Great City spawned suffering on an equally vast scale. The misery of urban poverty and, increasingly from the 1840s, the suffering of industrial workers and immigrants (commonly the same people) may not have exceeded the sum of pain abounding in earlier societies; but the suffering, if only because novel in form, became more visible and shocking. Noisome slums, wan factory children, families dissolved in whiskey wrenched humane feelings and stoked them to greater heat. The tantalizing dream that progress could wipe out such problems gave an added lift. These responses certainly did not create humanitarianism, but they did tighten its hold.

On the whole, moral efforts of church leaders proved remarkably successful. The churches, especially through the extradenominational voluntary associations pioneered by Evangelicals, got an impressively firm grip on the moral wobblings of American society. Despite the sometimes dizzying rate of change, religious leaders succeeded during the nineteenth century in grafting their moral ideals onto the American conscience, at least its middle-class portion, to perhaps a greater extent than ever before. And the effect was not limited to stricter morals. Church membership statistics are fragmentary and notoriously inaccurate, but the best guess is that adherence rose fairly steadily through the century; so, probably, insofar as impressionistic evidence permits judgment, did regularity of practice. Devoutness defies measurement, but by observable standards the American people were likely at their most religious in the second half of the nineteenth century.

Yet in choosing to respond to the challenge of social change with an overwhelmingly moralistic approach, church leaders also succeeded in making American religion more nearly a matter of morality than ever before. And they made morality itself more nearly a matter of improving the individual and society. Not many of them paused to ask whether their decision involved losses as well as gains.

Social Change and Rationalization

Deciphering moral responses to social circumstances is baffling enough. Still more uncertain is how socioeconomic change affected notions people had of what knowledge is and how to get it. Such commonplace, unarticulated epistemology is elusive anyway, likely to be unclear and inconsistent. Even professional philosophers relax their rigor when they leave their studies; the rest of us perpetually regard the bases of knowledge through a fog, though obviously one thin enough to let us find our way around for practical purposes. Any more rigorous epistemology would be unnecessary, perhaps paralyzing. But this fuzziness makes a historian's job tougher. Linking so amorphous a set of attitudes with shifts in social organization and material conditions is speculative at best.

Still, connections existed. Capitalism and technology did not induce any radical shifts in conceptions of knowledge, but they did encourage a gradual, subtle transposition of emphases and values. Some ways of knowing declined in respectability; others gained new prestige. Some kinds of truths grew less certain, others more secure.

The overall thrust, amid much ambivalence and backtracking, was toward a more empirical and rationally ordered style of thinking. Knowledge sank deeper roots in palpable physical reality, and the road to it grew straighter, plainer; more regular, logical, and concrete. This trend has already been noted in scientific, social, and religious thought in the seventeenth and eighteenth centuries. Even then this rationalization corresponded, though only very loosely, to the social realities of early capitalism. The swift exfoliation of commercial capitalism in America from the late eighteenth century, along with the growth of cities and the advance of technology, fostered much faster movement in this direction. Yet advance was anything but linear. Resistance, contradiction, and simple confusion are the norm when people try to come to terms with change. Nevertheless, a quick sketch must suffice to suggest the rough pattern, which a large book could not describe in its full complexity.

A version of natural selection governs the world of ideas. Ideas that "work"—that help in some way (perhaps very indirect) to cope with the physical or cultural environment—are more likely to survive. Those that work well for many people tend to proliferate. Empirical rationality fitted rather well the developing environment of commercial capitalism. A penchant for rational organization helped to bring success in an increasingly complicated and interwoven tangle of economic relationships. A sharp eye on specific concrete realities aided in taking advantage of rapidly changing markets. Bringing to affairs such a cast of mind, a man had an advantage in guessing the next turn of events, and successful prediction was key to gaining some measure of control over a very slippery future.

In the new ways of thinking that grew in importance from at least the seventeenth century onward, four specific elements stand out that seem to have some plausible connection with socioeconomic changes. First was the assumption that knowledge became reliable only when verified in experience. The uncertainties of commerce, where success hinged on a shrewd response to each unique set of shifting circumstances, made reliance on received wisdom less productive. A merchant or commercial farmer needed to form judgments on the basis of his own and his fellows' experience, rather than accept maxims handed down from the fathers. Accelerating commercialization and urbanization spread these conditions of life through much of society, thrusting millions into situations where traditional wisdom no longer made much sense—where, in short, they had to experiment.

Moreover, the nineteenth-century individual was avid for experimentation of all sorts: entrepreneurial, political, social, technological, intellectual; ranging from Fulton's steamboat to utopian communities like Brook Farm. No wonder that the very conception of knowledge came to include a larger dose of verification by experience, while the simple weight of traditional belief no longer seemed a guarantee of accuracy. Thinking about God did not escape this change. Emerson's obliteration of all authorities that stood between the soul and God, his utter repudiation of any basis for belief but personal experience, constituted an extreme case of a not uncommon inclination. In 1865 Charles Eliot Norton, editor of the nation's most respected magazine, the *North American Review,* spelled out his basic principle of belief for a Midwestern minister: "The relation between God and the soul is original for every man. His religion must be his own. No two men think of God alike. No man or men can tell me what I must think of him. If I am pure of heart, I see him, and know him;—& creeds are but fictions that have nothing to do with the truth."[22]

This rejection of traditional authority in favor of truths validated in experience bore on a second trait: the sense that empirical truths were more reliable than those that transcended physical reality. Again, some relation to social conditions seems likely. Rapid social change encouraged a man to focus attention on the here-and-now; the vicissitudes of trade impressed this lesson doubly on the man of business. Subsistence farming is a very mundane occupation, but its almost invariant routines allow generous opportunity for mental excursions elsewhere. The propect of bankruptcy, however, concentrates the mind wonderfully. City life and factory work—trolley schedules and power looms—also exacted closer attention to terrestrial things. The intangible perhaps grew, not less respected, but more remote. The truths that counted practically were the kind that a man could lay his hands on. Others, important but less convincingly solid, gravitated toward the custody of people supposed not to be involved with practical affairs: poets and women. Indeed, the Victorian ideology of womanhood incarnated just such a sexual division of intellectual labor. Religion specifically came to be regarded as in a special way women's work. This put ministers in potentially an awkward position vis-à-vis the world of male reality, and their invention of Victorian muscular Christianity may reflect some discomfort at being politely excused from hard realities.

A third characteristic of the new cast of mind was a greater thirst for precision in knowledge: for logically formulated, exactly specified propositions that offered a basis for accurate prediction. Newton's laws provided the celebrated model. A grain merchant in Buffalo was no Newton, the farmer whose wheat he shipped probably even less of one. Yet there was affinity. Commerce required criteria for making business decisions: rules for action that led, as precisely as possible given fluctuating markets, to predictable outcomes. These were hard to come by in the whirligig of spreading capitalism and, increasingly, technological innovation. Men often had to swing on hunch and instinct, and uncertainty only made them hungrier for predictability. Capitalists who could forge dependable principles to regulate their dealings, and apply them accurately, were usually the ones who prospered. "Prospered" sometimes puts it mildly. Andrew Carnegie's precise accounting system, hawklike regulation of costs, systematic assessment of employees, and logical coordination of production in his steel mills helped him to become one of the richest men in the world—and one of the most emulated. Capitalist development did not create rational organization and precision, but economic and technological pressures probably did widen their application, increase their apparent relevance, and tempt people to extend them further. Knowledge that failed to aspire to these standards often seemed by the mid-nineteenth century somehow second-rate, not entirely solid.

Lust for system and precision satiated itself in passionate embrace of statistics, the distinctively modern species of fact. Statistics larded a number of eighteenth-century books—Jefferson's *Notes on the State of Virginia* (1785) is the best-known American example—but systematic collection of numerical data was still uncommon, particularly in the United States, as late as the first federal census in 1790. The next few decades made up for lost time; by 1820, bookshelves groaned under fat volumes crammed with numbers. No charitable society with any sense of decorum dared parade its annual report without statistics to clothe its nude accomplishments. Even sacred affairs submitted to counting: the Boston Society for the Moral and Religious Instruction of the Poor dutifully inventoried in 1818 the memorization by pauper children of 54,029 Bible verses, 1,899 hymns, and 17,779 catechism responses.[23] The exact quantity of personal religious experiences was left unrecorded, though later revivalists filled this deficiency. Precision made it all seem more real; intolerance for the nebulous or mysterious was growing in the canons of knowledge. Mr. Gradgrind's schoolroom in *Hard Times* was no parody, only unusually thorough.

A fourth benchmark of modern thinking probably influenced by social change was the assumption that knowledge evolved historically. This perception, hardly breathing in the Middle Ages, had grown livelier by the late seventeenth century. Its spread paralleled the pace of social transformation. By the nineteenth century, the dullest citizen could scarcely fail to observe that things were not as they used to be and likely would not long remain as they now were. Along with social organization, economic methods, and technology, knowledge also was perceptibly changing. Beliefs held firmly a century or two earlier had grown outmoded, while new discoveries added daily to the sum of knowledge. When enlightened Victorians congratulated themselves that science and scholarship had purged their religious beliefs of old superstitions—a ritual they were fond of—they were only manifesting a historically conditioned sensitivity to the historical evolution of knowledge. Today's truths, it was widely accepted, were surer than yesterday's.

It is easy to observe that, by the mid-nineteenth century, the ideal of knowledge most appealing to educated Americans had become experimental, empirical, precise, predictive, and historically aware—and to conclude that social and economic change had something to do with the popularity of this archetype. It is harder to say what all this added up to.

Ultimately, what had occurred can only be pointed to, not explained: a shift at a very profound level in the way that the mind comprehends and orders at least certain kinds of experience. This change corresponded to, though was not necessarily determined by, a similar change in the actual social character of large areas of experience.[24] Beyond this conclusion a historian can hardly go. The next step leads into recesses of the mind too deeply buried for historical analysis to penetrate.

This new cast of mind—call it, for lack of any better term, "analytic-technical" thinking—implied a sharply revised and delimited version of "knowledge" and "truth." The analytic-technical mind favored calculation in factual, impersonal, measurable terms over more amorphous or inward ways of reaching truth. It devalued convictions that eluded demonstration in human experience (even if ultimately rooted in it) in favor of concrete truths explicable and controllable within the boundaries of experience. In effect, this way of thinking put stricter limits on what was "real" by casting suspicion on impalpable realities. By no means rooting out older habits, the analytic-technical approach nevertheless prospered with the advance of capitalist organization, urbanization, and technological influence.

The analytic-technical mind learned to admire itself especially in science. The new model of knowledge was experimental, empirical, precise, predictive, and historically cumulative. So was science. As the older, more all-embracing fields called natural philosophy and natural history narrowed into modern natural science in the first half of the nineteenth century, they approximated more and more closely to this ideal. Hostility to preconceptions and commitment to experimental method (that is, rejection of unexamined tradition and insistence on thinking things out for oneself); focus on physical evidence (that is, concern for what tangibly exists in this world); intolerance for unverifiable truths (that is, appreciation for definite decision making); demand for exact formulation of predictive theories and rigorous demonstration of them (that is, desire for reliable, precise rules of action); and careful building upon the verified work of previous scientists (that is, historical evolution of knowledge)—these standards, characteristics of scientific method as it approached its modern form, almost replicated the attitudes toward knowledge fostered by social and economic change since the sixteenth century and especially since the surge of commercial capitalism in America beginning about 1780. In a nutshell: science becoming modern could easily seem a refinement and extension of the analytic-technical cast of mind.

Growing respect for science then comes as no surprise. In the nineteenth century, its authority in some circles reached unprecedented heights. Auguste Comte literally made a cult of science; and, while he had few American disciples, by the 1850s a great many Victorians on both Atlantic coasts invested science with power and promise, by the 1870s even with sacredness, hard now to credit. The belief became common that only science could make the world intelligible: science seemed the avatar of all knowledge. The study of man and society became the "social sciences" after mid-century. The unlikeliest varieties of knowledge took refuge under the prestige of science. The eminent theologian Alexander Hodge, a conservative Presbyterian and no friend of contemporary science, defined theology as "the science of religion"—and he did not have in mind the comprehensive German sense of the word. By no means every Victorian worshipped science: a few detested it, and many harbored doubts. But the consensus of educated persons approached almost to a childlike trust in "the mighty enchantress, modern Science."[25]

Science appealed for many reasons; one of them was that it honed to razor keenness the modern cast of mind promoted by, among other things, the development of capitalism and technology. Victorians did not admire science as some sort of alien marvel (though its mysteries did grow steadily less accessible). They saw in it, if only obscurely, the apotheosis of ways of thinking central to their own dealings with the world. Its virtue partly resided in the fact that it seemed to do best much of what they more loosely tried to do. There was thus a temptation to give it a vague definition and expand it to universal applicability. A fairly conservative theologian, the Reverend Charles Mead of Andover Seminary, declared in 1870 that "it is the province of science to explain, not just some facts, but all facts. Whatever can be known is a proper subject of scientific inquiry." "No one," he added, "questions this."[26]

Actually, some did. They rebelled not just against the pretensions of the modern style of science but against the analytic-technical mind of which it was the purest expression, in fact against the whole business of markets and manufactories, cities and steam engines, that battened on such a way of dealing with the world. The rebels were not few, for they included not only the handful of self-conscious dissenters like Thoreau but also most of the people Thoreau denounced. Ambivalence usually marks personal reaction to change. Ambiguity of response, even contradiction, increases with depth of transformation. A mild shift in circumstances, even when welcomed, still evokes a touch of nostalgia for what is lost. Radical upheaval, however beneficial, generates considerable anxiety. The tearing down of a familiar world is upsetting, despite enthusiasm for the new world rising from the wreckage.

The wrecking ball of commercial capitalism, the uprooting pull of city life had the effect of a psychic earthquake. Even those who welcomed the new order—and profited from it—tried to resurrect some vestige of older times to cling to as a symbol of stability. Hence the magnificently incongruous spectacle of Gothic facades built to bless the hiss and clang of railroad stations, of Romanesque churches rising in the midst of sooty industrial cities. Hence Daniel Webster, the golden voice of Boston's millowners, setting himself up as a farmer in rural Marshfield.

City life and technology domesticated the natural world to an unprecedented extent, finally putting the relationship of man and nature on a new footing. So a cult arose to celebrate the mysteries and splendors of untrammeled nature. The new economic order demanded self-discipline, order, and impersonal cooperation. So novelists threw their characters into emotional transports; poets proclaimed the irreducible truth of individual genius. Analytic-technical thinking provided a lever for success in the new system. So the truths of intuition, worlds inaccessible to an earthbound mind, beckoned away. The landscapes of Constable and Cole, the verses of Wordsworth and Poe, the oratory of Burke and Everett, even the mass-produced chromoliths of Currier and Ives that replicated grandmother's farm in city parlors—all chanted a spell to soothe the uneasiness that sometimes crept up the spine when one stood on the brink of the unknown. To explain Romantic sensibility thus is to oversimplify grossly the complex roots of Cole's, Wordsworth's, or even Nathaniel Currier's art. It is also to point out an important truth. Urbanization, technology, and capitalism did nourish these seeming subversives in their own nest, a needed psychological counterweight to other progeny with a closer family resemblance to their parents.

A few renegades set their faces against merchants, machines, or cities; but most educated Americans gave modernity at the very least a half-hearted welcome. They harbored both rationalized and romantic attitudes. It is always an error to underestimate the human capacity to ignore contradiction, but in this case attitudes superficially at odds may have been symbiotic. Romantic flights from empirical rationality may have made the hard-headed new order easier to accept, just as playing at farmer gave Daniel Webster refreshment from Boston and Washington. In any case, few Victorians wanted to think of reason and emotion, individual genius and social cooperation, science and intuition as finally incompatible. They sought rather to harness these two sides of their culture together in a harmonious whole, to produce (in a quintessentially Victorian cliché, apparently coined by Longfellow) a well-rounded man.

Nothing could embody more distinctly the antiemotional, antiintuitive side of Victorian culture than its science. Yet, in *The Art-Idea* (1864), James Jackson Jarves insisted that, over and above "its material mission," science "talks face to face with spirit." By "unfolding the laws of being," it "carries thought into the infinite," up to God Himself. "As nature is His art, so science is the progressive disclosure of His soul."[27] "Carrying thought into the infinite" sounded very like Harriet Beecher Stowe writing of intuition. Yet, lest anyone assume that working scientists would all have scoffed at such stuff, it might be pointed out that Jarves's last sentence paraphrased the most eminent contemporary American scientist, Louis Agassiz. The compatibility should raise no eyebrows. For most of the middle classes, romantic attitudes remained for most purposes subordinate, even instrumental, to capitalist and technological rationality—a vacation. Yet even vacations suggest alternatives to humdrum routine, imply that one does not have to live all of life by the same standards.

This change of cultural climate set the context in which religious leaders were driven to reconsider the sources of knowledge of God. For centuries, rational-empirical approaches to reality had grown more attractive; now a quickening pace of socioeconomic change infused them with wider appeal. At the same time, social transformation helped to clarify and distinguish nonrational, nonempirical ways of grasping some kinds of apparent truth. The problem was how to fit the two together, to decide, indeed, if they fit together—or if different roads led to different truths. "I wish," sighed eighteen-year-old Lydia Maria Francis to her brother in 1820, "I could find some religion in which my heart and understanding could unite." The girl went on, as Lydia Maria Child, to a controversial career as novelist, editor, abolitionist, and religious writer. But thirty-five years later the same question remained with her. She believed that faith in God flowed from the heart, yet she still longed for "a science concerning the nature of the Divine Being, and the relations of human souls with him."[28]

Religious leaders faced no harder question. The analytic-technical mind beckoned in one direction, most clearly signposted by the scientific natural theology of William Paley. Romantic attitudes beckoned in another, toward the antirationalism of James Marsh and Horace Bushnell. Most of the guardians of belief were, understandably, anxious to keep up with modernity, to bridge the gaps and heal the conflicts between religion and modern society. And this commitment formed their choices. That was why heart-religion, even in Evangelicalism, tended to degenerate into mere emotional effusion, a release from too-dry rationality, rather than develop into a coherent nonrationalized basis for claiming assurance of God. That was why even Evangelical theologians tried to assimilate intuitionism to Scottish common-sense rationality, drew back in fear from the efforts of more adventurous writers to place knowledge of God beyond common sense. The majority of religious leaders were safe, cautious men. They decided that they could best secure knowledge of God by tuning it to the dominant harmonies of the modern world.

5

Christianity Confused, 1840–1870

America in 1840 was a Christian nation. The armies of Evangelicalism had seen to that. Yet the revivalists' successes had never entirely obliterated scepticism about Christianity. True, Evangelicals could rejoice that the "hardened forehead of Infidelity" gloried in "its own shame" chiefly among "the low and vulgar," and not among many of those.[1] But the doubts flaunted by a few querulous radicals were quietly shared by many others, including more respectable folk.

These believers in natural religion were like Canute before the Evangelical tide, but they do testify to a persistent, if not very persuasive, scepticism about Christianity. One of the stages in Orestes Brownson's pilgrimage from Presbyterianism to Rome was natural religion. The South Carolina politician James Henry Hammond (a loyal if unorthodox Christian) went so far as to claim that he had never known "anyone who had a free, lively, intelligent & thorough belief in even the essentials of Christianity."[2] Hammond's standards must have been preternaturally high. Still, while it would be wrong to exaggerate doubts about Christianity, it would be equally a mistake to ignore their existence. Disreputable and implausible as it seemed, such scepticism nevertheless dragged its battered existence into the triumphal epoch of Protestant America.

Then, in the bloom of resurgent Christianity, these aging doubts sprouted with new vigor. Novel questions were raised, or old ones intensified, about some of the most fundamental Christian doctrines. The result was certainly not to displace Christianity from its preeminence in American religion, nor was it to restore Deism to significance. But a process of rethinking began. Out of it came eventually a new Christianity, but first confusion and uncertainty—and a drift among many questioners toward non-Christian theism.

Humanitarianism

One of the earliest and most prolific sources of doctrinal doubts (though also one of the hardest to pin down in individual cases) was the growing humanitarian sensibility. The same revulsion from suffering that had undermined Calvinism corroded other, even more ancient, Christian beliefs. Victorians typically expected God to be kind, generous, and fair. In the context of their moralism, an inhumane God amounted almost to a contradiction in terms. Yet insistence on His humaneness was not easily reconciled with the old creeds.

What, for example, could one say about a Father who handed over His Son to torture and death to pay for crimes that he never committed? Yet the doctrine of the Atonement specified precisely this abomination. Original sin presented a similar picture of cruelty and caprice. Orthodoxy alleged that God had laden unborn generations with the guilt of their remotest ancestors. Was this kind, generous, and fair? Would a properly compassionate God deny salvation to heathen never reached by missionaries? Or, indeed, to heathen reached but unregarding? Or to honest Christians lost in doctrinal error? The Unitarians fled these beliefs altogether, as a libel on God's goodness. More orthodox Christians tried to soften and subdue such scandalous doctrines with various modifications and glosses. The reminders of theologians such as Nathanael Emmons that God's actions "transcend human norms of justice and injustice" fell largely on deaf ears.[3]

Lurking behind the uneasiness over these doctrines was a belief less elaborated in theology but touching closer to home: Hell. God, according to most churches, sentenced at least the worst sinners, possibly most of the human race, to inconceivable, eternal pain. This was not the soft touch that one now expected of God. Hell no longer fit smoothly into the divine scheme of things, as it had for Dante and Calvin. One friend of the distinguished theologian Horace Bushnell recalled that Bushnell had "revolted from the notion . . . of everlasting punishment. The great humanity of his heart could in no sectarian stress be made a sacrifice on the altar of a cruel God, which was no God to him." The abolitionist Lucy Colman, when a little girl in the late 1820s, pestered her mother about the goodness of God: how could He let children be slaves, and, above all, how could He subject anyone to "the worst of all calamities," burning forever "in actual fire." In her teens, Lucy Colman bolted from orthodoxy to the Universalists to escape this cruel doctrine.[4]

Within a few decades, Christians did not need to make her choice. In many of the major denominations, it became acceptable to preach nearly universal salvation or some kind of probation after death; by the 1870s, the theological flight from hell was in full swing. And, increasingly, people simply assumed that dead folk they cared about had gone to heaven.[5]

One liberal preacher, who had himself almost jettisoned hell, put the matter this way: "It was impossible for the community at the same time to abolish torture from punishment in this life and to believe that the Father retained it in the life to come." He exaggerated; most Christians apparently managed to reconcile hell with the abolition of flogging—and, for that matter, to retain in some form a belief in original sin, the Atonement, and other doctrines that confounded humanitarianism. Yet many did not. And the doctrines involved were not peripheral or novel but central and ancient in Christian teaching. Christianity's encounter with humanitarianism left it somewhat altered, more uncertain, more questionable. "Many a time have I sighed to think what a vast number of people were living in fear of that vile Hell," wrote a young New Englander in 1860, "and have wished that the world might cast off such dreadful creeds."[6] And that is just what the young man, John Fiske, did.

The Authority of the Bible

Where humanitarianism produced unease with specific doctrines, doubts about the Bible sometimes undermined confidence in Christianity altogether. As a professedly historical religion, Christianity required historical evidence of its claims. And, with certain very minor exceptions, this evidence, for Protestants at least, was to be found nowhere but in the Scriptures. Thus Christianity, at least in its traditional forms, stood or fell with the authority of the Bible.

The Bible's authority, moreover, had come to rest on a thoroughly literal reading of the text. The ancient and medieval Church understood the Bible at several levels. Allegorical, typological, moral, and mystical interpretations flourished alongside historical-literal readings. The hand of the Church kept the reins taut enough to prevent the Bible from becoming Babel. The Protestant Reformers rejected this traditional control; they left the meaning of the Bible in individual hands (in principle, at least) and at the same time exalted it as the sole foundation of faith. This mixture was potentially explosive—indeed, religious radicals like the Anabaptists touched it off. From the beginning, therefore, the cautious founders of Protestantism looked with a wary eye on readings that wandered very far from the obvious meaning of the text.[7]

In the seventeenth and eighteenth centuries, this suspicion hardened into outright literalism.[8] By 1800, Protestants in general and Evangelicals in particular read the Bible with a flat-footed literalness unparalleled in the annals of Christianity. Any apparent statement of fact, however incongruous with experience, was taken as fact, and fact stamped with divine authority.

This literalism was not obscurantist or simple-minded, as it sometimes appears in retrospect. On the contrary, it developed from an effort to make the Bible fit common sense: to insist on the rationality of divine revelation and to quash mystical exegesis that could be neither controlled nor clearly understood. Protestant literalism insisted that the ordinary human being could grasp the Word of God in ordinary human terms. As such, literalism formed part of the larger drive to secure religious belief by making it comprehensible, by keeping it within the bounds of human experience and understanding.

In this case the effort backfired, for literalism put the authority of the Bible at risk. Literalism implied that the Bible's truth depended on its factuality, but scientific developments in the early nineteenth century made Biblical "facts" increasingly questionable. Usually unintended, this scientific subversion came from several directions. Moses's account of the creation of the world in six days, detailed in the first chapter of Genesis, did not square with Pierre Simon Laplace's nebular hypothesis, which required a good deal more than six days for the formation of the solar system and was, to boot, uncomfortably vague as to God's role in the whole business. (Laplace distinctly did not regret his subversion.) But Laplace's theory, though broached at the turn of the century, roused little interest in America before the 1840s.[9]

In that decade, the Bible also ran into trouble from the "American school" of anthropology. These writers, some motivated mostly by racism but all invoking scientific evidence (principally cranial measurements), argued for "polygenesis," the separate creation of several distinct human races, as opposed to "monogenesis," the descent of all human beings from one primal pair. The most eminent American naturalist, Louis Agassiz of Harvard, lent his authority to their hypothesis. Polygenesis frankly declared that Genesis was seriously deficient: Moses had neglected to mention several other Adams and Eves. And most of the opposition to polygenesis arose because of its apparent slur on Scripture. Josiah Nott, one of the leading polygenesists, snarled that he needed "just to get the dam'd stupid crowd safely around Moses & the difficulty is at an end."[10] The crowd did not budge easily: it had too much invested in Biblical literalism. Neither the nebular hypothesis nor polygenesis raised a real storm, however, primarily because by the 1840s another disturber of the peace, geology, had already made a shambles of strict literalism.

Ominous rumblings were heard among natural historians in the last years of the eighteenth century, but it was Charles Lyell's *Principles of Geology* (1830–1833) that delivered the crushing blow to Biblical literalism. Lyell convincingly demonstrated that millions of years of slow workings of natural forces, not the six thousand years allowed by a strict reading of the Old Testament, had shaped the present face of the earth. If Lyell were right, the entire Creation narrative lapsed into mythology. The implications for Biblical authority—and for a Christian natural theology—were potentially devastating. Geology suddenly obsessed American theologians, and they began vigorously to backpedal on the issue of literal exegesis. In the 1830s, even Evangelicals softened their insistence on reading literally every single word; by the 1850s, the Mosaic chronology was rapidly becoming an antique. It took a while for the dust to settle, but by 1860 rigid literalism was largely left to the uneducated or the uneducable. A friend of Chauncey Wright recalled Wright's encountering a woman who "believed implicitly that the world was made in six days. He looked at her as if she were a new order of being, and I shall never forget the tone of his exclamation, *'Is it possible?'* " Wright was no Christian, but many a Christian minister shared his attitude toward literalism. The veracity of the Bible was rescued only by repudiating its total factuality.[11]

The rescue was, in fact, executed with little real difficulty. And the rapid recovery of the Bible's authority from this apparently devastating blow was not as remarkable as it might seem. Even in the heyday of literalism, some Christians (many Unitarians, for example) shied away from it. And an impressive, if dusty, repertoire of hermeneutical devices lay on the shelf: even eighteenth-century New England Calvinists had not wholly forgotten the existence of ethical, allegorical, and mystical readings of the Bible. Moreover, Calvin himself had cautioned against pushing literalism to dangerous extremes—Moses, he pointed out, had never intended to teach natural history—and American theologians knew of his authoritative warning. Even in 1816, a level-headed author could remind readers that what was historical and what metaphorical in the Old Testament was by no means transparent.[12]

Nor did anyone have to resort to mystical obfuscation to rescue the Biblical text. The commonest expedient was to argue, not implausibly, that the six "days" of Genesis symbolized vaster periods and hardly precluded God's working through secondary causes over immense stretches of time. Despite the hue and cry, few clergymen lost faith in the harmony of science and religion; indeed, by 1850 the conflict of Genesis and geology was often treated as an unfortunate misunderstanding, long since rectified. The more liberal ministers actually took comfort in Lyell's legacy. "Here is the grandeur of geology," wrote Horace Bushnell to his daughter in 1857, "that it looks on the hand of the Creator, and sees the stages by which he goes on."[13]

Nevertheless, the shock had been considerable. Most church members had grown up in a religion that treated the Bible essentially as a straightforward historical record. To find this belief false could raise questions about the religion itself. "Geological speculations" originally excited John Fiske's scepticism about Christianity, and he was not alone.[14] Nor, to be sure, was he typical. The collision of science and literalism rarely destroyed Christian faith. Yet it certainly shook complacency; the Bible, hence Christianity, never looked quite so plainly and simply true afterwards.

Christians had hardly absorbed this blow when a heavier one fell. German scholars in the first decades of the nineteenth century were pushing to new extremes a historical criticism of the Bible, the roots of which went back to the seventeenth. This "higher criticism" (as distinguished from the "lower," merely textual, criticism) used philological and historical expertise to try to determine the dates, authorship, and, ultimately, meaning of scriptural texts.[15] The results were challenging, to say the least. Doubts about the authenticity of Scripture had circulated freely in heterodox quarters since at least the late seventeenth century, but they could be dismissed as fanciful speculation (which was usually about right). Now stolid, solid Teutonic scholarship attacked the factuality of the Biblical text. Moses's authorship of the Pentateuch, long questioned by sceptics but piously assumed by orthodox Christians, became simply untenable after mid-century. Theologians were told to get used to at least a brace of Isaiahs. Meanwhile, Karl Richard Lepsius's *Chronologie der Aegypter* (1849) utterly demolished the chronology of the Old Testament.

Unsettling as this scholarship was, it did not directly challenge the New Testament revelation until David Friedrich Strauss brought the issue squarely home with *Das Leben Jesu* (1835–1836), translated into English by Mary Ann Evans in 1846. Strauss did not simply deny the literal accuracy of the New Testament; he came close to denying that Jesus had ever lived. He argued that the Gospels did not intend to relate a factual history; rather, they created a myth of a God-man: precisely the approach to religion to be expected from the prerational minds of a primitive people. This Christ-myth embodied profound religious truth, but it could hardly yield any historical knowledge. Indeed, Jesus and his real teachings remained unknowable—assuming that he had actually existed behind the primitive myth.

The initial American reaction to Strauss was itself fairly primitive. Reviewed in the United States quickly (as early as 1839) and vituperatively, *Das Leben Jesu* was denounced as a scholarly sham and damned as infidel, but scarcely treated knowledgeably or subtly. The Reverend William B. Clark fumed in 1863 that "this book is the great fountain from which nearly all the more recent infidelity has flowed." As far as this allegation went, Clark's bile pushed him well past the truth. But his ire was hardly surprising, considering that most Evangelicals regarded even critics more restrained than Strauss with the blackest suspicion.[16]

Yet suspicion was not the whole story. Some Americans proved more receptive. The Reverend Samuel Gilman, a Harvard man who went south in 1819 to become the minister of Charleston's Unitarian church, owned thirty volumes of Johann Gottfried Eichhorn's Biblical criticism and for a while spent an hour a day reading the German critics with the Reverend Jasper Adams, an Episcopalian minister and president of the College of Charleston. The historian George Bancroft studied the New Testament with Eichhorn himself in Göttingen between 1818 and 1820. By the 1840s, if not earlier, Harvard Divinity School professors regularly recommended the leading German authorities to their students. Evangelicals expected such behavior from Unitarians, but one of their own, the Reverend Moses Stuart, began cautiously to teach the new critical principles at Andover Seminary after 1812. By 1851, even the Evangelical journal *Bibliotheca Sacra* had officially embraced Biblical criticism. The embrace was, however, a fairly chilly one. Critical principles were never allowed to outrun doctrinal commitments, even by Stuart; and Stuart worked at the leading edge of Evangelical scholarship.[17]

Nor is it at all clear how widely these new ideas echoed. The Reverend Lyman Abbott thought that, before the 1860s, Biblical criticism interested only scholars; yet Chauncey Wright, then a young mathematician, and his roommate read together with evident fascination in 1854 a study of the historical Jesus. Fifteen years later Lester Ward, eventually a distinguished sociologist (and acid critic of religion) but then only a junior Treasury clerk, joined with friends in "a class for Biblical criticism." By that time, Ernest Renan's *Vie de Jésus* (1863) had appeared. Renan's book, suffused with religious sentiment but as destructive in its own way of historical Christianity as *Das Leben Jesu,* gripped American imaginations, according to Abbott, with "all the fascination of romance and became at once one of the popular books of the decade." So deep went the interest in Renan that, in the midst of the Civil War, the *Southern Literary Messenger* swallowed hard, abandoned its wartime embargo, and reprinted a Yankee review of the book. But what did readers make of such writings? The North Carolinian Ethelred Philips, marooned on a Florida plantation since 1835, was in the 1860s laboriously struggling, Greek dictionary in hand, to compare English versions of the Bible with recent German translations, and concluding, "The doctrines of the church are destined to undergo immense changes in a few years or they loose [*sic*] their influence on the well informed." Yet, while Philips in the backwoods pored over his copy of the controversial British *Essays and Reviews,* the new criticism ruffled the complacency of scarcely any of the far more cosmopolitan southern teachers and writers of theology. Stranger still, the Virginian scholar George Frederick Holmes, drawn to Strauss in 1850 because of his own interest in critical mythology, did not realize for many years that *Das Leben Jesu* had rather serious implications for Christian belief.[18] No one should jump to conclusions about the impact of the higher criticism on its readers. For most informed Christians, the higher criticism probably convinced them only that careful Biblical scholarship was needed to sort out literal from symbolic truth.

Nevertheless, for some readers the effect was radical. Extensive reading in the German critics, including Strauss, played a key role in Theodore Parker's abandonment of historical Christianity for naturalistic theism. And the books on Parker's shelves led Octavius Brooks Frothingham to a thorough study of the Tübingen School of New Testament critics, with results that Frothingham summarized in his memoirs: "The adoption of these opinions . . . compelled the adoption of a new basis for religious conviction. Christianity, in so far as it depended on the New Testament or the doctrines of the early Church, was discarded." Precious little of Christianity did *not* depend on the New Testament. What remained for Frothingham was "Theism" and "the spiritual nature of man with its craving for religious truth." It was not true, as one orthodox writer bitterly asserted in 1851, that many regarded "the Pentateuch as a collection of popular traditions, having scarcely any more foundation, in fact, than the legends of classical antiquity." Nevertheless, a few regarded even the New Testament in that light.[19]

Among those who did not dodge the implications of the higher criticism, whether remaining Christian or no, the new stress on the mythopoeic elements in Scripture fostered a new understanding of Biblical language, miles removed from the cut-and-dried literalism of Lyman Beecher's salad days. The symbolic strain in the Bible came to seem, not a historical excrescence incidental to the central message, but the quintessential voice of Scripture. "To understand," wrote Matthew Arnold in 1873, "that the language of the Bible is fluid, passing, and literary, not rigid, fixed, and scientific, is the first step towards a right understanding of the Bible." This view gained adherents especially among those Americans already influenced by Coleridge's idealist conception of religious knowledge. The doctrines of *Aids to Reflection* prepared the soil for an understanding of the Bible as adumbrating spiritual truths rather than describing mere physical events. It was no accident that Horace Bushnell, the disciple of Coleridge, became one of the early exponents of this symbolic conception of Biblical language. Such Christians (still adhering to traditional doctrines) found congenial Arnold's idea that the Bible consisted of "words *thrown out* at an immense reality not fully or half fully grasped by the writers, but, even thus, able to affect us with indescribable force." The Biblical narrative thus became, in the words of the young and still Christian Oliver Wendell Holmes, Jr., "a clothing of more concrete fact" over less tangible religious truths.[20]

The intent of Bushnell and others like him was to defend Biblical truth by placing it above the destructive currents of historical criticism. But their defense may have raised more questions than it answered, for where did one draw the line between historical fact and symbolic truth? Was, for example, the Resurrection an actual occurrence or only a symbol? Bushnell's position tended to devalue the very question and opened the way for more radical types who agreed that the "mythological stories of the Gospels" had "a real value" but were "quite unworthy of credit as facts."[21] And if the Gospels were "quite unworthy of credit as facts," the authority of the Bible as a historical foundation for Christian beliefs simply collapsed.

What to make of all this is problematic. The Bible was historically—and at no time more than between 1800 and 1850—"the religion of Protestants." Any weakening of its authority weakened belief in Christianity. Nevertheless, most Americans appear to have remained unshaken in their conviction of the Bible's historical veracity. Even theologians and Biblical scholars did not attend much to the higher criticism until late in the century; unavoidably aware of it, most of them kept it at arm's length. Yet, for thoughtful men and women, the Bible was no longer an unquestioned source of religious authority; it had become a form of evidence for Christianity that itself needed defending. And, for a small but articulate minority, the Bible no longer provided evidence of anything but human religious longings.

Christianity and Human History

The higher criticism was one particularly powerful instance of a general problem facing Christianity: an increased awareness of historical change. This sensibility, on the rise for centuries, reached a peak in the nineteenth century. Historicism bred a conception of truth as limited, relative, and changing. The Victorian worship of progress centered on this idea of ever-growing truth, and other versions of it lay everywhere at hand, ranging from John Henry Newman's theory of doctrinal development to Auguste Comte's three stages of knowledge to Herbert Spencer's evolutionism. Evangelicalism had its own version in millennialism.

Christianity professed at one and the same time to rest upon historical events *and* to embody unchanging truths. This claim rested on the belief that God, in the person of Jesus Christ, had intervened in human history; and it was, in fact, the historical events associated with Jesus that were believed to provide evidence of the divine intervention itself. The mixture of God and history gave Christianity a sort of exemption from relativism, even though its doctrines rested on historical evidence. Biblical literalism—along with the effort to make religious knowledge seem like scientific fact—put the Biblical events in a matter-of-fact atmosphere. In this milieu, historical evidence of Christian truth was conventionally understood in much the same way (reverence aside) as evidence of the exploits of Caesar or the intrigues of the Borgias.

Yet the very idea that *any* historical experience could provide absolute truth collided head-on with the accumulating evidence that historically-grounded "truths" shifted like the sands. To be sure, one could argue that human beings only gradually learned the full meaning of truths implanted long ago (roughly as Newman did). This potentially neutralized the corrosive effect of historical relativism on Christian doctrines. But even partial acceptance of the higher criticism had radical implications, for its very method of historical criticism presumed that the evidences of Christianity were subject to the same historical processes as other historical truths. And this presumption hinted that Christian truths likewise simply grew out of human history and would likewise be outgrown as the human race matured. What David Friedrich Strauss and Theodore Parker had made of this hint was scandalously well known. Ultimately at stake was the Christian claim of unique divine authority for Christian teachings. Were the radical critics right? Was absolute truth in human history a contradiction in terms? Thoughtful, well-read Christians could not ignore this question after mid-century.

Nor could they ignore the two developing fields of scholarship that offered at least parts of an answer: anthropology and the comparative study of religions. Both began to mature as scholarly disciplines around the middle of the century. Both, like the higher criticism, shared the historicist urge to explain human beliefs by explicating their historical origins. And both rattled the foundations of Christianity.

Speculations about the primitive condition of mankind, nothing new as such, exerted a new fascination after 1850. This curiosity sprang from several causes. Partly, Darwin's writings provoked interest in human evolution, not only physical but cultural as well. Partly, the strange tales borne by those offshoots of imperialism, explorers like Richard Burton and Henry Stanley, tantalized their chairbound readers. Probably most influential, discoveries in archaeology made theories about early man, for the first time, more solid than speculation and gave readers hope of learning the truth about their origins.[22]

Unfortunately, Palaeolithic peoples had left little more than bones, flints, and a few cave paintings; so one had to look elsewhere than in Danish bogs for evidence of their mental and social development. The "obvious" place to look was among people who still hunted with stone axes and arrowheads. The banker and anthropologist Sir John Lubbock adopted precisely this strategy in his immensely popular *Pre-Historic Times* (1865). The last three chapters examined "the Manners and Customs of Modern Savages" as illustrations of prehistoric mores and mentalities. Lubbock's next book, *The Origin of Civilization* (1870), devoted itself entirely to these surrogate cavemen.[23] Lubbock could treat modern tribesmen as cavemen because he assumed a single common pattern of human evolution, in which all wielders of stone axes stood at roughly the same early stage on the road to Victorian civilization.

This assumption of unilinear evolution infected virtually all of the early work in anthropology. It dominated, for instance, the outlook of the most consequential anthropologist of the 1870s, the dedicated Darwinist E. B. Tylor. Inevitably, when these authors and their readers looked at the customs and ideas of Tahitians or Kaffirs, they saw the primitive roots of their own manners and beliefs. The anthropologists of this generation devoted much of their attention to religion, Lubbock giving well over a third of *The Origin of Civilization* to the subject. Possibly this preoccupation echoed their own religious discomfort more than the concerns of the people they studied. In any case, primitive religion, like other primitive attributes, fitted into their evolutionary framework. The very method of these anthropologists' work demanded that they find "prehistoric" parallels for the practices of "higher" religions. As savage marriage customs revealed the obscure, often disgusting origins of chaste Victorian wedlock, so out of the mists of barbaric rituals emerged, like *Homo sapiens* from reptilian slime, the civilized Christianity of the nineteenth century.

Such theorizing left Christians in the lurch. Cultural evolution did not suggest a unique, divine, absolute truth. On the contrary, rites and doctrines central to Christianity began to look like savage survivals. Baptism appeared remarkably like one more purification ritual, the Eucharist like the widely diffused ceremonial eating of a god, even the Incarnation like many another myth of a God-man—"only the modified superstitions of barbarous ages, the natural offspring of man's primitive ignorance." And the broader implications of these resemblances devastated Christianity at the root. By propagating the assumption that cultural evolution could account for Christian beliefs, anthropologists undercut the Christian claim to special divine origin and sanction. George Frederick Holmes's battle-tested orthodoxy, which absorbed Strauss without crumbling, eventually collapsed under the strain of Lubbock and Tylor.[24]

Yet these anthropological insinuations were scarcely irrefutable. It bespeaks the spell cast by evolutionism that few questioned the dubious axiom on which all this speculation rested: that primitive societies still extant replicated evolutionary stages through which the Victorians' ancestors had passed—and that therefore Samoan religion revealed the development of Christianity. But even with this suspect premise granted, still the anthropological evidence was by no means decisive. Contradictory and confused travelers' accounts supplied the bulk of it. And the interpretations tortured out of these tales were equally conflicting.

Perhaps for this reason the early anthropologists themselves tiptoed around the troubling implications of their work. Tylor did take a certain quiet glee in sabotaging Christianity. But Lubbock, more widely read if ultimately of less consequence, held his speculations severely in check as soon as he crossed the border of the "higher" religions. Moreover, the primitive peoples and their beliefs appeared so outlandishly crude—"a melancholy spectacle of gross superstitions and ferocious forms of worship," in Lubbock's words—that their very primitiveness undercut psychologically the otherwise plausible evolutionary tie with Christianity.[25] Victorians found it hard to imagine as the same sort of phenomena the sacred bamboo of the Chittagong hill tribe and the Westminster Confession of the Presbyterian tribe. Without a Missing Link to bridge the gap between primitive religions and Victorian Christianity, anthropology could upset some Christians; but, in isolation, it could drive only the shakiest to abandon ship.

Anthropology was not, however, read in isolation. The great non-Christian religions came to public attention in the same period—and exerted, if anything, even more fascination.[26] Anthropology implied that Christianity could not be absolute divine truth because it was the historical product of cultural evolution. The study of comparative religion pointed to a similar verdict about Christianity, on different though disturbingly compatible grounds. "Christian truths" were, apparently, not unique to Christianity at all.

Enlightenment heterodoxy had inspired interest in non-Western religions. Already, at the end of the eighteenth century, liberal Christians in America used Islam in fictional tales as a stick with which to beat the orthodox. These stories never showed more than sketchy knowledge of Islam but may have introduced readers to the habit of comparing Christianity with other religions, an approach previously limited mostly to Deist critics of Christianity. The founding of the Asiatic Society of Bengal in 1784 opened a new era in European scholarship; its distinguished founder, Sir William Jones, became the first real Western Orientalist. In 1799, Joseph Priestley published the first serious work of comparative religion in America, *A Comparison of the Institutions of Moses with those of the Hindoos and other Ancient Nations;* but apparently only John Adams paid much attention. Nevertheless, knowledge of such things began to creep into the United States in the pages of general-interest magazines like the *Edinburgh Review*, the *Monthly Anthology*, and the *North American Review*. Rammohun Roy, a Hindu reformer who translated several Hindu scriptures into English, made a considerable splash in Unitarian circles in the 1820s. By 1845, even the Congregationalist *New Englander* had published a sketch of Buddhism, and, about the same time, that celebrated bluestocking Elizabeth Peabody was lecturing around Boston on the history of religions.[27]

Altogether this hardly amounted to a tidal wave of Oriental piety, but there was by the 1850s a good deal of awareness of non-Western religions and even some enthusiasm. Few fell as utterly under the spell as the young Harvard student Fitzedward Hall, the first American to edit a Sanskrit text; sent off to India by his father in 1846 to recover a runaway brother, Hall stayed there and ended as a world-famous philologist. But several of the American Transcendentalists also delved into these mysteries. Emerson became the first significant American writer actually to incorporate strains of Oriental thought into his own work and to try to reconcile Eastern and Western ideals. James Freeman Clarke's interest eventuated in 1871 in *Ten Great Religions*, a best-selling popularization of comparative religion. Nor did one have to inhabit the spiritual neighborhood of Concord. Max Müller's scholarship began to appear in the fifties; it influenced especially the religious radicals who organized the Free Religious Association in 1867.For those less inclined to mental exertion, Lydia Maria Child published in 1855 a pabulum of world religions called *The Progress of Religious Ideas, through Successive Ages*. Child's book seems not to have sold well; but articles on Buddhism, in particular, popped up regularly in the leading magazines. Even Ethelred Philips, cast away in the spiritual wastes of Florida during the Civil War, alluded knowingly to Islam. Poor Philips was in no position to know that in the fashionable world Moslems had sunk far below Buddhists.[28] The real outpouring of writing on comparative religion began just after 1870, but intellectually curious Americans were sensitized to the major non-Christian religions at least a decade earlier.

What the typical reader made of all this is hard to gauge. At the outset, few suspected much danger for Christian belief. The great Sir William Jones, indeed, had confidently predicted that his investigations would confirm rather than subvert Christian truth. And in 1837 Francis Wayland still blandly assumed that "heathen" religions patently floundered on a lower level of truth than the religion of Christ.[29]

Yet within a very few years such confidence came to seem badly misplaced. The general problem appeared in the line of attack that some Unitarians took against orthodox doctrines like the Trinity: "The Infinite Divinity dying on a cross . . . reminds us of the mythology of the rudest pagans." The Unitarians were playing with fire, for there were too many similarities between even their own Christian background and the beliefs of Buddhists and Hindus. A growing number of writers did not hesitate to draw such comparisons. The historic development of Christianity seemed, to these curious investigators, oddly paralleled in the other world-religions: monasticism, confession, virgin births, incarnate god-men. "Every reader knows," according to Emerson, "that almost every passage in our sacred books can be paralleled with a like sentiment from another book of a distant nation"; thus, "we find in our mythology"—our mythology!—"a key to theirs." Christianity, like all other great religions, amounted only to a "well-meant approximation" to some grander divine truth.[30]

Relatively few Christians drew such conclusions, but knowledge of other faiths proved shattering for some. President Andrew Dickson White of Cornell recalled that his belief in Christ's miracles, on which Christian truth seemed to depend, collapsed in the 1850s when he learned that Islam claimed the same sort of evidence for its doctrines. And Charles Eliot Norton, son of the "Unitarian Pope" Andrews Norton, found himself almost chuckling at the irony when a Westminster Abbey congregation prayed for the conversion of the heathen. Ministers understandably were growing alarmed. The frequent comparisons of Christianity with other religions often left "the impression that one was just about as good as another." "Out of this habit has come a vague scepticism"—a belief, as another clergyman worried, "that Christianity is losing its distinctive characteristics, and becoming simple humanitarianism or philanthropy; that it is resolving itself into that universal ethnic religion in which thoughtful minds of all ages and nations have agreed."[31]

The problem involved much more than the discrediting of doctrines. These two new fields of knowledge, anthropology and comparative religion, flowing together, generated a new image of the essential character of Christianity. They left the impression that Christianity, like the other world religions, resulted from the natural growth and development of human religious sensibilities or instincts. The whiff of mythology with which the higher criticism tainted the Bible heightened the perception. This notion of natural evolution did not ipso facto negate the truth of religion, for it dovetailed with the prevailing belief that God had implanted religious intuitions in the human mind. But the idea was toxic to the central dogma of historic Christianity: that God had intervened in human history to reveal a unique body of religious truths in the career of Jesus.

What made this view so persuasive to doubting Christians was not only the information that supported it. True, the nineteenth century added much new data in anthropology and comparative religion. But, after all, neither primitive peoples nor Oriental religions were unknown before the period. What mattered most was the evolutionary matrix into which intellectuals now tended to slot such facts. An earlier reader could dismiss curious coincidences between Christianity and other faiths as simply that. But to do so became difficult in "the atmosphere coming from the great thought of Darwin and Herbert Spencer,—an atmosphere in which history became less and less a matter of annals, and more and more a record of the unfolding of humanity."[32] Similarities of any sort now argued for continuity, not coincidence. And these specifically evolutionary ideas fitted neatly into the more amorphous, but even more widespread, faith in progress. This progressivism helped to make evolutionism seem natural and right, even in respect to religion.

Leaders of the Christian churches had certainly contributed to this outcome. They had confidently accentuated the methodological resemblances between religious knowledge and natural knowledge—and thus made it easier to discredit Christian beliefs by the methods of anthropology and comparative religion. They had often spoken of doctrines as if these were precisely definable matters of literal fact—and thus made externally similar non-Christian beliefs more likely to appear the same in essence. Most to the point here, they had nurtured, not merely a faith in progress, but at times a virtual identification of human progress with the mission of Christianity. Evangelical millennialism was the most obvious case, but less orthodox Christians were no less given to progressivist interpretations of Christianity. Unitarians, for example, saw the history of Christianity as quintessentially a story of the maturing of religious truth. "The dispensation of Moses, compared with that of Jesus, we consider as adapted to the childhood of the human race, a preparation for a nobler system, and chiefly useful now as serving to confirm and illustrate the Christian Scriptures." William Ellery Channing, who spoke these words, may have believed that Jesus's teachings provided "the last and most perfect revelation" of God's will.[33] But it was no great jump to thinking that Jesus's teachings might also one day be superseded.

Christianity now fitted all too well into a pattern of human religious development, exhibiting at every stage the unfolding of certain basic motifs: growing from crude notions of god and demon; proceeding through idolatry and polytheism; emerging into a higher monotheism and morality, embodied more or less nobly in Buddhism, Hinduism, Islam, and the varieties of Christianity; and headed—where? This idea itself was not new; it had appeared, for example, at the end of the seventeenth century. But its sophistication, evidence, and persuasive force were enormously magnified in the religious and secular climate of the mid-nineteenth century. Barton Cathcart felt its disconcerting power in Henry Ward Beecher's novel *Norwood* (1868): "As men look back upon nations in the olden time, and know that amid their fondest convictions they were in profound error—that their gods were myths, their histories half fables, and their theology a mere fiction, so now and then it came home to him with ghastly distinctness, that a time would come when men would look back upon him and his generation in the same manner."[34] There were, of course, other possible views of Christian history, and Barton Cathcart eventually recovered his equilibrium, as did most Christians. But some remained permanently shaken.

The Nature of Doctrinal Knowledge

This new scholarship—and the ease with which, in some quarters, it discredited Christian beliefs—pointed to a less obvious but nonetheless deepening difficulty: the problematic epistemological status of Christian faith. Could one *know* the kinds of things comprised in the tenets of Christianity? Miracles, accepted by most Christians as the strongest evidence of Jesus's divine mission, exemplified the problem. More and more people found them simply implausible: not credible themselves, much less credible as evidence of other beliefs. The critique of miracles had no more bite, logically, in 1850 than when Hume enunciated it a century earlier; but somehow it sank deeper.

One Presbyterian professor explained this growing scepticism by pointing to "the tendency of the higher scientific training, and of the most advanced philosophical speculation . . . to set aside the miraculous and the supernatural altogether." And there was a good deal to what he said. When John Fiske's grandmother asked him if he believed Christ was God, Fiske returned a scientism that stubbornly refused to look beyond the facts of physiology: "How can a man have two natures without having two medulla oblongatas? A double ego, a double centre of innervation is something to which I can not yet subscribe."[35]

Yet young Fiske's crude materialism—a scientific analogue to Biblical literalism—does not adequately indicate the problem. Doubt went deeper than miracles and sprang from something more pervasive than the extension of higher scientific training. The analytic-technical cast of mind increasingly influenced at least the educated classes. Though most precisely embodied in science and often identified with it, this outlook was by no means limited to scientists. It regarded empirical observation as the really secure ground of knowledge and, consequently, viewed more or less suspiciously any claims not so grounded.

This attitude, if fully realized, could not well tolerate any claim that God had physically interfered in human affairs. Such a breach of the observed natural order patently eluded empirical testing. Yet around just such a vaporous event Christianity revolved. And if this central dogma foundered, little remained of traditional Christian doctrine, at least as traditionally understood.

It was perhaps fortunate for the churches that this epistemological posture, rarely very self-conscious, was even more rarely adopted with consistency. For, when applied, it devastated doctrine. Charles Eliot Norton attributed the "decay of belief in creeds" to the "progress of science," specifically to the application of scientific method to religious questions. And by scientific method he meant "the method of all true knowledge, that of induction from the facts of particular observation." This position did not inherently exclude Christian beliefs from the realm of things knowable, but it insisted on a much more rigorous testing of the evidence and defined acceptable evidence much more narrowly. The younger Oliver Wendell Holmes, as a college student in 1858, described his generation as "almost the first of young men who have been brought up in an atmosphere of investigation."[36]

How widely such an attitude had spread is hard to say. But a Unitarian journal, *The Christian Examiner*, grew alarmed in 1866 at the number of Americans who had consciously adopted it. The magazine noted the "immense" sale to "solitary thinkers" of books "which treat, in a wholly philosophical spirit and without theological reference, of the fundamental questions in metaphysics, and in pure science; of what is knowable, and what the knowing powers are, and what is really known." "Works so dry, learned, and abstract, that one would think nobody but professors in colleges would read them, and only a few great libraries contain them, are sold by the thousand, edition after edition." And this "large and quiet class of readers and thinkers" evidenced a budding disenchantment with Christianity, "an alienation from public religion on the part of a very large and growing class of persons of character."[37]

Yet more than intellectual qualms pushed these sceptics away from Christianity. Epistemological doubts bred moral repugnance. If doctrines rested on shaky evidence, then belief in them meant bowing to the yoke of authority—the authority of tradition, the authority of the Bible, the authority of the church—rather than investigating for oneself. "Christianity," fumed the aging abolitionist Lucy Colman, "demands entire subordination to its edicts. Until the majority of the people are emancipated from authority over their minds, we are not safe." John Fiske agreed. Christianity entailed "a mass of metaphysical assumptions, wherein science was disowned, where reason was discredited, and where blind, unquestioning faith was regarded as the only passport to true Christian knowledge."[38] Infidelity became a moral obligation as well as an intellectual necessity. Relatively few focused their doubts about Christian knowledge as clearly as Colman or Fiske or even Norton, but their dissent reflected a basic pattern of cultural change.

However, the drift toward secularization of knowledge, toward suspicion of the intangible and invisible, does not itself explain the epistemological problems of Christianity. The division of knowledge into secular and religious spheres did not per se threaten doctrine. The problem arose, rather, from the application of secular standards to religious knowledge. And for this tendency scientists bore perhaps less responsibility than clergymen. Leaders of the church had, ever since the seventeenth century, encouraged the application of scientific methods to the work of theology. This formed part of their strategy for overcoming the effects of secularization, for holding together religious and natural knowledge, for preventing the world from slipping out of the grasp of religion.

Some Christians now insisted on following that road even if it led away from Christianity. The strategy had turned against its originators. As the scope of natural knowledge narrowed, the creeds began to be squeezed out of the realm of knowledge. By no means every Christian apologist recognized the problem, and those who did had usually never showed much enthusiasm for turning theology into a science in the first place. They were also the first to offer a way out of the impasse.

The solution pivoted on distinguishing the use of language to describe natural objects from the use of language to describe spiritual realities. This distinction, in turn, depended on an important transformation of language itself, in train for some centuries. Printing made it possible to regularize even the vernacular tongues, as learned Latin had been controlled in the Middle Ages; thus, for example, vernacular dictionaries began to appear and, by the eighteenth century, to proliferate. Among the loudest voices urging precision and definiteness in the use of language were those of scientists. In 1667, Thomas Sprat of the Royal Society had insisted on words "as near the mathematical plainness as possible."[39] The reference to mathematics was prescient. As science became more mathematized, its language grew ever more precise.

Yet in the eighteenth century and earlier, no clear distinction in kind had divided the language in which one discussed religion from the language in which one described mundane realities. Indeed, prior to the division of knowledge into intellectual specialties, a process that built up steam only in the nineteenth century, such distinctions could hardly exist: there was no "scientific" language, "philosophical" language, or even "ordinary" language. The words that one used meant the same thing, conveyed the same sort of reality, whether one applied them to the attributes of God or the habits of a salamander.

This unitary conception of language began to break down in the nineteenth century. Ultimately, the change stemmed from specialization of knowledge—a reflection, possibly somehow a result, of the intensifying economic division of labor. More immediately, pressures from both science and religion wedged the language apart.

By mid-century, science described the natural world with unprecedented definiteness. Mathematics best symbolized this achievement. The pathetic image lingers of Michael Faraday incapable of reading James Clerk Maxwell's formulation of Faraday's own researches. But even in the biological and medical sciences, still largely innocent of mathematics, exactness of both description and theoretical statement steadily increased. And science provided the commonest model for talking about physical reality.

Moreover, as scientific language grew increasingly exact, religious language by contrast seemed more and more vague. To be sure, natural theologians continued to speak of God in what passed for scientific language; and dogmatic theologians could split hairs with a diamond cutter's finesse. But behind their finespun speculations lay what could not be weighed, measured, or even observed.

Nor was science alone responsible for hewing language apart. In some respects, religion had equally drifted away from scientific language, though most American theologians bucked the trend. The Evangelical climate of Victorian intellectual life, with its enthusiasm for heart-religion, favored sentiment over precision in matters religious. This was more an impulse than a philosophy, yet some American religious writers followed it further. Coleridge's idealism suggested that spiritual realities, apprehended through intuitive Reason, eluded the categories by which the Understanding classified phenomena scientifically. This view chimed with Schleiermacher's claim that religious language referred in the first instance to subjective experience; precise definition removed dogma from this primal reality. Recently, Biblical critics had made it all too apparent that the language of the Bible did not measure up to the specificity of Joseph Henry's publications on electromagnetism. It was, in fact, from the Bible that much of the discussion of religious language took its start.

Whatever the pretensions of natural theologians, religious language looked less and less like the language one used to speak about physical reality. Growing awareness of the imprecision of religious language complemented the growing precision of scientific language; and there developed by mid-century a vague but common apprehension that scientists spoke one kind of language, ministers in the pulpit another, and people in everyday life perhaps something in between. It was this shift in linguistic understanding that made possible Matthew Arnold's description of the Bible's language as "fluid, passing, and literary" as opposed to "rigid, fixed, and scientific."[40] A century earlier, such a distinction could not have been conceived in quite those terms.

The American theologian most sensitive to these complementary developments—and able most effectively to turn them to apologetic advantage—was Horace Bushnell. Bushnell had imbibed Coleridge, digested Schleiermacher, and at least tasted the higher critics. If this were cannibalism, Bushnell made the most of it. Of course religious language is imprecise, he argued. Virtually all language is at its root more or less metaphorical. The subject of religion lies farther beyond our full comprehension than does the subject of science. And, to the extent that God more exceeds our grasp than does a rock, to that extent will the words of theology be less definite than the language of geology. "Words of thought or spirit are," according to Bushnell, "inexact in their significance, never measuring the truth or giving its precise equivalent." But words about God conceal another trap: "They always affirm something which is false, or contrary to the truth intended. They impute form to that which is really out of form." Thus, we can only gradually come to apprehend spiritual truth by acquaintance with a multitude of partly true, partly false, and often contradictory analogies that point to the truth. To expect to know divine truths with the same precision as astronomical data is therefore ridiculous. Christian doctrine does not pretend to scientific exactitude. Indeed, "the fixed forms of dogma" inherently distort truth. "Definitions cannot bring us over the difficulty; for definitions are, in fact, only changes of symbol, and, if we take them to be more, will infallibly lead us into error."[41] Bushnell never intended to segregate religious language as such, only to revivify the ancient axiom that God's ways eluded human grasp, but he effectively pushed Christian doctrine further away from scientific knowledge.

Orthodox Evangelicals regarded Bushnell as a rank heretic; but his heresy grew naturally in Evangelical soil with its heavy admixture of subjective religious experience. He had the nerve to draw out the unsettling implications. His radical view of religious language was seldom swallowed whole—after all, it did rather diminish the stature of the Apostles' Creed—and Bushnell himself seemed to back off somewhat in his later years. But something like his conception of religious language as metaphor became very familiar, not only in theology, but in the sermons of post-1850 Romantic Evangelicals like Henry Ward Beecher. By 1883, the Episcopal bishop Henry C. Potter, a Broad Churchman but by no means a Robespierre of the cloth, could blandly call the articles of the creed "symbols of belief."[42] Bushnell's kind of distinction between symbolic adumbration and physical description not only made room for the "heart." It also put Christian doctrine on a different ground than science, a ground where it did not have to provide the same exact knowledge as science.

Yet Bushnell's finger in the dike did not entirely plug the leak. His orthodox foes judged that he had actually widened it. On the one hand, to people already committed to subjective experience as the primal fount of religious knowledge, Bushnell unintentionally suggested a way out of Christianity. If Christian doctrines only approximated an indefinable truth—and if many contradictory expressions were needed to carry spiritual truths home to the seeker—then Christianity might be only one of many roads to God; and each individual had to find his own. This was precisely Emerson's point. And it was not coincidence that the American Transcendentalists were also disciples of Coleridge and had more than tasted the higher critics. They agreed with Bushnell that Christian doctrine, rightly understood, constituted a kind of knowledge indefinable with scientific exactness. So, however, did Buddhism.

On the other hand, to people already committed to narrow scientism, Bushnell's arguments seemed to admit that Christianity amounted to nothing more than an elaborate figure of speech, a flight of poetry, lovely to look at but hardly knowledge. John Fiske grew up in Bushnell's orbit; and he maintained that the "rhetorical work of Bushnell, with its total ignorance of physical science, did more to shake my faith than anything else."[43] Clergymen had long insisted on the commensurability of Christian belief and scientific truth. It was awkward now to turn around and claim that one could not speak of them in the same words. Bushnell offered too little, too late.

The Results

Most Christians weathered these storms without much battering; at least they ended up safely in their traditional port. Indeed, one suspects that the ordinary Christian never heard that there might be any reason to leave port. But from the 1830s onward, a small but increasing number of voyages away from Christianity led to a variety of non-Christian theisms.

The Transcendentalist heresy left the largest mark, chiefly because of its literary impact. But its search for God within the human breast reached people well outside the ambit of the Boston literati. The Transcendentalist appeal to nature (more precisely, to the human response to nature) went down especially well. Diluted Transcendentalism flowed so smoothly into major themes in mid-century Romantic Evangelicalism that only the specific gravity of the prose makes it easy to distinguish Henry Ward Beecher's sermons from some of Emerson's essays. Emerson, by far the most widely read of the Transcendentalists, provided a bridge between Christianity and undoctrinal theism; his essays made it easier for a young man or woman raised in an Evangelical home to realize that one could abandon Christianity without losing morality, spirituality, reverence, and the larger hope. The God revealed in Nature (where Evangelicals were already accustomed to look for breathings of the divine) offered all these. The trouble was that Transcendentalists had to fight the urge to go all the way and identify Nature with God; Thoreau never fought very hard, and Emerson often lost.[44] And if Nature *was* God, why bother to use two cognomens? At this point, the issue of Christianity's status faded, and a more fundamental question arose.

Transcendentalism appealed to people who had decided that science did not have much to do with religion; a far larger batch of heretics believed just the reverse. These were the Spiritualists, whose capacity for appearing ridiculous has largely obscured their significance. They were far from contemptible in their heyday between 1850 and 1875, and there were many of them. When Lucy Colman, herself then a Spiritualist, traveled the abolitionist lecture circuit in Michigan in the 1850s, she found that "Spiritualism was rioting, like some outbreak of disease. [Mediumistic] circles were the order of the day, and of the night." The Reverend Jonathan Harrison, after a survey of liberal religion in the Midwest in the late 1860s, reported "Spiritualism almost everywhere active and powerful." He thought the movement was "doing more than any other to prepare the way for the Church of the future."[45]

Spiritualism's distinctive doctrine was communication with the spirits of the dead, its animus doggedly scientific, peculiar as this combination may now sound. The pioneering psychiatrist Pierre Janet commented on the "analytic" attitude and "atmosphere of scientific curiosity" surrounding the movement; indeed, explicitly scientific investigation of spiritualist claims was a coeval natural growth from it. Characteristically, one leading Spiritualist, John C. Edmonds, was a sceptic of Tom Paine's stripe, and spoke regularly with his mentor in the spirit world.[46]

For Spiritualists wanted to carry the enterprise of natural theology to its ultimate conclusion: to provide empirical verification, rigorously scientific, of spiritual reality. Robert Dale Owen insisted that the "wonders of Spiritualism are not miracles." "I believe them all to be in accordance with great natural laws; and these are to be found only by patient and faithful searching." The favored hypotheses looked toward electricity or magnetism, appropriately invisible means of communication that also intrigued mesmerists, seeking their own scientific pathway to spiritual enlightenment. But the theory mattered less than the search. What was important was to believe that religion needed no miracles, that it did rest on secure knowledge, that it could pass the test of science—a test, many Spiritualists believed, that Christianity had failed.[47] But the Spiritualists, it appeared by 1870 or so, were not themselves having much luck persuading scientists.

Neither Transcendentalism nor Spiritualism are adduced here because of their lasting impact on American religion, but rather because they represent the kinds of gropings increasingly common among American Christians who found they could no longer believe in Christianity. Their old faith seemed to them a mythology descended from a more primitive age, with much of nobility but also much of cruelty in it, incapable of providing reliable knowledge of God. One impulse was to seek religious truth—"a religion independent of the accidents of time and place"—by listening "to the voice of God in the silence of our own souls" as Christ himself had done. The Transcendentalists took this route, but they were far from alone on an intuitionist pathway thickly if haphazardly blazed by Evangelicals. Another impulse was to look, as Spiritualists did, as John Fiske did, for scientific grounds for belief. Without such evidence, was it "honest for me to go [to church] and sit there on communion day and drink the wine and eat the bread while feeling it all to be mummery?"[48] These seekers, too, followed a road marked out by Christian theology: in this case, natural theology.

Most doubters appear to have followed neither impulse very consistently—or rather to have followed them both inconsistently—and drifted about uncertainly, neither repudiating the historic churches altogether nor feeling themselves at home there. Oliver Wendell Holmes, Jr., still apparently a believer in some sort of God in the early 1860s, vaguely identified "good" with the "general law" of the universe. About that time, the young writer Thomas Bailey Aldrich told his sweetheart, "I don't believe in parsons and forms, but I do most devotedly believe in leading a holy life here that we may live hereafter." Mary Grew, a Philadelphia abolitionist and suffragist, still called herself a Christian; but she managed it only because she insisted that creeds, rituals, indeed every distinctively Christian belief or practice had nothing to do with Christianity. Frederick Law Olmsted epitomized the whole awkward situation in a letter to his wife: "I would much prefer that the children never heard a sermon, if they could attend worship of a decorous character without it. And, among Sermons, the duller and least impressive, the better. I crave and value worshipfulness, but I detest and dread theology & formalized ethics." Charles Eliot Norton said it publicly in 1868: "But so far as the most intelligent portion of society at the present day is concerned, the Church in its actual constitution is an anachronism."[49] Some ministers may have questioned whether Norton's portion of society qualified as the most intelligent, but they could hardly have denied its disaffection.

Yet Norton was careful to point out that the rejection of the churches did not imply "a rejection of the authority of religion itself." Far from it: "Much of the deepest and most religious life is led outside [church] walls." And, in fact, abandonment of Christianity seldom involved loss of faith in God. Andrew Dickson White's experience was not atypical. An undergraduate at Yale during the 1850s, White found his religious beliefs slipping away from him; Christianity became less and less credible. At this crisis, he began to read W. H. Channing and Theodore Parker. Parker especially checked "all inclination to cynicism" and "strengthened my theistic ideas and stopped any tendency to atheism."[50] For the rest of his long and distinguished life, White evidently rested content here, secure in a cheerfully undoctrinal faith in God.

Still, the unsettlement of Christianity set off shock waves that rolled far beyond the articles of the creed. For one thing, ritual is psychologically closely connected with religious belief; deprive individuals of their rituals and you may unglue the whole structure of their beliefs. For another and less speculative thing, most Americans had imbibed Christianity with their mother's milk and grown up (unlike their Enlightenment ancestors) in an atmosphere that supported little public doubt of its truth. As Mr. Thwackum said, "When I mention religion, I mean the Christian religion; and not only the Christian religion, but the Protestant religion; and not only the Protestant religion, but the Church of England."[51] Omitting this last specification, Mr. Thwackum would have felt entirely at home in early Victorian America. The disruption of Christianity shattered this complacency. If the most securely held beliefs turned out to be a deception—and the most embarrassing kind, self-deception—then one ought to look carefully before committing oneself to other beliefs. Inevitably, deeper questions were asked. Even those who wanted very much to believe did not want to believe themselves gullible.

Moreover, and most important, the corrosives that had dissolved belief in Christian doctrines did not stop working with Christianity. In this respect, the experience of eighteenth-century Deists differed sharply from that of Victorian theists. The Deists' objections to Christianity, in the intellectual climate of the Enlightenment, still pointed to a natural-law God. But the moralism, historicism, and epistemological problems that now undermined Christianity pointed toward a blanker horizon.

It was a supreme irony that the Christian churches had, by their own teachings about God and the road to Him, contributed so richly to the mess in which they now found themselves. The Reverend Jonathan Harrison, a refugee from Methodism trying to find a resting place among the Unitarians, felt that "even atheism is a forward movement. It is better than the mental & moral state which precedes and produces it."[52]

Harrison's instinct was sure in one respect: the stage was now set for the rejection of God, for the emergence of agnosticism as a viable option in American culture. This process was complex, involving not one straightforward train of thought but the knarry intersection of several. It remains now to examine that "mental & moral state," to trace in detail those varied lines of ideas and impressions, suggest their interaction, and indicate their final outcome.

II

Modern Unbelief, 1865–1890

6

The Intellectual Crisis of Belief

It was 1867 when Jonathan Harrison, in Illinois, complained that "even atheism" would be "a forward movement." Such a movement of thought was even then gathering momentum, culminating two centuries of struggle between those who sought to secure belief by fixing it in comprehensible reality and those who denied that God fit those familiar terms. However, *atheism,* implying a positive denial of God's existence, did not precisely define this emerging outlook. Two years later Thomas Huxley, in London, would coin a fitter word, *agnosticism.* Huxley put a name on what had grown common enough to need a name: a permanent suspension of belief in God. This settled inability to accept the reality of God, rather than positive atheism, became the distinctively modern unbelief.

Within twenty years after the Civil War, agnosticism emerged as a self-sustaining phenomenon.[1] Disbelief in God was, for the first time, plausible enough to grow beyond a rare eccentricity and to stake out a sizable permanent niche in American culture. Two hundred years spent adapting belief to the cultural environment had paid off, in a way: unbelief now also fitted tolerably well into it—well enough to find sufficient intellectual and psychological nourishment to survive and reproduce itself. An agnostic subculture had taken root—not a geographic community, but a community of ideas, assumptions, and values.[2] This shared world view gave agnostics a coherent understanding of reality without benefit of God. That their world view *was* shared reinforced their agnosticism, for they knew that many others, and not insignificant men, agreed with their doubts. That it was a *sub*culture—that agnosticism was broadly continuous with the fundamental assumptions of the larger culture—made their unbelief convincing. For agnosticism did not represent a sharp break from Victorian culture, but rather one plausible outgrowth of it.

This particular offshoot grew from a mass of ideas and attitudes so tangled and matted as to be at points almost impenetrable. These intertwined roots can, for analytic purposes, be cut apart into three sections—three "mental and moral states," in Harrison's words, that engendered unbelief. They are (1) intellectual uncertainties about belief that produced the conviction that knowledge of God lay beyond human powers, if such a Being existed; (2) moral problems with belief that led to the rejection as immoral of belief in God and the erection of a nontheistic morality; and (3) the transfer of reverence from God to other ideals.

These three categories should not be taken as chronological stages in the development of agnosticism or even as actually distinct in the thinking of agnostics. They are only the historian's tools, instruments for dissecting a knotted growth of opinion, a subculture of unbelief otherwise too complex and intertwined to allow coherent discussion.

Indeed, these elements must be considered together, for no one of them could have sufficed to sustain unbelief. To be sure, in individual cases, one or another often tipped the balance toward agnosticism—and in that sense "caused" a person's unbelief. But the fibers of belief twined so thoroughly through the common life that ripping it out did not come easily; the emergence of unbelief appears to have been a very near thing. Just when modern unbelief was appearing, modern belief was also gaining coherence and vigor. Church membership was rising, more sophisticated theologies taking shape to meet the challenge of doubt. In these circumstances, agnosticism might have proved as evanescent as the few atheist voices of the Enlightenment, might never have found a voice at all. It was the concurrent force of different doubts that gave birth to agnosticism, the multiplicity of its springs that gave it endurance.

Of these sources, the intellectual problems of belief provide the clearest entryway into agnosticism. True, people seldom defined explicitly the basic rationale for their faith (if indeed only one existed and if indeed they were fully aware of it). So one cannot be sure which intellectual prop bore most of the weight of belief. But the arguments for God common in the mid-nineteenth century fell into three categories. First, but scarcely persuasive to anyone inclined to doubt, was the testimony of Scripture. Reeling under the higher criticism, revelation now required rehabilitation itself; the Bible might unfold a God already believed in but could hardly convince the mildest of sceptics that He existed.

The two other styles of argument carried much more conviction. One was the quasi-scientific, empirical demonstration of God's existence embodied in the argument from design. The other looked beyond the sensible world, into man's heart, and found there primal religious impulses or immediate intuitions of the divine, deeper than reason, that testified to the reality of God. These two approaches might appear oddly yoked, but most early Victorians thought them complementary: a devastatingly persuasive pair that made unbelief preposterous beyond words. Though not the only rationales for belief, "scientific" natural theology and various forms of intuitionism so dominated discussion that they almost inevitably leapt to mind whenever the plausibility of belief came into question.

And so they shall now, but against the background of some preliminary puzzles about religious knowledge that faced the Victorians.

Human Nature and the Knowledge of God

The anthropological speculations that had helped to unsettle Christianity did not cease at the last sentence of the Nicene Creed. If the idea of a God-man had evolved naturalistically from savage superstitions, then why not the idea of a God? Belief in a Deity might be nothing more than a savage survival. Such doubts fitted neatly the historicist pattern of Victorian thought. And after the impact of the *Origin of Species* (1859), evolutionary explanations gained, rightly or wrongly, even more force. John Stuart Mill acutely observed toward the end of the 1860s that religions "tend to be discussed, at least by those who reject them, less as intrinsically true or false than as products thrown up by certain states of civilization, and which, like the animal and vegetable productions of a geological period, perish in those which succeed it." A simile invoked by Jonathan Harrison fairly reeked of Tylor and Lubbock: his abandoned beliefs were, he declared, "as dead as—well, say the empire of the Mound Builders of the Mississippi."[3] Few anthropologists intended to scotch belief. But they conveyed the impression that religious beliefs, having evolved to meet purely natural individual and social needs, were entirely explicable in those terms.

It is hard to imagine what other impression the public might have got. The methodology of the new social sciences automatically foreclosed any attempt to determine the transcendental validity of religion. But this subtlety usually eluded people more given to admiration of science than reflection on its limits. Anthropology, vested with the authority of science, was often taken flatly to assert that belief in God amounted to no more than a human attempt to cope with the mysteries of nature. And some leading anthropologists, E. B. Tylor for instance, apparently intended it to be taken this way.

Even for those who realized that anthropology, as distinguished from anthropologists, did not and could not pronounce on the supernatural, these new studies cast a shadow on belief. If the idea of God could be accounted for naturalistically, supernatural explanations became supererogatory and therefore dubious. The "theistic theory" had "highly suspicious parentage." "Fetichism," the crudest idea of god, could be "easily traced to the laws of a primitive psychology"; and the subsequent steps to polytheism and monotheism seemed simple. Evolutionary explanations of the origin of belief in God, carrying the imprimatur of social science, thus acquired far more plausibility than ever before.[4]

And, as progress continued, would not human beings eventually outgrow their primitive fantasies? The John the Baptist of American agnosticism, Robert G. Ingersoll, thought so. "Every new religion has a little less superstition than the old, so that the religion of science is but a question of time." The suspicion crept in that someday everyone would regard belief as did a character in one of Henry Adams's novels: "very much as he would have looked at a layer of extinct oysters in a buried mud-bank." One perhaps begins to see why writers like Adams—or Carlyle or Ruskin or Charles Eliot Norton—created the myth of the Middle Ages as the Age of Faith, though all knew that, for sheer religious energy, the Reformation beat the thirteenth century cold. Belief seemed so much more at home in those misty feudal times. In Adams's own age of multiplying doubts, knowledge of God could appear wholly illusory, no more than a foible of human nature, a dying superstition. As Norton eventually came to conclude, "The loss of religious faith among the most civilized portion of the race is a step from childishness toward maturity."[5]

Indeed, the question had to be asked whether human nature included the capacity to have knowledge of God, even assuming

He existed. At this point, the inquirer left social science to wait upon the still more authoritative oracle of physical science. For it was a wave of discoveries in brain physiology in the 1860s that threw a new version of this old question into the laps of readers.

The relationship between mind and brain was indeed a very old question. It did not take nineteenth-century physiology to discover that a person stops thinking if his brain is smashed. And the consequent claim that the mind or soul has its seat in the brain went back to antiquity. At the end of the eighteenth century, Franz Joseph Gall broached the idea that particular mental functions and character traits resided in specific localities of the brain. Gall's science of "phrenology" (not his word), although snubbed by most scientists, enjoyed vast celebrity. It became something of a fad among American intellectuals in the 1830s and, vulgarized as "practical phrenology," a popular craze in the 1840s and 1850s.[6]

Through all of this hullabaloo, the authoritative position remained that laid down by the eminent physiologist Pierre Flourens: the understanding is unitary. Phrenology, despite its vogue, never penetrated deeply enough to disturb seriously the conviction that the human mind and soul involved something more ethereal than the cerebral cortex. To be sure, clerical radar often detected materialism in phrenology and pounded it accordingly. But Henry Ward Beecher, who evinced "a constitutional horror of the notion that mind was material," still remained an enthusiast of Gall's mental cartography.[7] Lacking a scientific imprimatur and remanded to the care of quirky popularizers, phrenology produced confusion more often than alarm.

Phrenology had barely sunk into intellectual disrepute before it became apparent that Gall's instincts were sharper than his science. In 1861, Pierre Paul Broca demonstrated that localized brain damage caused loss of speech—and thus presumably that the speech function resided in the specific damaged region. Broca's announcement opened a decade of revolutionary work in neurology, culminating in David Ferrier's crucial experiments in the early 1870s. The principle of cerebral localization appeared probable even before Ferrier's work; by the mid-seventies, it was a commonplace. The extent and character of localization remained in dispute but not the fact that the mind had a localized physical geography.[8]

Nor did the literate public remain uninformed. Oddly, these physiological discoveries were not integrated into the larger debates over human evolution then raging. But they were well enough publicized. Perhaps because phrenology had prepared the ground, cerebral localization reached lay readers almost as quickly as scientific. It struck nowhere near as many sparks as Darwin, but it made something of an impact—enough that orthodox writers went out of their way to refute at length its potentially materialist implications.[9]

One could still argue, as traditionally done, that an essentially spiritual mind or soul operated through the physical brain; but cerebral localization left this claim much less plausible. Physiology gave a specificity to the physical basis of mind that made assertions of some vague spiritual force breathing through the brain seem feeble, almost a last-ditch makeshift. Physiologists did not assert; they demonstrated—and with the sort of careful, concrete detail so persuasive to Victorians with a "modernized" outlook.

Moreover, all of this took place in an atmosphere impregnated by the new biology in which Darwin's name formed the centerpiece. The life sciences exhibited extraordinary creative vigor in the third quarter of the century. This energy, together with the sometimes spectacular results it produced, gave the biological sciences an unusual hold on the imaginations of many readers—not unlike the fascination of relativity in the 1920s or genetics today. A litterateur like Charles Eliot Norton, with no pretensions whatever to scientific competence, followed developments even in the less spectacular branches of biology.[10] Fifty years earlier the conclusions of cerebral localization would have carried the same implications but far less weight.

This work was reported and interpreted against the background of a new sensitivity to the animal nature of man. Comparative anatomy had, since the seventeenth century, detailed more and more fully the physical likeness of man and beast and, by beginning to explicate the mammalian nervous system, even breached that exclusively human preserve, the mind. In nineteenth-century biology, the barriers crumbled altogether. The new discipline of experimental physiology relied on animal experimentation to explain human bodily function. Not simply its discoveries but its very method struck at the distinction between man and beast. Ferrier's experiments were carried out on the brains of monkeys, but his conclusions immediately applied to people. Refusing to treat human beings as distinctive probably corroded their claim to uniqueness more rapidly than overtly denying it.

Physiology only exemplified a pattern common wherever biology touched on man. Comparative psychology so thoroughly confused the differences between human and animal intelligence that the muddle did not begin to get sorted out until near the end of the century. But it was Charles Darwin who most decisively thrust man into the embrace of his furry relations. Other biologists had uncovered likenesses; Darwin insisted that human beings had literally descended from animals: bone of our bone and blood of our blood.

And mind of our mind: already, in the second edition of his *Principles of Psychology* (1870–72), Herbert Spencer popularized a view of mind as simply the end product of the evolution of the animal nervous system. The "ultimate unit" of mind remained unknowable, in Spencer's scheme, as did the ultimate unit of matter; but this concession to the dictates of his peculiar philosophic system did nothing to rehabilitate the individual soul. Lester Ward adumbrated a similar but more crudely physicalist theory of mind in *Dynamic Sociology* (1883): "The nucleus of the highest nervous system is contained in the lump of protoplasm which moves about by the apparently spontaneous transformation of its gelatinous mass." In *The Physical Basis of Mind* (1877), G. H. Lewes took care to defend the mind from reduction to "purely physical processes." But he did so not "to admit the agency of any extra-organic principle," only "the agency of an intra-organic principle." There was no supernatural soul here, but only a physical function of a higher order than simple chemical reactions. A "mental process" was still "only another aspect of a physical process." Lewes spoke quite explicitly of the "Soul" as nothing more than the subjective experiencing of objective bodily phenomena.[11]

The influence of these ideas is hard to estimate. Spencer enjoyed an impressive vogue in the United States, though his formidable volumes and still more formidable prose may have encouraged readers to sample lightly. Lewes, however, was widely read, often cited by other writers, and frequently mentioned in private correspondence, on both sides of the Atlantic. And Spencer and Lewes provided only two of many expositions of the physical basis of mind. Even earlier, in 1870, James Russell Lowell was lamenting

> This nineteenth century with its knife and glass
> That make thought physical. . . .

The wide attention given William Carpenter's *Principles of Mental Physiology* (1874), which tried "to find some standpoint for free-will, morals, and responsibility, within touching distance of the brain cells," indicates how much these issues engaged public interest.[12]

Well they might have, for researches on the brain raised the most serious questions about the limits of human knowledge. A solely physical mind must operate according to strictly physical laws. Most specifically, if thought amounted to nothing more than "the product of the gray matter of the brain—the result of a change of form in inorganic matter taken into the system as food" (though the issue was seldom put quite so bluntly)—then by what laws of chemistry could the brain possibly achieve knowledge of any extraphysical reality? More generally, how could an animal, even a highly evolved one, break through the bounds of nature and secure knowledge of a God, if one existed—especially if that animal's mind had evolved specifically to fit it for physical survival, not supernatural inquiry? And, most broadly, if man no longer had a soul that elevated him above the merely physical, how could he have a spiritual life; and, without some sort of access to things supernatural, how could he claim to know that God existed? Darwin himself put the problem squarely: "Can the mind of a man, which has, as I fully believe, been developed from a mind as low as that possessed by the lowest animal, be trusted when it draws such grand conclusions?"[13]

Seldom, probably, did a sobered reader close the latest *Popular Science Monthly* with the stunned realization that he knew not God. Rather, as the idea of one's own animality sank in, a gradual, often unconscious change overtook one's unspoken assumptions about the powers and proper sphere of the human mind. The soul, immortality, and God might begin to seem to float out of reach of this grid of electrical nerve impulses called the brain.[14]

It is hard to know how much weight to give researches on the mind in the rise of unbelief, just as it is difficult to assess the role of anthropological writings. No one lost faith on these grounds alone; indeed, agnostics seldom explicitly mentioned either of these sets of problems as among reasons for discarding belief. Yet both lurked in the background of unbelief. Both the historicist account of belief as a naturally evolved mental product and the physiological account of mind as a physical organ insinuated that "knowledge" of God was not knowledge at all.

Both contributed to a failure of nerve: by no means a total loss of faith, but a weakening of confidence in human pretensions to know anything beyond the natural world. "Beyond nature man cannot go even in thought," wrote Robert Ingersoll.[15] But more played into this situation than science. Church leaders had so long trumpeted the absolute security of knowledge of God and pointed to science as its guarantor that the now apparent insecurity of that knowledge—the victim of that very science—could well leave a thoughtful believer trembling on a reed. This was not an ideal position from which to meet winds that now threatened to sweep away all knowledge of God.

Science and Knowledge of God

Before 1859, believers could rest secure in the conviction that the evidence for God was as certain as science itself. God remained central to thinking about important scientific questions. To be sure, scientists routinely distinguished their methods and their subject matter from those of theology. Nevertheless, such problems as the beginning of life and the origin of species required invoking some sort of creative force—which scientists and everyone else in fact thought of as God—or else they became incomprehensible. The adaptation of animals and plants to their environments provided both a central doctrine of natural history and obvious evidence of God's hand. Although scientists commonly thought of knowledge of God's nature as, technically, beyond science, they still believed that science pointed to Him; and, indeed, scientific explanations depended ultimately on the hypothesis of a First Cause.

Yet, by the end of the 1860s, science had little use for God. This was really no sudden transformation (though its last stages raised considerable noise around Charles Darwin). Rather, the excision of God from science culminated a long trend, the eventual outcome of which had been forecast long before by those disregarded prophets who warned that theologians had no business mixing God and science. And, in fact, ever since the seventeenth century, God—while remaining essential to the overall scientific enterprise—had become peripheral to progressively larger areas of scientific practice. After Darwin's *Origin of Species* appeared in 1859, God rapidly became redundant in the whole business.

Darwin's work played the largest part in the eviction of God. The Darwinian hypothesis of natural selection explained two of the three great instances of divine activity in biology—the origin of species and the adaptation of animals and plants to their environments—without reference to God. The theory of natural selection was hardly impregnable, but it broke the magic spell. Darwin showed that, in the one large area of science where God still retained an active explanatory function, He was not needed after all. A purely naturalistic account of the central phenomena of natural history could be laid out in a scientifically credible way.

Ten years later, Thomas Huxley proposed a solution to the great remaining mystery of biology, the origin of life. The basic unit of life, he claimed, was protoplasm. Having formed by purely chemical processes from inorganic material, protoplasm then aggregated into more complex forms, wiggling up the evolutionary tree until it appeared in frock-coat and spats. There was nothing very original or consequential in Huxley's speculations, but they created a tremendous stir at the time. John Morley, editor of the *Fortnightly Review,* where Huxley's musings first appeared in print, recalled fifty years after that no other article "in any periodical for a generation back," with possibly one exception, "excited so profound a sensation." The *New York World,* a penny daily, trumpeted "New Theory of Life" and reprinted the full text. Huxley's Ur-life formed the center of a scientific and popular controversy that raged into the 1880s. Lester Ward erected an elaborate description of the evolution of life on this gelatinous foundation.[16] As with Darwinism, the effect turned not on the final validity of the hypothesis—Huxley's was flabbier than its protagonist—but on its credibility. Darwin and Huxley might both be wrong, but they were plausible. They had proved that the big problems could be explained without God, and they had thus shown God to be unnecessary in biology. And if God was superfluous in the science of life, then He could call no part of science home.

Even His primal creative function—His role as First Cause—dissipated into mist. Most scientists, qua scientists, simply stopped talking about such metaphysical questions. Many of the amateurs of science, taking their cue from Herbert Spencer, solemnly if vaguely invoked Force as the primal creative power inherent in the universe, discarding "a divine Creator, a guiding intelligence, and a controlling purpose" in favor of "a force that is physical, persistent, ultimate, unintelligent, unconscious, unknowable." This "modern theory of forces" stemmed from the law of the conservation of energy, enunciated in the 1840s—a concept that had a fascination for some nonscientists almost equal to its scientific importance. Those who invoked Force as a creative power believed themselves to be speaking science.[17] That they were, for the most part, speaking hokum only underlines again the enormous appeal of scientific explanations.

What really mattered was not that an agnostic had ready at hand a scientific explanation for the origin of life, the formation of the solar system, or any other specific problem; rather, it was that he had the impression that science could provide one—if not right away, then eventually. Awareness of the details of any particular theory was not key; awareness that such theories existed was. The scientific endeavor to understand reality—in both its professional and its vernacular versions—appeared to be dispensing with God.

Even the fundamental concept of scientific law had altered in a way that left God out. In its origins, the idea of natural laws presumed a Lawgiver. The very word *law* reveals this assumption of a personal governor. Although, by the early nineteenth century, scientists thought of laws as empirically discovered regularities, rather than in more explicitly theological terms, they still believed that law manifested God, for these universal and invariable causes reflected a regular order that could only have come from the hand of a divine Orderer. And this Orderer had to *will* the law-described behavior of the universe—execute His laws, as it were—for dead matter could not move of itself.[18]

In the Darwinian universe, however, all the varieties of life developed as unintended consequences of chance variations. Evolutionists might speak of a "law" of natural selection, but this term only disguised a roulette wheel that earlier would have ranked as a natural law in no one's book, not even a French materialist's. Asa Gray of Harvard, though Darwin's friend and defender, could scarcely digest so bizarre a notion. He went on insisting on "faith in an order" as "the basis of science" and assuring his readers that this inevitably led to "faith in an Ordainer, which is the basis of religion."[19] Gray remained loyal not only to Christianity but to the Enlightenment; Darwin repudiated both. For the existence of order in nature, in the traditional sense, was precisely what Darwin put in question.

Natural selection reflected and speeded an expulsion of all metaphysical assumptions from the concept of natural law. One scientific popularizer warned his audience not to read too much into scientific talk of law; "for law is not an agent, but a conception, an intellectual summation in respect of the order of things." Indeed, a law might represent nothing more than a very high degree of statistical probability.[20] No one could say that a God had not determined these regularities. But the regularities themselves—and that was all science could know—no longer implied a God.

"Principles of order, so pervasive, so permanent, so inflexible, lose their personal character, become a nature of things, and wholly separate the mind of man from God," warned the Reverend John Bascom of Williams College. What worried Bascom delighted the agnostic Robert Ingersoll. The fact that "the universe is governed by law," trumpeted Ingersoll, is not proof of God's existence but "the death-knell of superstition."[21] Although many scientists clung to the faith that their work pointed to God, God no longer formed a necessary part of the scientific understanding of reality.

God's absence from scientific work constituted no logically valid argument against His existence, but it did mean one less reason to believe in Him. And precisely because both scientists and theologians had long assumed His necessity in science, His sudden departure could not but shake confidence. "Physical science, at the present day, investigates phenomena simply as they are in themselves. This, if not positively atheistic, must be of dangerous tendency. Whatever deliberately omits God from the universe is closely allied to that which denies him."[22] This naturalizing of scientific explanations did not of itself sever the sturdy and reassuring connection between science and belief, because leaving God out of statements about physical reality did not prohibit scientific statements about metaphysical reality. But the weakening of the link was undeniable.

Nor was this the end of the problem. To the strongest ties that bound science and belief, Darwin applied an ax. No demonstration showed more forcefully how science led to nature's God than the argument from design. No proof of God compelled more nearly universal assent than the argument from design. No theology exuded more confidence than the argument from design. And no theology ever collapsed so rapidly. Darwin punctured it, and its plausibility fizzed away like air from a leaky balloon.

Just before Darwin, two species of design arguments flourished, a dominant utilitarian one and a less popular idealist version, both of which by separate paths led the scientific inquirer inexorably to God. The utilitarian species, stemming from Ray and Paley, hinged on two points. First, the complexity of living organisms evidenced design, and design implied a Designer. Second, the design of organisms fitted them to prosper in their specific environments, and this precise adaptation showed the benevolent concern of the Designer for His creatures. The idealist species of design focused not on complexity and adaptation but on the fundamental structures that pervaded nature: for example, the basic anatomy shared by all vertebrates. Not usefulness but uniformity mattered. Indeed, the very uselessness of male nipples showed a symmetry, a harmony, a fundamental plan carried through without regard to function. Thus, nature revealed intelligent planning; it embodied the thoughts of God.

Darwin not only disabled the dominant species, he laid waste the whole genus. Darwin showed how, through purely natural selection, organisms developed from the very simple to the extremely complex. And far from proving divine benevolence, adaptation to environment was nothing more than the mechanism and product of natural selection. Those scattered organisms that chanced to develop variations better fitting them to their environments survived and reproduced. The multitude of organisms that varied unfavorably or not at all survived less often and accordingly reproduced less often. Ultimately, the old form died out altogether, and a new variety, eventually a new species, emerged, better adapted to the environment—but only at the cost of millions of ill-adapted organisms dying of starvation, predation, and disease. Darwinian natural selection thus explained not only the appearance of benevolent design in complex organisms adapted to specific environments but also the uniformities ramifying through nature. These were not the enfleshed thoughts of God but the branching out of an evolutionary tree, through eons of trial and error, from a common ancestor.

If this were design, its sloppiness and inefficiency suggested gross incompetence; and if this were benevolence, the designer exercised it with a paradoxical delight in suffering. Darwin had shown that this cast-iron proof of God had a gaping hole in the bottom, that the scientific evidence of design had a wholly naturalistic explanation. Moreover, the wastefulness and suffering entailed in evolution made it harder to believe that God could be responsible for the process: the humanized God of the nineteenth century, the God who was expected to act like a perfect and all-powerful human being, could not plausibly have set in motion Darwinian evolution. Perhaps more shocking, Darwin implied that man was an accident, the human presence on earth a mere chance. Was this *design?*

It was, of course, still possible to believe in God. Darwin himself did when he published the *Origin of Species*.[23] After all, natural selection did not explain why there should be order in the universe or why there should be a universe at all.[24] Admittedly, even order appeared less certain after Darwin made chance the mainspring of biology. And Darwin had blasted the natural theologies in which confidence had been vested: those that had tried to mimic science and carefully grounded themselves in detailed physical evidence. But he did not torpedo every possibility of natural theology. Moreover, the *Origin* itself was far from conclusive. The fossil evidence for evolution was closer to nonexistent than overwhelming. Darwin had no solid clue as to the mechanism that produced variations. And it shortly became clear that natural selection required more eons than Lord Kelvin and contemporary physics allowed. Indeed, many gentlemen of the cloth went blithely along spinning their design arguments as if Darwin had drowned on the voyage of the *Beagle*.[25]

Yet these problems did not deflate Darwinism, far less revive the quasi-scientific proofs of God. Darwin had plausibly accounted for the appearance of design in purely naturalistic terms. The sheer audacity of this stroke shook confidence in natural theology and impressed people with the independent explanatory power of science. Less ready now to assume that the lack of a naturalistic explanation required invoking the hand of God—particularly since science had dispensed with God in its own work—people grew readier to trust that science would eventually unravel present mysteries. The gaps in Darwin's theory suggested limited knowledge rather than divine activity. It was natural theology, not natural selection, that found itself becalmed.[26]

More specifically, Darwin's effect on design arguments could not be countered by pointing out his failure to prove his hypothesis. Simply by offering a plausible alternative explanation, Darwin had destroyed the proof value of design. God was no longer the only persuasive way to account for appearances of design. No wonder that an unbeliever in 1871 declared Darwinism "the most complete revolution which modern science has effected." One could still believe that evolution manifested God—as many scientists did—but to do so became an act of faith. One Christian apologist tried to slide around Darwin by pointing out that "evolution, if rightly understood, has no theological or anti-theological influence whatever."[27] But that was just the point. After Darwin, there was no longer a scientifically persuasive argument for God.

Nor, more troubling still, could there be. Recovery from this blow was not possible. For Darwin's overthrowing of the design argument in particular, and the omission of God from science in general, manifested a basic change in the epistemology of science: a narrowing of the range of valid scientific knowledge so as to exclude all inferences about supposed nonphysical realities. The older idea of science, prevalent through the early decades of the century, envisioned a spacious and rather laxly policed territory of scientific knowledge. Science meant something like "orderly and methodically digested and arranged" knowledge of nature. No fortified frontiers prevented science from exploring metaphysical as well as physical questions about the natural world. To Francis Wayland, president of Brown University, for example, science included all "the knowledge of the laws of nature and of the modes in which they may be applied to increase the happiness of man."[28] No notion prevailed that this knowledge excluded conclusions unverifiable by direct physical consequences. So long as "laws" or "facts" (of which God was one) rested ultimately on observation of nature, they qualified as scientific knowledge. That science was still commonly called natural philosophy before 1850 signified more than a semantic accident. Natural philosophy shared the metaphysical concerns of all philosophy.

So broadly constructed a version of science flourished because standards of evidence and proof were similarly generous. Science typically concerned itself with physical data perceptible to the senses, but no barrier shut out other modes of knowing scientifically. Psychology, for instance, got most of its facts from introspection yet fell at least on the borders of science. As late as 1874, the erudite Presbyterian conservative Charles Hodge of Princeton did not conceive of science as limited to observable physical evidence.[29] Most scientific work did not wander so freely; the point is that science did permit some fairly elastic conceptions of "fact."

Yet a good deal of tightening up took place in the decades before 1850. Research, even in natural history, exhibited greater precision. More and more scientists in other fields began to speak the exact language of mathematics. The Cambridge geologist Adam Sedgwick defined science in 1833 as "the consideration of all subjects, whether of a pure or mixed nature, capable of being reduced to measurement and calculation."[30] Probably Sedgwick did not really intend to outlaw every phenomenon that defied counting or weighing. But his drift was revealing—and carried an implication that ought to have set natural theologians and Sedgwick himself back on their heels. For the creation could be measured, but the Creator could not. A process of self-limitation was already in train by which natural philosophy would shed its transcendental concerns and become "science" in the modern sense.

Sedgwick's student Charles Darwin did more than anyone else to bring this process to fruition (and earned in the process his teacher's undying enmity). Except for an enigmatic allusion on the last page, the Creator appeared nowhere in the *Origin of Species*. Darwin was, at least in 1859, not an agnostic; he certainly had no wish to deny God. But, as a scientist, he shrank from questions unanswerable in terms of observable, regular physical consequences and refused to treat as knowledge beliefs about the nonphysical.

Darwin soon found a great deal of scientific company. In effect, science by fiat redefined its meaning of "natural" so as to preclude the traditional necessity of a supernatural on which nature depended. It did this de facto, not by denying the supernatural, but by refusing to consider as within the bounds of scientific knowledge anything but the physical. This was at root why scientific laws had to be reconceived as merely observed regularities rather than manifestations of divine will. By no means every well-read person understood what had happened, but one furious Presbyterian certainly did. Scientists, wrote Charles Hodge, perversely refuse to recognize that "there are other kinds of truth than the testimony of the senses." Instead, they limit themselves to "the external world": "A scientific fact is a fact perceived by the senses." The Johns Hopkins physiologist Henry Newell Martin fully agreed with this last statement; his "business was to study the phenomena exhibited by living things, and leave the noumena, if there were such, to amuse metaphysicians."[31] Martin could afford to be snide. He had won. As far as science went, knowledge had shrunk to physical knowledge.

Nor should this contraction have surprised anyone, had the earlier warnings of the critics of natural theology been heeded. Since the seventeenth century, science had striven not just to describe nature but to control or at least predict its course. The prodigious American physicist Joseph Henry defined as essential to a "scientific truth" its enabling "us to explain, to predict, and in some cases to control the phenomena of nature." But what could be accurately predicted was inherently limited to what could be carefully and precisely observed; that is, to physical reality. Thus, this predictive drive demanded ever more rigorous verification by physical evidence of scientific hypotheses. Hypotheses projected beyond human experience of the natural world—even if formed by it—are worthless, George John Romanes insisted, because we have no way of testing them.[32] The very purpose of modern science forced it gradually but inexorably to narrow its focus to physical reality alone. Darwin made this obvious at last—and owed much of his notoriety to the fact.

Darwin, then, not only torpedoed the argument from design but made clear that the whole enterprise of natural theology had foundered in very deep waters. The very idea of a scientific natural theology involved now a contradiction in terms. For science qua science, by definition, could now offer no foundation for belief in God.

Science hardly banned belief; indeed, most American scientists remained Christians. But they looked less and less to science for support of their faith, as science repudiated any claims to pronounce on such subjects. Increasingly, Christian scientists and clerical apologists concerned themselves not with proving God but with showing that science did not disprove Him. The botanist Asa Gray, a devout Presbyterian and ardent Darwinian, reconciled the two beliefs by severing them, arguing that science as such had no more bearing on religious truth than religion had on science. Only by such utter heresy to the tradition of natural theology could Gray preserve both his science and his Christianity. Gray's friend Chauncey Wright took this hint and elaborated it into a philosophical theory of the neutrality of science.[33]

Where science had once pointed beyond nature to God, it now pointed only to nature, behind which lay, if anything, the Unknowable. One might choose to call nature or force or the Unknowable by the name of God. But science offered no justification. Only the "illegitimate pretensions of natural theology" asserted that there could be scientific knowledge of God.[34] Thus, the enormous prestige and influence of scientific support for belief were cut away.

The loss of scientific knowledge of God would not necessarily have proved devastating, save for one fact. Religious leaders had, since Newton, insisted on linking science and God. In the half century before Darwin, the certainty of knowledge of God through science had been drummed into Christians more insistently than ever before. Natural theologians—ministers and scientists alike—had hoped thereby to capitalize on the rising stock of science, on the ever-growing confidence in its approach to knowledge.

Now those who thought science could find God were trapped by their own self-assurance. To be sure, many believers had never taken the bait, and they escaped the debacle. But the rest suffered a blow to the head. Assertions of absolutely certain knowledge turned into a desperate scramble for reassurance. Natural theology had invested huge sums of confidence in scientific knowledge. If it now turned out that science could give no knowledge of God, the question had to be asked whether knowledge of God was possible at all.

Nonscientific Knowledge of God

The estrangement of science from theology threw believers back onto whatever other resources of knowledge remained available to them, and in the main this meant intuition.[35] Intuitionist arguments for God, either appealing directly to apprehensions of divinity (as Emerson did) or to such interior signatures of God as the human conscience (as orthodox Evangelicals did), had always enjoyed a good press among Victorians. After about 1865, intuition often seemed the only rock to cling to.

Lyman Abbott, a thoughtful man caught in the wreckage of scientific theology, concluded after digesting Spencer that "if I was to retain any really forceful belief in God and immortality, or even in practical morality, I must believe in the trustworthiness of spiritual experience." A man less completely bowled over by science, Harvard's former president the Reverend Thomas Hill (himself a scientist), admitted in 1874 that the "clear sight of the invisible things of God, even his eternal power and Godhead, is not by vision of the outward eye." Indeed, absent a "power in the soul to see what is divine, theology would be as impossible as a knowledge of painting is to the blind." An "almost sacrosanct air" thus hung about the idea of intuitions in the 1870s and 1880s, as John Dewey recalled. "Somehow the cause of all holy and valuable things was supposed to stand or fall with the validity of intuitionism." It was this urgent need for nonscientific grounds of belief that pushed the growing influence of Schleiermacher and his American disciple Bushnell in late nineteenth-century American theology.[36]

Yet the intuitionism on which believers had to fall back could barely carry the weight. Several American theologians had already incorporated Schleiermacher's elaboration of man's feeling of dependency and Coleridge's stress on personal religious experience into their own understandings of faith. But these ideas had not been developed or deployed for the purpose of demonstrating the existence of God, and they were not up to the task without extensive overhaul. The intuitionist arguments for God laid out even in theological textbooks in the decades around mid-century were perfunctory and crudely developed. In less rigorous fora, in sermons and in ordinary discourse (if letters can be taken as evidence), intuitionism hardly approached intellectual coherence. Infected by the romantic sentimentalism of heart-religion, these palsied evidences seldom amounted to more than effusions about the awakened heart.

Intuitionism tottered because its validity and God's existence had been too much taken for granted; but, even more, its feebleness was the ultimate consequence of a longstanding preference among churchmen for proof that looked scientific. This is not to deny the very great importance of religious experience for Evangelicals and others but only to point out its superficial development as an apologetic. Admiring natural theology as the irrefutable demonstration of God, church leaders had put so much energy into it that they had neglected to cultivate carefully other paths; the avenues opened by Kant, for example, led mostly to virgin territory. So avid were theologians for concrete natural knowledge that they commonly even treated intuitions as if these constituted some kind of empirical evidence: thus, the fondness for Scottish moral-sense arguments. When heretics—Emerson, Parker, Bushnell—tried to give real independence to intuition, the scuttling about in more orthodox circles resembled nothing so much as a henhouse visited by a weasel.

This lust for empirical proof proved, in the end, nothing less than disastrous for belief. After science separated itself from God, doubting Victorians had left, not a subtle and firmly grounded alternative, but stunted arguments and evocations of heartfulness. Philosophers and theologians soon began to throw up new defenses to guard the intellectual plausibility of belief. By the 1890s, some of these looked pretty impressive: notably that spelled out by William James in "The Will to Believe" and those theologies that pointed to the complex roots of belief in the whole range of human experience. But for two or three decades after the mid-sixties, the nonscientific arguments for God appeared pitifully undernourished to a sceptical observer; yet they needed every ounce of their strength.

For in those decades intuitionism was squeezed within a constricting epistemology that raised the question whether intuition qualified as knowledge at all. A general tightening of standards of knowledge took place, hard to define and equally hard to ignore. And in this stricter conception of the knowable, natural science—now professing ignorance of God—took pride of place. From a believer's point of view, it was bad enough when science proclaimed that it had no knowledge of God, but far worse when science also seemed the avatar of knowledge.

Indeed, science often appeared identical with knowledge: "Its sphere is boundless; and where science cannot reach there is nothing but sheer emptiness." Herbert Spencer, of course, insisted that science comprehended "all positive and definite knowledge of the order existing among surrounding phenomena"—that is, everything knowable. But a considerably less dogmatic man, the paleontologist O. C. Marsh, told the American Association for the Advancement of Science in 1877 that "science is only another name for truth." No wonder that some theologians muttered bitterly that "science has of late assumed absolute authority in the domain of the knowable, and has summarily ordered religion into close confinement."[37] The line waggishly attributed to the Master of

Balliol might have come from a zealot of science: "What I do not know isn't Knowledge."

Nor was this attitude confined to men of science; in less exulting tones, it issued from the mouths of those who were anything but. No one would have accused Charles Eliot Norton of scientism. Yet, writing in 1868 (in an article in which he attributed the "decay of belief in creeds" to the "progress of science" and specifically to the application of scientific method to religious questions), Norton described scientific method as "the method of all true knowledge, that of induction from the facts of particular observation." In effect, for many thoughtful people (and many not notably thoughtful), science had ballooned to encompass all of knowable reality as its legitimate, even exclusive, terrain. "The scientific sense in man never asserted its claims so strongly," Matthew Arnold wrote; and theology could not escape its imperatives. "The licence of affirmation about God and his proceedings, in which the religious world indulge, is more and more met by the demand for verification."[38]

The mana of science glowed more brightly with each passing year. Adulation owed much to scientific achievements in explaining nature. It owed even more to the spectacular progress of technology, with which the public closely associated science, however mistakenly. The "magic wand" of science infused with happiness and enlightenment whatever it touched. William James bemoaned this undiscriminating cult of science in his 1878 Lowell Lectures: "Many persons nowadays seem to think that any conclusion must be very scientific if the arguments in favor of it are all derived from twitchings of frogs' legs—especially if the frogs are decapitated—and that, on the other hand, any doctrine chiefly vouched for by the feelings of human beings—with heads on their shoulders—must be benighted and superstitious."[39]

Complain as James might, he was whistling in the wind. So powerful seemed scientific knowledge that many believers gladly signed over to it rights of eminent domain over God. This was the animus wishfully embodied in Spiritualism, but not in Spiritualism alone. Christian Science also, however unscientific in fact, fell under the spell of the name. The father of the economist John R. Commons, a small-town editor in the Midwest after the Civil War, in fact traversed the entire route from Spencerism to Spiritualism to Christian Science. Jonathan Harrison, himself at one time a dabbler in Spiritualism, wrote in 1878 that he had for years urged the "full acceptance of the scientific method in religious teaching and thought."[40]

No one pushed this scientific search for God further than Francis Ellingwood Abbot, minister, editor, scholar, and "free religionist." "Theism and Atheism are in the scales," warned Abbot, "and Science holds the balance." Abbot possessed no mean philosophic talent, and he exercised it tirelessly in his effort to show that "the universal method of Science" held the only hope for belief in God. Knowledge could come only from science; thus, "the future of theology" depended utterly on "its coalescing with science."[41] Abbot only carried to an extreme a groping common among liberal believers for some kind of plausibly scientific basis for their belief. Their search illustrated how convincing science's exclusive claim to knowledge had become. Their mistake was that, in looking for proof of God in science, they were pursuing a will-o'-the-wisp.

Devotees of science did not necessarily think that science could know everything (though one entertains suspicions about Abbot in this regard). Not even science could penetrate to the essences of things; those realities remained forever impervious to human probing. So, increasingly, seemed all metaphysical possibilities. The message of scientific agnostics like Thomas Huxley was precisely that science could know nothing about God. The point was that science could know everything within the reach of human knowledge: "There is but one method of discovering truth, namely the scientific method."[42]

Most of those who subscribed to this faith imbibed it from the manifestoes of scientism rather than from any intimate acquaintance with science itself. Around 1865 or 1866 Oliver Wendell Holmes, Jr., found in reading G. H. Lewes the notion that "the only proper method by which truth may be discovered is by observation and experiment." Lewes's claim evidently resonated with Holmes's own experience and preconceptions, for it became a settled conviction. Holmes's agnosticism dated from about this time, and in later years he attributed it to "the scientific way of looking at the world." He realized, however, that the meaning of this scientific way had changed for his generation, grown more rigorous and more corrosive of belief. As Holmes pointed out, his father, the distinguished physician, had received a scientific education, which he himself had not. "Yet there was with him, as with the rest of his generation, a certain softness of attitude toward the interstitial miracle—the phenomenon without phenomenal antecedents, that I did not feel." Part of this difference in attitude, Holmes speculated, might have been temperamental; but "I think science was at the bottom."[43]

The ironic twist in Holmes's case—and many others—was that "science" had this earthshaking impact on a man who in truth knew very little of science and entertained notions of its workings rather remote from reality. Yet he convinced himself that "scientific" standards provided the only route to knowledge and that they made God intellectually implausible. Like his friend Chauncey Wright (who had a much firmer grasp of science), "he called for proof of the invisible, and would accept of no half proof."[44]

Measured against this demand, intuitions often seemed feeble stuff; and even these weak reeds science explained away. Darwinian evolution treated mental development as the result of an organism's resolving concrete problems of coping with its environment. In this context, all real knowledge shrank to knowledge of that environment; that is, the natural world: "Man has no ideas, and can have none, except those suggested by his surroundings." Intuitions could give no special insight beyond this realm. They too, like all human faculties, had evolved naturally. The moral sense, for instance, did not display the hand of God but the effect of natural selection.[45]

Not every believer went gentle into this good night: quite the reverse. The *Princeton Review* in 1864 raged that some writers expected knowledge of God to meet absurdly restrictive criteria. Knowledge, realistically, meant simply "a firm belief of what is true on appropriate grounds addressed to our reason"; and knowledge of God fulfilled that standard.[46] Evidently this appeal to common experience persuaded the vast majority of Christians (if they did not ignore the problem entirely), for they went on thinking that they knew about God. But not all were soothed.

The essence of the problem, according to the Presbyterian theologian Charles Hodge, was that scientists had so steeped themselves in the study of nature that they believed in nothing but natural causes. They failed to appreciate "the strength with which moral and religious convictions take hold of the minds of men." The "facts of religious experience," he insisted, must "be accepted as facts." But Hodge's appeal to "facts" revealed the poverty of his theological resources—as did the many complaints of theologians that their "science of the facts of religion" was being unwarrantedly pushed out of the narrowing circle of science.[47] Stripped of the magic name of science, they scarcely knew where to turn.

Religious leaders had themselves to blame if some members of their flock inclined to give science a quitclaim to knowledge. The seductiveness of scientific knowledge did not flow inevitably from the rise of modern science. It grew from deep roots in Anglo-American culture. The successes of science—and the territorial imperative of scientists—certainly contributed. But so did men of the church.

It was, after all, theologians and ministers who had welcomed this secular visitor into the house of God. It was they who had most loudly insisted that knowledge of God's existence and benevolence could be pinned down as securely as the structure of a frog's anatomy—and by roughly the same method. It was they who had obscured the difference between natural and supernatural knowledge, between the tangible things of this world and the impalpable things of another. By the mid-nineteenth century they had, really, no effectual model of knowledge except science. John Henry Newman, who fumed at science, nevertheless had to define truth by reference to science. No wonder that science kept chipping away at religious knowledge, at the stories of the Bible or the doctrines of the creeds: belief was supposed, by theologians themselves, to be subject to scientific canons of knowledge, however much some of them protested otherwise.[48] We have grown so accustomed to science as the archetype of knowledge that we regard this attitude as natural; it takes an effort of historical imagination to realize that theology helped to make it natural. Was it such a surprise that when theologians took science as the standard of reality, scientists and others should do the same?

Perhaps knowledge existed beyond science, but it seemed shakier, less secure, less real than science. The "superior exactness" attributed to science gave an air of "vagueness" to theology. Knowledge no longer seemed as easy to attain as it had a half century earlier. Scientists had ever more rigorously to verify their hypotheses by empirical data. And, as professional science divorced itself from amateurism, this toughness impressed much of the generally educated public, painfully aware of the distance between scientific restraint and theological garrulity. There was much that science did not pretend to know. "Mystery for mystery," said one of Henry Adams's fictional scientists, "science beats religion hollow." But scientists were not afraid to say, "I don't know"—especially about what Huxley contemptuously dismissed as "questions of lunar politics"—because, when they knew, they expected really to *know*.[49]

This sense of the difficulty of knowledge, this demand for systematic verification and willingness to suspend belief while waiting, pervaded Victorian agnosticism—and it reflected far more than a narrow adulation of science. For science was admired, not as an exotic technique wholly disjoined from ordinary thinking, but as somehow epitomizing the criteria that sensible people ought always to use to separate truth from fancy. Scientific standards were invoked, not as bringing scientific methods to bear on non-scientific questions, but as applying universal rules of knowledge. The narrowing of scientific knowledge was only the leading instance of a general constriction of what qualified as knowledge.

People spoke of a conflict between science and religion because in that pairing the contrast of old and new was most clearly seen. Yet in fact what undermined the intellectual grounds of belief in God was not so much science as such but a set of assumptions about knowledge similar to, but broader and more amorphous than, those of science. Crudely formulated, often not articulated at all, these notions typically leaked out in dribs and drabs or in nothing more than unspoken assumptions. Eluding precise delineation, they nevertheless remain crucial for understanding the fortunes of belief.

It was the growing prevalence of these assumptions—and the eagerness of churchmen to grant them—that led people to admire science so deeply and even to apply its canons consciously to religion. To be sure, the successes of science also nourished these broader assumptions in a kind of dialectical exchange. And science embodied them most attractively and powerfully. Moreover, it provided the most direct avenue by which they entered the culture, not only through elite science, but through such quasi-scientific activities as phrenology, mesmerism, health reform, and medical practice. Nevertheless, American culture had not simply given itself over to science. Rather, there had emerged, with science as midwife, a new, more rigorous, and more confined way of understanding what constituted knowledge and how it could be got.

What most distinguished this new epistemology was its worldliness, its orientation toward the concrete, measurable fact. The stress lay, as in science, on control and prediction; and thus the mind grew puzzled at elusive, intangible matters that evaded human grasp. "Tangible facts; material objects; truths, laws, and principles, demonstrable either directly by the senses or deducible from such as are demonstrable": these, said Lester Ward, are what is wanted. These provide "materials for the intellect to deal with," the "proper objects of knowledge." Away with softheaded fancies! "The only safe knowledge is knowledge of *things*. . . . The only real knowledge is knowledge of *nature*."[50] This was the knowledge of science but also the ideal knowledge of modern life: historically cumulative, empirical, experimental, and precise.

Thus Ward crowned the victor after two centuries of conflict about the nature of knowledge. This new epistemological model had deep historic roots: in the process of secularization that had pried apart natural and supernatural, in the economic changes that had created a new social basis for understanding reality, in the shaping of a powerful new science, and in the strategies of religious leaders who wanted above all else to make God fit man's new world. In consequence, the very meaning of "belief" narrowed. The connotations of trust and reliance inherent in "belief in God" diminished; the cognitive dimension of belief expanded. Accurate knowledge of God became at once both more urgent and more problematical.

By the later nineteenth century, these new, tighter principles of knowledge had come to suffuse modern culture, as the analytic-technical cast of mind extended its hold. And "knowledge" here involved not some abstracted Humean criteria but a solidly felt assurance of reality suited to practical living. With his usual perspicacity, Huxley understood this and, with his usual glee at the squirming of clergymen, gloated over it. The number of people, he pointed out, "driven into the use of scientific methods of inquiry [he intended the phrase loosely] and taught to trust them, by their education, their daily professional and business needs, is increasing and will continually increase." And the result for religious belief? "The phraseology of Supernaturalism may remain on men's lips, but in practice they are Naturalists."[51]

Huxley perhaps overrated the consistency of his fellow men; a lot of naturalists in daily life remained supernaturalists in more than words. But he hit squarely one situation that helped to make agnostics. "Experience, observation, and reason" provide "the only basis of knowledge," Robert Ingersoll believed; consequently, "I care nothing about the 'future' world." He intended instead "to make the best" of this one.[52] Knowledge aimed at precision: God was undefinable. Knowledge looked for what was tangible or observable: God was impalpable and invisible.

These stricter presuppositions of knowledge did not operate in isolation; they corroded belief all the more severely because they reinforced a growing confusion at the heart of Victorian religion. Hints of this difficulty appeared in the writings on religious language of such men as Coleridge, Schleiermacher, and their American admirers James Marsh and Horace Bushnell. They argued that language employed to speak about God differed from that used in science—as, for that matter, it differed from the everyday language used to describe physical realities. God so far exceeded human comprehension that religious truth eluded exact verbal expression. Matthew Arnold stressed that "*approximate,* not scientific," language was not only "lawful" in religion but "indeed is all we can attain to."[53] Arnold was no Christian; but Bushnell, who certainly was, echoed his view. Words could only grope toward and point to ineffable divine realities, for the intellect could never approach a full understanding of God.

Only symbolic language allowed man to taste God. Metaphors, "signs and images," could give the mind a glimpse of what the heart could better absorb. But this "analogic property" of words "transcends speculative inquiry." Grasping divine truth required, therefore, "not reason, or logic, or a scientific power, so much as a right sensibility," what Bushnell called an "aesthetic talent." And Bushnell welcomed the problematic implication: "Religion has a natural and profound alliance with poetry."[54]

Bushnell did not think that conflating religion with poetry left knowledge of God any less secure. To the contrary, he (and those who thought like him) regarded the "highest and freest forms" of truth as flowing, not from the "natural understanding," but from "spirit and life." He was not, in this respect, so very far from Emerson, who also believed that intuitive experiences, scarcely expressible in words, opened the doors on religious truths barred to the mundane intellect.[55] Unorthodox though it was, this position looked safe enough, as long as intuition was believed to give knowledge.

Many of Bushnell's colleagues thought him barely a Christian—and no one had any doubt about Emerson—but both articulated a theme central to nineteenth-century religion. The doughty conservative Charles Hodge warned that such heresies made God impossible to prove. But many people were coming to think roughly like Bushnell, for the cult of the "heart" made religious belief peculiarly susceptible to being conceived as a matter of feeling, sensibility, and ideals. Henry Ward Beecher, perhaps the closest thing to an archetype of the mid-Victorian Christian, styled himself a Calvinist; yet he insisted that Calvin had labored under "an inordinate share of intellect" and too small a "share of heart." Beecher scorned "facts which appeal to my senses as the lowest possible truth, and as appealing to the lowest avenue of my mind." He worshipped, rather, truths that could not be "incarnated" in "a logical statement." Indeed, he went Bushnell one better; for

Beecher, the highest truths remained altogether inexpressible. Beecher became, not surprisingly, the leading exemplar of the new, self-consciously artistic pulpit style that developed around 1850. These effusive rhetoricians strove to clothe religious truth "in the language of a poem."[56]

When preachers preached poetry, it was perhaps not shocking that some members of their congregations drifted into regarding religious belief as more like poetry than scientific knowledge. The analogy was not wholly novel. An emotional response to God had, after all, always been crucial to religion, and from the late seventeenth century the aesthetics of the sublime had linked this reaction specifically with art. But the comparison with art had ranked as a fairly minor theme before the mid-nineteenth century. Then it moved close to the center of how people conceived religion. James Russell Lowell, for instance, viewed religion as essentially poetic. By 1880, even Hodge's Presbyterians no longer disdained the appeal to the muses.[57] For most believers, such an attitude raised no troubling questions; for the fact that religion was preeminently poetry did not mean that it was any less fact.

Yet the idea of religious belief as aesthetic response appeared in a very different light when tighter epistemological canons excluded God from science, intuitions from knowledge. Theologians like Bushnell were striving to reverse what they regarded as an excessive rationalizing of belief; to return belief to a foundation in a wider conception of knowing; to root it, as Jonathan Edwards had tried, in the entire human personality. But, because of the stunted development of intuitionism, because of the theological surrender to empirical knowledge, there hardly existed a vocabulary in which to argue for some kind of "poetic" cognition of reality. Poetry was poetry, not fact. Its domain was affective, not cognitive. Beecher, consistently enough, came to regard religion as "intrinsically an emotion, a disposition." If talk about God amounted *only* to poetry (which Beecher denied), then it did not qualify as fact. It seemed instead equivalent to the emotions inspired by a Beethoven symphony or an Old Master. Most believers still clung to the conviction that their belief rested somehow on objectively demonstrable knowledge. But some concluded that "the sources of our belief are, in large degree, inscrutable." "No two men think of God alike," wrote Charles Eliot Norton in 1865. "No man or men can tell me what I must think of Him."[58] Within four years Norton was an agnostic.

For it was hard to believe that a poetic faith, even if somehow more than an upwelling of emotion, provided solid ground for belief in God. Christianity, more than most religions, had defined itself in cognitive terms. To believe in God meant, not simply to rely on and bow down to a divinity somehow apprehended, but to have an assurance of God's reality that satisfied the reasoning powers. Mystical, or at least nonrationalist, traditions had balanced this proclivity through most of Christian history. From the late seventeenth century onward, however, church leaders had seized on science for proof of God, had labored to demonstrate His existence empirically, had even tried to transmute intuition into science, and had scowled dissenters down as heretics. They had abandoned those nonrational, sometimes noncognitive, roads to belief, left them weed-grown traces of once broad avenues. Churchmen seldom explicitly denied that faith might be convincing without cognition, but generations of sermons and theology texts had left the distinct impression that belief required cognitive knowledge.

Now, to more and more people, belief in God seemed to express feeling rather than to state knowledge. Chauncey Wright called faith in God "a sentiment, not a faculty of knowledge." Henry Adams described it as a form of "imaginative and emotional expression," "a state of mind, like love or jealousy." Lester Ward defined it as "the embodied and organized state of the emotions." The neurologist George Beard said bluntly that "to prove a religion would be to kill it—to transfer it from the emotions, where it belongs, to the intellect, where it can find no home."[59]

Belief had slipped into a convenient new category, which helped not only to explain it but to explain it away. "The poetry of faith is as indispensable as the prose of information, and while science furnishes the latter, religion supplies the former." Grouping religion solely with emotional and aesthetic feelings distinguished it from knowledge, as knowledge became more precise and concrete, and thus stamped belief as fanciful. But this did not necessarily devalue religion. After all, Victorians admired Duty above almost all else and fashioned an idol of the Heart; and these things sprang from feeling, not knowledge. Indeed, Lowell regarded religion and poetry as superior to intellect, precisely because they revealed the heart. Even the scientist John Tyndall, bête noire of the orthodox, declared that religion, "in the region of *poetry* and *emotion*," added "inward completeness and dignity to man."[60]

This exaltation of religion as feeling made it easier to accept the loss of God as reality. On the one hand, it gave belief an understandable function, explained the historic centrality of the God-idea. Agnostics did not have to overcome the preposterous spectacle of millions of people duped for thousands of years by a meaningless fantasy. On the other hand, they did not have to deny their own religious feelings in order to preserve their self-respect; they could give up God without abandoning the penumbra of feelings surrounding God that usually meant very much to them. "There is nothing irrational," wrote Charles Eliot Norton, "in a sentiment or emotion." Religion, which Norton understood as a man's devotion to his highest objects, retained "absolute claim over the whole of his life."[61]

Yet, however important, faith remained what Matthew Arnold called "the poetry of life." Although the supreme artistic creation, essential as a source of inspiration and moral values, religion was not to be confused with knowledge of any reality outside of man's affective life. "The test of a true faith," Chauncey Wright insisted, "is emotional and moral, not intellectual."[62]

Knowledge and Belief

In 1850, the intellectual ground of belief in God had seemed like bedrock; by 1870, it felt more like gelatin. There had diffused through much of Anglo-American culture a chastened perception of what kinds of things human beings could possibly know. The shape and boundaries of reality had thus acquired sharper, narrower definition. And, within these limits, the apparent certainty of science made other claims to knowledge seem second-rate, even feeble. Caught in this vise was belief in God—not "belief" in some abstract universal sense, but the particular species of belief native to the nineteenth century: a type that had trouble reaching out for knowledge of God beyond nature precisely because it had attached itself so firmly to this world.

Most Americans persuaded themselves that they still had some grasp of God. Some clung to an older idea of knowledge that left room for God within science. As late as 1900, so prominent a scientist as Joseph LeConte could describe science as "a rational system of Natural Theology." Others held open the door to some kind of nonempirical knowledge, though, since their culture lacked words to talk about such a thing, they could only point confusedly in its general direction. "The very wisdom and wonder of the universe and its laws," wrote the poet-novelist Bayard Taylor shortly before his death in 1878, "prove conclusively to me that the intuitions of power and knowledge in ourselves, which we cannot fulfill here, *assure us* of continued being." But "I cannot demonstrate" it, he had to add. Many believers remained contentedly inconsistent—demonstrating perhaps a healthy animal scepticism as to whether we really know why we know. They just put God, in effect, into a separate compartment, regulated by older, more expansive standards of knowledge. James Russell Lowell blandly confessed, "I continue to keep my eyes shut in certain speculative directions."[63]

Yet some would not or could not keep their eyes shut. Charles Eliot Norton eulogized his friend the poet Arthur Hugh Clough as "too intellectually sincere to hold to the old beliefs in spite of himself, as Lowell tries to." Frederick Law Olmsted frankly said, "I don't know," and left it at that. A story told of Ralph Waldo Emerson in the 1870s was no less characteristic. Emerson was staying with a Dr. Reid, professor in a seminary near Steubenville, Ohio. After a stream of Emersonian conversation, the professor began to wonder whether the man held any religious convictions whatever and put the question squarely: "Mr. Emerson, do you believe in God?" "Really," Emerson replied, "it is beyond my comprehension." Decades later, Charles Norton, an old man, looked back over the last half of the nineteenth century and concluded that the "greatest spiritual change" of his era consisted in "the change in our conceptions of the relation of man to the universe, and of the possibility of knowledge of anything whatsoever that lies outside the narrow limits set for us by our senses and by the constitution of our mental powers."[64]

By the time Norton wrote, the prospects for knowledge of God looked less desperate than in the years when his agnosticism developed. For one thing, scientific knowledge—the certainty of which had helped to make other knowledge insecure—seemed a good deal less certain. Indeed, much earlier, in the formative years of agnosticism, thoughtful theorists of science had qualified their enthusiasms with reminders of the elusiveness of reality. But these warnings had largely gone by the boards; admiration for science and its achievements blocked too many ears. Huxley and Spencer set the popular tone. The chemist John William Draper, for example, "believed that there was no limit to understanding the world in natural rather than supernatural terms."[65] The muddle of classical physics at the turn of the century shook such naive confidence, though these problems took time to sink into lay consciousness. By the later 1920s, in the paradoxical universe of twentieth-century physics, one began to glimpse the ultimate randomness of reality and wonder whether science could comprehend the universe without self-contradiction. The suspicion then grew that "nature's" most basic laws involved human impositions on nature: workable metaphors pointing to a reality that must finally elude us. This perspective was not so very different from the terms in which Bushnell had described our knowledge of God.

Moreover, a warier, subtler rationale for belief had also emerged, based on a more sophisticated, complex view of the grounds of belief and evidence for God. Religion was shocked into abandoning its pre-1859 naiveté, just as science would later shake off its own innocence about its knowledge. An orthodox minister in 1877 confronted "The Difficulties of the Concept of God" in a very different spirit than most would have in 1857. "The difficulties make the thinker feel, with a sense of awful mystery, the inadequacy of his attempts perfectly to compass the Eternal with forms of sense and understanding." And after this admission, there followed no invocation of science or Scottish intuitions, no apodictic delineations of the Deity's character, but a multiplex suggestion that an unambitious belief might be grounded philosophically in the structure of being, psychologically in its emotional resonance, and practically in its effects on one's life. "I know not the whole of God, and many things, therefore, I dare neither to affirm nor to deny; but what I do know of Him, I find so grounded in my very being, so comforting to the heart, so fruitful in the life, that I affirm it beyond the possibility of trustworthy denial."[66] As philosophers and theologians followed such paths, by 1900 it was becoming clear that the new epistemology provided an intellectual foundation for new forms of belief as much as for unbelief.

In the 1870s and 1880s, though, this was far from clear. Science was dominant, and theology found itself stripped of the intellectual resources that it relied on for credibility. Looked at with the cold eye of empiricism, belief's claims to knowledge stood naked as a babe.

To some extent, these problems of knowledge reflected cultural transformations rooted in social change, which had little or nothing to do specifically with religion. The new stress on empiricism, on prediction and control in knowledge, grew up in symbiosis with more complex economic structures, technological change, and urbanization. That these changes speeded up and penetrated more widely in the nineteenth century helps to explain the timing of agnosticism's appearance. Not surprisingly, American agnosticism was really native to the Northeast, the section most heavily industrialized and most dominated by large cities (though more than factories and cities played into northeastern inclinations).

By contrast, southerners, residents of a region less caught up in these currents, appeared more comfortable with divine mystery and less swept away by science. Granted, the Northeast was also the intellectual center of the nation, the earliest recipient of most new ideas; but by no means all southerners languished in gothic ignorance. Yet one scholar of southern Protestantism reports that "intellectual abstractions and scientific theories" scarcely ruffled belief until well after 1900; and the sermons and reminiscences of well-educated southern clergymen reflect little intellectual turmoil or sense of challenge during the 1870s and 1880s, in either their congregations or their own minds: a sharp contrast to the experience of their northern brethren. Educated southerners did not lack access to new ideas; they lacked interest. The libraries of the University of North Carolina owned Darwin and Huxley, but few students or professors cared to read them.[67] Given the contrast between Northeast and South, it would be myopic to ignore the social roots of the new ideal of knowledge.

Yet the social roots of the new epistemology do not explain why it applied so neatly to religion, nor why belief sometimes succumbed so easily to its claims. The church played a major role in softening up belief. Theologians had been too unwilling to allow God to be incomprehensible, too insistent on bringing Him within the compass of mundane human knowledge, too anxious to link belief with science, too neglectful of other roads to knowledge, too insensitive to noncognitive ways of apprehending reality—too forgetful, in short, of much of their own traditions as they tried to make God up-to-date. And the leaders of the churches got away with this as long as science depended on God, as long as the new conception of knowledge that science exemplified did not reach its ultimate conclusion. But when it did, theology paid the price for ignoring the complexity of the question of God, for suppressing the transcendent mystery that was supposed to exceed human understanding. One might say that most theologians had lost faith long before any Victorian agnostics.

It is not obvious that this intellectual crisis of belief in God would, of itself, have produced agnosticism. After all, the inability to mount arguments in favor of a belief does not necessarily give reason to abandon it, especially if the belief is well engrained. But the matter takes on a different color if the belief also comes to appear somehow pernicious or offensive—if the intellectual softness becomes mixed with moral revulsion. And this was what happened to belief in God.

7

The Immorality of Belief

In January 1865, Leslie Stephen committed his religious creed to his journal. "I now believe in nothing, to put it shortly; but I do not the less believe in morality."[1] Most Victorian agnostics found themselves in Stephen's position—clinging, as other beliefs grew shaky, all the more tightly to moral principles. So unquestionable seemed morality to them that they never dreamed of subjecting moral convictions to the same rigorous standard of proof demanded of other religious beliefs. Yet unbelief had not produced this moral fervency; agnostics shared it with Victorian Christians and theists. Moralism was the peak that still stood, prominent in its isolation, after other beliefs had eroded.

Well it might stand prominent, for moralism played a large role in wearing away those other beliefs. Belief in God actually came to seem immoral; and revulsion from its immorality gave a powerful impulse to rejection. The newly perceived flimsiness of knowledge of God set Him on the edge of the ashcan; moral repugnance helped to push Him in. Indeed, moral revulsion appears often to have been a greater spur to unbelief than intellectual scepticism. Robert Ingersoll's agnostic sermons were composed mostly of diatribes against the wickedness of Jehovah and His henchmen. Charles Norton's letters spoke seldom of problems of evidence or logic, often of the "unmanliness" of belief.

Yet to divorce moral from epistemological problems is artificial, even misleading. Indulging in God repelled Norton as unmanly precisely because of belief's intellectual flabbiness. Yet it was a moral principle—that a person *ought* not to believe on insufficient evidence—that dictated the intellectual standards applied to belief and thus made knowledge of God problematical in the first instance.[2] There is no gain in trying to unriddle whether the chicken or the egg came first. The point is to understand how believing in God came to seem—there is really no avoiding the word—sinful.

Theodicy

How could a good God create a world tormented by suffering and evil? This paradox—the theodicy problem—is perhaps as old as monotheism. In the wake of the disastrous Lisbon earthquake of 1755, it had engaged some of the greatest writers of the Enlightenment; their quarrel, which thrust theodicy into the center of modern thought, still echoed a century later. To be sure, a person's sensitivity to the problem of evil is in part a matter of temperament. The dilemma disturbed Theodore Parker, for example, in his young manhood; but his "broad health and common-sense, his unconquerable hope, his great humanity"—that is, his congenital optimism—enabled him to put his perplexities aside.[3]

Yet sensitivity to suffering is also historically conditioned. For those susceptible to the distemper, the problem of evil grew more virulent by the mid-nineteenth century than even a half-century earlier. W. E. B. DuBois undoubtedly exaggerated, but perhaps understandably, when he declared the nineteenth century "the first century of human sympathy."

The awareness of suffering awakened by social change deepened after the Civil War. When people looked around them, they were more likely than before to perceive the world as brimming with pain. This shift in perception possibly owed something to the war itself, almost certainly to industrialization and especially urbanization.[4] Whether social changes actually increased the sum of suffering in the short term is uncertain; in any case, the question is moot. For they created shockingly unaccustomed forms of suffering and, by thrusting hundreds of thousands together into new urban agglomerations, raised the ancient misery of poverty into much greater visibility. Wan children bound to the loom for twelve hours a day; girls still clutching dolls as they hawked their bodies; ragged women sewing trousers for six or seven cents a pair; these tragedies played out against the background of festering slums where drunkenness, wife-beating, disease, and starvation stalked crowded tenements—the panorama was hideous but ineluctable.

Such horrors could make an individual ask whether any God could have created such a world. New York City's grim slums forced the theodicy problem on the young Reformed Jew Felix Adler in the 1860s. The puzzle of theodicy led to his first questioning of God's existence and started him on the journey out of theism into Ethical Culture.[5] To be sure, many managed to turn their faces away from the poor quarters of the great cities or contrived to rationalize somehow man's inhumanity to man. Perhaps it was perverse to blame God when His creatures abused their free will to subvert His benevolent intentions. But Adler was not alone in his unease.

Nor, frankly, did nature's works present a happier picture than man's. And God could not escape responsibility for them. The Victorians were hardly the first to notice the suffering blindly inflicted by nature, nor to ponder its implications for belief in God. But they saw the agony on a wider canvas than earlier generations. The time-scale of life, previously compressed within a few thousand years, suddenly shot backwards for hundreds of thousands, even millions, of years. Geology unburied the grim fossil memorabilia of the bloody competition for survival, eons of individual deaths and racial extinction: a natural history of pain. It was Charles Lyell's *Principles of Geology* (1830–1833) that lay behind Tennyson's "Nature, red in tooth and claw with ravine." Like Tennyson, many Victorians shuddered at (in Mill's words) the "blind impartiality, atrocious cruelty, and reckless injustice" that "abound to excess in the commonest phenomena of Nature."[6]

Darwin's doctrine of natural selection imputed hideous irony to this suffering; for Darwin made pain not a byproduct of creation but the very mechanism by which life developed. The refreshing beauties of nature, its endless delights, not merely masked but, vampire-like, fed on suffering. Competition to survive was the mainspring of evolution. Nature's tools for fashioning the varieties of life were bloodshed, starvation, disease, the wholesale extinction of billions of lives, perhaps millions of species. "The 'Plan' of Nature I detest," cried Robert Ingersoll, in one of the few outbursts of his usually calculated emotion that seems to spring directly from the heart. "Competition, and struggle, the survival of the strongest, of those with the sharpest claws and longest teeth. Life feeding on life with ravenous, merciless hunger—every leaf a battlefield—war everywhere." Later, when Darwin's correspondence was published, Charles Norton glumly agreed with his assessment of "the clumsy, wasteful, blundering, low and horribly cruel works of nature," adding only that "the same principle" holds in human history.[7] Norton was typical in perceiving more suffering than his ancestors had—and in perceiving it as inherent in the order of things rather than as a perversion of a benevolent creation.

Yet the theodicy problem did not grow more difficult only because suffering loomed larger. Suffering in any quantity had become less tolerable. Charles Peirce somewhere said that, as the eighteenth century is named the Age of Reason, so the nineteenth should be called the Age of Pain. Humanitarianism, at best sporadic in earlier times, rose to a universal concern; those who ignored it in practice usually at least paid it the tribute of hypocrisy. Looking back over the experience of his generation, Oliver Wendell Holmes, Jr., declared in 1895:

> We have learned the doctrine that evil means pain, and the revolt against pain in all its forms has grown more and more marked. From societies for the prevention of cruelty to animals up to socialism, we express in numberless ways the notion that suffering is a wrong which can be and ought to be prevented, and a whole literature of sympathy has sprung into being.[8]

As Holmes observed, humanitarianism involved more than a sensibility; it was a moral principle. Suffering was not just repugnant but evil. This transformation of earthly suffering into a great moral wrong owed something to both the secularizing pressures of social change and the enthusiasm of churchmen in responding to those changes. And it was this moral dimension that made pain a stumbling-block for belief. For the more deeply one believed pain an evil, the more one puzzled over how a good God could allow it to exist—worse still, as in Darwin's universe, make it essential to His plans. Was it coincidental that in the South—where church leaders had shied away from social reform, had less thoroughly incorporated sympathy for suffering into their moral teachings, had indeed at times seemed willfully callous to the plight of the poor and the black—the theodicy problem seemed to press less hard, and unbelief took root later and more shallowly than in the North? Northern ministers "preach another Gospel," as the Methodist bishops of the South rightly declared in 1866.[9] And that Gospel put the Creator in an awkward position.

For what kind of Deity would create a universe of pain, a world of evil? "I have had some trouble," Ingersoll dryly reported, "in regarding evil as having been intended by infinite Goodness." The problem here was not that the Creator of "crawling, creeping horrors" lay beyond Ingersoll's imagining. To the contrary, Ingersoll waxed eloquent for hours detailing every repellent lineament of His character. The difficulty was that any Deity who would choose to create the world Ingersoll inhabited was morally intolerable. God must be good: that was the foremost demand placed on Him—and good not in some mysterious way that transcended human understanding but good in the ways of the ordinary human world. "I will call no being good," wrote John Stuart Mill in his influential *Examination of Sir William Hamilton's Philosophy* (1865), "who is not what I mean when I apply that epithet to my fellow creatures; and if such a creature can sentence me to Hell for not so calling him, to Hell I will go." God did not measure up to Mill's standards. Elizabeth Cady Stanton wrote to her son in 1880: "How anyone, in view of the protracted sufferings of the race, can invest the laws of the universe with a tender loving fatherly intelligence, watching, guiding and protecting humanity, is to me amazing." And if she could not find a "tender" God, Stanton would admit no God at all: "I see nothing but immutable inexorable law, grinding the ignorant to powder."[10]

Declarations of unbelief often sounded more like acts of moral will than intellectual judgments. Ingersoll said that "I cannot worship a being" whose "cruelty is shoreless." Darwin was so appalled by the harshness of natural selection that he could no longer bring himself to believe in God: better that this horror should have sprung from blind chance. Or listen to Henry Adams, reacting to his sister's death: "The idea that any personal deity could find pleasure or profit in torturing a poor woman, by accident, with a fiendish cruelty known to man only in perverted and insane temperaments, could not be held for a moment. For pure blasphemy, it made pure atheism a comfort."[11]

Adams went to the heart of the matter. Belief in God seemed not merely implausible but blasphemous. In a world of pain, no humanitarian could with entire comfort worship its Creator. This dilemma had become, by the later nineteenth century, especially excruciating. Many believers had attributed to God their concern to ease human suffering; church leaders had joined in divinizing humanitarianism. And now the very principles thus sanctified turned on their baptizers. God became the victim of those who insisted on His human tenderness.

Authority

Beyond the theodicy problem, believers in God encountered a quite different sort of moral perplexity. In revulsion from suffering, the accent fell more on God's failings than the believer's. The specific character of the Deity believed in, rather than the general character of the process of believing, seemed wrong. But for some people, by the 1860s, the very idea of belief in the supernatural had come to seem in principle shady, offensive to moral sensibilities.

This attitude grew in part from the broader moral problem of individual freedom versus social authority. Whatever words one chooses—"individualism," an "inward turning," or some sort of fuller appreciation of personality—it is hard to overlook a deepened sense of individual autonomy in the nineteenth century. Exaltation of the individual as decision maker (and parallel denigration of tradition and authority) had roots in social change: specifically, as suggested earlier, in the imperatives of an entrepreneurial market society, which gave high marks for individual initiative. To be sure, more bureaucratic forms of social organization and the increasing anonymity of city life and mass culture challenged the reality of this individualist ideal, especially after mid-century. Ironically, such pressures seem only to have heightened the felt value of the individual, once established. Even the classic Tocquevillean American, buckling to public opinion, was supposed (in his own mind) to kowtow only by free and independent choice. And, still more to the point, to accuse Americans of unthinking conformity à la Tocqueville was taken to be criticism.

On the level of formal ideas, admiration for science also played a part in pumping up respect for individual judgment and cutting down tradition and authority. Despite more ambiguous actual behavior, scientists had learned to pride themselves on a posture of rigorous scepticism: *vide* the very model of a modern major scientist, Thomas Huxley.

One could ferret out still other sources of this individualist ethic; what emerges in the end is that the autonomy and integrity of the individual constituted for Victorians a crucial moral principle. (At least for Victorian males: the Victorian ideal of womanhood placed the female in a more ambiguous position of subordination to the family. But two points are worth noting: first, that feminists from the beginning demanded as essential the winning of autonomy from husbands; second, that the family supposedly existed largely to nurture in children—and recharge in men—a character that would let them stand morally on their own two feet.)[12] This sense of the sacredness of the individual appeared, for example, in the respect accorded privacy, a sensibility first canonized in the nineteenth century. Samuel P. Putnam, a Congregationalist minister who eventually lost his belief in God, found that his sensitivity to his parishioners' privacy cramped his ministerial work: "I never did like to ask anybody about the state of their soul. I was of the opinion that it was none of my business[!]. Religion is so entirely private and individual, that to me it cannot be a subject of conversation."[13]

As Putnam's uneasiness suggests, individual autonomy seemed especially crucial in a person's dealings with his Maker. Romantic religion, Evangelicalism in particular, pushed ultimately toward this conclusion, despite countervailing pulls toward a more traditionally public faith. For all the social ritual surrounding revivalism, the end of the exercise was to put the individual alone and face-to-face with his God. And, as the Calvinist doctrine of predestination faded, it was the individual, not God, who made the choice. A more radical religionist, like Emerson, demanded more uncompromising autonomy: the trappings of organized religion were likely to hinder, not help, an individual's search for God. Martin Luther might have been surprised to learn, as he could have from any number of Victorian writers, that his greatest contribution was freeing the individual soul from religious authority.

As Putnam's eventual loss of faith further hints, rejection of authority in favor of individual judgment appealed peculiarly to those who became unbelievers. Emerson exerted powerful influence on several American agnostics, among them Charles Eliot Norton. "There is no man in America," Norton wrote in 1866, "whose writing seems to me, at this time of so much value as his." What Norton valued above all in Emerson was his "fidelity to his own ideals," his "unflinching assertion of the supreme right of private judgment; of the wrong done to human nature by 'authority' in matters of religion." In the same vein Ingersoll complained, "The trouble with most people is, they bow to what is called authority; they have a certain reverence for the old because it is old." What "a blessed thing" to find someone with "individuality enough to stand by his own convictions." These were exactly the terms in which Norton praised his dead friend, the poet (and agnostic) Arthur Clough. Clough refused to "listen to the claim of an authority which did not derive its validity from its harmony with the dictates of his own moral sense." Always the strongest feature of Clough's "life and inner development was his utter truth to himself."[14]

Norton was not yet an agnostic when he planted that banner, and the question becomes how this moral conviction might have pushed him and others toward unbelief. A clue appears in the attitude of unbelievers (and many "liberal" believers) toward organized religion. The "overshadowing authority of the Church," as a Cornell professor put it, seemed to bind the individual down, put him in a false position of mouthing other people's beliefs, prevent him from developing and giving vent to his own ideas and convictions. The modern church enforced "pulpit dictation" mostly by weight of tradition and fear of hell rather than legal coercion; but this only made submission more shameful. Individuals voluntarily sacrificed their inner selves on the altar of unthinking conformity, *chose* to make themselves slaves. "The Christian virtues are the slave virtues: meekness, obedience, credulity, and mental non-resistance."[15]

Throwing off the bonds of the churches often brought, therefore, an overwhelming feeling of moral relief and triumph—the satisfied glow that comes when, against heavy pressure, one has chosen the right. Truth to oneself left the "infidel" morally purified. The feminist leader Elizabeth Cady Stanton, eventually an agnostic, spoke thus of her own liberation from Christian orthodoxy:

> In the darkness and gloom of a false theology, I was slowly sawing off the chains of my spiritual bondage, when, for the first time, I met [William Lloyd] Garrison in London. A few bold strokes from the hammer of his truth, I was free! Only those who have lived all their lives under the dark clouds of vague, undefined fears can appreciate the joy of a doubting soul suddenly born into the kingdom of reason and free thought. Is the bondage of the priest-ridden less galling than that of the slave, because we do not see the chains, the indelible scars, the festering wounds, the deep degradation of all the powers of the God-like mind?[16]

In conventional Victorian mythology, this kind of trampling on individual conscience belonged peculiarly to the Church of Rome. But that distinction no longer seemed so clear to unbelievers. In 1870, during the Vatican Council's debate on papal infallibility, Charles Norton wrote from Italy a commentary that would have scandalized most Americans. Rome, he said, had no real quarrel with Protestants. Norton drew the line instead "between the Church and the unchurched," all churches standing for the principle of authority, those outside their bounds for the principle of freedom in opinion. Three years earlier, Norton had insisted that the times demanded "a free Church," to which all "trying to express their highest convictions in life" could come "and be welcomed on equal terms, whether they call themselves Unitarians or Trinitarians,

Christians or unbelievers."[17] This curious organization, not surprisingly, never attained incarnation beyond Norton's musings, and within a couple of years Norton himself had ceased to dream about it.

For by then Norton, as other agnostics would do, had taken his free thinking one step further. It had been a dogma of the radical Enlightenment that the heavy hand of the churches cramped human freedom; but the threat came from the institutions and traditions of Christianity, not from belief in God. For Voltaire or Franklin, no man could be mentally freer than a Deist. But for some Victorians, the autonomy of the inner self was so precious—and so precarious—that submission to any external authority, even God, potentially endangered the moral integrity of the person. Partly the sheer fact that belief in God was traditional made it dubious. There was also fear that belief in God encouraged authoritarian leanings, that any "religion that has a personal God outside of humanity to worship and to please is quite apt to get appointed an officer to regulate the people." But, more fundamentally, there seems to have been uneasiness about looking to a God as source of right and wrong, rather than making those decisions for oneself—unwillingness to countenance any ultimate authority in the universe. Samuel Putnam clearly articulated this position and so concluded that "to vindicate liberty I must dethrone God."[18]

Yet it seems doubtful that many agnostics really carried their moral individualism this far. Most treated their still believing friends as perfectly respectable—provided that those friends stood in some tension with the churches and gave the impression of having worked out their beliefs for themselves.

Revulsion from authority in most cases prepared for, rather than produced, agnosticism. It helped to push the doubter into radical freethinking, a posture of revolt against established beliefs about God. It stripped from belief any claim to moral superiority, left it even exuding a faint aroma of moral decay. Thus weakened, belief in God more easily succumbed to other, closely related but more fundamentally corrosive, moral qualms.

Truth

Tirades against the rape of individual conscience often ended with the writer praising a conviction even more deeply felt than hostility to authority: the individual's duty to seek the truth and to be satisfied with nothing less. Indeed, respect for individual autonomy and for truth, not precisely twin values, certainly bore a family resemblance. Victorian agnostics often cast their opposition to authority in terms of its tendency to obstruct truth seeking. Charles Norton, summing up the "deepest spiritual conditions" of his generation, linked these two values by pointing to Arthur Clough's "liberal temper, his questioning habit of mind, his absolute devotion to truth, and his sense of her many-sidedness."[19] To understand the moral objections to belief in God is, in large measure, to appreciate the premium that Victorians placed on Truth.

To value truthfulness was hardly novel. People had for some centuries referred to Satan as the Prince of Liars, and the title was never intended as a compliment. But faithfulness to truth had now ascended in the hierarchy of moral principles, close to, if not to, the pinnacle. The prominence of truthfulness in their code of honor distinguished Victorians from, for example, their eighteenth-century ancestors who, while hardly enthusiasts for deceit, did not rate honesty nearly so highly among a gentleman's attainments. Honesty had ranked no higher than seventh in Benjamin Franklin's list of virtues, and Franklin abjured only "hurtful" deceit. In 1829, in contrast, Orestes Brownson declared as the first article of his personal creed, "I believe that every individual of the human family should be *honest*." Twenty years later, Brownson still insisted that "fidelity to what one believes to be true, moral courage in adhering to our convictions before the world, is the greatest want of our times." Little Jane Addams's father told her, around 1870, "You must always be honest with yourself inside, whatever happened." And his principle of "mental integrity above everything else" seems to have stuck with her as the primary moral lesson of her childhood.[20]

Moreover, "truth" tended to connote secure knowledge rooted in verifiable fact. Few denied that philosophical abstractions or the insights of poets might have value; but truth had more and more often an air of factuality about it. Churchmen themselves had encouraged this restriction by relying on natural theology and empiricist versions even of intuitionism: "Men have grown tired of speculation, and the reason seeks some solid ground upon which to rest its foot."[21] Truthfulness meant not so much loyalty to the Inner Truths of the Cosmos—here agnostics did *not* follow Emerson—but the more down-to-earth business of discriminating the provable from the merely possible or desirable. Devotion to truth implied, above all, respect for fact.

"Devotion" is the right word. Committing oneself to a statement of truth became, for those most sensitive to honesty, almost a religious transaction. Thomas Huxley said that "the most sacred act of a man's life is to say and to feel I believe such and such to be true.'"[22] The matter-of-fact tone of this utterance (and of Huxley's writings at large) itself conveyed his intolerance for embroidered realities. By no means all people gripped by this ideal voiced it as explicitly as Huxley, even to themselves; it surfaced more as attitudes and inclinations than fully formed ideas and convictions. Nor were Victorians immune to hypocrisy, the tribute that vice always pays to virtue: truthfulness, like all ideals, being honored as often in the breach as in the observance. In everyday life, not even Huxley genuflected at each utterance of fact. But clearly the ancient, humble virtue of honesty had gained new power to shape basic moral decisions.

Deepened reverence for truth probably grew partly from social and economic roots. It would be hard to believe, for example, that respect for fact had nothing to do with that analytic-technical cast of mind described earlier. Certainly the morality of truth showed the kind of geographic and generational variations that social change would produce. The southern code of honor, not a whit less demanding than any Yankee's, seems nevertheless to have laid less weight on exact honesty.[23]

Likewise, to speak very approximately, Americans born after about 1825 seem to have felt more strongly the strictures of truth's imperative. James Russell Lowell, anything but orthodox himself, intimate with men such as Leslie Stephen who gagged at unprovable truths, nevertheless complacently told the latter in 1874 that "I find no fault with a judicious shutting of the eyes."[24] Lowell came to intellectual maturity around 1840. Oliver Wendell Holmes, Jr., grew up in the same neighborhood and an equivalent cultural milieu, but two decades later. One cannot imagine Holmes defending the practice of closing his eyes to unpleasant facts; indeed, few things could have outraged him more. The difference was not one between deceit and honesty but rather a narrowing of the grey area between the two, growing intolerance for fuzziness around the truth, devaluing of the merely probable with respect to the provable, greater insistence on distinguishing what one wished to be true from what was in fact true—all this adding up to a shift in moral tone not less significant for its subtlety. It was no coincidence that another member of Holmes's generation, William James, coined the term "tough-minded."

The model of the new truthfulness was science, and the Victorian conception of science gives the clearest outline of the ideal of truth. No other human pursuit laid such stress on exact accuracy and strict proof. Above all, no other endeavor seemed to exhibit so pure a form of dedication to the truth, in both its honesty in telling the truth and its devotion to finding new truths. The inviolability of truth not merely existed for science as a desideratum but inhered in its very approach to the world; "this love of truth, for its own sake, . . . lies at the very foundation of all scientific methods." The Johns Hopkins physicist Henry Rowland declared that he cherished "in a scientific mind most of all that love of truth, that care in its pursuit, and that humility of mind which makes the possibility of error always present more than any other quality." Only science "values the truth as it should be valued."[25] When Victorians tried to say what they meant by truth, they almost instinctively groped in the direction of science, if not explicitly borrowing from it. Admiration for science shaped the moral ideal of truthfulness, just as this moral ideal contributed to the immense respect in which science was held. And here perhaps lies one clue to the widespread uneasiness—in the teeth of all talk of reconciliation and even cooperation—that a primal conflict divided science and belief.

For it was in the context of religion that moral dilemmas about truthfulness most often arose. Orestes Brownson's insistence on honesty, Jane Addams's discussion with her father, James Russell Lowell's apologia to Leslie Stephen had all concerned questions of religious belief. Cornell's president Andrew Dickson White, author of the controversial *History of the Warfare of Science with Theology*, remembered well his moral outrage during his student days at Yale at the "demand" at chapel services to recite an unprovable creed.[26]

Belief in God raised no problem of honesty as long as it seemed obviously true. But narrower standards of knowledge applied after mid-century shook this conviction. Intellectual difficulties thus raised moral uncertainties. (This was by no means a one-way street: the moral ideal of strict truthfulness had encouraged in the first place application of tighter canons of truth.) The Metaphysical Society at Johns Hopkins heard around 1880 a paper on "The Ethics of Belief" stressing "the dishonesty of treating as positive fact, dogmas which are matters of doubt or dispute"—echo of the English mathematician W. K. Clifford's celebrated article of the same title. Two years earlier, a physician addressing a convention of freethinkers had pointed to "a love of knowledge, amounting to sincerity of mind; a desire to escape the false, and wisely live in the true" as a foundation of his agnosticism. In the same vein, Norton had linked Clough's unorthodoxy to "his mental integrity" that "was too strong to yield to the pressure of arguments in which fancy had a larger share than reason."[27]

It is important to understand as clearly as possible the dynamics of this moral rejection of belief. These agnostics were not saying simply that sincere unbelief is better than insincere belief; in the seventeenth century Pierre Bayle had already said that. They were insisting, rather, that it is always and everywhere wrong to *believe* what we do not *know*. An individual who sincerely accepts an unprovable "truth" might be guiltless, but only if he had good reason to regard his belief as demonstrated knowledge.[28]

Agnosticism amounted to unbelief only because doubts about knowledge of God combined with this moral demand that there be no doubts. Sceptics of earlier centuries—late Renaissance fideists, for instance—had argued that man could not attain knowledge of God. But this did not destroy their belief in God, since they held it acceptable, even necessary, to believe things not accessible to knowledge: knowledge not being the only or even a reliable road to assurance of truth. A key to Victorian unbelief was precisely the newly rigorous moral principle that only knowledge provided truth and that believing in what one could not know was immoral. Those who were a little softer on this rule (John Fiske, for example) remained theists, however vaguely. Those who conformed morally (like Charles Eliot Norton) marched sternly into agnosticism: once a Puritan always a Puritan.

Even the most austere morality, however, did not ban religious impulses. In truth, flaunting them may have allowed slightly envious literary men to remind scientists that a firmer grip on truth did not give science a monopoly of all that mattered in human life. "Ah, my dear fellow, the heart is never a positivist," Norton declared. In daily life no one could avoid acting on unproved beliefs, on the impulses of the heart, tempered by experience and disciplined by what knowledge one had; and there was nothing wrong with this. Norton's friend Chauncey Wright helped to erect the foundations of pragmatism on this practical reality. The point that Wright stressed (and William James would later obscure) was to recognize the difference between "the desirableness of a belief and the evidence thereof."[29] For to treat unprovable hopes as facts played traitor to truth.

The utterances of clergymen came under the most withering scorn, for they seemed to propagate the widest variety of improbabilities with the smuggest self-assurance. "To men whose religion is the result of serious personal experience and deliberate conviction, and to whom the fit expression of religious thought and sentiment seems one of the highest and most difficult of intellectual efforts," said Norton as he teetered on the edge of unbelief in 1868, "the perfunctory manner and loose thinking common in the pulpit are scarcely tolerable." When Henry Ward Beecher made the mistake of declaring in the pulpit that, if convinced immortality were a fiction, he would seal his lips about it, Lester Ward jumped on him. "This may do very well for clergymen, but . . . we believe in the superiority of truth over error, however unpleasant the former, however pleasing the latter." To many agnostics, like Ward, Christianity sacrificed truth for pleasing illusions, indulged in cowardly self-deception rather than facing facts. Henry Adams made one of his characters cry out, "Why must the church always appeal to my weakness and never to my strength!"[30]

Yet, honestly, was liberal theism any better? In the severe light of verifiability, even the theist's amorphous faith in a vague Spirit, if asserted as truth rather than hope, looked "weak and shameful."[31] Lydia Maria Child, as amorphous a theist as ever believed, felt herself hemmed in between thirst for faith and dread lest she "accept delusion for truth." Did not believers in any sort of God commit what Norton called "the great sin" of "insincere profession"?[32]

All belief in God struck agnostics as a kind of subornation of the truth. Its attraction seemed to lie in cheap and easy comforts: immortality, so that one did not have to face the fact of death; divine purpose in the universe, so that one could evade the ultimate meaninglessness of one's own life. All one had to give up was the truth. To claim these things as certain, when patently unprovable, seemed a peculiarly despicable moral bribery, an appeal to the lower side of human character, an offer to trade cheering illusions for an individual's integrity. Put simply, belief taught cowardice, selfishness, and lying.

Not all agnostics felt so strongly—few regarded their believing friends as vicious—but belief wrenched the moral sensibilities of all of them more or less in this way. When Samuel Putnam considered "the infinite abyss" without a single "gleam of hope" in which humanity would ultimately vanish, religion revolted him. "O the weakness, the falsehood of religion in view of this terrific destiny!" Putnam would have nothing to do with this "cry of the child against the night," this "coward's sentimentality." He insisted on looking truth in the face. Frederick Law Olmsted, in contrast, reacted much more calmly. He admitted the possibility that believers might be closer to the mark than he; but his moral standards would not let him profess to believe what he himself did not know to be true. Thomas Huxley, too, declared the primacy of truthfulness in terms that left no doubt of the moral superiority of agnosticism: "However bad our posterity may become, so long as they hold by the plain rule of not pretending to believe what they have no reason to believe because it may be to their advantage so to pretend, they will not have reached the lowest depths of immorality."[33]

Progress

Sheer moral repugnance aside, laxity about truth offended because it seemed to retard human progress; condemnation of belief as dishonest blended into its rejection as profaning another major principle of Victorian moralism. For progress did not merely describe human history and predict its future; it functioned as a central moral value. Anything that put brakes on progress smacked of evil. And belief seemed to gum up the wheels of progress for more than one reason.

Progress involved more than steam turbines and sanitary engineering. Physical improvement and increasing wealth allowed amelioration of intellectual and moral conditions through the spread of schooling, widening of human sympathies, wiping out of social evils like prostitution and drunkenness, elevation of human aspirations. Progress meant, above all, this moral progress. In placing progress as the keystone in the arch of morality, agnostics were not departing from their religious backgrounds, rather carrying on a tradition well established by Evangelicals and other churchmen in the first half of the century. And in seeing material progress as the mother of moral progress, they were echoing countless preachers and theologians. "Progress," wrote a Unitarian minister in 1853, "is the law of life; progress not even, uniform, and rectilinear, but steady and constant; progress from feeble and rude beginnings onward."[34]

True, faith in progress had lost some ebullience by 1865. The Civil War chastened many intellectuals. Moreover, in the long evolutionary perspective of Darwin's and Spencer's writings, achievement of major improvements faded into a much more distant future than in antebellum expectation. Nevertheless, it would be altogether wrong to imagine that the steam had leaked out of faith in progress. Evolutionary doctrines—anthropological, biological, cosmic—actually gave more definite shape and scientific authority (however misconceived) to visions of progress. Writers now reckoned the struggle upwards to be tougher and more protracted, spoke more often of the minuteness of any one man's contribution; but they had by no means lost confidence in progress.

Progress had, however, become more tightly contained within the natural and human worlds, continuing a drift well marked before mid-century. Evangelical millennialism (and non-Evangelical analogues) had viewed evidences of human progress as benchmarks of movement toward the Kingdom of God, human manifestations of a larger divine plan. A mutation of this vision evolved after 1865 into an evolutionary theology, offspring of the marriage of Darwinism and Christianity performed by liberal Evangelicals like Lyman Abbott.[35] But because such doctrines increasingly depicted the substance of the "Kingdom of God" as the betterment of human life, it was not always easy to distinguish any necessary divine element in what often looked like a purely secular moral hope.[36]

As far back as the 1830s, Orestes Brownson had found that his "firm belief in progress" and "strong desire to contribute to the welfare of my fellow-men" had caused him to give "very little thought" to God, indeed to recognize Him "only in human nature."[37] Not surprisingly, then, as expectations of the coming Kingdom of God receded in the minds of uncertain Christians, evolutionary expectations of a naturalistic equivalent filled their place: a sort of human millennium to be achieved by eons of human striving. The pledges dangled by religion seemed increasingly remote, hypothetical, even illusory as compared with the palpable improvements exhibited at the Crystal Palace in 1851 or the Philadelphia Centennial Exposition in 1876.

Agnostics felt this commitment to progress as deeply as any other Victorians. Even so cautious and socially conservative a man as Charles Eliot Norton retained "an ardent confidence in Progress as an end." In identifying morality and progress, agnostics differed from most believing Victorians in only one respect: they had carried to completion the trend toward secularizing progress. They sharply distinguished real progress—"rational and scientific progress"—from any mythical divine hand in history.[38] God did not spin the wheels of Progress.

In fact, the reverse seemed true. Even theists and liberal Christians commonly regarded the church as historically an obstacle to progress, whatever its present stance. John Fiske was perhaps extreme in describing Christianity's past as "the history of fraud, superstition, misery and bloodshed; until these last two centuries, when its power has dwindled almost to nothing." But this gothic tale was only a peculiarly lurid redaction of the nineteenth-century mythology, rooted in the Enlightenment, that pitched the paladins of progress—Bruno, Luther, Galileo, Servetus, and the rest—into epic struggle with sadistic inquisitors, lecherous cardinals, and fanatic Puritans.

> Men of generous culture or of great learning, and women of eminent piety and virtue, from the humble cottage to the throne, have been led out for matters of conscience and butchered before a mad rabble lusting after God. The limbs of men and women have been torn from their bodies, their eyes gouged out, their flesh mangled and slowly roasted, their children barbarously tortured before their eyes, because of religious opinion.

So runs a brief sample of church history from Joel Moody's *Science of Evil*.[39] This stuff was Ingersoll's meat and drink. More refined agnostics, especially those like Olmsted who still had a soft spot for Christianity, muted their tantrums against the Inquisition, even exempted from blame liberal members of the modern clergy. But, in whatever tone, they all assumed irrepressible conflict between church and progress.

Nor—and this proved crucial—did the conflict stop when a believer passed out of the church. As Moody said, it was not so much the institutions of the church as the "*normal* action" of the "religious faculty," inherently "blind and irrational," that stood in the way of progress. Lester Ward reckoned that individual "superstitions" (his term for any supernatural belief) seldom had much direct effect on human welfare, except in "exerting a lowering influence of a general character upon those who entertain them." But the cumulative force of religious belief was to retard human advancement.[40] Other agnostics agreed with Ward, pointing to two reasons why.

First was the habit of credulity that belief in the unknowable supposedly produced in the believer. The earliest glimmer of antipathy to religion in Ward's youthful diary came in the record of a speech, delivered in 1867, in which he weighed the consequences of infidelity against the harm that flowed from too easy belief. The problem was that belief in God came dangerously close either to wishful thinking or to blind submission to tradition or authority. In either case, a person's ability to see clearly and unflinchingly, to think straight and solidly, became warped or rusted. Once a believer admitted the unknowable, there was no limit to what he might swallow. Accepting beliefs because of their "consoling nature," Mill warned, "would sanction half the mischievous illusions recorded in history or which mislead individual life."[41] Ward apparently thought that religious belief softened the brain—literally.[42]

In view of the moral imperatives of progress, credulity amounted to nothing short of disaster. Progress depended on right habits of mind: careful analysis, hard-headed respect for fact, clear distinction between what is and what one would wish to be—roughly speaking, the intellectual style most cogently embodied in science. Scepticism, as a *North American Review* writer noted in 1877, purified and strengthened thought, for it forced the discarding of weak and unworthy beliefs.[43] Indulgence in myths, fantasies about the unseen hearkened back to the Dark Ages. Man had taken centuries to climb into the light. Belief in God blasphemed against that achievement and obstructed the ascent that remained.

Moreover, belief sapped energies desperately needed for the climb. This appears to have been the mature Ward's chief moral objection to belief: "By whatever amount the energies of man are expended in efforts to influence supernatural beings, by so much will they be withdrawn from the legitimate work of ameliorating his temporal condition." Ward's concern echoed widely among agnostics, from the celebrated Ingersoll to an obscure Mr. Toohey. Chauncey Wright warned in 1867 that, when we assent to belief in God (or for that matter positively deny that He might exist),

> we feel ourselves carried, not by evidence, but by the prejudices of feeling. We fall into one or another form of superstitious belief. Suspension of judgment appears to me to be demanded, therefore, not merely by the evidence, but as a discipline of character,—that faith and moral effort may not waste themselves on idle dreams, but work among the realities of life.[44]

Progress demanded life in the tentative mood, incessantly questioning, straining every fiber toward betterment of the species. Belief undercut this stance, encouraged complacency, distracted attention from the struggle at hand.

Belief, so Samuel Putnam alleged, boiled down to pure selfishness. Dream of your own eternal happiness; forget the rest of mankind.[45] Putnam's charge amounted to barefaced calumny, when one thought of ministers like Charles Loring Brace of the New York Children's Aid Society. Yet his underlying logic appealed to agnostics. Yielding to dreams of a God who will help us out, softening one's mind by indulging unprovable beliefs *was* selfish, for such moral holidays did make it harder to do one's bit for progress. Once stripped of confidence in knowledge of God, agnostics found themselves caught between moral obligation to advance humanity and a belief in God that impeded progress. This was no dilemma. Any decent Victorian knew which way to turn.

No Compromise with Evil

"The test of a true faith," the retiring philosopher Chauncey Wright had written in 1864, "is emotional and moral, not intellectual. Our respects must decide what is worthy of belief. Not what claims our respect, but what gains it, is our true faith, and the basis of our religion; and nobility of character is the sole end and criterion of its validity." Grounded in the supremacy of morality, Wright's position could hardly have been more characteristically Victorian. For those who agreed with him that the existence of God lay outside "the domain of real knowledge," the burning question necessarily became whether belief in a Deity indeed did gain respect, foster nobility of character.[46]

This query, sincerely pursued, yielded no easy answer. Few regarded belief as wholly corrupting. Yet no thoughtful and honest person could ignore the conflict between what belief entailed and what Victorian morality demanded. A movement like the Social Gospel, strenuously committed to proving in practice the moral force of Christianity, could serve as one way of resolving the conflict.[47] Unbelief was another.

Sharpness of conflict depended largely on individual milieu. Personal influences could, of course, prove crucial in any given case; but impersonal cultural and social patterns also appeared. Strong early associations with religion, not surprisingly, predisposed an individual to moral concern and thus to agnosticism (among other possibilities). Jonathan Harrison and Samuel Putnam both began their careers as ministers; Robert Ingersoll's father was a Congregationalist clergyman; Charles Norton's father ranked among the most influential Unitarians. In fact, an unusually high proportion of nineteenth-century agnostics emerged from clerical backgrounds.[48] Likewise, as geographic variations in moral outlook noted earlier suggest, social and economic changes created an environment in which moralistic religions were more likely to flourish, hence moral problems with belief more apt to arise. Far more agnostics seem to have originated in the New England-New York-Pennsylvania region than anywhere else.[49]

As these patterns hint, churches themselves laid much groundwork for moral revulsion from belief. Responding to the pressures of modernity over the past two centuries, church leaders had increasingly chosen to make religion conform to the needs and demands of the modern world, rather than to try to understand that world in relation to a God outside of history and beyond human wishes. This strategy aimed to keep religion on top of social change, and one of its results was naturally a closer focus on worldly behavior; that is, a moralization of religion. Specifically, nineteenth-century theologians and ministers, ignoring warnings from dissenters, attributed to God the humanitarian and progressive ideals of their age. At the same time, they defined belief in intellectual terms inherited from Enlightenment religion, analogous to the powerful world view of modern science. This stance not only (as explained in the previous chapter) created uncertainty about knowledge of God; more to the point here, it also brought to the fore moral issues revolving around questions of authority and factual truth. Above all, church leaders had come to insist that God must be moral—and not in His own terms, whatever those might be, but in humanly understandable ones.

Moralization of God had reached an unexampled extent by 1850 and, if anything, continued to expand thereafter. Probably, rising religious doubt around mid-century only intensified the churches' moralism. Simply as a matter of tactics, ministers battling Parkers and Ingersolls liked to bolster Christianity by trumpeting its power for good, prophesying moral collapse if it fell. But this sermonizing was something of a sideshow: Christians puzzling over their own problems of belief had more deeply felt troubles at heart. An overriding stress on morality as the essence of religion eased their plight. Moralism distracted attention from questionable creeds, reduced controverted doctrinal issues to secondary importance. Or so worried Christians could tell themselves.

For whatever reasons, moralism became more central in Anglo-American culture, at least its educated middle-class ranges, in the decades after 1850 than at any previous period. It was hardly coincidental that the second half of the century saw the greatest flowering of ethical studies in the annals of Anglo-American philosophy, from John Stuart Mill's *Utilitarianism* in 1853 to G. E. Moore's *Principia Ethica* in 1902. There is no evidence that Victorians on either side of the Atlantic actually behaved better than their ancestors or descendants. That is not the point. An intensely self-conscious moralism—we call it, generically, "Victorian"—loomed larger in their world view.

At first glance, taking in the corruption of the Grant administration, the wholesale purchase of state legislatures by bargain-hunting businessmen, this claim seems more than odd, at least in respect to the United States. Yet what is in question here is not the buccaneering of Jay Gould or Boss Tweed but the response of the educated classes; and the air of crookedness that lingers around the Gilded Age owes as much to voluble middle-class revulsion from dishonesty as to the undeniable knavery that provoked outcry. American intellectuals, at least, probably threw more of their energy into reform of political morality, strictly defined, in the fifteen years after the Civil War than at any time before or since. And prominent among these reformers were such high-minded agnostics as Henry Adams, Charles Eliot Norton, and E. L. Godkin.

Their presence was no surprise, for the moral athleticism of their godly forebears persisted among agnostics, as did the conviction that morality constituted the essence of religion: a bar before which God Himself must stand accountable. During the Civil War, Charles Norton, then still floating in a vaguely Emersonian Unitarianism but about to slide into agnosticism, confessed a religion consisting of enthusiasm for "the goodness of God" and "his moral government of the world." Even among Evangelical children who had utterly repudiated their fathers' truths, moralism clung like a barnacle, more tenacious than God. Matthew Arnold barely conceded a wispy Power behind the universe; but his definition of religion—*"morality touched by emotion"*—uncannily resembled the staunchly Evangelical Francis Wayland's epitome of faith forty years earlier: a disposition, pervaded by affection, to obey God's moral laws. But one scarcely needs to resort to an American educator like Wayland to explain Arnold, whose own father, Thomas, headmaster of Rugby School, ranked among the most successful purveyors of Evangelical moralism in early Victorian England.[50]

So basic was moralism for agnostics that even notorious sceptics did not think to be sceptical of morality. This double standard provided some of the more curious scenes in the literature of religious controversy. Ingersoll could run on for pages detailing how belief in immortality failed to meet scientific standards of evidence and then solemnly assert a moral claim that would have fizzled utterly by the same test. Huxley, at least, did not advance moral principles as "facts" in a scientific sense. But he thought them universally binding on grounds that he himself would have derided as wishful thinking if used to maintain a belief about God. Looked at neutrally, Huxley's moral beliefs had no firmer foundation than his friendly antagonist Charles Kingsley's faith in God. Yet morality occupied so central a place in Huxley's own mindset that he simply could not doubt morality, as he could God. John Stuart Mill actually slipped into saying that the moral perverseness of a belief ought to cause it to be rejected as false—though what the morality of a belief had to do with its factuality he never did explain.[51]

By no means everyone succumbed so entirely to the moralization of religion as to make human moral purposes the test of God's acceptability. The Florida planter Ethelred Philips for most of his sixty-nine years tried to decipher the Chinese puzzle of God, drifting at times very close to agnosticism. Yet to the end he retained his faith that every event "takes place in perfect accord with the purposes of God." He was able to hold on to this belief, one suspects, because he never imagined that his ideas of what is wisest and best were the same as God's (perhaps in part because he was a southerner). "*His* ways are not like ours," he wrote to his cousin in 1864, "and tho the 'judge of all the earth must do right,' it does not follow that it should be in accordance with *our* ideas of right."[52] This sense of the strangeness and remoteness of God was nurtured by many like Philips who remained unconvinced, whatever some preachers said, that God could be measured by man. It would ultimately provide a basis for a modern belief, a kind of cousin to modern unbelief, erected on the ruins of early nineteenth-century Christian self-confidence.

Yet many did follow their preachers' advice, much further than the preachers intended, and measured their belief in God honestly against the moral principles supposed to be its essence. Measured honestly, belief failed. "The last superstition of the human mind," wrote Samuel Putnam, recalling his own step into unbelief, "is the superstition that religion in itself is a good thing, though it might be free from dogma. I believe, however, that the religious feeling, as feeling, is wrong, and the civilized man will have nothing to do with it." An immoral religion—and that is precisely what belief came to seem to agnostics—revolted the mind, violated the very definition of religion, profaned the deepest convictions of any good Victorian. After the "shadow of religion" had "disappeared forever" from his life, a sense of profound relief overcame Putnam. "I felt that I was free from a disease."[53]

Thus, certain chickens came home to roost. Theologians and ministers were not wrong to relate faith in God to ethics; for surely no human beings will worship a God who has no bearing on their moral struggles, and just as surely belief must express itself in practice. The great error of church leaders—their blasphemy, to put it in their terms—was to forget the tension that must exist between man's wishes and the intentions of any Deity who might plausibly be imagined to have created our universe. They had let gather dust the ancient wisdom that creation transcended human grasp. The delusion that man could feel at home with the nature of the universe led inevitably to a rude awakening, a cold splash of reality.

Yet it would be wrong to jump to the conclusion that the perceived immorality of belief would alone have produced unbelief. That conclusion misjudges the deep rootedness of belief in God and distorts the connectedness of things in the human psyche. Questioning of belief's morality seriously began when knowledge of God's existence started to seem shaky. And unless some new foundation for morality were assured, very few Victorians could have allowed themselves to condemn the old one as immoral. Only the emergence of a secular morality made it safe—in the subliminal reaches of the Victorian (perhaps one should say the human) mind—to assert the immorality of belief in God.

8

A More Excellent Way

Religion waxed fat and prosperous in the Gilded Age. Dwight Moody shored up traditional Evangelicalism; Henry Ward Beecher crafted a more flexible Protestantism, at peace with Darwin; Isaac M. Wise reconstructed Judaism to fit modernity; James Cardinal Gibbons helped to build an American Catholicism to house millions of immigrants. Gothic spires rose over American cities, and church memberships towered to new heights.

Yet doubters saw rot. Revival rantings and suave discourses alike papered over the preacher's incapacity to know anything about his purported God. Gilt-edged hymnbooks praised the mercies of the Lord, but nature and history told another story. The proud towers rose precariously on moral weakness; belief mortgaged man's future for childish fables in stained glass. The splendid temples were whited sepulchres. This, doubters did not doubt.

Yet they could not let go their last grip on God without something to put in His place. In 1874 Chauncey Wright, challenged to explain why life existed, answered: "Why, for nothing, to be sure! Quite gratuitously." This would not do—certainly not for Wright, who regarded moral purpose as the driving force of life. The writer Bayard Taylor insisted that "merely *negative* argument" would never settle questions of religion: doubters could not "at once" toss aside even Christianity "when nine-tenths of the morality we have (such as it is—but we cannot spare it) comes through that doctrine."[1]

This need to find a fresh basis for morality occasioned the first confession of agnosticism in Charles Eliot Norton's letters. He wrote to Ruskin his worries about "allowing my children to grow up without acquiring the usual *sentiment* in regard to God, to Christ, to immortality . . . without being subjected to the usual motives of religion." Could he give them "strong enough moral conceptions" to steel them against temptation, nourish upright character, "without connecting these conceptions with religious sanctions"? And then Norton, a man not normally at a loss for rules of life, ended by begging, "What advice can you give me?" Little wonder that, a few years later, Norton praised an essay of Leslie Stephen's for providing, not merely a "negative" critique of belief, "but a deeply felt, and ably thought statement of 'Why we are not so,' and of the rectitude and superior manliness of our position."[2]

Agnostics needed very much to feel the "rectitude" of their position. For them, even more than for most Victorians, existence grew intolerable without moral meaning, for their religion was morality. Just as the moral blasphemy of belief pushed them away from God, so a moral void might frighten them back again: rejection of belief as immoral amounted to worse than an exercise in futility if one traded a defective basis of morality for none at all. Doubters could not abandon God without assurance that morality endured. Yet, abandoning God, they had solely the materials of humanity out of which to construct moral purpose. Agnosticism could rise only on a secure—yet purely human—morality.

Morality Naturalized

Agnostics did not need to start fresh. Ancient tradition linked morality to natural law; and antebellum churchmen, anxious to justify God's ways to secular man, had elaborated from this heritage an appealingly modern variant. This scientific machinery enforced morality through the agency of natural laws, especially those of physiology and psychology. To the extent that natural law now incorporated God's moral purposes, to the extent that it became, in practice, guideline and executor of morality—to that extent morality was potentially separable from God. It is no exaggeration to say that many antebellum Protestants, without ever realizing it, teetered on the brink of a secular morality.

The career of Henry Clarke Wright provides a case in point.[3] Wright began as a Congregational minister in West Newbury, Massachusetts, in the 1820s; but in 1833, alarmed by Unitarian influence in the schools, he gave up his parish for home missionary work. He soon grew more interested in education as a means of promoting public morality. In the mid-thirties, his moral concern drew him into abolitionism, from which he moved into the peace movement; peace became his primary motif in the 1840s, as he lectured through the country. Temperance had also long engaged Wright, like many other Evangelicals, and that movement's emphasis on the laws of bodily hygiene launched him into dietary reform. In 1845, he published a book on this subject, and "scientific" advice on health became a continuing theme in his lectures. By the early 1850s, Wright had established himself as a lecturer and writer on a variety of reform topics, centering on the relation between the body and human happiness: diet, sex, marriage, child rearing. By this time he seldom mentioned God, though continuing to believe in a vague Deity. He now couched moral exhortations in supposedly scientific laws of human physiology. Wright apparently still regarded himself as a Christian, but he had long stopped being one in any recognizable sense. Yet it is impossible to say when; and that is the point: religious moralism led Wright smoothly by degrees into purely secular morality, which substituted for his original religious commitment.

The life of Jonathan Harrison differed from Wright's in almost every detail, yet the same underlying logic drove it.[4] Born in 1835, he preached to Methodist congregations in the Old Northwest in the 1850s. But around 1861 he left the Methodists, convinced that even those notably undogmatic Christians allowed doctrine to overshadow the essence of Jesus' religion: morality. Harrison edited a newspaper for a while but by 1864 had returned to the ministry; he spent many of his remaining years preaching to various liberal churches, ending as the fuzziest sort of Unitarian. He wandered in and out of divers reform movements, including (as with Wright) temperance and dietary reform. Oddly for a minister, Harrison seems almost never to have mentioned God; he preached morality instead. It is not entirely clear that he believed in God as anything more than an idealization of nature, perhaps of human aspiration. Certainly he did not hesitate to work side by side with unbelievers, insisting that an atheist could be as moral as any Christian.

Neither Wright nor Harrison cared much about God except as moral force; and His moral function became subsumed within the natural world. Both men pointed up, by carrying to extremes, the potential for secularization in antebellum Protestantism. Both illustrated how its natural-law moralism could lead out from Christianity. (It could and did lead as well to a redefined Christianity, but that is another story.) Christians who became agnostics (possibly including Harrison) followed that road a little farther but started from the same identification of religion with morality, the same conflation of morality with natural law.

Yet, until after mid-century, morality wholly independent of God seems not to have been viable. One reason was that, in purely scientific terms, God explained the existence of natural law itself: science still deemed a Lawgiver necessary to create law. The evaporation of this scientific assumption, discussed earlier, need not detain us here. Suffice it to say that, especially after Darwin's implications sank in, many people no longer believed God necessary to explain why natural law should punish drunkards with cholera. This effect was part of the structure of nature, and that was that. Unbelievers afflicted with uncontrollable metaphysical lusts could slake them by taking a cue from Herbert Spencer and weaving natural laws out of elemental Force.

Yet the assumption that natural law could exist without God did not imply that natural-law morality could. God-based moralism not only explained how natural laws enforced morality; it also provided an origin for the specific moral rules recognized by human beings—directions far more elaborate and lucid than any messages clearly deducible from natural laws. This moral code came from God and was impressed on the human conscience, as even non-Christian theists believed, and revealed in Scripture, as Christians additionally professed. Natural law merely embodied and reinforced an independently known morality.

So complex a morality could have come from nowhere else but the hand of God. After all, the laws of human physiology and psychology, while certainly moral instruments, were pretty blunt instruments. They taught moral lessons but often so indirectly that many sinners never learned them. Human beings had only lived on earth for a few thousand years—or so received opinion ran in the earlier part of the century. Yet the most ancient writings, records almost coeval with man himself, already contained elaborate moral rules. It passed credibility to believe that the earliest human beings could have directly and immediately translated the subtle moral teachings of natural law into even a rough-hewn code of morality.

As long as human existence remained compressed into a few millennia, as long as no extended history of human development existed, God continued necessary to explain the origin of morality and to certify its enduring character. Morality mattered far too much for its origins and its grip on the human conscience to be left misty, uncertain, insecure.

In the middle third of the century, a far more expansive view of human history took shape. The new time-scale of geology allowed, not a few thousand, but hundreds of thousands of years for human development. Work in anthropology and archaeology told a tale of mankind creeping upward by minute steps, ascending from primitive origins to painfully achieved civilization. A blurred picture gradually appeared: human institutions and mores slowly evolving over hundreds of thousands of years from rude, almost animal habits of Hottentots and Fuegians to the noble and sophisticated morals of Victorian civilization. Enlightenment writers had bruited about cruder versions of this genealogy of morals, but their speculations lacked the persuasive evidence of Victorian geology and anthropology. By the 1860s, these varied notions had coalesced into a new history of human moral development, a tale that any reasonably alert reader could scarcely avoid.

The story was fascinating and, above all, plausible. The collective experience of primitive tribes gradually produced common moral feelings, these eventually being codified into moral principles, under pressure of either the usefulness of certain behaviors or the dread of powers seen and unseen. Eventually norms so developed and their associated feelings—"from generation to generation insisted on by parents, upheld by public opinion, sanctified by religion, and enforced by threats of eternal damnation"—became effectively innate in human nature. Sir John Lubbock actually used the word "intuitive," inviting (presumably unconsciously) his readers to substitute this new understanding for the dominant religious theory, borrowed from Scottish philosophy, of an innate moral sense implanted by God. An unbeliever could reinterpret the intuitional foundation of morality in purely naturalistic terms—and do so without even challenging the assumption that morality rested securely on primal intuitions, much less unsettling the ethical superstructure supposed to arise from these intuitions. The Scottish tradition, always concerned to make God's morality intrinsic to human nature, thus collapsed into thoroughly secular natural morality. Darwinian evolution gave a boost to evolutionary theorizing of all sorts, including this brand; but evolutionary moralists usually looked upon morality as a product less of natural selection than of broader human needs, yet still one shaped within the constraints that nature placed on man. Jonathan Harrison, though dismissing Darwinism as a "miserable sham," embraced evolution as the key to understanding the slow moral growth of the human race.[5]

Thus became available the missing link in secular moralism. Here was an explanation of the origin of human moral codes that allowed time for slow and haphazard adaptation of social and individual mores to the demands of natural laws. "Any transgression of the laws of Nature," warned the fiery young agnostic Lester Ward, "is sure to be followed by punishment. It makes no difference whether you call such transgression sin, evil, vice, or immorality"; in any case, "immutable laws" impose the sanction. Indeed, the fact that natural laws punished sinners only *most* of the time, a disturbing anomaly in a divinely designed moral system, made perfect sense if morals had grown to fit the *usual* effect of natural laws. Ward did not mean that nature itself was morally good—most agnostics, unlike their religious forebears, thought it neutral at best—but that man had gradually built his own morality in learning to live with nature. So here, too, was an explanation that tied morality to the most basic patterns in the evolution of human nature. As the mathematician W. K. Clifford put it, "The voice of conscience is the voice of our Father Man who is within us; the accumulated instinct of the race is poured into each one of us, and overflows us, as if the ocean were poured into a cup."[6] A wholly secularized morality now made sense and seemed secure, had grown intellectually plausible, emotionally tolerable.

Above all, here was an explanation of morality in which God became superfluous. Doubters could now extract God entirely from their hitherto almost wholly secularized morality. Charles Eliot Norton, one of the earliest American agnostics, declared, "Our morals seem to me to be the result and expression of the secular experience of mankind"—a claim that Norton's English friend Leslie Stephen systematized in *The Science of Ethics* (1882). Norton was an intensely moral man, but of a special type, his morality reflecting the humanizing trend in Victorian religion. When speaking of morality, he always talked of duties that human beings owe to one another, never of duties owed to God or to some universal principle above man. Norton's moral vision included nothing like Jonathan Edwards's "benevolence toward being in general." Norton said, "Let us love and serve one another," and that injunction defined the limits of his morality. Frederick Law Olmsted put it more baldly. "I don't know [about God] and I don't care. I am occupied quite enough with 'the duty that lies nearest to you.' " This morality lacked any superhuman objects, and it had now become possible to explain and secure it without invoking God.

Belief and morality now stood apart. In Norton's opinion, "The question of the existence of God must be regarded as . . . one which has no intrinsic relation with moral character."[7] Samuel Putnam, the erstwhile Congregationalist minister turned agnostic, put it more bluntly: "Religion and morality are distinct." Putnam also put more weight than most agnostics on ratiocination, as opposed to "intuitive" response, in explaining moral judgments; but he ended in very nearly the same place. We know something is wrong, he wrote, not because God has decreed it, but because "the intellect declares it to be wrong, interpreting the experience of the race." A writer in Lester Ward's *Iconoclast* summed up: "The truth is that no profession of faith or lack of faith has anything to do with a man's morals. . . . Away," he cried, "with the bug-bear that to be good we must be pious!"[8]

Indeed, most agnostics carried this claim further. Not only was God needless to morality but agnosticism revealed a higher moral vision, a more excellent way than imagined by the best of believers. Infuriated by a pious attack on John Stuart Mill in the *New York Times* in 1873, Frederick Law Olmsted threw back an image of secular sainthood:

> Are the men who consecrate their lives to the propagation of Christian theology much more inclined to understand and weigh well the arguments of those who differ from them, much less apt to misrepresent them than Mill? Are they bolder than he, or more earnest, in seeking truth for truth's sake? Who do you think in our time has had a stronger desire that man should live together in peace, in justice & brotherly kindness than Mill?

"May my last end be like his."[9]

Humanity Idealized

Belief in God offered moral advantages beyond merely a plausible explanation of the origins of morality. From belief could flow a moral vision capable of inspiring life, instilling confidence, imparting direction. Faith in God could give persistence to stick to one's last, a framework of larger moral purpose, an ideal worthy to set the pattern for one's own finest aspirations. Indeed, failure of their own belief in God to realize this promise gave agnostics one large motive to forsake it.

Unbelief had somehow to succeed where God had not. Social evolution explained moral origins; it did not give meaning to life. Yet without this larger hope, only nihilists would reject God. In his letter to Ruskin in 1869, Charles Norton was groping for just such a moral foundation for life: the answer he needed to give his children. He found it. Norton, like other agnostics, grew to regard unbelief as morally tolerable, even attractive, precisely because he imbibed a new, secular moral ideal. Crystallizing in the first half of the century, this entirely human vision of a higher good infiltrated—and eventually for unbelievers supplanted—its religious progenitor.

The unbelievers' ideal eludes simple definition. It constituted, more often than not, no clear-cut and exclusive ethical standard, but amorphous attitudes, loosely linked. The specific injunctions accepted by agnostics displayed no startling novelty; any listener could have plucked them straight out of the sermons of Henry Ward Beecher or Phillips Brooks. The sceptics' ethos likewise grew from values cherished by Christians; but, where believers had called these aspirations divine, agnostics saw them as purely human. At the heart of this agnostic constellation of beliefs and values lay two articles of faith—by no means always clearly articulated, but certainly definable, if with some difficulty and more translucently than transparently. The first principle was the nobility of uncompromised pursuit of truth. The second was commitment to human progress.

The two ran together, more or less. So blurred were their points of intersection, so much did these vary from one agnostic to another, that the connections allow only the broadest of generalizations. Roughly speaking, on a self-conscious and logical level, unbelievers, like believers before them, conceived pursuit of truth as leading to growth of knowledge, thence to progress. And, conversely, progress led humanity ever closer to truth. The historian George Bancroft, no agnostic, had explained in 1854: "The necessity of the progress of the race follows, therefore, from the fact, that the great Author of all life has left truth in its immutability to be observed, and has endowed man with the power of observation and generalization."[10] Delete the great Author, and Robert Ingersoll would have answered Amen.

On a psychological level, the two principles interrelated more subtly. Faith in progress gave a motive for action, a goal toward which one could bend one's efforts. Devotion to truth, in contrast, functioned more passively. It provided a kind of oil of holiness with which to anoint progress, a chrism of sanctity that redeemed this commitment to human improvement—and the agnostics who consecrated themselves to it—from any taint of seeking merely material good, any self-accusation of giving in to spiritually unworthy goals. Agnostics, too, hungered and thirsted after righteousness.

Nor were any fresh canons of holiness required; these lay ready at hand in the preachments of Christians. According to an 1873 analysis of "Modern Culture," the "cultivation of this devotedness to truth constitutes the very highest order of mental culture": "It is this which ennobles a man, which destroys the brute within him, and brings out his humanity as refined gold, which lifts him above the grovelling of a self-interest which chains his spirit to the earth, which assimilates him to Christ his living Head, who is himself the very embodiment of truth." For this writer, as for most of his readers, the ideal of truth meshed with Christianity. But he valued truth for bringing out man's "humanity"; and omission of the last sixteen words—entirely possible without diminishing the fervor—leaves a purely human standard. The omission came easily to those to whom science suggested a "human criterion of truth": that is, "the unanimous consent of the entire human race."[11] Thomas Huxley, blanching perhaps at the rhetoric of "refined gold," would have endorsed the sentiment. Robert Ingersoll would not even have squirmed at the rhetoric.

In fact, Ingersoll deployed his own brand of bombast to dramatize the moral superiority of agnosticism. "Give me," he cried, "the storm and tempest of thought and action, rather than the dead calm of ignorance and faith! Banish me from Eden when you will; but first let me eat of the fruit of the tree of knowledge!" In one metaphor he depicted unbelievers as "intellectual discoverers" sailing unknown seas in search of "new isles and continents in the infinite realms of thought." What isles they charted mattered less to Ingersoll than that they had found a figurative infinity of human endeavor to replace the lost infinity of Deity. In another metaphor (his recurring favorite) Ingersoll described "a deadly conflict" that had raged throughout history. The handful of uncompromising champions of truth faced "the great ignorant religious mass." Straining against fear and mental slavery, suffering prejudice and martyrdom, this glorious band dragged by painful inches a reluctant humanity closer to truth.[12]

There could be no higher vocation than to enlist in the struggle. By no means every agnostic orated about infidel truth-seekers thrown to the devout and bloodthirsty lions; rather than flaunt their nobility, many simply insisted, with a kind of modest moral snobbery, that believers did not fully appreciate the great difficulty of truth and its supreme importance. Charles Norton wrote about the delusive "consolations of religion" with quiet but utter self-confidence. "You and I," he told Leslie Stephen, "who have given them up, stand really upon firmer ground." But whatever their tone, all unbelievers agreed on the "duty," resting "directly upon us as individuals," to seek "earnestly, fearlessly, and carefully" for the truth. This duty served, in the words of the "free religionist" Francis Abbot, as "a faith diviner still" than Christianity.[13]

Dedication to truth appealed partly because of other virtues it demanded. Abbot, defining his "faith diviner still," wrote of "intellect daring to think, unawed by public opinion." And Charles Norton admired in Darwin's work "above all the honesty and manliness of his plain speech." Norton spoke often of "manliness" in connection with his agnosticism, contending, for example, that religious belief "enfeebled the spirit of manliness." Lester Ward echoed the theme, contrasting "the manly independence" of the "empiricist" with "the idle respectability characteristic of the dogmatist."[14] Manliness meant, for these Victorians, self-sufficiency, toughness, unflinching courage. (Just possibly, Victorian belief in women's natural affinity for religion led men to choose this word; however, Victorians habitually used "manliness" to refer to moral toughness in any context.)

By rejecting the easy consolations of religion, by facing the truth no matter how grim, agnostics in their own eyes had climbed a moral Everest inaccessible to believers. Thus Charles Norton, in his characteristically restrained tone, said: "To accept the irremediable for what it really is, not trying to deceive one's self about it, or to elude it, or to put it into a fancy dress, is to secure simple relations with life, and tends to strengthen the character without, I trust, any hardening of heart or narrowing of sympathies." The former minister Samuel Putnam cast much the same point in his apocalyptic pulpit style. "The very moment man recognizes the evil of his lot, that very moment the grandeur of his being arises. For he can love; he can endure; he can perish without terror."[15] This faith a man could live by. This consecration to truth no saint could excel.

Even better, this devotion did not spend itself in monkish asceticism. It involved self-denial, to be sure—surrendering the pleasant illusion of a God who made everything turn out right. But this was good Protestant self-denial, sacrifice for the welfare of others, in fact for the good of all mankind.

Devotion to truth merged at this point into a commitment of

even more consequence in the agnostics' moral world: the intellectual and moral advance of the race. Not that all agnostics were Pollyannas about the future. Unlike many antebellum enthusiasts—and some of his more exuberant contemporaries—Jonathan Harrison entertained no illusion that a New Jerusalem lay just around the corner. He regarded progress as "rather a convenient conception (often a misleading one) than an ascertained fact." "I do not expect," he wrote, "to do more than add the lightest increment to the soil from which better things will sometime grow."[16] But this chastened hope powered his life.

Charles Norton likewise held only shakily to a belief in progress, yet he never let it slip from his grasp. Though he usually spoke as if humanity was inching forward, he had his moments of doubt. He certainly did not share, as he observed of himself, "that confident spirit of cheerful optimistic fatalism of which Emerson is the voice and prophet." Yet the very doubtfulness of the outcome gave all the more motive to throw oneself into the struggle: a better world would take shape only if individual human beings scratched it out of the unyielding rock. The "true end of life," Norton insisted, lay in a man's contributing "his mite of individuality to the improvement of the common ideals." Norton knew "that the progress will be very slow and irregular." But "in the long run I have no fear in regard to improvement in the general morality of the race."[17]

Nor did other agnostics. Most, in fact, indulged rosier expectations than Norton and Harrison. Lester Ward never doubted that his age of "rational and scientific progress" was pushing away the dead hand of religion to clear the way for the liberating power of science. And Ingersoll prophesied a future in which "man, gathering courage from a succession of victories over the obstructions of nature, will attain a serene grandeur unknown to the disciples of any superstition."[18]

Agnostics regarded their unbelief as indispensable to this achievement. Indeed, more than one agnostic described his attack on religion expressly as part of "the great work of elevating and ameliorating the condition of the people." Like believers, agnostics looked to science, technology, economic growth, and the diffusion of knowledge as the engines of progress. But powering these was a questioning, inquiring, doubting habit of mind, liberating individuals from mental bondage to tradition, freeing them to build a newer world—exactly the mental outlook that, agnostics liked to think, made them agnostics. Just as religious credulity clogged the gears of progress, agnostic scepticism greased them. *The Icon-*

oclast nailed to its masthead a motto from Buckle: "Until doubt began progress was impossible." Ingersoll echoed the idea; the "first doubt," he said, "was the womb and cradle of progress, and from the first doubt, mān has continued to advance." Thus, humanity had advanced, he concluded, in direct proportion to the decrease of religious influence; and the race would reach his version of the millennium only if (as he confidently expected) it discarded its delusions about God.[19]

Agnostics held a card high enough to beat any hand believers laid down—though possibly they had stacked the deck. If "all our moral worth depends on our knowledge and labor, not on faith and belief," then agnostics indeed could throw themselves more completely than any believer into the struggle for a better world. If "idleness, ignorance and misery dwell in the idea that a personal God does all," then unbelievers did have a firmer basis for moral endeavor than religion could offer. Had not the "leading thinkers of our time" conceded "that the only ultimate object which can be successfully maintained for human effort is the improvement of the human race upon this planet"? As Ingersoll was fond of saying, we cannot help God, so we had better stop pretending and help our fellow man.[20]

To spread light among the ignorant, to purify the seamy metropolis, to quell disease and suffering, to rescue the poor from their brutish warrens, to end the injustice that sundered society—one did not actually have to *do* this sort of thing. Most Victorian agnostics were human beings like the rest of us, not secular saints. Unbelievers who lived the kind of life they idealized were as rare as Christian preachers of charity who actually divided their riches among the destitute. Yet one could believe that, by doing one's own work carefully and well, by aiding others within one's limited range, one contributed in the small way possible to the greater human endeavor, justified one's own life. And such, perhaps, is the real purpose of this sort of moral ideal: to help a person to understand the larger meaning of his or her efforts, to give assurance that a life is not ultimately wasted.

Progress did for unbelievers what God did for believers. The existence of God reassured believers that the universe had a purpose, that their own hopes and efforts were not ultimately pointless. An agnostic had to conclude that the final purpose, if any, of the cosmos eluded human knowledge. But one could still feel that one's own strivings did not evaporate into nothingness, that they held an infinitesimal but salient place in the pilgrimage of the race. Chauncey Wright recalled the religious monuments of an earlier era. The "grand cathedral" of the Middle Ages hid "the squalid hovel." The "monument of our age," however, "the religious edifice on which thousands of busy hands and studious minds are laboring," was nothing less than the material and moral well-being of future generations—and the inculcation in them of an enduring "pious care" for their own posterity. "Will it be a less glorious monument or less deserving of future admiration than the cathedral?"[21] Rhetorical questions do not need answers.

This touch of self-sacrifice suffused agnosticism with a pious glow, left belief slightly sordid by comparison. "We do not expect to accomplish everything in our day; but we want," said Ingersoll, "to render all the service possible in the holy cause of human progress." No hoggish rooting after personal immortality for agnostics; their "grand philosophy" taught them, as Elizabeth Cady Stanton put it, "to lose sight of ourselves and our burdens in the onward march of the race." Unbelievers kept an almost proprietary grip on that grand Victorian ideal of self-effacing duty. George Eliot once suggested, as the mark of a more advanced religion, that it would abandon beliefs that appealed to human egotism: it was no coincidence that she was an agnostic. She had gone through the same experience that led an American agnostic to insist that "the moment that one loses confidence in God, or immortality in the universe," one becomes "more self-reliant, more courageous, and the more solicitous to aid where only human aid is possible."[22]

Yet the upbeat note plays false to the feelings of a great many agnostics. Stolid determination and gritted teeth, fading into stoicism as the years rolled on, describe better the outlook of Norton or Harrison. Yet even for these, the real sceptics—perhaps especially for them—the hope of helping generations to come was their spring in a desert land. At most times William James was the least grim of men; but in the late 1860s he slipped into a disabling depression, where he found all confidence in his own will and all faith in God slipping away from him. In the hour of darkness, the "rock" on which "I find myself washed up when the waves of doubt are weltering over all the rest of the world" proved to be his ability to lend posterity a helping hand.

> And if we have to give up all hope of seeing into the purposes of God, or to give up theoretically the idea of final causes, and of God anyhow as vain and leading to nothing for us, we can, by our will, make the enjoyment of our brothers stand us in stead of a final cause; and through a knowledge of the fact that that enjoyment on the whole depends on what individuals accomplish,

> lead a life so active, and so sustained by a clean conscience as not to need to fret much.

It did not matter much how an individual "add[ed] to the welfare of the race."

> You may delight its senses or "taste" by some production of luxury or art, comfort it by discovering some moral truth, relieve its pain by concocting a new patent medicine, save its labor by a bit of machinery, or by some new application of a natural product. You may open a road, help start some social or business institution, contribute your mite in *any* way to the mass of the work which each generation subtracts from the task of the next; and you will come into *real* relations with your brothers—with some of them at least.[23]

James in 1868, others permanently in his condition, did not merely tout progress as a far, far better thing than godly morality; they needed it to keep them afloat. When God fell silent, this cautious, clipped breed of progress—this frail helping hand across the generations—gave them their only answer to the existential question. Nothing else kept them from the edge of the void. Whether they would otherwise have found the courage to stare into emptiness is an open question.

John Stuart Mill, who stood somewhere between the grim and the gay, may have captured most feelingly the moral meaning of progress for all agnostics:

> A battle is constantly going on, in which the humblest human creature is not incapable of taking some part, between the powers of good and those of evil, and in which every even the smallest help to the right side has its value in promoting the very slow and often almost insensible progress by which good is gradually gaining ground from evil, yet gaining it so visibly at considerable intervals as to promise the very distant but not uncertain final victory of Good. To do something during life, on even the humblest scale if nothing more is within reach, towards bringing this consummation ever so little nearer, is the most animating and invigorating thought which can inspire a human creature.

That this high act of faith was destined, concluded Mill, "to be the religion of the Future I cannot entertain a doubt."[24] Unbelievers sometimes betrayed irritation with churchmen who, they felt, lacked their own moral engagement and seriousness. They perhaps had some right to impatience.

Truth, Progress, the whole panoply of godless morality did not spring full-blown from the brow of Ingersoll. The intertwined branches, truth and progress, spread from the central trunk of nineteenth-century American culture. These derivations, sketched earlier, need little attention here. But both the substance and the emotional power of the unbelievers' morality become clearer when one traces more carefully one line of its genealogy.

The new morality looked into the mirror of science and saw its clearest reflection. Agnostic writings brim with praise of not just the intellectual achievements but the moral content of science. Science, in the persons of Charles Darwin and Herbert Spencer, had, after all, revealed that progress was the law of life and of the cosmos. "The future happiness of our race, which poets had hardly ventured to hope for, science boldly predicts." Progress became, in Sir John Lubbock's perhaps slightly overheated imagination, not simply a consummation devoutly to be wished, but "the necessary consequence of natural laws."[25]

More to the point, science seemed the main engine powering progress. The Chinese, having no science, had no progress—or so believed the distinguished physicist Henry Rowland. In part, science caused progress because of "the great mechanical and material inventions" that it generated. But, more profoundly, it was the method of science that produced advance. What Robert Ingersoll called "the Holy Trinity of Science"—"Reason, Observation, and Experience"—pointed individuals toward human happiness as the only good and gave them the tools to construct it. "Science is in its nature progressive," wrote the polemical chemist John William Draper, and he only echoed an apparent truism.[26] The approach of science—building on a constantly cumulating store of knowledge, ever testing, refining, and extending, leaving errors and refuted hypotheses permanently behind—embodied steady and irreversible progress.

Science's method achieved moral as well as material progress. Some such conviction drifted through even Charles Norton's distinctly literary mind when he attributed the profusion of "moral barbarians" in the United States to "the unsettled condition of the science of social morals among us." Chauncey Wright asserted that a stiff dose of science could cure the ills of America's festering cities.[27] Practitioners of social science in our own century have, at least until recently, labored to squeeze their work dry of moral intent. But Victorians created the whole enterprise as a consciously ethical assault on social problems; they aimed to unleash science on obstacles to moral improvement, and "social scientists" roosted in settlement houses as comfortably as in universities.

Science spoke just as influentially for truth. Not only agnostics like Norton valued Darwin's honesty and plain speaking. A liberal Christian like Lyman Abbott found "a fairness of statement in Darwin, an eagerness for truth in Huxley" that seemed "sometimes conspicuously absent from the writings of the churchmen." This was not coincidental. Sniffing out truth was the business of scientists; nothing, in theory, mattered more to them. Only the scientific mind, Henry Rowland said, "values the truth as it should be valued and ignores all personal feeling in its pursuit."[28] The distance between reality and Rowland's ideal should not obscure its great appeal.

For the scientific approach to the world did (and does) place a high premium on the pursuit of truth; its techniques, however fallible in application, stress the weeding out of error. "Love of truth," as one writer put it in 1873, "lies at the very foundation of all scientific methods." Science, its votaries claimed, could sweep out errors that religion had never even recognized precisely because science had more respect for truth: it utterly repudiated all preconceived restrictions on thought, submitted every theory to the test of observed fact. The agnostic British scientist John Tyndall, the black beast of orthodox American clergy, infuriatingly claimed that science was purifying religion by freeing it from error.[29]

Yet it is not clear that science in any fundamental sense produced this secularized morality. The question defies precise answer. One can safely say that science gave many agnostics a tangible standard that helped them to sort out their own moral thinking. But it seems equally likely that science itself benefited from its apparent congruence with this secular moral ideal, its popularity owing something to the fact that it neatly encapsulated certain moral views originating and becoming widely influential outside of science. The vogue of science may have owed more to these new moral values than the new morality did to science.

Certainly not every agnostic worshipped science. Charles Norton believed that the "progress of science" had left Protestantism "vacant of spiritual significance" and genuinely admired the moral qualities inherent in scientific method. Yet he also thought that science offered no moral panacea, had "obviously nothing but a stone to offer to the ignorant and dependent masses." His later career at Harvard involved considerable muttering against the encroachments of purportedly scientific scholarship on the humanities. Jonathan Harrison felt a deeper suspicion. He detected "a gladiatorial jauntiness & unseriousness, & a fatal narrowness of thought in Spencer, Huxley, Darwin, Tyndall & all their coadjutors, when dealing with religion and social morality." Harrison traced this fault to the severance of science from faith in a moral cosmos. Fundamentally, he argued, "modern science" had no answer to a man who said simply that he chose to believe, not in "decency, self-restraint, culture, justice," but in their opposites. Science might exhibit some admirable moral qualities, but it provided no foundation for morality.[30] At times science even appeared to undermine moral agency, as in the determinism propagated by the notorious German mechanistic materialists.

Harrison and Norton were not antiscience; they simply recognized its moral limits—and so did many other agnostics. Even Robert Ingersoll, who was a science-worshipper, seemed to feel that the poet, not the scientist, would displace the priest in the better world a-coming. And, contrary to the fevered nightmares of some conservative churchmen, John Tyndall himself made "no exclusive claim" for science, indeed, exhorted hearers of his scandalously agnostic 1874 address to the British Association for the Advancement of Science not "to erect it into an idol." Science, he freely admitted, could never satisfy the "unquenchable claims" of man's "moral and emotional nature." Small wonder, then, that someone like Norton insisted that "it is the poets who help us most" in achieving moral progress. More tellingly, perhaps, a close look at any of the whirling dervishes of scientism (say, John William Draper) reveals an astonishingly loose conception of science; its very flaccidity and all-encompassing sweep arouse the suspicion that their vision of "science" as moral savior did not arise entirely from science.[31]

"Scientific" morality seems in truth less a creation of science than a secularization of religion. Science, in effect, received the moral and emotional mantle passed on from religion. An undergraduate orator at the University of Wisconsin in 1885 sounded exactly like Lyman Beecher, retuned in an agnostic key. "Social Science is the Healer, the life-thrilled Messianic Healer of the human race. It is the herald on the misty mountaintop, proclaiming, through all this burdened earth, that THE KINGDOM OF MAN IS AT HAND."[32]

The religious ancestry of "scientific" morality shows through in the ease with which committed Christians fell under its spell, as suggested earlier in the case of the sanitary reformer John Griscom. The anthropologist Lewis Henry Morgan, a devout Presbyterian, sketched in *Ancient Society* (1877) a vast panorama of human progress, all of which he traced to "the slow accumulation of experimental knowledge": in other words, science. Morgan attributed progress ultimately to "the plan of the Supreme Intelligence." But the sole reference to the Supreme Intelligence occurred on the last page of more than 550.[33] It was not a very large step to omit the Supreme Intelligence altogether from moral progress, as Henry Clarke Wright more or less had done and Jonathan Harrison did definitively. Reforms intensely religious, often specifically Evangelical, in origin thus gradually metamorphosed into utterly secular scientific efforts for improvement. Sanitary reform never lost its moralism, but it ended by fighting germs instead of sin. Such entirely worldly morality, legitimated more or less by science, was perfectly compatible with belief in God. But it could also—and for most agnostics did—stand alone as the finest exemplar of truth and progress.

The agnostics' linking of morality with science reveals a good deal about their values and moral priorities, and it makes clearer why their secular moralism broadcast so much glitter and excitement. But, in the end, the apotheosis of truth and progress owed more to churches than laboratories.

No wonder, then, that agnosticism seemed far superior to morality based on God. Agnostics could feel that they had put behind them all the rot and perverseness of the churches, yet, while sloughing the dross, had preserved the gold. Scepticism, as a *North American Review* writer asserted in 1877, purified and fortified thought, for it forced abandonment of weak and unworthy beliefs; indeed, there was virtually a chorus of agnostics chanting that they were "purifying" belief.[34]

For unbelief appealed as almost painfully upright. Agnostics displayed no crabbed narrowness of spirit, as among the orthodox, but a spirit of exploration, a fresh openness to the human adventure. Nor could agnostics be accused of deceiving themselves with sweet illusions, as could believers. Having nothing to gain except opprobrium and everything to lose including the prospect of heaven, agnostics could—and commonly did—feel themselves as actors in the heroic mode.

Agnosticism became, in Samuel Putnam's view, "the grandest sacrifice to truth that is possible for humanity to make. It is not merely an intellectual conviction, it is a moral power." In a celebrated lament, W. K. Clifford reminded religionists of the agonies that agnostics endured: "We have seen the spring sun shine out of an empty heaven, to light up a soulless earth; we have felt with utter loneliness that the Great Companion is dead."[35] Doubtless Clifford (and other agnostics who rang changes on his theme) genuinely suffered. But the suspicion will not down that he took a certain pride in displaying his wounds: bloody proof that agnostics did not simper and, by inference, that believers did.

In this posture appeared the crucial achievement that made agnosticism possible. To Chauncey Wright, not merely "the evidence" but "discipline of character" demanded agnosticism. It impressed Samuel Putnam as "the last and best conviction of the human mind"; and Norton seconded that opinion, regarding the putting aside of religious faith as "a step from childishness toward maturity." Putnam recalled that he felt "a vast relief" when he cut his last ties to God and "breathed the joy of recovered liberty and virtue." But perhaps Charles Norton, looking back in old age, summed up most universally, in his quiet way, the sentiments that gave agnosticism its appeal: "One may sigh for all that one loses in giving up the old religion, as one sighs for the disappearance of any romantic sentiment that once held possession of the heart. But the new irreligion is the manlier, honester & simpler thing, and affords a better theory of life and a more solid basis for morality." Unbelievers did not endanger morality in embracing agnosticism, for it "appeal[ed] directly to the highest qualities of [human] nature."[36] The moral risk lay with belief.

From Christianity to Agnosticism

Revisiting after a century battlefields where the dead now rest in peace, one sees what the haze of gunsmoke and rattle of artillery then obscured. It was a civil war. Agnostics did not repudiate the churches' morality; they inherited it. They did not stray from the paths of righteousness posted by antebellum preachers; they followed them religiously.

To be sure, not every jot and tittle of the agnostics' law came from the tablets handed down by Lyman Beecher. Few ministers, for example, laid as strong a stress on truth as unbelievers did. The cult of truth probably grew more from science than religion—and from those deeper social changes discussed earlier, at work underground like Marx's old mole. Yet science did not grow up divorced from religion. Preachers, hungry for the millennium, joined in, even led, the cheering for science. It really comes as no surprise to find a conservative Protestant in the 1840s chiding the superstitious who set their faces against science, polishing up the tale of Galileo, martyr for science.[37] Nor should one forget another fact: truth became sacred in tandem with the ideal of progress.

And progress lay close to the churchman's heart. The enthusiasms of antebellum millennialists do not need to be rehearsed again; no more do the less apocalyptic versions of progress celebrated by non-Evangelical preachers. Church leaders invested God's moral purposes quite specifically in the progressive development of the human race. They saw no heresy in this, for they believed history itself to display the hand of God, guiding human destiny indirectly through secondary causes. Critics who wondered how anyone could see so clearly what God had in mind got short shrift.

The guardians of belief thus paved the road to unbelief. Few ministers, of course, drifted anything like as far as his "firm belief in progress" carried Orestes Brownson: "I recognized God, but only in man, and I held that he exists for us only in human nature."[38] Other elements of their creed, and the weight of tradition, held the clergy back. But their teachings about progress, their interpretation of it in humanitarian terms, gravitated in Brownson's direction. The secularizing of history, completed in the picture of human evolution that took shape after mid-century, allowed agnostics to move past even Brownson. Yet they gained the courage to stare into an empty cosmos largely by clinging like grim death to the moral vision of humanitarian progress drilled into them by their catechists.

The churches' faith in progress, however, only capped a longer and larger trend. For generations now, a growing number of ministers and theologians had understood the need to get right with modernity. The most influential had courted modernity by playing down the antique teaching that God transcended human grasp and human purposes, that His ways were not man's. They had talked instead of God's congruence with the business of this world. They had spoken mostly of morality rather than spirituality, of religion's uses in the palpable human world rather than its difficult and tenuous straining toward some purported other realm. They had intimated—some almost said it right out—that God really mattered to human beings because He underwrote and rewarded morality. With this strategy church leaders kept religion in tune with the secular world, but sometimes at the price of allowing this world to call the tune for God.

This did not always happen, by any means. Moralistic, worldly belief did not necessarily end in total secularization, much less unbelief. To cite but one example, the first generation of American agricultural chemists, who came of age with the initial cohort of agnostics, melded faith in Christianity and scientific progress in an intense and unified sense of vocation. Indeed, some Christians found in moral activism refuge from storms of doubt, escape from their crises of faith. One writer in 1877 plausibly claimed that "the growing development within the church of that conception of religion in which character is central and supreme" was successfully warding off the danger to belief from "free thought."[39]

The Social Gospel, in its several varieties, offered a particularly inviting escape route. To say so is not to make light of the moral sensitivity and deep concern about injustice that inspired the Social Gospel, that drove ministers and laypeople to make of the church above all an instrument of social reform. Yet, as William Hutchison has shrewdly observed, many troubled church leaders did snatch the tenets of social Christianity "as fragments to be shored against the ruins of traditional faith."[40]

Deeds and words bear him out. The jurist and reformer Ernest H. Crosby embraced social religion amid a personal crisis of belief. As Frederick Law Olmsted was sliding into agnosticism, his closest friend, the Reverend Charles Loring Brace, turned away from shaky doctrines and threw himself into social work among the street urchins of New York. In such social salvation he found the essence of Christianity—a discovery elaborated through nineteen centuries in his *Gesta Christi,* a chronicle of Christianity's contributions to human welfare and a counterblast to sceptics who decried the church as perpetual enemy of progress. The theologian Theodore Munger made explicit the connection between the falling stock of belief and rising fortunes of social religion. By reconceiving "spiritual processes" in moral rather than "magical" terms, theology, he hoped, might dissolve the antagonism between faith and science. The fiery Catholic priest Edward McGlynn prescribed social activism as a specific against the likes of Ingersoll.[41]

Yet, if a religion devoted to human betterment could steer one person away from the shoals of unbelief, it could guide another right onto them. The economist Henry Carter Adams, son of a leading Iowa minister, gradually discovered that his vocation as social reformer provided a satisfying substitute for his father's God; and God slowly faded from his calculations. If God mattered chiefly as a moral force, and if a better moral alternative existed, why cling anachronistically to an intellectually implausible and morally unpalatable Deity? Carrying one giant step further the leanings of many ministers, agnostics identified religion wholly with the moral aspirations of man. From that standpoint they easily fell into thinking, as George Eliot did, that "the idea of God, so far as it has been a high spiritual influence, is the ideal of a goodness entirely human."[42] In fact, agnostics had come to believe that a goodness entirely human provided a *higher* spiritual influence than any idea of God.

More than a little irony lurked here. Leaders of the church were surely not wrong to insist that belief had to express itself in practice, that faith and morality were linked, that any God worth credence had to provide some grounding for human moral striving. But they had neglected tensions in their own ancient traditions between God's will and human purposes, between a transcendent ungraspable Deity and human effort to decipher divine intentions—or, to translate from the theological idiom, between a cosmos meaningless so far as we can see and our endless need to construct meaning. Theologians had made their God too much a mirror of man—and risked making man an adequate substitute.

"I grow more and more contented," concluded Charles Norton, "to accept the fixed limitations of human nature, and find room enough for the highest and longest flights of human wings within the vast spaces legitimately open to man." Agnostics were without God; but they were not, stressed Professor J. E. Oliver of Cornell, without religion.

> We have or may have a religion of unselfish devotion to others and to our own highest ideals; a religion of character, of abiding enthusiasm for humanity, and of complete intellectual honesty. Into our little human lives it will bring something of the grandeur of these infinite surroundings, a high purpose amid which and for which we live.[43]

"The grandeur of these infinite surroundings"—Oliver sounded here a telling note. For, morality secured, a sense of reverence remained the one thing needful. Agnostics only had to find something to worship, and they could obliterate the last vestigial trace of God.

9

Sanctity without Godliness

Although Victorian moralism dulls awareness of the axiom, religion involves more than ethics. True, many nineteenth-century Christians valued God mostly as creator and caretaker of the moral law. It was this work by which, so to speak, God was to be judged. But not even the most single-minded Evangelical moralist, not even the Francis Wayland who called morality the "only business" of religion, really succeeded, or wished to succeed, in atomizing the remains of a fuller, many-sided religion. Even Wayland wanted, needed, more from belief than a code of laws.

For, questions of ultimate truth aside, belief satisfies deep psychic needs. When loss brings grief, belief in God consoles; "God shall wipe away all tears from their eyes." When alien and uncontrollable forces shatter life, God assuages fear, quells terrifying chaos; for He is supposed to understand mysteries that we do not. When uncertainty and insecurity overwhelm, belief in God is a compass that orients a person in a larger reality, that gives some sense of one's location and role in the universe. Perhaps most universally, God offers a sacred center on which to release feelings of awe, dependency, exaltation, and reverence springing from the deepest wells of the mind. Amid the babel of beliefs about Deity, these emotions flow on like the eternal Mississippi; and God was the name of the ocean into which they drained.

Not even the most exalted morality could completely replace Him. No substitute could offer the ultimacy of God's reassurance, the absoluteness of a divine object of reverence. But agnostics had to find a replacement that met enough of these primal needs to satisfy spiritual hunger. Without it, agnosticism withered into an impossibly cramped and shriveled emotional dead end; with it, unbelief became fully tenable. Most unbelievers recognized this need. But they utterly divorced religious feelings from any association with that mythological figure on whom more "primitive" folk than themselves trained them. A vital part of subjective emotional life, true religion did not depend on the putative existence of a Deity, indeed had nothing to do with objective reality and rational understanding. "Faith and reason are in conflict only among the theologians," wrote Charles Norton. "There is nothing irrational, as there is nothing strictly rational, in a sentiment or emotion."[1] So these impulses, once directed toward the idea of God, were now played on other, nontheistic objects.

In fact, agnostics discovered a variety of springs of reassurance and objects to revere. Science, art, and nature each provided consolation, comfort, and a kind of holiness. Personal background or mental bent inclined some unbelievers to lean toward one, others toward another. But these ideals were not jealous gods, indeed mixed fairly easily; and agnostics drew satisfaction promiscuously from whichever one or ones offered most help in given circumstances.

Unbelievers did not thereby renege on their unbelief. Superficially, agnostics may appear only to have switched God for secular ideals in a kind of theological shell game, merely to have transferred allegiance to new gods. This facile view belittles both believers and unbelievers. A literally infinite gap separates God from any humanly created ideal. Admittedly, the worldly concern of Victorian religion can gull one into missing this rather basic fact, but agnostics did not miss it. They knew, even took a grim satisfaction in knowing, that they had given up, in their conception of both cosmos and personal destiny, the ultimacy that only a God can provide. Unbelievers did not devise a new god. They found a way of living without God.

Science

In the zeal of the true moralist, morality somehow adds up to more than morals. This certainly held true of the secular moral ideal of Truth and Progress with which agnostics displaced divine morality. To kneel before truth in humble reverence, to lose oneself in grander strivings of the race, to find solace in the better world arising for future generations—these emotions transformed a moral code into a posture toward the universe, turned it into something very like a religion. Agnostics themselves spoke of the moral and intellectual betterment of mankind as a "religious faith," a faith "more worthy of admiration" than any directed toward God. The "altar of superstition," Robert Ingersoll cried, must fall before "the grand tranquil Column of Reason." The Jewish agnostic Felix Adler in 1876 actually refurbished the religious temple as a secular church: the Society for Ethical Culture.[2] Most unbelievers, though, warmed to no sort of ecclesiasticism, sought their spiritual satisfactions elsewhere.

Since truth and progress hovered usually in the vicinity of science, science radiated their mana with special intensity. Science had the extra charm of starring in the great costume drama of agnostic theatricals: the Warfare of Science and Religion. It appealed, therefore, as a kind of antichurch, the perfect religion for the irreligious. By no accident did both friends and foes of science fall into the habit of likening scientists to priests, science itself to a church or temple. By no means every agnostic blindly worshipped science. Not only a litterateur like Charles Norton but even an ideologue of science like Thomas Huxley retained healthy cynicism about the nobility of flesh-and-blood scientists. Nevertheless, most unbelievers looked up to science as embodying, to a greater or lesser degree, their most revered ideals.

Science seemed "worthy of all reverence"—a truism Herbert Spencer thought obvious to any but "the most perverted intellect." Charles Peirce called the ethos of science—its devotion to the discovery of truth—essentially religious. John Dewey, who both elaborated Peirce's pragmatism and perfected his agnosticism, claimed that linkage of science with moral development had conferred upon science "the religious value once attaching to dogma."[3] Even for those slightly perverted intellects to whom the study of nature seemed worthy of only *some* reverence, science often helped to fill the emotional vacancy where God used to dwell.

Holiness implies saints, and the cult of science bred them in job lots. What Hugh Honour calls "the sanctification of genius" in the nineteenth century encouraged writers to canonize secular clones of Christian holy men. There were the Desert Fathers, Roger Bacon and Copernicus, toiling alone in the barrens of medieval superstition; the founders of scientific monasticism, Francis Bacon and John Locke, laying down the rules of investigation and knowledge; the great Evangelists, Newton and Darwin, transcribing the gospel of nature; and above all the roll of the martyrs: the Alexandrian scholars scattered by the Church, Giordano Bruno at the stake, Galileo before the Inquisition, Joseph Priestley hounded from England. When John William Draper intoned this secular "Faith of Our Fathers" in 1874, one of his critics spied exactly what he was up to: "What a glorious army of martyrs this Church of the Scientists is!"[4] Here were paragons of holiness a free mind could venerate, a communion of saints unbelievers could aspire to enter.

Nor were all the saints scientists, and this fact is crucial. The sixteenth-century unitarian heretic Michael Servetus went to the stake in freethinkers' hagiography almost as often as his near contemporary, the "scientist" Giordano Bruno.[5] Ingersoll set up the politico-religious radical Thomas Paine next to the scientist Alexander von Humboldt in the pantheon of "intellectual heroes" to which he called his audiences to worship; for Paine, too, had helped to transform the "gloomy caverns of superstition" into the "temples of thought."[6] Neither Ingersoll nor any other agnostic sharply distinguished men of science from other benefactors of humanity. Unbelievers revered science not as sacred in itself but as the purest distillation of truth and progress, and they likewise venerated its saints as selfless seekers of the holy grail of human betterment.

For the real deity behind the veil was humanity itself, conceived in its collective development. There were not many Americans baptized in Auguste Comte's Religion of Humanity. (There were some, the journalist David Croly being the nearest thing to an American vicar of Comte's church.) But, like Comte's Positivist religion, the faith of many unbelievers set Humanity on the altar in place of God. When progress became a purely human millennialism, reverence for progress was no longer worship of God but veneration of humanity. And precisely because antebellum believers had so often worshipped their God incarnated in man's efforts and aspirations, it was easier for postwar unbelievers simply to revere man. Francis E. Abbot extended rather than extirpated his Protestant heritage when in 1871 he called his Free Religion "organized Faith in Man." But it was a considerable extension: ultimate meaning resided in the destiny of the human race, not in anything transcending it. "My doctrine," said Ingersoll, "is this: All true religion is embraced in the word Humanity."[7]

Art

Almost all unbelievers admired science, but not all equally. Science could seem a high and essentially spiritual pursuit; it could also seem, despite devotion to truth and progress, obsessed with material truth and corporeal progress. If science drew the human spirit down toward matter—by no means generally conceded—then some other power must lift man toward the ideal. Otherwise science made a shabby religion, the collective advance of humanity dwindling into a tinker's faith of better pots and pans. Even enthusiasts of science, perhaps not insensitive to the danger, felt the need for at least some complementary inspiriting force.

Ars longa, vita brevis. For some agnostics, art became this elevating force. Or, one should say, Art. Art required the initial capital, for it soared over the crass, petty, transient, lowercase affairs of daily life like the eternal purifying Dove. Art was not Walt Whitman or (inconceivably) Zola, but Dante and Raphael. The best painting, poetry, and music drew out the best in human beings: ennobled their struggles, uttered their most sacred feelings, distilled their finest aspirations out of the muck of mundane life. Immersed in art, one lost sight of the minuteness of individual limits in the lasting grandeur of the race. Reverencing art, one revered the spiritual in humankind.

Agnostics had no monopoly on these sentiments. Something very like a Religion of Culture flourished in the latter part of the century among the upper and middle classes on both sides of the Atlantic, without much regard to traditional religious beliefs. Art museums and concert halls became, in the then-current phrase, temples of culture. Orthodox priests of this cultus (most notably Matthew Arnold in England and Charles Eliot Norton in America) preached art as a means of moral as well as spiritual grace, anathematized any art vacant of moral intent. A heretical minority (identified especially with the Oxford critic Walter Pater, to some extent in retrospect with Henry Adams, and gathering strength in the fin de siècle) inclined toward a purer aestheticism. In both strains of the art cult, a certain ambiguity, perhaps not always unintended, often left unclear whether "spiritual" implied supernatural. In any case, the acolytes of art, whether Christians or Jews, theists or agnostics, revered art as spirit enfleshed.

Agnostics were most reverent of all. Lacking the Holy Spirit, they needed all the more the human spirit, idealized in art. It was more than coincidence that the most-attended American apostle of the gospel of art—Norton—was an agnostic. So was Adams, author of *Mont-Saint-Michel and Chartres*, its most exquisite American product. Nor was it chance that both men found their artistic ideals in the Middle Ages. For in that Age of Faith, in Mont-Saint-Michel, in Chartres, in Dante's *Divine Comedy*, art seemed precisely the expression of religion, religion the intimate companion of art. Henry Adams lost faith in God, but he could still pray to the Virgin of Chartres. When God faded, religion literally turned into "a form of art" for Norton's student Bernard Berenson: "Taken as objective reality it is the art of the unaesthetic; but taken consciously as subjective it is perhaps the highest form of beauty."[8] Unbelievers, needing religion, transformed it into art, metamorphosed art by the same prestidigitation into religion.

As avatar of human spiritual values, art ascended the throne abdicated by God. An ideal worthy of reverence, it gave consolation in sorrow, hope in dark times, strength in adversity. For Henry Adams or Charles Eliot Norton, the sanctuary lamp had long since flickered and died in Chartres and San Marco; but venerating the cathedrals themselves remained truly meet and just, right and helpful unto salvation. Only man had replaced God as the savior.

Oddly, God's official agents had helped to arrange for His displacement. Linkage of art and spirit sprang from a very old tradition (lately spruced up in Romantic literature); church leaders had recently drawn this connection in a specifically religious context. The tendency had always lurked in the cult of the heart, so prominent in Victorian religion, especially its Evangelical variety. Toward mid-century, possibility became actuality. In a few cases, it was serious grappling with deep paradoxes of belief that pulled religion and art together. Trying to drive home the lesson that words could never describe a God Who transcended human understanding, Horace Bushnell drew analogies between theology and poetry. But Bushnell's drift toward mysticism was exceptional in the nineteenth century, particularly among more or less orthodox Christians.

Far more common—and more influential in shaping prevailing conceptions of religion—was the facile identification of art and spirituality in a preacher like Henry Ward Beecher. Beecher wanted to make his hearers more, not less, certain about their grasp of God. He wanted to solidify Deity as scientific evidence of God grew shakier. His rhapsodies about poetry aimed to convince congregations, not that God whispered in mysterious voices, but that He announced Himself loud and clear every time they sighed over a page of Tennyson. In such sermons, analogies with art became a way of pulling God out of transcendence and pushing Him more fully into the human sphere. And, to the listener, poetry did not sound so very different from religion.

Yet, while it is easy to detect Christian origins of agnostic reverence for art, it is not so easy to judge how much this faith signified for American agnostics. For a few—Adams, Berenson, possibly Norton—human artistic effort, broadly understood, became the primary source of consolation, the chief object of reverence. Toward the century's end its appeal apparently increased. But the religion of art probably never provided the major theme for very many unbelievers. It sounded, rather, as a recurring secondary motif, a counterpoint to the human glories of science and the awesome music of nature.

Nature

In *The Varieties of Religious Experience* (1902), William James wrote of "a new sort of religion of Nature, which has entirely displaced Christianity from the thought of a large part of our generation." James had in mind specifically veneration of evolution, but he could as well have been referring to a number of reverent approaches to nature. He went on to note that it was scientists and amateurs of science who cultivated most fervently the habit of bowing down before nature. Scratch a Victorian science-worshipper, and underneath was often a man genuflecting to nature. When Herbert Spencer declared science "worthy of all reverence," he did not mean by science what scientists *did* so much as what their work *revealed*. And he used the word "revelation" in deliberate analogy to Christian revelation. A veritably religious "duty" obliged man to "receive with all humility" the "established order of the Universe"—to fall on his knees before nature.[9]

Nature shows many faces; agnostics really worshipped two: its beauty and its power. In revering natural beauty, they followed in the ancient footsteps of Christian nature mystics. These men and women had found union with Deity in intensely aesthetic communion with nature: nature's loveliness ravished Jonathan Edwards's soul and left him weak with love for God, a species of exaltation that echoed back through the centuries. Usually much attenuated, this association of natural beauty with spiritual experience partly underlay the nineteenth-century romantic attitude toward nature. The pioneering landscape architect Frederick Law Olmsted thought of his naturalistic parks as wells from which people would draw moral vigor and spiritual refreshment. Olmsted was an agnostic, but the point is that one did not need to be to adopt his posture.

For a highway ran from Christian nature mysticism through vaguely theistic romanticism to out-and-out unbelief, and reverence for nature carried the traveler the whole way. Young Bernard Berenson probably had in mind this kind of aesthetic-religious experience when in 1884 he lumped together agnosticism and pantheism. The poet Richard Henry Stoddard lived on the same border between pantheism and agnosticism. He never made up his mind whether he believed in the wispiest of deities or none at all, but the distinction hardly mattered, since he trained his religious feelings on the beauty of nature without much regard to whatever lay behind it.[10]

Yet, *pace* their debts to mysticism, agnostic nature worshippers were not, properly speaking, mystics at all. Although sensitive to the mystery in nature, although seekers of "spiritual" exaltation in its beauties, they did not look for a deeper reality there, for any supernatural truth cloaked in natural splendor. They sought their psychic gratifications wholly within the boundaries of nature; they revered beauty, not God's beauty.

This aesthetic worship seldom by itself fully satisfied; and its thinness did not simply result from the stumbling block that Darwin had placed to finding loveliness in this nasty world. Natural beauty was evanescent, insubstantial, and all too obviously an individual's imposition on nature rather than nature's own meaning. It lacked crucial elements of continuity, externality, and power. Unlike God, it did not stand perpetually above man and command his obedience, so it could hardly fill the void left by His departure. The beauty of nature, rather, typically added a thrill of delight to a religious sensibility stoked mostly with other fuel.

The awful power of nature, the inexorable workings of its law, could pound reverence into almost any heart. Here, too, agnostics followed in the well-worn path of Christian mystics and Romantic poets. And it was under this grim aspect that nature most often won veneration from unbelievers—even became, in an odd way, a source of consolation. The terrible authority once attributed to Jehovah unbelievers now lodged in nature itself. At the climax of his novel *Esther*, Henry Adams brought his heroine face to face with Niagara Falls, "the huge church which was thundering its gospel under her eyes." All the religious doubts and personal troubles with which Esther was then wrestling appeared in the waterfall's roar "an impertinence." "When eternity, infinity and omnipotence seem to be laughing and dancing in one's face, it is well to treat such visitors civilly, for they come rarely in such a humour."[11]

Like Adams (at least in this mood), many agnostics transferred religious sensibilities from God to the eternal omnipotence of nature. Herbert Spencer revered what he called the Unknowable: the unsearchable power behind the laws of nature. His American disciple John Fiske proceeded to deck the Unknowable out as God; others (including Spencer himself) refused to make that leap of faith, yet did not cease playing their emotions on ineffable *Kraft*. Other unbelievers, though, sought a more definable power to worship; and they treated the laws of nature as, in William James's phrase, "objective facts to be revered."[12]

It may seem passing strange that devout Darwinians could find bloody nature a fit object of reverence. Who would worship chaos and cruelty? This paradox dissolves when one realizes that agnostics had in this case severed the link between majesty and morality. They no longer expected, as believers did, to find goodness and power in the same Being. Indeed, agnostic reverence for amoral nature puzzles in the first place only if one assumes that unbelievers were actually looking for a new god. They were not; they really were unbelievers. They fell down in awe before nature; they did not, most of them, draw their ethics from it. Nature inspired humility, not morality. Indeed, in his Romanes Lectures on evolution and ethics, Huxley insisted that nature was the last source from which we ought to imbibe our ethics.

Yet the same Huxley preached an attitude of humble submission to nature, a posture irrelevant to the moral issue. This stance toward the universe had nothing to do with Huxley's science (if that be understood as objective study of nature, as Huxley thought); it had everything to do with his religion. That neither Huxley nor anyone else could elude the dictates of nature was simply a matter of fact. That Huxley should warm to this constraint manifested a basically religious urge. Agnostics like Huxley sought in Stoic acceptance of nature the same emotional gratification that believers found in submission to Deity. And, like the Stoics, they thus transformed everyman's fate into a religious stance toward the cosmos.[13]

They fully recognized this posture as religious. Their reverence for nature expressed a kind of secularized Calvinism: man must not only accept as inevitable the will of the almighty but give glory to nature for damning him. Thomas Huxley had a small son, Noel, in whom he delighted, more, apparently, even than most parents. In 1860 the boy died. To the despondent father his friend Charles Kingsley sent a message intended to console, pressing on him as some comfort the possibility of a future life. In a touching, enormously courageous letter Huxley replied that "if wife and child and name and fame" were all lost in consequence, "still I will not lie," and went on to say: "Science seems to me to teach in the highest and strongest manner the great truth which is embodied in the Christian conception of entire surrender to the will of God. Sit down before fact as a little child, be prepared to give up every preconceived notion, follow humbly wherever and to whatever abysses Nature leads." Another of the great agnostic scientists, John Tyndall, invoked in less desperate circumstances the same Biblical phrase in a letter to Michael Faraday. "I often think," he wrote, "that the qualities which go to constitute a good christian are those essential to a man of science, and that above all things it is necessary to become 'as a little child.' "[14]

In the teeth of inevitable buffetings by nature's omnipotent caprice, submission could bring comfort, even contentment. Huxley evidently found it so. However horrid the wounds nature inflicted, by accepting them with resignation a man rose to his full stature. Humility, as in the Christian parable, turned into triumph: "And the last shall be first." Moreover, reverent submission to nature reminded an unbeliever that he himself belonged to this larger whole. To feel integral to the flow of nature made its vicissitudes less disturbing, less threatening to one's personal weal. Thus it was with Adams's Esther in the crisis of her father's death. She "gently" turned aside the church's offer of consolation, "floating on, with her quiet air of confidence as though she were a part of nature itself, and felt that all nature moved with her."[15] In willing submission to nature came at last the peace that passeth all understanding.

Never, though, did unbelievers bow before nature with unalloyed reverence. Nature's cruelty mocked its beauty; its amorality flouted their own precious moralism; its unconcern for humanity stung their sacred faith in human progress. Man's grandeur blossomed in the hopeless fight against nature. Yet it was the final hopelessness of the contest—and one's conceding this fact—that made the continuing struggle so grand. Victory ended in submission, submission that was victory. Reverence for nature existed in symbiosis with hostility to it. The tension defined the limits of nature worship but did not subdue it, rather raised it to Stoic heroism.

Yet, for all its echoes of Marcus Aurelius, agnostic reverence for nature owed as much to Christian as pagan forebears. As a broad generalization, this assertion amounts almost to a truism: orthodox Christians, like believers in most other religions, had always, one way or another, worshipped God in nature. Hence, for agnostics, once God evaporated, only nature remained. But agnostic nature-worship also sprang specifically from modern Protestant theology. In coming to terms with the world picture of modern science, the most influential theological leaders had tried to integrate religion and science—to defend belief, not by declaring its autonomy, but by insisting that scientific methods led ineluctably to God. This marriage gave life to the quasi-scientific natural theology typified by William Paley's argument from design.

And this natural theology nudged believers toward assuming that nature displayed more or less directly the face of God. In older theologies, divinity at once infused nature, yet remained masked in it. Not in this one; for (conventional pieties aside) the modern relation of God and nature entailed no vivid and forceful mystery. Nature's elaborate interdependency, its reliable cosmic rhythms, showed the clear purposes of the Creator, made public His benevolence, revealed His transparent beauty and power. Of course, natural theologians repeated formulae about God's ultimate incomprehensibility and certainly believed what they said. But the image of nature they projected stood at odds with such ritual invocations. Jonathan Edwards had worshipped a God hidden somewhere behind the images of nature, shadows that revealed an edge of His visage but left Him mostly in darkness; William Paley and his Victorian successors admired a God Who smiled candidly out from the mirror of nature. True, nature and nature's God did not always display, especially by the middle of the nineteenth century, Enlightenment rationality. Put most starkly, Emerson's God, even Henry Ward Beecher's, was hardly Paley's.

Yet, though Emerson and Beecher shook off much of Paley's rationalism, they did not shed his vision of nature mirroring God. The shift from a rational image of nature (and God) toward a romantic one did not break this more fundamental continuity. Even Emerson's mystical Swedenborgian doctrine of correspondences—that every natural reality corresponds to a spiritual reality—was a variety of mysticism that tended to conflate God and nature. In his essay "Fate" in *The Conduct of Life* (1860), Emerson approached even Huxley's doctrine of submission to nature itself, identifying his impersonal God with impersonal natural law. As for Beecher's sort, they clung like limpets to a personal God above nature, yet continued to revere nature as the direct and explicit revelation of His character. Any man who could speak of a hollyhock as a moral and accountable being surely surprised no one when he claimed that we *know* in nature the "feelings, tastes, and thoughts" of God.[16]

In Transcendentalist heresy and Evangelical romanticism as much as in the argument from design, nature came often to stand as an almost adequate representation of God. "Often" and "almost" are important qualifiers here. A still-kicking Calvinist like Charles Hodge seethed at the notion that creation could depict the Creator. Horace Bushnell, on the opposite wing of Evangelical theology, likewise warned against the adequacy of any human conception of God. Even Beecher would never have let slip that nature fully expressed God. Christian theology never expressly identified God and nature; but the point is that natural theology and nature-preaching had implanted within Protestantism an increasingly strong leaning in this direction. Ministers often forgot Calvin's warnings, misunderstood Edwards, ignored Bushnell; natural theologians wanted not just to glorify God in nature but to *see* Him there. By the mid-nineteenth century, a string of signposts plainly marked the road that led away from God toward bare nature.

It was the most obvious thing in the world for agnostics to follow that route. A natural progression, though certainly not an inevitable one, led from the seventeenth-century progenitors of scientific natural theology (men like Boyle and Ray), through Paley, to Emerson and Beecher and thence to Charles Norton, Henry Adams, and Robert Ingersoll. Nature never fully substituted for God, but it did partly fill the void. And this replacement came as a gift from believers to unbelievers.

The Children of This World

With these emotional surrogates for God in place, unbelief became truly viable. A religion of humanity (ritualized in science), a cult of art, the worship of nature provided agnostics the psychic gratifications they had used to seek in God. No neat creedal lines separated these godless denominations; unbelievers were free to worship at all three altars. Most did, distributing their piety as temperament and circumstance inclined them. They found in this way objects of reverence and sources of consolation sufficient to permit them to let go of their Father in heaven.

Already rendered intellectually incredible and morally repugnant, belief in God thus faded in favor of an entirely human morality and a religion of this world. Agnosticism often had a tentative character, befitting the outlook of people who had grown suspicious of cosmic claims, who had learned to live contented with the limits of human knowledge. Tentativeness indeed seemed its great superiority to Chauncey Wright: "Suspension of judgment appears to me to be demanded, therefore, not merely by the evidence, but as a discipline of character,—that faith and moral effort may not waste themselves on idle dreams, but work among the realities of life."[17] However chastened, unbelief had grown sturdy enough to stand on its own feet—and endure. Agnostics, so they believed, had put away childish things. Where once they had seen through a glass darkly, they now thought they saw face to face.

What stands out most vividly, in this last turning of the story as in earlier twists, is the role of believers in nurturing unbelief. To be sure, developments external to religion produced the climate in which unbelief grew. The rise of modern science challenged believers to rethink the intellectual bases of their belief. Social and economic change stripped away much of the insulation that protected belief from corrosion, and it created an environment in which old conceptions of God made less sense, even became repugnant. The topography of unbelief reflected these influences. Unbelievers appeared most often in intellectual locations exposed to science, economic locations shaped by new means of production and distribution, geographic locations unsettled by industrialization and urbanization.[18]

Yet, in the final analysis, these forces only raised new questions; it was religious leaders who gave the answers. If a pedestrian flings himself in front of a moving automobile, one does not usually charge the driver with responsibility for the ensuing smash-up, even though without the car no disaster would have occurred. Responses to external pressures, not the pressures themselves, shaped belief—though no one should underestimate the strains on religion in a world growing modern. Change pushed the guardians of belief into confusing, often painful, dilemmas. Tradition offered no sure answers, yet answers had urgently to be found. In the end, the most influential church leaders tried to protect belief by making peace with modernity, by conceiving God and His purposes in terms as nearly compatible as possible with secular understandings and aims. A minority insisted that a transcendent God must utterly elude human grasp; their case, their God seemed too out of step, too remote. In the extreme case, the modernizers came close to making religion a thing of this world and creating a God in the image and likeness of man.

Such efforts to defend belief by fitting it to man's world did not have to end—usually did not end—in agnosticism. They generated distinctively modern forms of belief, such as the Social Gospel and evolutionary theologies; reaction against them, in our own century, produced a perhaps even more modern resurgence of orthodoxy.

Yet attempts to modernize belief did often leave it exposed to the standards of judgment of a purely human criticism and made God morally and emotionally dispensable. Charles Eliot Norton did not see himself as turning his back on religion, but as building on it, purifying it, going beyond God to a higher faith:

> In the decline of the power of the churches, and in the rejection of their authority, many . . . see a rejection of the authority of religion itself. But this is far from being the case. On the contrary, the increased sense of personal responsibility, which is the direct effect of individual freedom, leads rather to an increase of the religious sentiment. The formal religion of tradition and habit gives place to the vital religion, which is a new growth in each man's soul, and the expression of his sincere devotion to the object which he acknowledges to have absolute claim over the whole of his life.[19]

The natural parents of modern unbelief turn out to have been the guardians of belief. In a mind like Norton's, one comes at last to realize that it was religion, not science or social change, that gave birth to unbelief. Having made God more and more like man—intellectually, morally, emotionally—the shapers of religion made it feasible to abandon God, to believe simply in man.

Epilogue

By the 1880s, unbelief had assumed its present status as a fully available option in American culture. Agnostics by no means lurked under every blackberry bush; only the imaginations of overwrought bishops saw a "flood of infidelity" sweeping "over our land." Yet it was true that many Americans no longer believed in God. Surveying American culture at the end of the eighties, the English observer James Bryce found, not merely in "the cultivated circles" of the metropolises, but even in most of the smaller cities, "a knot of men who profess agnosticism." Except for places in the West and South, "where aggressive scepticism would rouse displeasure and might affect a man's position in society," Americans seemed free "to hold and express any views" of religion that they pleased. Bryce exaggerated the nonchalance with which respectable society treated professed unbelief but hit pretty close to the mark. One Christian writer even lamented in 1884 "the pressure of fashionable reluctance to believe."[1]

The new viability of unbelief did not mean (*pace* some vitriolic infidels) that belief had lived out its allotted career in human evolution and was fast sinking into decrepitude. It was, to the contrary, flourishing in impudent good health. Church membership in the United States grew dramatically between 1860 and 1910, and nothing suggests any diminution of fervor among these multiplying believers.[2] The point is not that unbelief had begun to drive out belief, but that unbelief had become one readily available answer to the question, What about God? Indeed, public conflict surrounding the rise of agnosticism had largely subsided by the late 1880s—one of several indications that unbelief had passed through its initiatory rites and settled in as part of the cultural landscape.[3]

Its position has essentially remained the same, although contemporary unbelief differs in important respects from its late Victorian counterpart. Unbelievers today (and, for that matter, believers) are less likely than their great-grandfathers to assume that progress is linear and universal, that science's standard of knowledge is generally applicable, or that science's effect is uniformly beneficent. Perhaps most notably, unbelief has lost the sense of crusade and commitment that Victorian agnostics infused in it; religion now simply fails to command attention among most unbelievers, except when some antievolutionist or the like prods them awake. Unbelievers have largely stopped asking, even caring about, the question of God. The banner-waving atheism of Madalyn Murray O'Hair imparts the disorienting sensation of being flung back to the age of Ingersoll.

Yet, amid all the differences, a fundamental continuity connects Ingersoll's day with our own. Belief became then for the first time, remains still, *subcultural.* To be sure, opinion surveys invariably show that most Americans believe in God—so the "believing" subculture includes most members of the whole culture. But belief no longer functions as a unifying and defining element of that entire culture; it no longer provides a common heritage that underlies our diverse world views. Religion had already become for Charles Eliot Norton by 1867 "the most private and personal part of the life of every man."[4] The idea that believing in God is a matter of individual choice would have sent Norton's Puritan forebears, even his Unitarian father, spinning in their graves. Yet, ever since Norton's generation, upbringing and experience have led some people to choose belief, others unbelief.[5] The numbers inclining each way matter far less, from the historian's point of view, than the fact that the decision is open.

We are still trying to digest this revolution. Unbelief has transformed the hopes, aspirations, purposes, and behavior of millions of unbelievers. It has affected believers almost as remarkably. Wrangling over prayer in public schools is only one minor eruption, pointing to a major shift of the tectonic plates on which our culture moves. The option of godlessness has dis-integrated our common intellectual life, both in formal disciplines like philosophy, science, and literature and in those informal habits of mind by which we, as a culture, experience and order our world. God used to function as a central explanatory concept. As cause and purpose, the idea of God shaped and unified natural science, morality, social theories, psychology, political thought into one vaguely coherent (though very loosely assembled) approach to understanding humankind and the cosmos. Disagreement, often radical, of course raged in every corner of intellectual life: there is no blinking the fact that Giordano Bruno and the reverend gentlemen of the Inquisition had some irresolvable differences. But at the most fundamental level, God provided the frame of an agreed-upon universe in which to argue. Our web of shared assumptions has not unraveled altogether—without some unity, a culture collapses. But the traditional linchpin is missing; our culture, in this sense, now lacks a center.

For those who have accepted personally the agnostic option, the disappearance of God has meant still more. If divine purpose does not inhere in the cosmos, then human beings must define the meaning of their own brief lives amid a pointless vastness. Hence arises the distinctively modern angst. And, since life without purpose makes it difficult to define the meaning of any human endeavor, this problem has made modern culture, whenever concerned with value rather than fact, restless and volatile. Consider modernism in the arts, experimental almost by definition, incessantly exploring novel styles, seeking new meanings, or rejecting meaning altogether in fantastic nihilisms like Dada. Modernism hardly owes its soul utterly to the Victorian invention of agnosticism, but could modernism exist in a culture confident of divine purpose? The emergence of unbelief has rewired the neural circuits of our society.

So vast a transformation almost demands explanation by some equally tremendous, ineluctable Grand Cause. We rebel at the idea that accidental or inconsequential events, fallen together by happenstance, set the parameters of our lives. Still, again and again, reality kicks our self-esteem. True, some of the preconditions of modern unbelief did rise to world-historic proportions—for example, industrialization, the scientific revolution—but even those, examined closely, dissolve into complex webs of contingency. And others of unbelief's causes never amounted to more than local nineteenth-century disturbances, long since faded from popular memory, kept alive only by assiduous historians. No self-evidently resistless tide of inevitability swept God aside. Rather, a shifting constellation of contingent developments, anything but predestined, flowed together to shape our present state of mind.

Nonetheless, a pattern of sorts does emerge, slowly taking shape over the space of three centuries or more. This configuration makes most sense if cast in terms of the intellectual and emotional functions that belief fulfilled. Roughly speaking, one aspect of God—the Ruler of Nature Who satisfied the desire to understand our surroundings and ourselves—was abstracted into naturalistic scientific explanations. The study of nature yielded no longer evidence of God but simply knowledge of nature. Another side of God—the Moral Governor Who satisfied the need for good order and the longing for a better—was identified with purely human activities and aspirations. Humanitarianism, science, progress could operate without divine sanction. A third dimension of God—the mysterious Lord of Heaven Who struck human beings with awe and humility—was much diminished, as believers shifted the main focus of their concern from God's transcendence of earthly things to His compatibility with humanity, its wants, its aspirations, its ways of understanding. What remained of awe before divine mystery was transformed into reverence for such surrogates as nature, art, and humanity itself. In dialectical interplay, each of these "humanizing" trends fostered the others, and thus naturalistic explanations and ideals slowly came to satisfy cultural and personal needs once met by belief in God.

Yet even this threefold transformation did not drive inexorably to unbelief. Emergence of unbelief depended more specifically on how this larger pattern worked itself out in a few decades after the middle of the nineteenth century. At that time, a crisis in the intellectual credibility of God coincided with a rising moral revulsion from belief to render belief both implausible and unpalatable from a purely human point of view. And, at the same time, a set of wholly secular moral ideals and objects of reverence was taking shape that could stand in for God, even appear superior to what belief had to offer. None of these events makes entire sense in isolation from the others. For example, the precipitous drop in God's credibility resulted in part from tightened moral principles (about truthfulness) that redefined legitimate standards of evidence; those same moral convictions contributed to the secular ideal of Truth and Progress that outshone religious morality; and finally that ideal became itself one of the objects of reverence that displaced God—yet the tightening of those moral principles in the first place owed much to the intellectual (as distinguished from moral) response to science! This complicated network reflects not circularity but dialectical dependency. Every one of these elements in unbelief nurtured and shaped the others, as it in turn drew nutriment and definition from them. Nor could any one of them alone—or indeed all of them working separately—have given birth to unbelief. It was out of their interweavings that modern agnosticism emerged.

In a broader view, this interplay (and its parts) manifested a very deep shift in religious sensibility. So did the larger, longer-term transformation from which it emerged. Thinking about God had moved away from the nonhuman and transcendent, toward the human and worldly. And it is this new posture toward God, this growing worldliness of belief, that crops up more often than anything else when one tries to explain unbelief.

Some of the conditions making for this sea change in sensibility amount almost to historical commonplaces. Secularization, the spread of capitalism, the influence of modern science, industrialization—such developments play a shaping role in almost every broad historical explanation of religious change in the modern era, as they do in this book. But these supporting actors too often usurp center stage. Their role needs clearer definition. Although such pressures forced believers to confront certain choices, even tempted them to choose some paths and not others, ultimately human beings made the choices; and not all of them chose the same direction. Every theological proposition or posture mentioned in these pages had its advocates, it doubters, its bitter opponents.

The crucial ingredient, then, in the mix that produced an enduring unbelief was the choices of believers. More precisely, unbelief resulted from the decisions that influential church leaders—lay writers, theologians, ministers—made about how to confront the modern pressures upon religious belief. Not all of their selections resulted from long thought and careful reflection; part of our humanity, after all, is that we have much in common with lemmings. But they were choices. And the choices, taken together, boiled down to a decision to deal with modernity by embracing it—to defuse modern threats to the traditional bases of belief by bringing God into line with modernity.

Whatever the wisdom of hindsight, this strategy was far from contemptible. Anyone who believes in God will want that belief, that God, to have some bearing on the world in which we breathe, think, live, and die. Reconciling belief with the standards of science, attending more to the immediate moral relevance of religion than to its incomprehensible mysteries, were ways of keeping belief meaningful in a radically changing environment.

In tailoring belief more closely to human understanding and aspiration, however, many religious leaders made a fatal slip. They were not wrong to think that any significant faith would have to express itself in moral practice. But they often forgot that their God's purposes were not supposed to be man's. They were not mistaken in believing that any resilient belief must ground itself in human thought and experience. But they frequently forgot the tension that, by definition, must exist between an incomprehensible God and the human effort to know Him. They were hardly fools to insist that any God must be lord of this world, but they did not always remember that this world could not define Him. They forgot, in short, that their God was—as any God had to be to command belief over the long term—radically other than man.

Put slightly differently, unbelief emerged because church leaders too often forgot the transcendence essential to any worthwhile God. They committed religion *functionally* to making the world better in human terms and *intellectually* to modes of knowing God fitted only for understanding this world. They did this because, trying to meet the challenge of modernity, they virtually surrendered to it. These ministers and theologians well understood that belief could not continue in its old tracks. They did not grasp firmly enough that it did not simply have to jump to the new, that belief could modify secular wisdom in the very process of adapting to it. Sometimes overstatement clarifies by the act of caricaturing. In that spirit, one might borrow a page from the churchmen's own book and say that they chose to worship Mammon more than their God. No wonder, then, that some people eventually gave up God altogether in favor of Mammon.

Some religious leaders had protested this course at every turning, and it did not take long after the emergence of agnosticism for alert believers to realize that they had indeed badly misset their compasses. A sharp swerve then carried religionists away from scientific natural theology and emotional heart-religion toward an attempt, both subtler and chastened, to base belief in human experience. William James's *Varieties of Religious Experience* (1902) stands as the landmark of this effort. Somewhat more slowly, even liberal church leaders gave up their facile identification of human betterment with the Kingdom of God—though it took fifty years and the prodding of Karl Barth and Reinhold Niebuhr really to shake them loose. Panic and a lot of jury-rigging marked the first efforts to reconstruct the basis of belief. But most believers rode unperturbed through the storm on faith and instinct. And by the early twentieth century they again had respectable grounds for their faith. That, however, is another story.

Given the diverse elements that converged to breed unbelief, one cannot help wondering whether different timing of events might have produced a different outcome. After World War I, progress, especially moral progress, no longer seemed so secure. Had the European order collapsed in bloodshed fifty years earlier, the ensuing moral uncertainty might have made the agnostics' secular morality less attractive, just as in actuality faith in moral progress made it more appealing. Similarly, Charles Darwin's work secured the final victory of a conception of scientific knowledge tightly limited by physical observation—and therefore excluding God. If natural selection had not been promulgated until the 1890s (by which time the cracks in classical physics had grown too wide to paper over), this new conception of scientific knowledge might never have acquired the air of certainty that made knowledge of God appear so flimsy in contrast. God in some ways looked more improbable in the Age of Huxley than the Age of Einstein; but by the time the science-intoxicated had begun to moderate their claims, unbelief had already established itself.

I indulge in these speculations, not to appear Delphic, but to return with more concreteness to a particular point. On the one hand, it is clear that belief in God could not have endured in anything very like the form it had taken in the Middle Ages or early modern period. It could not have rested on the same epistemological bases or retained the same conceptual content, for these would have slowly ceased to make sense as the ways of thinking associated with modern science and modern social organization began to take wider hold.

On the other hand, it is by no means clear that the disappearance (for many people) of old forms of belief under the pressure of these intellectual and social changes had inevitably to leave unbelief in its wake. Nothing compels people to think about "God" in the same ways that they think about geology or cost accounting. We do not, for example, think about "love" in these ways; yet we have not ceased, most of us, to commit ourselves to another person for life on the nonrational basis of "love." (That many of us eventually apostasize does not destroy the analogy.) Too often we yield to the historian's greatest temptation: to confuse what did happen with what had to happen. It was not the inexorable juggernaut of history that crushed belief. It was, rather, the specific responses to modernity chosen by thousands of specific believers which made belief vulnerable.

Whether the emergence of unbelief was a good thing or a bad may become clearer to us in a few more centuries. But that it was an important thing is already clear. Neither belief nor unbelief should be adopted unthinkingly, but only after the most serious reflection. The history of unbelief makes clear that the choice matters, for it influences our entire outlook. As to what the choice should be, a historian is lucky enough to be able legitimately to plead professional incompetence.

Readers, notoriously perverse, will find their own lessons in this story; but I think that two merit pointing out. Those who wish to believe in God ought to realize that, if belief is to remain plausible over the long haul, they cannot regard God as if human, sharing human interests and purposes, accessible to human comprehension. And both believers and unbelievers ought to keep in mind that no one way of knowing reality is the last, best form of human knowledge—more: that no one form of knowing can possibly navigate the labyrinth of reality.

Yet perhaps, after all, there is really only one lesson here. The universe is not tailored to our measurements. Forgetting that, many believers lost their God. So may we all run into trouble.

Notes

Preface

1. Charles Eliot Norton to John Ruskin, 8 October 1869, in Charles Eliot Norton Papers, Houghton Library, Harvard University.

2. William A. Clebsch puts it neatly when he refers to "the full optionality of being religious" that became the case in the nineteenth century (*Christianity in European History* [New York, 1979], p. 189).

3. See, e.g., Emmanuel Le Roy Ladurie, *Montaillou, village occitan de 1294 à 1324* (Paris, 1975), pp. 468–500, and A. N. Galpern, *The Religions of the People in Sixteenth-Century Champagne* (Cambridge, Mass., 1976), esp. chaps. 2–3.

4. I say "continuing absence" because passing doubts of the reality of the unseen have apparently disturbed even the most devout believers in all centuries.

Prologue

1. Emmanuel Le Roy Ladurie, *Montaillou, village occitan de 1294 à 1324* (Paris, 1975), esp. chaps. 19–22.

2. This conclusion derives both from my inability to locate a single probable case of sustained disbelief in God before the Reformation and from the extreme rarity of cases for two centuries thereafter (more about this latter point in chapters 1 and 2). If unbelievers were extremely rare in the seventeenth century—a climate much more conducive to doubt about God than that of the Middle Ages—it seems highly unlikely that they appeared earlier. Much about medieval religion, especially that of the common people, remains obscure, despite ingenious and impressive recent historical research. For a good brief summation of what seems to be the emerging consensus on this subject, see Jean Delumeau, *Catholicism between Luther and Voltaire: A New View of the Counter-Reformation*, trans. Jeremy Moiser (London, 1977), pp. 154–74.

3. St. John of the Cross, *The Dark Night of the Soul* (c. 1585), in *The Complete*

Works of Saint John of the Cross, Doctor of the Church, ed. P. Silverio de Santa Teresa, C.D., trans. and ed. E. Allison Peers (Westminster, Md., 1953), 1:315–457.

4. Lucien Febvre, *Le problème de l'incroyance au XVIe siècle: la religion de Rabelais* (Paris, 1942), esp. pp. 362–63, 491–97.

5. Febvre vividly evokes the last days of this lost world in ibid., pp. 363–80.

6. This primal attitude did not, of course, suddenly disappear at the close of the Middle Ages (if that can be defined) but persisted long both in bastions of traditionality and coexistent with newer ideas. Cf. Alan Macfarlane, *The Family Life of Ralph Josselin, a Seventeenth-Century Clergyman: An Essay in Historical Anthropology* (Cambridge, 1970), pp. 171–75, 188–89, 193.

Chapter 1: A New Age

1. Samuel Pepys, *Diary*, ed. Robert C. Latham and William Matthews (London, 1971–76), 18 August 1667.

2. Ibid., 13 January, 8 and 9 February 1668.

3. Ibid., 23 July 1664.

4. Ibid., 30 April 1668 and 15 July 1666.

5. Economic change also affected the growth of the nation-state as well as the course of the Reformation, so the neat distinction implied here is somewhat artificial. But at this point it is convenient to distinguish the direct influence of economic change on the church from its indirect effects.

6. Carlo Ginzburg, *The Cheese and the Worms: The Cosmos of a Sixteenth-Century Miller*, trans. John and Anne Tedeschi (Baltimore, 1980), pp. 30–31, 51, 60. Elizabeth Eisenstein, *The Printing Press as an Agent of Change*, 2 vols. (Cambridge, 1978), provides a thorough if perhaps at times exaggerated account of the influence of printing.

7. My account of Pepys throughout this chapter is based on Richard Ollard, *Pepys: A Biography* (New York, 1974), and Arthur Bryant, *Samuel Pepys*, 3 vols. (Cambridge, 1934–39), as well as on the incomparable *Diary*.

8. Jean Delumeau, *Catholicism between Luther and Voltaire: A New View of the Counter-Reformation*, trans. Jeremy Moiser (London, 1977), pp. 41, 227.

9. John Bunyan, *Grace Abounding to the Chief of Sinners* (1666), in *Grace Abounding . . . and The Pilgrim's Progress*, ed. Roger Sharrock (London, 1966), p. 33. For the influence of books and reading in Bunyan's milieu, see Margaret Spufford, "First Steps in Literacy: The Reading and Writing Experiences of the Humblest Seventeenth-Century Spiritual Autobiographers," *Social History* 4 (1979): 407–35.

10. Thomas S. Kuhn, *The Copernican Revolution: Planetary Astronomy in the Development of Western Thought* (Cambridge, Mass., 1957), chaps. 1–4, explains the development of this cosmology and describes its final form.

11. Alexandre Koyré, *From the Closed World to the Infinite Universe* (Baltimore, 1957).

12. John Donne, "The First Anniversarie," in *The Complete Poetry of John Donne*, ed. John T. Shawcross (New York, 1967), pp. 270, 277–78.

13. Koyré, *Closed World*, p. 6. For the idea of the Copernican universe as an absolute monarchy, see S. F. Mason, "The Scientific Revolution and the Protestant Reformation-I," *Annals of Science* 9 (1953): 72–79.

14. Kuhn, *Copernican Revolution*, pp. 128–30, 213–19; Hugh Kearney, *Science and Change, 1500–1700* (New York, 1971), pp. 96–107, 130–140; Frances Yates, *Giordano Bruno and the Hermetic Tradition* (London, 1964), esp. chap. 13.

15. On the development in general of this view of the universe, see Kearney, *Science and Change*, chap. 5. For Galileo, mechanism was a matter of assumptions rather than a coherent system; see, e.g., his *Dialogue Concerning the Two Chief World Systems*, trans. Stillman Drake, 2d ed. (Berkeley, 1967). Descartes was the first to propound a mechanistic general system to replace Aristotle's, in his *Principia philosophiae* (1644).

16. The standard biography is now Richard S. Westfall, *Never at Rest: A Biography of Isaac Newton* (Cambridge, 1980). See also Frank E. Manuel, *A Portrait of Isaac Newton* (Cambridge, Mass., 1968), pp. 73–74, 380; idem, *The Religion of Isaac Newton* (Oxford, 1974), esp. pp. 48–49, 78. The quotation comes from a letter of Leibniz to Newton's bulldog, Samuel Clarke, quoted in Koyré, *Closed World*, p. 236.

17. Edgar Zilsel, "The Genesis of the Concept of Physical Law," *Philosophical Review* 51 (1942): 245–79, esp. 246–47.

18. Among the many works on the history of history, the two most useful for my point here are Donald R. Kelley, *Foundations of Modern Historical Scholarship: Language, Law, and History in the French Renaissance* (New York, 1970), and F. J. Levy, *Tudor Historical Thought* (San Marino, 1967).

19. Arthur B. Ferguson, *Clio Unbound: Perception of the Social and Cultural Past in Renaissance England* (Durham, N.C., 1979); Peter Gay, *A Loss of Mastery: Puritan Historians in Colonial America* (Berkeley, 1966), chap. 3.

20. Caroline Robbins, *The Eighteenth-Century Commonwealthman* (Cambridge, Mass., 1959), pp. 91–102.

21. Joyce Oldham Appleby, *Economic Thought and Ideology in Seventeenth-Century England* (Princeton, 1978), esp. pp. 37–41, 50.

22. Much of this shift fits within Max Weber's celebrated term, appropriated from Friedrich Schiller, the "disenchantment of the world."

23. See, e.g., Barbara J. Shapiro, *Probability and Certainty in Seventeenth-Century England: A Study of the Relationships between Natural Science, Religion, History, Law, and Literature* (Princeton, 1983). Carlo M. Cipolla provides concrete instances of this more empirical outlook in a very different context in *Faith, Reason, and the Plague in Seventeenth-Century Tuscany*, trans, Muriel Kittel (Ithaca, 1977). Sprat is quoted in Walter J. Ong, S.J., *The Presence of the Word: Some Prolegomena for Cultural and Religious History* (New Haven, 1967), p. 69.

24. Walter J. Ong, S.J., *Ramus, Method, and the Decay of Dialogue: From the Art of Discourse to the Art of Reason* (Cambridge, Mass., 1958).

25. Ibid., pp. 72–73, 92, 135–36.

26. For the congruence of Ramism specifically with a commercial outlook, see Walter J. Ong, S.J., "Ramist Method and the Commercial Mind," in *Rhetoric, Romance, and Technology: Studies in the Interaction of Expression and Culture* (Ithaca, 1971), pp. 165–89. A good example of how complex the relationships were that in fact obtained between economic position and mental attitudes is provided by Natalie Zemon Davis, "The Sacred and the Body Social in Sixteenth-Century Lyon," *Past and Present*, no. 90 (February 1981): 40–70, esp. 67–68.

27. Pepys, *Diary*, 10 June 1667. The best source for Pepys's scientific interests is Marjorie Hope Nicolson, *Pepys' Diary and the New Science* (Charlottesville, Va., 1965).

28. The book was *Microscopium statisticum quo status imperii Romano-Germani repraesentatur*, cited in Ollard, *Pepys*, pp. 53, 345.

29. Wilfred Cantwell Smith, *The Meaning and End of Religion* (New York, 1963), chap. 2, sec. 5.

30. John Bossy, "The Counter-Reformation and the People of Catholic Europe," *Past and Present*, no. 47 (May 1970): 51–70.

31. Cf. A. N. Galpern, *The Religions of the People in Sixteenth-Century Champagne* (Cambridge, Mass., 1976), p. 157; Philip Benedict, "The Catholic Response to Protestantism: Church Activity and Popular Piety in Rouen, 1560–1600," in *Religion and the People, 800–1700*, ed. James Obelkevich (Chapel Hill, 1979), p. 175.

32. *Oxford English Dictionary*, s.v. "belief," "believe."

33. Smith, *Meaning and End of Religion*, p. 40, notes Herbert's effort. Cf. the transition from a communal and mysterious religion to one more individualistic and rationally ordered depicted in John Bossy, "Essai de sociographie de la messe, 1200–1700," *Annales: Economies, sociétés, civilisations*, 36 (1981): 44–70.

34. Keith Thomas, *Religion and the Decline of Magic* (New York, 1971), pp. 168–70; William Turner, *A Compleat History of the most remarkable Providences. . . .* (1697), quoted in ibid., p. 96.

35. Diary of Rev. Ralph Josselin, 1 March 1663, quoted in Alan Macfarlane, *The Family Life of Ralph Josselin, a Seventeenth-Century Clergyman* (Cambridge, 1970), p. 22; Francis Bacon, "Of Atheism" (1625), in *The Works of Francis Bacon*, ed. James Spedding (London, 1857–74), 6:414. The best thing on the problem of atheism in this period is G. E. Aylmer, "Unbelief in Seventeenth-Century England," in *Puritans and Revolutionaries: Essays in Seventeenth-Century History Presented to Christopher Hill*, ed. Donald Pennington and Keith Thomas (Oxford, 1978), pp. 22–46. George T. Buckley, *Atheism in the English Renaissance* (Chicago, 1932), is still worth a look. Don Cameron Allen, *Doubt's Boundless Sea: Skepticism and Faith in the Renaissance* (Baltimore, 1964), casts a wider net and is a sound analysis; see esp. pp. vi, ix.

36. Richard H. Popkin, *The History of Scepticism from Erasmus to Spinoza* (Berkeley, 1979), is the standard study of this Pyrrhonist tradition. G. E. Aylmer thinks Marlowe probably was an atheist ("Unbelief," p. 23n); but see Buckley, *Atheism*, chap. 10, where a detailed analysis reaches the opposite conclusion.

37. John Milton, "Paradise Lost," in *Complete Poems and Major Prose*, ed. Merritt Y. Hughes (New York, 1957), pp. 363–67 (VIII, 15–178) and, e.g., pp. 270 (III, 481–83), 308 (V, 266–68), and 422 (X, 651–57). See also the editor's discussion at pp. 187–92 and Kuhn, *Copernican Revolution*, pp. 194–95.

38. Macfarlane, *Josselin*, pp. 15, 172–76, 179–81, 193–94; Ong, *Ramus*, p. 279; Ollard, *Pepys*, pp. 333–35. On seventeenth-century scientific ideas of natural law, see J. E. McGuire, "Boyle's Conception of Nature," *Journal of the History of Ideas* 33 (1972): 523–42.

39. John Bunyan provided a good example of these often very distressing yet transient fits of unbelief in his spiritual autobiography. He recalled "a very great storm [that] came down upon me." "Whole flouds of Blasphemies" were "poured upon my spirit, to my great confusion and astonishment" and "stirred up questions in me, against the very *being* of God, and of his onely beloved Son; as whether there were in truth a God or Christ, or no?" Yet "afterwards the Lord did more fully and graciously discover himself unto me" (Bunyan, *Grace Abounding*, pp. 33, 38).

40. Michael Heyd, "The Reaction to Enthusiasm in the Seventeenth Century: Towards an Integrative Approach," *Journal of Modern History* 53 (1981): 258–80, stresses this point.

41. Boyle, quoted in Kearney, *Science and Change*, pp. 176–77.

42. Quoted in Herschel Baker, *The Image of Man* (Cambridge, Mass., 1947), p. 209.

43. Samuel Pepys, "Notes from Discourses touching Religion" (MS, n.d.), quoted in Ollard, *Pepys*, p. 329.

44. Anne Bradstreet's harrowing phrase, quoted in Philip Greven, *The Protestant Temperament: Patterns of Child-Rearing, Religious Experience, and the Self in Early America* (New York, 1977), p. 49. The historical literature on this rise of moralism, stemming from Max Weber's seminal essay *Die protestantische Ethik und der Geist des Kapitalismus* (1904–5), is unusually frustrating: argumentative as to why the rise occurred but obscure as to what actually happened. However, recent close studies of medieval and early modern religious practice confirm the general pattern of a "new moralism." See, e.g., Peter Burke, *Popular Culture in Early Modern Europe* (London, 1978), chap. 8, esp. pp. 207–12. More generally, see William A. Clebsch, *Christianity in European History* (New York, 1979), chap. 5.

45. Pepys, *Diary*, 6 January 1663, 3 March 1662.

46. On late seventeenth-century confidence that study of human nature and human relations would reveal divine moral law, see Norman Fiering, *Moral Philosophy at Seventeenth-Century Harvard: A Discipline in Transition* (Chapel Hill, 1981), p. 7.

Chapter 2: Enlightenment and Belief, 1690–1790

1. Kenneth Ballard Murdock, *Increase Mather, the Foremost American Puritan* (Cambridge, Mass., 1925), pp. 147–48, 264–66; Kenneth B. Murdock, *Selections from Cotton Mather* (New York, 1926), p. xxviii; Robert Middlekauff, *The Mathers: Three Generations of Puritan Intellectuals, 1596–1728* (New York, 1971), p. 283; I. Bernard Cohen, *Franklin and Newton* (Philadelphia, 1956), p. 207. The phrase "New Learning," favored by Samuel Johnson of Connecticut long before "Enlightenment" was coined, suggests something of its exciting freshness.

2. Samuel Eliot Morison, *Harvard College in the Seventeenth Century* (Cambridge, Mass., 1936), 1:214–51; Theodore Hornberger, *Scientific Thought in the American Colleges, 1638–1800* (Austin, 1945), chap. 4; Joseph J. Ellis, *The New England Mind in Transition: Samuel Johnson of Connecticut, 1696–1772* (New Haven, 1973), pp. 23–26, 45–49. "Muddy-headed Pagan" is Cotton Mather's phrase in *Manuductio ad Ministerium* (Boston, 1726), p. 48. To simplify matters I have committed a slight anachronism: Yale did not receive its name until 1718, a year after it moved to New Haven.

3. Francis L. Broderick, "Pulpit, Physics, and Politics: The Curriculum of the College of New Jersey, 1746–1794," *William and Mary Quarterly*, 3d ser., 6 (1949): 42–68. For the South, see the data about southern libraries compiled in Richard Beale Davis, *Intellectual Life in the Colonial South, 1585–1763* (Knoxville, 1978), 2:592–93, and note the conspicuous absence of Newtonianism in chap. 7, "Science and Technology." Little is known about the early curriculum at William and Mary, but there is nothing to suggest that it was advanced in natural philosophy. See Herbert B. Adams, *The College of William and Mary: A Contribution to the History of Higher Education*, U.S. Bureau of Education, Circulars of Information, no. 1 (Washington, 1887), esp. p. 20. The quotation is from Mather, *Manuductio*, p. 50.

4. Howard Mumford Jones, *Revolution and Romanticism* (Cambridge, Mass., 1974), p. 73.

5. The classic case where divine intervention seemed essential was the creation of new life forms after the original creation, but this necessity only became obvious

with the beginnings of clarification of the fossil record toward the end of the century.

6. W. T. Davison, "Providence," in *Encyclopaedia of Religion and Ethics,* ed. James Hastings (New York, 1908–27), 10:415–20; Gershom Scholem, "Providence," in *Encyclopaedia Judaica* (Jerusalem, 1971), 13:1279–86. For Puritan particular providences, see, e.g., William Bradford, *Of Plymouth Plantation,* ed. Samuel Eliot Morison (New York, 1952); John Winthrop, *Journal,* ed. James Kendall Hosmer, 2 vols. (New York, 1959).

7. Sir John Pringle to Boswell, 10 February 1767, in James Boswell, *Boswell in Search of a Wife, 1766–1769,* ed. Frank Brady and Frederick A. Pottle, Yale Editions of the Private Papers of James Boswell (New York, 1956), p. 29.

8. Boswell's Journal, 4 August 1764, in James Boswell, *Boswell on the Grand Tour: Germany and Switzerland, 1764,* ed. Frederick A. Pottle, Yale Editions of the Private Papers of James Boswell (London, 1953), p. 49.

9. Charles Chauncy, *Earthquakes a Token of the Righteous Anger of God* (Boston, 1755), pp. 7–9, 16–23, cited in Edward A. Griffin, *Old Brick: Charles Chauncy of Boston, 1705–1787* (Minneapolis, 1980), pp. 105, 201.

10. David Hume, "The Natural History of Religion" (1755), in *The Philosophical Works of David Hume* (Boston, 1854), 4:446. There seems to be no general study of this development, but see Jacob Viner, *The Role of Providence in the Social Order: An Essay in Intellectual History* (Philadelphia, 1972).

11. Robert Nisbet, *History of the Idea of Progress* (New York, 1980), is the latest work in a scholarly lineage that goes back to J. B. Bury's classic *The Idea of Progress: An Inquiry into Its Origin and Growth* (London, 1920), which, despite its flaws, remains the most satisfactory general treatment of the subject. On the growing consciousness of social change over time during the Renaissance, see Arthur B. Ferguson, *Clio Unbound: Perception of the Social and Cultural Past in Renaissance England* (Durham, N.C., 1979), esp. chaps. 10, 11. On the development of the idea of progress in the eighteenth century, see Peter Gay, *The Enlightenment: An Interpretation* (New York, 1966, 1969), 2:98–125, and John Passmore, *The Perfectibility of Man,* 2d ed. (New York, n.d. [1st ed., 1970]), esp. chap. 10.

12. Bernard Le Bovier de Fontenelle, "Digression sur les anciens et les modernes," in *Oeuvres complètes,* ed. G.-B. Depping (Paris, 1818), 2:361–62; Anne Robert Jacques Turgot, "Discours sur les progrès successifs de l'esprit humain," in *Oeuvres,* ed. Eugene Daire and Hippolyte Dussard (Paris, 1844), 2:598.

13. Edward Gibbon, *The Decline and Fall of the Roman Empire* (1776–88; London, n.d.), 2:431 ("General Observations" following chap. 38).

14. Franklin to Joseph Priestley, 8 February 1780, quoted in Gilbert Chinard, "Progress and Perfectibility in Samuel Miller's Intellectual History," in *Studies in Intellectual History* (Baltimore, 1953), pp. 119–20; John R. Howe, Jr., *The Changing Political Thought of John Adams* (Princeton, 1966), pp. 39–40. I know the song only from a Folkways record, *Election Songs of the United States.*

15. James West Davidson, *The Logic of Millennial Thought: Eighteenth-Century New England* (New Haven, 1977), provides the best elucidation of this knarry subject; see Passmore, *Perfectibility,* pp. 173–74, for Joseph Priestley's rather extreme version.

16. On astrology, witchcraft, divination, etc., in eighteenth-century America, see Herbert Leventhal, *In the Shadow of the Enlightenment: Occultism and Renaissance Science in Eighteenth-Century America* (New York, 1976), and Jon Butler, "Magic, Astrology, and the Early American Religious Heritage, 1600–1760," *American His-*

torical Review 84 (1979): 317–46. Christopher M. Jedrey, *The World of John Cleaveland: Family and Community in Eighteenth-Century New England* (New York, 1979), chap. 4, gives a good picture of how intellectually cut off a rural community was, even within easy distance of a cosmopolitan center where Enlightenment thinking flourished.

17. Alan Charles Kors, *D'Holbach's Coterie: An Enlightenment in Paris* (Princeton, 1976); Henry F. May, *The Enlightenment in America* (New York, 1976), pp. 241–42, 326; W. H. Reid, *The Infidel Societies of the Metropolis* (London, 1800), cited in Susan Budd, *Varieties of Unbelief: Atheists and Agnostics in English Society, 1850–1960* (London, 1977), p. 11. Barlow apparently recanted his atheism when he became disillusioned with the French experiment after Napoleon's coup d'état.

18. On America, see G. Adolf Koch, *Republican Religion: The American Revolution and the Cult of Reason* (New York, 1933), and Herbert M. Morais, *Deism in Eighteenth Century America* (New York, 1934). Koch mentions two apparent exceptions to my generalization about the absence of unbelievers (pp. 83–84, 148–67); but one case is dubious, based on very thin evidence from a hostile source, which I have found nothing to substantiate; and the other was a British import after the French Revolution who did believe in a First Cause but thought it irrelevant to human beings. Hume's statement occurs in the well-known anecdote related in a letter from Diderot to Sophie Volland, 6 October 1765, in *Correspondance*, ed. Georges Roth, vol. 5 (Paris, 1959), 133–34. (Diderot evidently liked the story, for he also told it to the British legal reformer Samuel Romilly, who recounted it in his *Memoirs*, 2d ed. [London, 1840], 1:179. The bite of the tale lies in the fact that Hume happened to utter these words while at table with perhaps a majority of the professed atheists in France.) Jacob Viner agrees with Hume that England had no known atheists of consequence; see Viner, *Role of Providence*, p. 13.

19. Gay, *Enlightenment*, 2:526.

20. Thomas Jefferson to John Adams, 11 April 1823, in Lester J. Cappon, ed., *The Adams-Jefferson Letters* (Chapel Hill, 1959), 2:591–92.

21. Quoted in Norman Hampson, *The Enlightenment* (Harmondsworth, Middlesex, 1968), p. 114. The best study of Toland is Robert E. Sullivan, *John Toland and the Deist Controversy: A Study in Adaptations* (Cambridge, Mass., 1982). On La Mettrie, see Aram Vartanian, *La Mettrie's L'Homme Machine: A Study in the Origins of an Idea* (Princeton, 1960).

22. Frank E. Manuel, *The Eighteenth Century Confronts the Gods* (Cambridge, Mass., 1959); Hume, "Natural History of Religion."

23. Jean Delumeau, *Catholicism between Luther and Voltaire: A New View of the Counter-Reformation*, trans. Jeremy Moiser (London, 1977), p. 227.

24. Thomas Symmes, quoted in Perry Miller, *The New England Mind: From Colony to Province* (Cambridge, Mass., 1953), p. 396; David Lundberg and Henry F. May have analyzed the contents of eighteenth-century American libraries in "The Enlightened Reader in America," *American Quarterly* 28 (1976): 262–93.

25. Quoted in W[alter]. Jackson Bate, *Samuel Johnson* (New York, 1977), p. 277, where the circumstances of the letter are detailed.

26. "Epitaph. Intended for Sir Isaac Newton."

27. Jonathan Edwards, *The Great Awakening*, ed. C. C. Goen, vol. 4 of *Works of Jonathan Edwards*, ed. John E. Smith (New Haven, 1972), 249; James Hoopes, "Jonathan Edwards's Religious Psychology," *Journal of American History* 69 (1983): 849–65.

28. Lundberg and May, "Enlightened Reader"; Norman Fiering, "The First

American Enlightenment: Tillotson, Leverett, and Philosophical Anglicanism," *New England Quarterly* 54 (1981): 309–10; Leslie Stephen, *History of English Thought in the Eighteenth Century* (London, 1876), 1:119–29 (quotation from p. 123).

29. Jonathan Mayhew, *Seven Sermons* (Boston, 1749), quoted in Charles W. Akers, *Called unto Liberty: A Life of Jonathan Mayhew, 1720–1766* (Cambridge, Mass., 1964), p. 70; Mayhew, *Seven Sermons,* quoted in May, *Enlightenment in America,* p. 57; Jefferson to John Adams, 22 August 1813, in Cappon, *Adams-Jefferson Letters,* 2:368.

30. Akers, *Called unto Liberty,* pp. 103–4; Gay, *Enlightenment,* 1:396–97.

31. It is significant that Protestants, among whom the rationalizing of belief proceeded more rapidly than among Catholics, tended to distinguish the two words earlier, while Catholics continued to refer to "the Faith" as involving the whole complex of intellectual convictions, trust in God, and church tradition.

32. Stephen, *English Thought,* remains the fullest exposition of the major writings of the Deist controversy; but Sullivan, *Toland,* now provides the best understanding of English Deism in its historical setting.

33. The limitation to "most Deists" is necessary. A few of the more radical entertained doubts about an afterlife.

34. The victim was Thomas Aikenhead, a medical student about nineteen years of age, executed for denying the Trinity and the authority of Scripture. This was the last British execution for heresy, and Toland was never in danger of such an extreme fate.

35. Benjamin Franklin, *Autobiography,* ed. Leonard W. Labaree et al. (New Haven, 1964), pp. 64–65, 71; Carl Van Doren, *Benjamin Franklin* (New York, 1938), pp. 14–16. The fullest study of Franklin's religion is Alfred Owen Aldridge, *Benjamin Franklin and Nature's God* (Durham, N.C., 1967).

36. Lyman Beecher, *Autobiography of Lyman Beecher* (1864), ed. Barbara M. Cross (Cambridge, Mass., 1961), 1:27. There are two histories of American Deism, neither adequate: Koch, *Republican Religion,* and Morais, *Deism in America.* A new study is badly needed, for the role of Deism in America is poorly understood.

37. Eliza Lucas Pinckney, quoted in Philip Greven, *The Protestant Temperament: Patterns of Child-Rearing, Religious Experience, and the Self in Early America* (New York, 1977), p. 225.

38. Cotton Mather, *The Christian Philosopher: A Collection of the Best Discoveries in Nature, with Religious Improvements* (London, 1721), p. 6.

39. Harold Fruchtbaum, "Natural Theology and the Rise of Science" (Ph.D. diss., Harvard University, 1964), chap. 1.

40. Margaret C. Jacob, *The Newtonians and the English Revolution, 1689–1720* (Ithaca, 1976), pp. 15–16; Fruchtbaum, "Natural Theology," pp. 179–98, 216–28. Let me repeat that Newton himself, with his mystical leanings, did not think of God as an engineer. For his less than crystal-clear ideas about the use of science in apologetics, see William H. Austin, "Isaac Newton on Science and Religion," *Journal of the History of Ideas* 31 (1970): 521–42.

41. Charles E. Raven, *John Ray, Naturalist: His Life and Works* (Cambridge, 1942), esp. chap. 17.

42. F. C. Lesser, *Insecto-Theologie,* and J. A. Fabricius, *Wasser-Theologie,* are cited in John Dillenberger, *Protestant Thought and Natural Science: A Historical Interpretation* (Garden City, N.Y., 1960), p. 152; Johann Gottfried Herder, *Aelteste Urkunde des Menschengeschlechts,* in *Sämtliche Werke,* ed. Bernhard Suphan, 6 (Berlin, 1883), 202n.

43. Quoted in A. Rupert Hall, *The Scientific Revolution, 1500–1800: The Formation of the Modern Scientific Attitude,* 2d ed. (London, 1962), p. 295.

44. Charles Coulston Gillispie, *Genesis and Geology: A Study in the Relations of Scientific Thought, Natural Theology, and Social Opinion in Great Britain, 1790–1850* (Cambridge, Mass., 1951), p. 33.

45. Mather, *Christian Philosopher*, p. 294.

46. Unpub. Newton MS, c. 1692–93, printed in J. E. McGuire, "Newton on Place, Time, and God: An Unpublished Source," *British Journal for the History of Science* 11 (1978): 121.

47. John Calvin, *Institutes of the Christian Religion*, trans. John Allen (London, 1813), 1:61–62, 66–67, 69–75 (bk. 1, chap. 5, secs. iv, viii, xi-xii, xiv-xv); T. F. Torrance, *Calvin's Doctrine of Man* (1957; Westport, Conn., 1977), chaps. 11–12; Edward A. Dowey, Jr., *The Knowledge of God in Calvin's Theology*, 2d pt., corr. (New York, 1965), pp. 72–86.

48. See Johnson's autobiography in Herbert Schneider and Carol Schneider, eds., *Samuel Johnson* (New York, 1929), 1:3–49, and Ellis, *New England Mind*, esp. chaps. 2, 3, 7, 8, 11. The quotation is from a note that Johnson appended in 1715 to his Aristotelian *Technologia*, written the previous year, printed in Schneider and Schneider, *Johnson*, 2:186.

49. Adams to Jefferson, 20 January 1820, and 14 September 1813, in Cappon, *Adams-Jefferson Letters*, 2:560, 375.

50. Sullivan, *Toland*, pp. 80–81; Stephen, *English Thought*, chap. 3, sec. 76–81. Stephen regarded Dodwell as a sneaky Deist. Henry F. May thinks him probably a sincere Christian: *Enlightenment in America*, p. 23.

51. May, *Enlightenment in America*, pp. 59–60; Norman Fiering, *Jonathan Edwards's Moral Thought and Its British Context* (Chapel Hill, 1981), p. 97.

52. W. R. Ward, "The Relations of Enlightenment and Religious Revival in Central Europe and in the English-Speaking World," in *Reform and Reformation: England and the Continent, c1500–c1750*, ed. Derek Baker (Oxford, 1979), pp. 284–85.

53. Ibid., p. 281; Wesley quoted in Frederick Dreyer, "Faith and Experience in the Thought of John Wesley," *American Historical Review* 88 (1983): 13–14; Hoopes, "Edwards's Psychology."

54. Cotton Mather, *Christianity Demonstrated* (Boston, 1710), pp. 23, 26, quoted in Middlekauff, *Mathers*, p. 304.

55. Thomas Reid, *Essays on the Active Powers of the Human Mind* (1788) and *Essays on the Intellectual Powers of Man* (1785), in *The Works of Thomas Reid* (Charlestown, Mass., 1813–15), vols. 3, 4.

56. Ronald Grimsley, *Rousseau and the Religious Quest* (Oxford, 1968).

57. Ibid., p. 28.

58. Franklin, *Autobiography*, pp. 146–48, 153–54, 167; Aldridge, *Franklin and God*, esp. chaps. 14, 16.

59. If one looks at the most self-conscious level of ideas—"high" intellectual life—moral philosophy constituted "the essential component of the nonscientific American Enlightenment," according to the most careful recent student of that subject in colonial America. Norman Fiering, *Moral Philosophy at Seventeenth-Century Harvard: A Discipline in Transition* (Chapel Hill, 1981), p. 300.

60. Jonathan Edwards to Rev. Thomas Prince, 12 December 1743, in Edwards, *Great Awakening*, p. 544.

61. Thomas Jefferson, *The Life and Morals of Jesus of Nazareth* (Washington, 1904); Franklin, *Autobiography*, pp. 146–52, 158; Rivarol, quoted in Jones, *Revolution and Romanticism*, p. 59n.

62. Grimsley, *Rousseau*, passim; the quotation is from p. 76.

63. Quoted in Akers, *Called unto Liberty*, p. 74.

64. On this point, see especially Joseph Haroutunian's minor classic *Piety versus Moralism: The Passing of the New England Theology* (New York, 1932). Haroutunian, it must be said, failed to appreciate the compelling need to come to terms with the new world view of the Enlightenment, and his consequent lack of sympathy with his subjects led to unjust harshness.

65. See Fiering, *Moral Philosophy*, pp. 300–302.

66. G. Stanley Hall, "On the History of American College Textbooks and Teaching in Logic, Ethics, Psychology, and Allied Subjects," *Proceedings of the American Antiquarian Society*, 2d ser., 9 (1894): 152, quoted in D. H. Meyer, *The Instructed Conscience: The Shaping of the American National Ethic* (Philadelphia, 1972), p. 43.

67. *Lettres persanes* (1721), quoted in Hampson, *Enlightenment*, pp. 104–5.

68. Humphrey Primatt, *A Dissertation on the Duty of Mercy and Sin of Cruelty to Brute Animals* (London, 1776), pp. 321–22; Wesley, quoted in David Owen, *English Philanthropy, 1600–1960* (Cambridge, Mass., 1964), pp. 67–68.

69. Quoted in Akers, *Called unto Liberty*, p. 74.

70. Daniel Whitby, *A Discourse* (London, 1710), p. 84, quoted in H. Shelton Smith, *Changing Conceptions of Original Sin: A Study in American Theology since 1750* (New York, 1955), pp. 12–13; Griffin, *Old Brick*, pp. 124–25, 170–76. See D. P. Walker, *The Decline of Hell: Seventeenth-Century Discussions of Eternal Torment* (Chicago, 1964), for foreshadowings of these complaints.

Chapter 3: A God of Mind and Heart, 1790–1850

1. This is the title of Dwight's verse satire of Deists (1788).

2. Daniel Walker Howe, *The Unitarian Conscience: Harvard Moral Philosophy, 1805–1861* (Cambridge, Mass., 1970), p. 84.

3. For some of these similarities see ibid., as well as Anne C. Rose, *Transcendentalism as a Social Movement, 1830–1850* (New Haven, 1981), chap. 1.

4. Jay P. Dolan, *Catholic Revivalism: The American Experience, 1830–1900* (Notre Dame, 1978), esp. pp. 11–22, 32–40, 91–93, 109–11, 176, 187–88, 190–91.

5. Joseph Henry, "Address to the American Association for the Advancement of Science" (1850), in *A Scientist in American Life: Essays and Lectures of Joseph Henry*, ed. Arthur P. Molella et al. (Washington, 1980), p. 46. "Biology" in this context is slightly anachronistic, the word in its scientific meaning apparently not entering English until 1819 and not becoming fairly common before the 1840s (*Oxford English Dictionary*, s.v. "biology"); the common term at the time was natural history. On miracles, see for example Walter F. Cannon, "The Problem of Miracles in the 1830's," *Victorian Studies* 4 (1960): 5–32.

6. Charles Grandison Finney, *Lectures on Revivals of Religion* (1835), ed. William G. McLoughlin (Cambridge, Mass., 1960), pp. 15, 21.

7. William G. McLoughlin, Introduction to ibid., p. xxv; ibid., p. 13; Jonathan Edwards, *A Faithful Narrative* (1737), in *The Great Awakening*, ed. C. C. Goen, vol. 4 of *Works of Jonathan Edwards*, ed. John E. Smith (New Haven, 1972), p. 157. McLoughlin calls attention to this contrast in Finney, *Revivals*, p. 13n.

8. David D. Hall, "The Uses of Literacy in New England, 1600–1850," in *Printing and Society in Early America*, ed. William L. Joyce et al. (Worcester, Mass., 1983), pp. 20–47.

9. Ralph Waldo Emerson, *Nature*, in *Collected Works of Ralph Waldo Emerson*, vol. 1, ed. Robert E. Spiller and Alfred R. Ferguson (Cambridge, Mass., 1971), p. 10.

10. James McCosh, *The Method of the Divine Government, Physical and Moral*, 4th ed. (New York, 1855), pp. 170, 178, 112.

11. Quoted in Gay Wilson Allen, *Waldo Emerson* (New York, 1981), p. 80.

12. Jonathan Stearns, *Female Influence, and the True Christian Mode of its Exercise* (Newburyport, 1837), p. 11, quoted in Nancy F. Cott, *The Bonds of Womanhood: "Woman's Sphere" in New England, 1780–1835* (New Haven, 1977), p. 126; ibid., p. 126n; Barbara Welter, *Dimity Convictions: The American Woman in the Nineteenth Century* (Athens, Ohio, 1976), pp. 21–41, 83–102. "Cult of true womanhood" is Welter's now-famous phrase.

13. George M. Marsden, *The Evangelical Mind and the New School Presbyterian Experience* (New Haven, 1970), p. 9; cf. pp. 34, 38–39.

14. E.g., Mary P. Ryan, *Cradle of the Middle Class: The Family in Oneida County, New York, 1790–1865* (Cambridge, 1981), pp. 99–101; Joseph F. Kett, *Rites of Passage: Adolescence in America, 1790 to the Present* (New York, 1977), p. 106.

15. Lyman Beecher, *Lectures on Scepticism* (Cincinnati, 1835), p. 132. There has been in recent years an explosion of writings on American "civil religion." The conceptual terms were set by Robert N. Bellah's essay "Civil Religion in America," *Daedalus* 96, no. 1 (Winter 1967): 1–21; a good collection is Russell E. Richey and Donald G. Jones, eds., *American Civil Religion* (New York, 1974). On republican ideology of the American Revolution, the central work is Bernard Bailyn, *Ideological Origins of the American Revolution* (Cambridge, Mass., 1967), followed by Gordon S. Wood, *The Creation of the American Republic, 1776–1787* (Chapel Hill, 1969). The recent spate of revisions and intellectual relocations of republican ideology (centering on its relation to capitalism and liberal individualism) do not diminish the force of my point here; if anything, they amplify it.

16. Michael B. Katz conveniently brings together the main themes of recent work on early public school systems (to which he has largely contributed) in "The Origins of Public Education: A Reassessment," *History of Education Quarterly* 16 (1976): 381–407.

17. Cf. Nathan O. Hatch, *The Sacred Cause of Liberty: Republican Thought and the Millennium in Revolutionary New England* (New Haven, 1977).

18. Lyman Beecher, *Sermons Delivered on Various Occasions* (Boston, 1828), pp. 138, 143–44; Francis Wayland, *The Elements of Moral Science*, 2d ed. (1837), ed. Joseph L. Blau (Cambridge, Mass., 1963), p. 147.

19. James McCosh, *The Scottish Philosophy* (New York, 1875), pp. 86–87, quoted in J. David Hoeveler, Jr., *James McCosh and the Scottish Intellectual Tradition: From Glasgow to Princeton* (Princeton, 1981), p. 31; Wayland quoted in Blau, Introduction to Wayland, *Moral Science*, p. xxviii.

20. David S. Reynolds, *Faith in Fiction: The Emergence of Religious Literature in America* (Cambridge, Mass., 1981), p. 5; Walker quoted in Howe, *Unitarian Conscience*, p. 7; Henry Adams, *The Education of Henry Adams* (Boston, 1918), p. 34; Frederick Law Olmsted to Charles Loring Brace and Charles Wyllys Elliott, 1 December 1853, in Olmsted Papers, Library of Congress.

21. Wayland, *Moral Science*, p. 110.

22. Ibid.

23. Quoted in Arthur Alphonse Ekirch, Jr., *The Idea of Progress in America, 1815–1860* (New York, 1944), pp. 48, 70.

24. Gilbert Chinard, "Progress and Perfectibility in Samuel Miller's Intellectual History," in *Studies in Intellectual History* (Baltimore, 1953), pp. 117–18; McCosh, *Divine Government*, p. 512. It is difficult to learn about the attitudes of people who did not write for publication or achieve some celebrity. Diaries and letters of those

who belonged to neither intellectual nor social elites seldom suggest exuberant views of progress, though perhaps only because speculations on that scale were rarely recorded: see Lewis O. Saum, *The Popular Mood of Pre-Civil War America* (Westport, Conn., 1980), chap. 1. And at no level of society was faith in progress of the race incompatible with stoicism about one's personal fate, an attitude common in an age when medicine could do little to relieve chronic suffering or prevent early death. Nor do I mean to suggest that faith in progress was universal among even the educated elite, only that it very widely prevailed.

25. Peter Cartwright, *Autobiography*, ed. W. P. Strickland (Cincinnati, n.d. [1856]), pp. 51–52. The best account of American millennialism's development is James West Davidson, *The Logic of Millennial Thought: Eighteenth-Century New England* (New Haven, 1977).

26. See J. F. C. Harrison, *The Second Coming: Popular Millenarianism, 1780–1850* (New Brunswick, N.J., 1979). Harrison suggests that popular premillennialism (millenarianism, as he terms it), in contradistinction to the orthodox postmillennialism of socially dominant religious groups, was in part "a struggle to assert values which are alternative to the dominant culture of the Enlightenment" (p. 230)—an insight that reinforces the idea of educated Evangelicals as propagators of the Enlightenment.

27. Lyman Beecher, *Autobiography* (1864), ed. Barbara M. Cross (Cambridge, Mass., 1961), 1:185; Beecher, *Sermons*, p. 99; Finney, *Lectures*, p. 306.

28. I have stolen this phrase from Ernest Lee Tuveson, *Redeemer Nation: The Idea of America's Millennial Role* (Chicago, 1968), p. 51.

29. Samuel Hopkins, *A Treatise on the Millennium* (Boston, 1793), reprinted in Gordon S. Wood, ed., *The Rising Glory of America, 1760–1820* (New York, 1971), pp. 48–51.

30. Ibid., pp. 49–51.

31. Rev. R. H. Beattie, *A Discourse on the Millennial State of the Church* (Albany, 1849), quoted in Tuveson, *Redeemer Nation*, p. 88.

32. This drift can be traced in Frank H. Foster, *A Genetic History of the New England Theology* (Chicago, 1907); see, e.g., pp. 282, 287–89. It is more forcefully stated in Joseph Haroutunian, *Piety versus Moralism: The Passing of the New England Theology* (New York, 1932). For Emmons, see H. Shelton Smith, *Changing Conceptions of Original Sin: A Study in American Theology since 1750* (New York, 1955), p. 64.

33. Beecher, *Lectures*, p. 29.

34. Beecher, *Sermons*, p. 17n; David Harrowar, *A Sermon on the Total Depravity of Infants and Their Entire Dependence on Sovereign Grace, for Eternal Salvation* (Utica, 1815), p. 13, quoted in Ryan, *Cradle of the Middle Class*, p. 69; John Calvin, *Institutes of the Christian Religion*, trans. John Allen (Philadelphia, 1928), 2:516.

35. Marie Caskey, *Chariot of Fire: Religion and the Beecher Family* (New Haven, 1978), pp. 46–48; Beecher, *Autobiography*, 2:102–6.

36. Beecher, *Autobiography*, 1:370–73; Caskey, *Chariot of Fire*, p. 77.

37. Harriet Beecher Stowe to Catharine Beecher, 1857, in Charles Edward Stowe, *Life of Harriet Beecher Stowe* (Boston, 1891), p. 322; Caskey, *Chariot of Fire*, pp. 117–87; Harriet Beecher Stowe, *The Minister's Wooing* (New York, 1859).

38. Finney, *Lectures*, esp. chap. 1, and see McLoughlin's Introduction, p. xxv; Cartwright, *Autobiography*, p. 29.

39. Sermon by Rev. William Stith, 1753, quoted in Richard Beale Davis, *Intellectual Life in the Colonial South, 1585–1763* (Knoxville, 1978), 2:739; Williston Walker, *The Creeds and Platforms of Congregationalism* (New York, 1893), pp. 553–65. After

the Civil War, strict Calvinism found its chief citadel among the Old School Presbyterians, entrenched around Princeton Theological Seminary; but even that bastion was weakening by the turn of the century.

40. Finney, *Lectures,* p. 9; McCosh, *Divine Government,* p. 9.

41. William Ellery Channing, *Unitarian Christianity* (1819), reprinted in Conrad Wright, ed., *Three Prophets of Religious Liberalism: Channing, Emerson, Parker* (Boston, 1961), pp. 69–70.

42. The Lincoln quotation is from the Second Inaugural; Emerson, 1828, quoted in Allen, *Emerson,* p. 115.

43. Beecher, *Lectures,* p. 149.

44. Charles E. Rosenberg, *The Cholera Years: The United States in 1832, 1849, and 1866* (Chicago, 1962), chaps. 2, 7.

45. Griscom is quoted in Charles E. Rosenberg, *No Other Gods: On Science and American Social Thought* (Baltimore, 1976), pp. 112, 114, 239. (Carroll Smith-Rosenberg is coauthor of the chapter in question.)

46. McCosh, *Divine Government,* p. 197; Emerson, *Nature,* p. 27.

47. Rosenberg, *No Other Gods,* p. 139; quotations are from pp. 111, 139.

48. Leslie Stephen, *History of English Thought in the Eighteenth Century* (London, 1876), 1:411.

49. Beecher, *Lectures,* pp. 52, 125; Charles Darwin, *Autobiography,* ed. Nora Barlow (New York, 1958), p. 59.

50. McCosh, *Divine Government,* pp. 2–13, 17–19; Beecher, *Lectures,* pp. 66–67. The list for the 1850s, certainly partial, includes Tayler Lewis, *Lectures on the Evidences of Christianity* (1852); Edward Hitchcock, *The Religion of Geology* (1852); Thomas Ewbank, *The World a Workshop* (1855); Lewis again, *The Six Days of Creation* (1856); James Walker, *God Revealed in the Process of Creation* (1856); Mark Hopkins, *Science and Religion* (1856); another Hitchcock, *Religious Truth Illustrated from Science* (1857); and the first part of Louis Agassiz, *Essay on Classification* (1859)—not to mention magazine articles. Theological and philosophical differences separated these texts, but these are irrelevant to the point here: the wide popularity of the approach to God through science.

51. Louis Agassiz, *Essay on Classification* (1859), ed. Edward Lurie (Cambridge, Mass., 1962), p. 12. On the idealist strain in Anglo-American natural theology, see Peter Bowler, "Darwinism and the Argument from Design: Suggestions for a Reevaluation," *Journal of the History of Biology* 10 (1977): 29–43. McCosh distinguished clearly between these two approaches to design—which he called the "principle of special adaptation" (Paley) and the "principle of order" (Agassiz)—and considered them complementary (*Divine Government,* p. 125).

52. Accomplished historians of theology give a wrong impression on this point by focusing (understandably and for their purposes rightly) on those seminal religious writers of this period who were suspicious of rationalizing theology (Schleiermacher, Coleridge, Kierkegaard, et al.). Such thinkers achieved their major influence in England and America only after the mid-century crisis of belief.

53. The phrase "scientific evidence" (as distinct from "science") is chosen because a distinction was commonly drawn between *theological* proofs based on science and *scientific* conclusions as such, held to be strictly confined to the naturalistic subject matter of the individual science. E.g., Mark Hopkins, *Science and Religion* (Albany, 1856), p. 24: "The inference from any particular science that there is, or is not, a God, is not part of that science" (quoted in Stanley M. Guralnick, "Geology and Religion before Darwin: The Case of Edward Hitchcock, Theologian and Geologist," *Isis* 63 (1972): 540).

54. Beecher, *Lectures,* p. 53.

55. [Andrew Preston Peabody], "The Intellectual Aspect of the Age," *North American Review* 64 (1847): 274–76; cf. Susan Faye Cannon, *Science in Culture: The Early Victorian Period* (New York, 1978), esp. chap. 3.

56. James D. Dana, "Thoughts on Species," *Bibliotheca Sacra* 14 (1857): 859–62; J. F. W. Herschel, *A Preliminary Discourse on the Study of Natural Philosophy* (London, 1831), p. 7.

57. Ibid., p. 18; McCosh, *Divine Government,* p. 17.

58. Clement Read, "Charge Delivered to John Rice," p. 33, in John H. Rice, *An Inaugural Discourse, Delivered on the First of January 1824* (Richmond, 1824), quoted in E. Brooks Holifield, *The Gentleman Theologians: American Theology in Southern Culture, 1795–1860* (Durham, N.C., 1978), p. 81; sermon of Lyman Beecher, preached at the installation of Rev. Bennet Tyler, Portland, Maine, April 1829, printed in part in Beecher, *Autobiography,* 2:144–46.

59. William Meade, *Old Churches, Ministers, and Families of Virginia* (1857; Philadelphia, 1900), 1:29, quoted in Holifield, *Gentleman Theologians,* p. 51; *Southern Literary Messenger* 2 (1836): 768.

60. A. Hunter Dupree, *Asa Gray, 1810–1888* (Cambridge, Mass., 1959), pp. 21–22, 45; Henry Holt, *Garrulities of an Octogenarian Editor* (Boston, 1923), p. 33; Albert Post, *Popular Freethought in America, 1825–1850* (New York, 1943).

61. Dumas Malone, *The Public Life of Thomas Cooper, 1783–1839* (New Haven, 1926), pp. 15–16, 339–42, 347–48; Allen, *Emerson,* pp. 99–101. Despite the absence of evidence, one might be tempted to suspect the existence of underground unbelief. All available evidence runs against this suspicion. Typically: between 1813 and 1816, the Reverend John Frost of Oneida County, New York, recorded conversations during pastoral visits. He interviewed a number of sceptics, notably undeferential to his office, who did not hesitate to deny very fundamental doctrines (e.g., immortality). But none of them seems to have doubted the existence of God (Ryan, *Cradle of the Middle Class,* p. 75). On usage of the term "infidelity" in this period, see Martin E. Marty, *The Infidel: Freethought and American Religion* (Cleveland, 1961), p. 52.

62. Quoted in Irving Bartlett, *Daniel Webster* (New York, 1978), p. 291; [J. Torrey, ed.], *The Remains of the Rev. James Marsh, D.D., Late President, and Professor of Moral and Intellectual Philosophy, in the University of Vermont; with a Memoir of His Life* (Boston, 1843), pp. 19–20.

63. Mary Bushnell Cheney, comp., *Life and Letters of Horace Bushnell* (New York, 1880), pp. 56–58.

64. Ibid., p. 60.

65. Beecher, *Lectures,* Lecture 6, "The Attributes and Character of God"; the quotation is from p. 139.

66. Woods to James Marsh, 11 January 1830, in John J. Duffy, ed., *Coleridge's American Disciples: The Selected Correspondence of James Marsh* (Amherst, 1973), pp. 106–7; Beecher, *Sermons,* pp. 217–66 (my emphasis).

67. Rice to James Marsh, 14 April 1829, in Duffy, *Coleridge's Disciples,* p. 88.

68. Wayland, *Elements of Moral Science,* p. 107; *North American Review* 16 (1823): 357.

69. Bancroft is quoted in Russel B. Nye, *George Bancroft, Brahmin Rebel* (New York, 1944), p. 131; Beecher, *Lectures,* p. 102.

70. On interiorization of consciousness as a long-term development, see Walter J. Ong, S.J., *Fighting for Life: Contest, Sexuality, and Consciousness* (Ithaca, 1981), pp. 187–201.

71. Marsh to Coleridge, 24 Febuary 1830, in Duffy, *Coleridge's Disciples,* p. 108;

ibid., p. 8. See also Richard Henry Dana to Marsh, 14 July 1832, and 31 December 1834, in ibid., pp. 137, 170–71.

72. Marsh to Dana, 8 March 1838, in ibid., p. 218; [Torrey], *Remains of Marsh*, pp. 42–43, 113–14; Marsh to Coleridge, 23 March 1829, in ibid., pp. 136–37; Marsh to Dana, 21 August 1832, in Duffy, *Coleridge's Disciples*, p. 140.

73. Quoted in Rene Wellek, *Confrontations: Studies in the Intellectual and Literary Relations between Germany, England, and the United States during the Nineteenth Century* (Princeton, 1965), p. 173.

74. Bushnell was also affected by Schleiermacher, but Coleridge appears to have been the larger influence, especially on those aspects of Bushnell's theology relevant to this book.

75. McCosh, *Divine Government*, p. 9.

76. Ibid., p. 20; Francis Bowen, *Principles of Metaphysical and Ethical Science*, 2d ed. (1855), quoted in Howe, *Unitarian Conscience*, p. 95.

77. Preliminary draft of the Burial Hill Declaration of Faith, reprinted in Walker, *Creeds and Platforms*, p. 558.

78. Quoted in Charles H. Foster, *The Rungless Ladder: Harriet Beecher Stowe and New England Puritanism* (Durham, N.C, 1954), p. 107; Clifford E. Clark, Jr., *Henry Ward Beecher: Spokesman for a Middle-Class America* (Urbana, 1978), p. 25.

79. Lyman Beecher's charge at the ordination of Charles Beecher, 1844, printed in Beecher, *Autobiography*, 2:360–61.

80. Cheney, *Bushnell*, pp. 200–201.

81. Rev. Charles Lowell to James Russell Lowell, 16 June 1836, quoted in Martin Duberman, *James Russell Lowell* (Boston, 1966), pp. 62–63.

Chapter 4: Belief and Social Change

1. I follow conventional usage in referring to modern economic structures and attitudes (and their noneconomic ramifications) as products of capitalism. Socialist economies, of course, exhibit similar traits. As a matter of chronological priority, capitalism (and these modern traits) preceded socialism—and will, *a fortiori*, precede any other economic reifications of human activity yet to be devised. Whether this precedence was also a logical and necessary priority (as the later Marx maintained)—and whether, consequently, the social attitudes discussed herein are somehow inherently capitalist in nature and only appeared *because of* capitalism—is another question altogether, and one which carries the questioner beyond reality as it can actually be investigated. What I want to make clear is that, in associating attitudinal and value changes with capitalist economic organization, I am not asserting anything about necessary connections or about whether the chicken produced the egg or vice-versa. I am only observing actual historical conjunctions of certain kinds of economic organization and certain attitudes and values.

2. Robert G. Ingersoll, "Progress" (1864), in *The Works of Robert G. Ingersoll* (New York, 1900), 4:460; Horace Bushnell, 1846, quoted in Mary Bushnell Cheney, comp., *Life and Letters of Horace Bushnell* (New York, 1880), pp. 169–70.

3. David Hume, "The Natural History of Religion" (1755), in *The Philosophical Works of David Hume* (Boston, 1854), 4:428–32.

4. Dates are from William L. Langer, ed., *An Encyclopedia of World History*, 4th ed. (Boston, 1968), p. 603, and William H. Harris and Judith S. Leavey, eds., *The New Columbia Encyclopedia* (New York, 1975), s.v. "lighting."

5. Gerard Manley Hopkins, "God's Grandeur" (1877), in W. H. Gardner, ed., *Poems of Gerard Manley Hopkins*, 3d ed., corr. (New York, 1961), p. 70.

6. Lyman Beecher, *Autobiography* (1864), ed. Barbara M. Cross (Cambridge, Mass., 1961), 1:22; Lucy N. Colman, *Reminiscences* (Buffalo, 1891), pp. 9–10; Lyman Abbott, *Reminiscences* (Boston, 1915), p. 17.

7. Donald M. Scott, *From Office to Profession: The New England Ministry, 1750–1850* (Philadelphia, 1978); Walker is quoted in Ronald Story, *The Forging of an Aristocracy: Harvard and the Boston Upper Class, 1800–1870* (Middletown, Conn., 1980), p. 66.

8. Frederick Rudolph, *The American College and University: A History* (New York, 1962), pp. 231–32.

9. Henry Adams to Charles Francis Adams, Jr., 11 April 1862, in Worthington Chauncey Ford, ed., *A Cycle of Adams Letters, 1861–1865* (Boston, 1920), 1:135; John William Draper, *History of the Conflict between Religion and Science* (1874; New York, 1898), pp. 321–23.

10. Rudolph, *American College*, pp. 232–33; A. Hunter Dupree, *Science in the Federal Government: A History of Policies and Activities to 1940* (Cambridge, Mass., 1957), esp. chaps. 7–11, 13; Sally Gregory Kohlstedt, *The Formation of the American Scientific Community: The American Association for the Advancement of Science, 1848–1860* (Urbana, 1976); Ethelred Philips to James Philips, 26 February 1869, James J. Philips Papers, in the Southern Historical Collection, University of North Carolina Library, Chapel Hill.

11. Charles Hodge, *What is Darwinism?* (New York, 1874), p. 135. The two great monuments of this polemical genre, deceptively quaint in retrospect, are John William Draper's *History of the Conflict between Religion and Science* (1874) and Andrew Dickson White's *History of the Warfare of Science and Theology in Christendom* (1896). Thomas Huxley's anticlerical essays also got a great deal of play in the United States. None of the clerical responses, of which there were many, achieved the same celebrity; but for typical examples see the *Southern Review* 1 (1867) through 25 (1879), passim.

12. Rudolph, *American College*, p. 232; James Turner, *Reckoning with the Beast: Animals, Pain, and Humanity in the Victorian Mind* (Baltimore, 1980), chaps. 5–6; Donald Fleming, "Charles Darwin, the Anaesthetic Man," *Victorian Studies* 4 (1961): 219–36.

13. A. D. Moore, "Henry A. Rowland," *Scientific American* 246, no. 2 (February 1982): 150–55; A. W. Coats, "Henry Carter Adams: A Case Study in the Emergence of the Social Sciences in the United States, 1850–1900," *Journal of American Studies* 2 (1968): 177–97. On fragmentation of cultural life along professional lines, see, in an expanding body of literature, Thomas Bender, "The Cultures of Intellectual Life: The City and the Professions," in John Higham and Paul K. Conkin, eds., *New Directions in American Intellectual History* (Baltimore, 1979), pp. 181–95; Burton J. Bledstein, *The Culture of Professionalism: The Middle Class and the Development of Higher Education in America* (New York, 1976); Daniel H. Calhoun, *Professional Lives in America: Structure and Aspiration, 1750–1850* (Cambridge, Mass., 1965); and Thomas L. Haskell, *The Emergence of Professional Social Science: The American Social Science Association and the Nineteenth-Century Crisis of Authority* (Urbana, 1977). This genre sometimes gives the impression of utter breakdown of any civic cultural life in the later nineteenth century. A useful corrective is a work like Helen Lefkowitz Horowitz, *Culture and the City: Cultural Philanthropy in Chicago from the 1880s to 1917* (Lexington, Ky., 1976).

14. See Ann Douglas, *The Feminization of American Culture* (New York, 1977), esp. pp. 81–85.

15. Benjamin Franklin, *Autobiography*, ed. Leonard W. Labaree et al. (New Haven, 1964), p. 163.

16. Among the better recent attempts to relate moralism, specifically Evangelical moralism, to economic change are Paul E. Johnson, *A Shopkeeper's Millennium: Society and Revivals in Rochester, New York, 1815–1837* (New York, 1978); Mary P. Ryan, *Cradle of the Middle Class: The Family in Oneida County, New York, 1790–1865* (Cambridge, 1981), and Anthony F. C. Wallace, *Rockdale: The Growth of an American Village in the Early Industrial Revolution* (New York, 1978). Wallace and Johnson perhaps overstress the imposition of more rigorous morality on workers, scanting their own willing embrace of it. Ryan is good on this point; see esp. p. 103. Another useful corrective is Paul G. Faler, "Cultural Aspects of the Industrial Revolution: Lynn, Massachusetts, Shoemakers and Industrial Morality," *Labor History* 15 (1974): 367–94.

17. The classic observation of this relationship is Whitney R. Cross, *The Burned-Over District: The Social and Intellectual History of Enthusiastic Religion in Western New York, 1800–1850* (Ithaca, 1950), which may fairly be regarded as godfather to works like Ryan, *Cradle of the Middle Class*, and Johnson, *Shopkeeper's Millennium*.

18. Lyman Beecher, *Lectures on Scepticism* (Cincinnati, 1835), p. 111.

19. Charles Loring Brace, *The Dangerous Classes of New York and Twenty Years Work Among Them* (New York, 1872); Michael B. Katz, "The Origins of Public Education: A Reassessment," *History of Education Quarterly* 16 (1976): 381–407.

20. Paul Boyer, *Urban Masses and Moral Order in America, 1820–1920* (Cambridge, Mass., 1978); Carroll S. Rosenberg, *Religion and the Rise of the City: The New York City Mission Movement* (Ithaca, 1971); Joseph F. Kett, *Rites of Passage: Adolescence in America, 1790 to the Present* (New York, 1977), chap. 4 (quotation from p. 107).

21. Ryan, *Cradle of the Middle Class*, chap. 3 and pp. 115–16. Paul G. Faler, *Mechanics and Manufacturers in the Early Industrial Revolution: Lynn, Massachusetts, 1780–1860* (Albany, 1981), pp. 103–4. Abolitionism in particular provoked a great number of riots; see Leonard L. Richards, *"Gentlemen of Property and Standing": Anti-Abolition Mobs in Jacksonian America* (New York, 1970).

22. Norton to Jonathan B. Harrison, 15 August 1865, in Charles Eliot Norton Papers, Houghton Library, Harvard University.

23. Patricia Cline Cohen, "Statistics and the State: Changing Social Thought and the Emergence of a Quantitative Mentality in America, 1790–1820," *William and Mary Quarterly*, 3d ser., 38 (1981): 35–55.

24. The historian Daniel Calhoun has grappled with a similar problem in *The Intelligence of a People* (Princeton, 1973), a venturesome, problematic, original, and highly important book, too little attended to because it fits no standard field of historical inquiry. Calhoun demonstrates at least a real possibility that the character of intelligence—the mental processes by which people reached conclusions—changed substantially over the course of the eighteenth and nineteenth centuries. Although Calhoun did not concern himself directly with the particular mental shifts discussed here, his conclusions imply a close linkage between socioeconomic transformations and the mind's mode of dealing with experience.

25. A[lexander]. A. Hodge, *Outlines of Theology*, 2d ed. (New York, 1878), p. 15; William Brackett, "Modern Science in its Relation to Literature," *Popular Science Monthly* 15 (1879): 178.

26. Charles M. Mead, "The Uncertainties of Natural and Religious Science," in *Boston Lectures, 1870: Christianity and Scepticism* (Boston, 1870), pp. 103–4.

27. *Oxford English Dictionary*, s.v. "well-rounded"; James Jackson Jarves, *The Art-Idea* (1864), ed. Benjamin Rowland, Jr. (Cambridge, Mass., 1960), p. 40.

28. Lydia Maria Francis to Rev. Convers Francis, 31 May 1820, in *Lydia Maria Child: Selected Letters, 1817–1880*, ed. Milton Meltzer et al. (Amherst, 1982), p. 2,

and Lydia Maria Child to same, 27 February 1856, in *Letters of Lydia Maria Child* (Boston, 1883), pp. 7, 74.

Chapter 5: Christianity Confused, 1840–1870

1. J. M. Mathews, *The Bible and Men of Learning* (New York, 1859), p. 44. The lectures that compose this volume were delivered in 1844.

2. Orestes A. Brownson, *The Convert* (1857), in *Works*, ed. Henry F. Brownson (Detroit, 1882–1907), 5:28–29; Hammond quoted in Drew Gilpin Faust, *A Sacred Circle: The Dilemma of the Intellectual in the Old South, 1840–1860* (Baltimore, 1977), p. 67.

3. H. Shelton Smith, *Changing Conceptions of Original Sin: A Study in American Theology since 1750* (New York, 1955), esp. pp. 64, 75–78.

4. Rev. C. A. Bartol, quoted in Mary Bushnell Cheney, *Life and Letters of Horace Bushnell* (New York, 1880), p. 185; Lucy N. Colman, *Reminiscences* (Buffalo, 1891), pp. 5, 8.

5. "The Doctrine of Eternal Punishment," *North American Review* 126 (1878): 323–57 (a symposium exhibiting the range of Christian beliefs about hell at that time); Geoffrey Rowell, *Hell and the Victorians: A Study of the Nineteenth-Century Theological Controversies Concerning Eternal Punishment and the Future Life* (Oxford, 1974); Philippe Ariès, *The Hour of Our Death*, trans. Helen Weaver (New York, 1981), p. 435. Alexander Campbell, one of the founders of the Disciples of Christ, calculated that the ratio of souls who would be saved in the millennium to souls lost in the past would be 17,465.33 to 1 (Ernest Lee Tuveson, *Redeemer Nation: The Idea of America's Millennial Role* [Chicago, 1968], p. 58).

6. Lyman Abbott, *Reminiscences* (Boston, 1915), p. 469; John Fiske to Mother [Mrs. E. W. Stoughton], 20 March 1860, in Ethel F. Fisk, ed., *The Letters of John Fiske* (New York, 1940), p. 34.

7. Robert M. Grant, *The Bible in the Church: A Short History of Interpretation* (New York, 1960), chaps. 1–10.

8. Jerry Wayne Brown, *The Rise of Biblical Criticism in America, 1800–1870: The New England Scholars* (Middletown, Conn., 1969), p. 5; Hans W. Frei, *The Eclipse of Biblical Narrative: A Study in Eighteenth and Nineteenth-Century Hermeneutics* (New Haven, 1974), pp. 18–41, 55–56.

9. Ronald L. Numbers, *Creation by Natural Law: Laplace's Nebular Hypothesis in American Thought* (Seattle, 1977).

10. William Stanton, *The Leopard's Spots: Scientific Attitudes toward Race in America, 1815–1859* (Chicago, 1960); Nott to James H. Hammond, 25 July 1845, Hammond Papers, Library of Congress, quoted in John McCardell, *The Idea of a Southern Nation: Southern Nationalists and Nationalism, 1830–1860* (New York, 1979), p. 78.

11. Charles Coulston Gillispie, *Genesis and Geology: A Study in the Relations of Scientific Thought, Natural Theology, and Social Opinion in Great Britain, 1790–1850* (Cambridge, Mass., 1951); Herbert Hovenkamp, *Science and Religion in America, 1800–1860* (Philadelphia, 1978), pp. 132–45, 165; George M. Marsden, *The Evangelical Mind and the New School Presbyterian Experience: A Case Study of Thought and Theology in Nineteenth-Century America* (New Haven, 1970), p. 143; Catherine L. Howard, quoted in James Bradley Thayer, ed., *Letters of Chauncey Wright, with Some Account of His Life* (Cambridge, Mass., 1878), p. 121.

12. Alan Heimert, *Religion and the American Mind: From the Great Awakening to*

the Revolution (Cambridge, Mass., 1966), pp. 197–99; *North American Review* 3 (1816): 209–12. Luther's position was similar to Calvin's. See R. Hooykaas, *Religion and the Rise of Modern Science* (Edinburgh, 1972), pp. 114–22, and John Dillenberger, *Protestant Thought and Natural Science: A Historical Interpretation* (Garden City, N.Y., 1960), pp. 29–34.

13. See, e.g., E. P. Barrows, "The Mosaic Six Days and Geology," *Bibliotheca Sacra* 14 (1857): 61–98; Bushnell to his daughter, 27 November 1857, quoted in Cheney, *Life of Bushnell*, p. 412.

14. Fiske to Herbert Spencer, 20 February 1864, in John Spencer Clark, *The Life and Letters of John Fiske* (Boston, 1917), 1:294.

15. The most penetrating account of the rise of the higher criticism is Frei, *Eclipse*, though Frei's analysis runs at a tangent to my questions; for a straightforward summary, see S. L. Greenslade, ed., *The Cambridge History of the Bible: The West from the Reformation to the Present Day* (Cambridge, 1963), pp. 265–87.

16. Brown, *Biblical Criticism*, p. 140; William B. Clark, "Doubt, Faith, and Reason," *New Englander* 22 (1863): 80. Lyman Beecher's attitude in his *Lectures on Scepticism* (Cincinnati, 1835), pp. 32–33, and his *Autobiography* (1864), ed. Barbara M. Cross (Cambridge, Mass., 1961), 2:148, typified the Evangelical response throughout this period: suspicion, if not outright hostility, even when forced to come to terms with historical criticism to some extent.

17. E. Brooks Holifield, *The Gentlemen Theologians: American Theology in Southern Culture, 1795–1860* (Durham, N.C., 1978), p. 64; Russel B. Nye, *George Bancroft: Brahmin Rebel* (New York, 1944), pp. 35–38; Octavius Brooks Frothingham, *Recollections and Impressions, 1822–1890* (New York, 1891), p. 29. Brown, *Biblical Criticism*, provides the best account of these developments.

18. Abbott, *Reminiscences*, p. 482; Chauncey Wright to Mrs. J. P. Lesley, 16 November 1854, in Thayer, *Letters of Wright*, p. 37; Lester Ward, *Young Ward's Diary*, ed. Bernhard Stern (New York, 1935), p. 308; *Southern Literary Messenger* 38 (1864): 38–47; Ethelred Philips to James Philips, 21 January 1866, and 5 January 1870, James J. Philips Papers, in the Southern Historical Collection, University of North Carolina Library, Chapel Hill; Neal C. Gillespie, *The Collapse of Orthodoxy: The Intellectual Ordeal of George Frederick Holmes* (Charlottesville, 1972), p. 70. Historians have tended to assume that Abbott was right about the limited penetration of the higher criticism. But readers of these Germans keep cropping up in odd places. For example, Frederick Law Olmsted, during his tour of the South in the early 1850s, reported a Tennessean named Samuel Perkins Allison who "was reading secretly (as he confessed to us) Strauss' life of Christ and some of [Theodore] Parker's books." Olmsted to Charles Loring Brace and Charles Wyllys Elliott, 1 December 1853, in Olmsted Papers, Library of Congress.

19. John Weiss, *Life and Correspondence of Theodore Parker* (New York, 1864), 1:passim; Frothingham, *Recollections*, pp. 57–59; Eleazar Lord, *The Epoch of Creation: The Scripture Doctrine contrasted with the Geological Theory* (New York, 1851), quoted in *United States Magazine and Democratic Review* 29 (1851): 353.

20. Matthew Arnold, *Literature and Dogma* (1873), in *Dissent and Dogma*, vol. 6 of *Complete Prose Works of Matthew Arnold*, ed. R. H. Super (Ann Arbor, 1968), pp. 152, 250; Horace Bushnell, "Preliminary Dissertation on Language," in *God in Christ* (Hartford, 1849), esp. pp. 68–69, 74–75, 93–94; Holmes, quoted in Mark DeWolfe Howe, *Justice Oliver Wendell Holmes: The Shaping Years, 1841–1870* (Cambridge, Mass., 1957), pp. 57–58.

21. David A. Wasson, quoted in Mrs. John T. [M. E.] Sargent, ed., *Sketches*

and Reminiscences of the Radical Club of Chestnut Street, Boston (Boston, 1880), p. 23. Wasson (1823–1887) was a radical minister with a checkered ministerial and literary career.

22. The folklorist Andrew Lang recalled that discoveries of Palaeolithic remains played the largest role in invigorating anthropology in the decade 1860–1870 (Lang, "Edward Burnet Tylor," in *Anthropological Essays presented to E. B. Tylor in Honour of his 75th Birthday, Oct. 2, 1907* [Oxford, 1907], pp. 3–4, quoted in Richard M. Dorson, *The British Folklorists: A History* [London, 1968], p. 207). Modern prehistoric archaeology might be said to have entered the English-speaking world in 1847. In that year, Lord Ellesmere published a translation of Christian Thomsen's path-breaking 1819 guide to the collections of the Danish National Museum: the first application to prehistoric artifacts of the categories Stone Age, Bronze Age, and Iron Age, the first coherent scheme of prehistory and the foundation for all that followed. Sir John Lubbock refined this division in the 1860s by subdividing the Stone Age into Palaeolithic and Neolithic (Glyn Daniel, *Man Discovers His Past: A Survey of Archaeological Findings* [New York, 1968], pp. 8–12; John Lubbock, *Pre-Historic Times, as Illustrated by Ancient Remains, and the Manners and Customs of Modern Savages,* 2nd ed. [London, 1869], pp. 2–3).

23. Lubbock, *Pre-Historic Times,* esp. chaps. 13–15, and *The Origin of Civilization and the Primitive Condition of Man. Mental and Social Condition of Savages* (London, 1870). On these formative years of anthropology, see Godfrey Lienhardt, *Social Anthropology,* 2d ed. (London, 1966), chap. 1; J. W. Burrow, *Evolution and Society: A Study in Victorian Social Theory* (Cambridge, 1966), pp. 80–81, 115–16, 118–36, 228–59; Fred Eggan, "One Hundred Years of Ethnology and Social Anthropology," in *One Hundred Years of Anthropology,* ed. J. O. Brew (Cambridge, Mass., 1968), pp. 121–27; and T. K. Penniman, *A Hundred Years of Anthropology,* 3d ed. (New York, 1965), chaps. 3–4.

24. [Lester F. Ward?], "The Situation," *The Iconoclast* 1, no. 1 (1870): 1, and cf. no. 4: 3; Gillespie, *Collapse of Orthodoxy,* esp. 234–35, 238, 241–42.

25. Lubbock, *Origin of Civilization,* p. 114.

26. The standard study for America is now Carl T. Jackson, *The Oriental Religions and American Thought: Nineteenth-Century Explorations* (Westport, Conn., 1981); more generally, see Raymond Schwab, *La Renaissance orientale* (Paris, 1950).

27. David S. Reynolds, *Faith in Fiction: The Emergence of Religious Literature in America* (Cambridge, Mass., 1981), pp. 15–20; Jackson, *Oriental Religions,* pp. 25–39; Van Wyck Brooks, *The Flowering of New England, 1815–1865* (New York, 1936), pp. 19–20, 229; "Buddhism," *The New Englander* 3 (1845): 182–91. Brooks records that the first Hindu work to appear in America was a version of the *Sakuntala* printed in the *Monthly Anthology;* this would have been between 1803 and 1811.

28. *Dictionary of American Biography,* s.v. "Fitzedward Hall"; Jackson, *Oriental Religions,* pp. 46, 125, chap. 6; Ethelred Philips to James Philips, 12 January 1865, Philips Papers.

29. Burrow, *Evolution and Society,* pp. 44–45; Francis Wayland, *The Elements of Moral Science* (1837), ed. Joseph L. Blau (Cambridge, Mass., 1963), pp. 117–18.

30. William Ellery Channing, "Unitarian Christianity Most Favorable to Piety" (1826), in *Works,* 3:173, quoted in Daniel Walker Howe, *The Unitarian Conscience: Harvard Moral Philosophy, 1805–1861* (Cambridge, Mass., 1970), p. 42; Ralph Waldo Emerson, "Religion" (1867), in Sargent, *Sketches and Reminiscences,* pp. 3–4, 6. Typical of such comparisons were [James Freeman Clarke], "Buddhism; or, The Protestantism of the East," *Atlantic Monthly* 23 (1869): 713–28, and Lydia Maria

Child, "Resemblances between the Buddhist and the Roman Catholic Religions," *Atlantic Monthly* 26 (1870): 660–65.

31. Andrew Dickson White, *Autobiography* (New York, 1905), 2:527–28; Journal of Charles Eliot Norton, 20 December 1872, in Sara Norton and M. A. DeWolfe Howe, *Letters of Charles Eliot Norton, with Biographical Comment* (Boston, 1913), 1:434; Edward Hungerford, "Buddhism and Christianity," *The New Englander* 33 (1874): 268–86; Samuel Harris, "The Christian Doctrine of Human Progress Contrasted with the Naturalistic," in *Boston Lectures: Christianity and Skepticism* (Boston, 1870), pp. 23–24. Harris was president of Bowdoin College.

32. White, *Autobiography,* 1:42.

33. William Ellery Channing, "Unitarian Christianity" (1819), in Conrad Wright, ed., *Three Prophets of Religious Liberalism* (Boston, 1961), p. 48.

34. Henry Ward Beecher, *Norwood; or Village Life in New England* (New York, 1868), p. 266.

35. J. Leslie Porter, "Miracles," *Bibliotheca Sacra* 118 (1873): 254; John Fiske to Mother, 20 March 1860, in Fisk, *Letters of Fiske,* p. 32.

36. Charles Eliot Norton, "The Church and Religion," *North American Review* 106 (1868): 378–79; Holmes, quoted in Howe, *Holmes,* p. 44.

37. "Popular Creeds and the Nation's Life," *Christian Examiner* 80 (1866): 1–2.

38. Colman, *Reminiscences,* p. 7; Clark, *Life of Fiske,* 1:103n.

39. Walter J. Ong, S.J., *The Presence of the Word: Some Prolegomena for Cultural and Religious History* (New Haven, 1967), pp. 65, 69.

40. Arnold, *Literature and Dogma,* p. 152. Ironically, considering his role in this transformation, Coleridge himself strove to prevent the separation of scientific and literary language, fearing that such a divorce would devalue the authority of poetry. See Timothy J. Corrigan, "*Biographia Literaria* and the Language of Science," *Journal of the History of Ideas* 41 (1980): 399–419.

41. Bushnell, *God in Christ,* pp. 48, 55, 72.

42. Henry C. Potter, "The Revision of Creeds," *North American Review* 136 (1883): 101–5.

43. Quoted in Clark, *Life of Fiske,* 1:113.

44. See especially Emerson's essay "Fate" in *The Conduct of Life.*

45. Colman, *Reminiscences,* pp. 13, 25; Harrison to Charles Eliot Norton, 8 February 1867, in Norton Papers, Houghton Library, Harvard University. Recent research has begun to recover the meanings of Spiritualism. See especially R. Laurence Moore, *In Search of White Crows: Spiritualism, Parapsychology, and American Culture* (New York, 1977).

46. Henri F. Ellenberger, *The Discovery of the Unconscious: The History and Evolution of Dynamic Psychiatry* (New York, 1970), p. 399; Ariès, *Hour of Our Death,* p. 459; Moore, *White Crows,* pp. 19–21. Spiritualism among less-educated people may not have had so strong a scientific bent. See Lewis O. Saum, *The Popular Mood of Pre-Civil War America* (Westport, Conn., 1980), pp. 48–52.

47. Robert Dale Owen, 1867, quoted in Sargent, *Sketches and Reminiscences,* p. 25; Robert W. Delp, "A Spiritualist in Connecticut: Andrew Jackson Davis, the Hartford Years, 1850–1854," *New England Quarterly* 53 (1980): 346; Lydia Maria Child to Lucy Searle, 1862, in Child, *Letters of Lydia Maria Child* (Boston, 1883), p. 167; Robert C. Fuller, *Mesmerism and the American Cure of Souls* (Philadelphia, 1982), esp. chap. 3. By no means all Spiritualists believed Christianity to have flunked the test of science. There were many Christian Spiritualists, who were fond of explaining events like the Resurrection in electromagnetic terms.

48. Benjamin Jowett, Journal (c.1870), quoted in Melvin Richter, *The Politics of*

Conscience: T. H. Green and His Age (Cambridge, Mass., 1964), p. 99; Lydia Maria Child to Lucy Osgood, 11–19 February [?] 1856, in *Lydia Maria Child: Selected Letters, 1817–1880,* ed. Milton Meltzer et al. (Amherst, 1982), p. 278; Fiske to Mother, 20 March 1860, in Fisk, *Letters of Fiske,* p. 32.

49. Holmes's Civil War Diary, quoted in Howe, *Holmes,* pp. 105–6; Aldrich to Lillian Woodman, 17 August 1864, in Aldrich Papers, Houghton Library, Harvard University; Mary Grew, "Essential Christianity" (c.1872), in Sargent, *Sketches and Reminiscences,* p. 121; Olmsted to Mary Perkins Olmsted, 29 July 1863, Olmsted Papers; Norton, "Church," p. 382.

50. Norton, "Church," pp. 381–82; White, *Autobiography,* 2:535.

51. Henry Fielding, *The History of Tom Jones, a Foundling* (1749; Harmondsworth, Middlesex, 1966), p. 129 (bk. 3, chap. 3).

52. Harrison to Charles Eliot Norton, 7 August 1867, in Norton Papers.

Chapter 6: The Intellectual Crisis of Belief

1. The evidence presented by historians agrees as to when unbelief in God became a truly viable possibility in German, French, and Anglo-American culture: the 1860s and 1870s. My own sense is that America lagged slightly behind Europe. See Owen Chadwick, *The Secularization of the European Mind in the Nineteenth Century* (Cambridge, 1975), p. 184; Bernard M. G. Reardon, *From Coleridge to Gore: A Century of Religious Thought in Britain* (London, 1971), p. 13; Stow Persons, *Free Religion: An American Faith* (Boston, 1947), esp. p. 101; Sidney Warren, *American Freethought, 1860–1914* (New York, 1943), pp. 23–24. Letters and diaries of the period display this rather sudden upsurge of concern about problems of belief. For example, comments about unbelief peppered James Russell Lowell's correspondence in the 1870s; these references, uncommon before the seventies, faded away in the 1880s, although Lowell kept up correspondence with the same people (Charles Eliot Norton, ed., *Letters of James Russell Lowell,* 2 vols. [New York, 1894]).

2. One gets a sense of the boundaries, subtle but real, of this agnostic subculture in reading the correspondence of good friends of common cultural background who were on opposite sides of the divide. For example, after Leslie Stephen, an outspoken agnostic, published his *Essays on Free Thinking and Plain Speaking* in 1873, James Russell Lowell, very heterodox but still a believer in God, wrote to him of his "great interest" and "great satisfaction." Nevertheless, Lowell would not follow Stephen into agnosticism, partly because Lowell was willing to grant more validity to human intuition than Stephen and partly because "I find no fault with a judicious shutting of the eyes." This difference in standards of evidence made all the difference, yet in other respects Lowell and Stephen moved in the same world (Lowell to Stephen, 16 May 1874, in Norton, ed., *Letters of Lowell,* 2:125). The path toward agnosticism commonly ran from some more or less traditional version of Christianity through, successively, a very liberal, creedless Christianity and some form of spiritualism or theism. (See, e.g., the numerous short biographies of unbelievers and other religious radicals in Samuel P. Putnam, *Four Hundred Years of Freethought* [New York, 1894], pp. 681–829.) This path could lead all the way into agnosticism, as it did for Charles Eliot Norton; stop at a vague theism, as for Norton's good friend Lowell; or leave the traveler straddling the fence, as was apparently the case for another good friend of Norton's, Jonathan Harrison. These patterns will, I trust, become clearer in the succeeding pages.

3. John Stuart Mill, "Theism" (c.1868–1870), in *Three Essays on Religion* (London,

1874), pp. 126–27; Jonathan Harrison to Charles Eliot Norton, 6 April 1875, in Norton Papers, Houghton Library, Harvard University.

4. Physicus [George John Romanes], *A Candid Examination of Theism* (London, 1878), pp. 88–89; cf. Lester F. Ward, *Dynamic Sociology* (New York, 1883), 1:194–98.

5. Robert G. Ingersoll, "Individuality" (1873), in *The Works of Robert G. Ingersoll* (New York, 1909), 1:192; Frances Snow Compton [Henry Adams], *Esther: A Novel* (New York, 1884), p. 219; Charles Eliot Norton to Goldwin Smith, 14 June 1897, in Sara Norton and M. A. DeWolfe Howe, *Letters of Charles Eliot Norton with Biographical Comment* (Boston, 1913), 2:248.

6. Robert M. Young, *Mind, Brain, and Adaptation in the Nineteenth Century: Cerebral Localization and Its Biological Context from Gall to Ferrier* (Oxford, 1970); John D. Davies, *Phrenology, Fad and Science: A 19th-Century American Crusade* (New Haven, 1955). The term "phrenology" was coined by Gall's student, collaborator, and popularizer, Johann Kaspar Spurzheim; Gall himself did not use it.

7. Henry Ward Beecher, *Norwood; or, Village Life in New England* (New York, 1868), p. 51; William G. McLoughlin, *The Meaning of Henry Ward Beecher* (New York, 1970), pp. 46–49. Clerical nervousness about phrenology's materialism is recorded in Davies, *Phrenology*, chap. 13, and Theodore Dwight Bozeman, *Protestants in an Age of Science: The Baconian Ideal and Antebellum American Religious Thought* (Chapel Hill, 1977), pp. 92–93.

8. Young, *Mind, Brain, and Adaptation*, chaps. 4, 6, 7, 8.

9. Robert M. Young, "The Role of Psychology in the Nineteenth-Century Evolutionary Debate," in *Historical Conceptions of Psychology*, ed. Mary Henle et al. (New York, 1973), pp. 180–204. See, e.g., Claude Bernard, "On the Functions of the Brain," *Popular Science Monthly* 2 (1872–73): 64–74, and Henry de Varigny, "Cerebral Localization; or, the New Phrenology," ibid. 18 (1880–81): 599–610; and see, for examples of attacks by Presbyterians, *Princeton Review*, n.s. 1 (1878): 606–32; by Methodists, *Southern Review* 20 (1876): 85–116, 302–24; and by Catholics, *Catholic World* 32 (1880): 747–56.

10. Norton refers, e.g., to the experimental physiologists John Scott Burdon Sanderson and Charles Edward Brown-Séquard in his letters to Sir John Simon, Norton Papers.

11. Herbert Spencer, *The Principles of Psychology*, 3d ed. (1880; New York, 1887), 1:59–62, 66–67, 148–59; see also Spencer, *The Principles of Biology* (1866–67; New York, 1886), 2:375, 387; Ward, *Dynamic Sociology*, 1:361; George Henry Lewes, *The Physical Basis of Mind* (Boston, 1877), problem 3, chaps. 1–3, esp. pp. 365, 376–77, 386. In arguing that the organization of the organism made it more than simply the sum of the underlying physical processes, Lewes faintly foreshadowed the positions developed by the early twentieth-century physiologists C. S. Sherrington and Walter B. Cannon.

12. James Russell Lowell, "The Cathedral" (1870), in *The Writings of James Russell Lowell* (Cambridge, 1890), 10:49; J. C. Bucknill, "Mental Physiology," *Popular Science Monthly* 5 (1874): 705.

13. J. Milner Fothergill, "The Mental Aspects of Ordinary Disease," *Popular Science Monthly* 6 (1874–75): 562; Nora Barlow, ed., *The Autobiography of Charles Darwin, 1809–1882* (New York, 1958), p. 93.

14. See, e.g., An Agnostic, "Confessions of an Agnostic," *North American Review* 129 (1879): 284–85.

15. Ingersoll, "The Gods" (1872), in *Works*, 1:27.

16. T. H. Huxley, "On the Physical Basis of Life," *Fortnightly Review*, n.s. 5

(1869):129–45; Gerald L. Geison, "The Protoplasmic Theory of Life and the Vitalist-Mechanist Debate," *Isis* 60 (1969): 273–92; John, Viscount Morley, *Recollections* (New York, 1917), 1:90; Ward, *Dynamic Sociology*, 1: chap. 4.

17. R. B. Welch, "The Modern Theory of Forces," *Princeton Review*, n.s. 4 (1875): 399. One did not have to be scientifically foggy to take this position; Spencer adopted it, but so did George John Romanes (Physicus [Romanes], *Theism*, chap. 4). On the career of the concept of force, see Ronald E. Martin, *American Literature and the Universe of Force* (Durham, N.C., 1981).

18. See, e.g., J[ohn]. F. W. Herschel, *A Preliminary Discourse on the Study of Natural Philosophy* (London, 1831), which was probably the most influential discussion of such issues published in the first half of the century; cf., for an authoritative American statement, Joseph Henry, "Address to the American Association for the Advancement of Science" (1850), in *A Scientist in American Life: Essays and Lectures of Joseph Henry*, ed. Arthur P. Molella et al. (Washington, 1980), pp. 47–48. On scientists' conceptions of natural law and its relation to God, see Michael Ruse, "The Relationship between Science and Religion in Britain, 1830–1870," *Church History* 44 (1975): 505–22, esp. 508–9, and Susan Faye Cannon, *Science in Culture: The Early Victorian Period* (New York, 1978), pp. 267–68.

19. Asa Gray, *Darwiniana: Essays and Reviews Pertaining to Darwinism* (1876), ed. A. Hunter Dupree (Cambridge, Mass., 1963), p. 194.

20. "Matter, Life, and Mind," *National Quarterly Review* 38 (1879): 47; see, e.g., Murray G. Murphey, *The Development of Peirce's Philosophy* (Cambridge, Mass., 1961), pp. 333–34.

21. John Bascom, "The Natural Theology of Social Science," *Bibliotheca Sacra* 25 (1868): 270; Robert G. Ingersoll, "Humboldt" (1869), in *Works*, 1:95–96.

22. "The Logical Relations of Religion and Natural Science," *Princeton Review* 32 (1860): 574.

23. Darwin's belief has been a controverted question, but see Dov Ospovat, "God and Natural Selection: The Darwinian Idea of Design," *Journal of the History of Biology* 13 (1980): 169–94.

24. John Bascom made this point in "Natural Theology of Social Science," p. 2.

25. See, e.g., *Bibliotheca Sacra* 24 (1867): passim.

26. Herbert Hovenkamp, *Science and Religion in America, 1800–1860* (Philadelphia, 1978), p. 49.

27. *The Iconoclast* 2, no. 17 (1871): 1; W. R. Thompson, "Evolution," *Catholic World* 34 (1882): 692.

28. Herschel, *Preliminary Discourse*, p. 18; Francis Wayland, 1835, quoted in Joseph L. Blau, Introduction, in Wayland, *Elements of Moral Science* (1837), ed. Blau (Cambridge, Mass., 1963), p. xxiv.

29. Charles Hodge, *What is Darwinism?* (New York, 1874), passim.

30. Cannon, *Science and Culture*, p. 234; for U.S. scientists specifically, see pp. 73–81; Sedgwick is quoted in Patricia James, *Population Malthus: His Life and Times* (London, 1979), p. 446.

31. Laurence R. Veysey, *The Emergence of the American University* (Chicago, 1965), pp. 133–35; Hodge, *What is Darwinism?*, pp. 126–27, 140; Martin is quoted in Hugh Hawkins, *Pioneer: A History of the Johns Hopkins University, 1874–1889* (Ithaca, 1960), p. 295.

32. Henry, "Address," p. 50; Physicus [Romanes], *Theism*, p. 73.

33. See Edwards A. Park et al., "The Relation of Theology to Other Sciences,"

Bibliotheca Sacra 33 (1876): 288–89; A. Hunter Dupree, *Asa Gray, 1810–1888* (Cambridge, Mass., 1959), pp. 275, 290; [Chauncey Wright], "Natural Theology as a Positive Science," *North American Review* 100 (1865): 177–85.

34. [Wright], "Natural Theology," 181.

35. Owen Chadwick has noted this fallback onto forms of intuition as a general European phenomenon of the 1860s and 1870s: Chadwick, *Secularization*, pp. 183–84.

36. Lyman Abbott, *Reminiscences* (Boston, 1915), p. 450; Thomas Hill, "Theology a Possible Science," *Bibliotheca Sacra* 31 (1874): 22; John Dewey, "From Absolutism to Experimentalism," in George P. Adams and William Pepperell Montague, eds., *Contemporary American Philosophy* (New York, 1930), 2:15. For an early instance of the groundswell of interest in Schleiermacher, see Egbert C. Smith, "From Lessing to Schleiermacher, or from Rationalism to Faith," in *Boston Lectures, 1870: Christianity and Scepticism* (Boston, 1870), pp. 276–311.

37. "Matter, Life, and Mind," p. 46; Herbert Spencer, *First Principles of a New System of Philosophy*, 2d ed. (New York, 1870), p. 102; Marsh is quoted in Paul F. Boller, Jr., "The New Science and American Thought," in H. Wayne Morgan, ed., *The Gilded Age*, rev. ed. (Syracuse, 1970), p. 252; James T. Bixby, "The Know Nothing Position in Religion," *Bibliotheca Sacra* 38 (1881): 435.

38. Charles Eliot Norton, "The Church and Religion," *North American Review* 106 (1868): 378–79; Matthew Arnold, *St. Paul and Protestantism* (1869–70), in *Dissent and Dogma*, vol. 6 of *Complete Prose Works of Matthew Arnold*, ed. R. H. Super (Ann Arbor, 1968), pp. 8–9.

39. "Science vs. Theology," *The Iconoclast* 1, no. 2 (1870): 2; James is quoted in Ralph Barton Perry, *The Thought and Character of William James* (Boston, 1935), 2:30.

40. John R. Commons, *Myself: The Autobiography of John R. Commons* (1934; Madison, 1963), p. 14; Jonathan Harrison to Charles Eliot Norton, 1 May 1878, in Norton Papers.

41. Francis Ellingwood Abbot, "Positivism in Theology," *Christian Examiner* 80 (1866): 240, 252, 255; cf. Abbot, *Scientific Theism* (London, 1885).

42. Putnam, *Four Hundred Years*, p. 505.

43. Mark DeWolfe Howe, *Justice Oliver Wendell Holmes: The Shaping Years, 1841–1870* (Cambridge, Mass., 1957), pp. 17–18, 210.

44. James Bradley Thayer, ed., *Letters of Chauncey Wright, with Some Account of His Life* (Cambridge, Mass., 1878), p. 67.

45. Ingersoll, "The Gods" (1872), in *Works*, 1:26; Physicus [Romanes], *Theism*, pp. 27–34, details the putative evolution of the moral sense.

46. "Can God be Known," *Princeton Review* 36 (1864): 144.

47. Charles Hodge, *Systematic Theology*, 3d prntg. (1871; New York, 1887), 1:16, 2:15–16; Charles M. Mead, "The Uncertainties of Natural and Religious Science," in *Boston Lectures, 1870*, pp. 103–5.

48. Cannon, *Science in Culture*, pp. 274–75; Stanley M. Guralnick, "Geology and Religion before Darwin: The Case of Edward Hitchcock, Theologian and Geologist," *Isis* 63 (1972): 542.

49. Mead, "Natural and Religious Science," p. 108; Compton [Adams], *Esther*, p. 191; Huxley, "Physical Basis," 144.

50. Ward, *Dynamic Sociology*, 1:69–70.

51. Thomas H. Huxley, *Science and Christian Tradition: Essays* (New York, 1898), pp. 37–38.

52. Ingersoll, "Humboldt" (1869), in *Works*, 1:93; Ingersoll to Mr. Ellis, 8 August

1883, in Eva Ingersoll Wakefield, ed., *The Letters of Robert G. Ingersoll* (New York, 1951), p. 268. Ingersoll intoned this triad, "reason, observation, and experience"—"the Holy Trinity of Science"—repeatedly throughout his career.

53. Matthew Arnold, *Literature and Dogma* (1871–73), in *Dissent and Dogma*, p. 381.

54. Horace Bushnell, *God in Christ* (Hartford, 1849), pp. 40, 42, 74; Bushnell is quoted in Mary Bushnell Cheney, ed., *Life and Letters of Horace Bushnell* (New York, 1880), pp. 200–201. The fullest explication of Bushnell's linguistic thinking is Donald A. Crosby, *Horace Bushnell's Theory of Language in the Context of Other Nineteenth-Century Philosophies of Language* (The Hague, 1975); see also Philip F. Gura, *The Wisdom of Words: Language, Theology, and Literature in the New England Renaissance* (Middletown, Conn., 1981), chap. 2.

55. Bushnell, *God in Christ*, p. 96. One of the most thoughtful and erudite of early American agnostics, much influenced by Emerson, zeroed in on precisely this point in the latter's writings: Charles Eliot Norton to E. L. Godkin, 31 January 1868, in Norton and Howe, *Letters of Norton*, 1:298.

56. Hodge, *Systematic Theology*, 1:202–3; Beecher is quoted in Introduction to William G. McLoughlin, ed., *The American Evangelicals, 1800–1900: An Anthology* (New York, 1968), p. 20; Henry Ward Beecher, *Norwood; or, Village Life in New England* (New York, 1868), pp. 52, 269; Donald M. Scott, *From Office to Profession: The New England Ministry, 1750–1850* (Philadelphia, 1978), pp. 144–47 (quotation from Beecher's *Yale Lectures on Preaching* [1872], pp. 226–27).

57. Martin Duberman, *James Russell Lowell* (Boston, 1966), pp. 62–63; R. W. B. Lewis, *The American Adam: Innocence, Tragedy, and Tradition in the Nineteenth Century* (Chicago, 1955), p. 191; J. C. Shairp, "Poetry versus Agnosticism," *Princeton Review* 5 (1880): 286–302.

58. Henry Ward Beecher, "The Revision of Creeds," *North American Review* 136 (1883): 19; Harrison to Norton, 19 February 1875, Norton to Harrison, 15 August 1865, in Norton Papers.

59. Chauncey Wright to Francis E. Abbot, 9 July 1867, in James Bradley Thayer, ed., *Letters of Chauncey Wright, with Some Account of His Life* (Cambridge, Mass., 1878), p. 103; Henry Adams to Mabel LaFarge, 6 October 1894, in *Letters to a Niece and Prayer to the Virgin of Chartres*, ed. Mabel LaFarge (Boston, 1920), p. 75; Adams is quoted in Introduction to ibid., p. 18; Compton [Adams], *Esther*, p. 201; Ward, *Dynamic Sociology*, 1:11; George M. Beard, "The Psychology of Spiritism," *North American Review* 129 (1879): 65.

60. Octavius Brooks Frothingham, "Reasonable Religion," p. 26, in *Beliefs of the Unbelievers and Other Discourses* (New York, 1876); John Tyndall, "Address" (1874), in George Basalla et al., eds., *Victorian Science: A Self-Portrait from the Presidential Addresses to the British Association for the Advancement of Science* (Garden City, N.Y., 1970), p. 474.

61. Norton to Harrison, 3 June 1866, in Norton Papers; Norton, "Church and Religion," p. 382.

62. Arnold, *Literature and Dogma*, p. 232; Wright to Abbot, 20 December 1864, in Thayer, *Letters of Wright*, p. 61.

63. Joseph LeConte, "Autobiography," p. 2, Elizabeth Furman Talley Papers, in the Southern Historical Collection, University of North Carolina Library, Chapel Hill; Bayard Taylor to Paul Hamilton Hayne, n.d. [1877?], in Marie Hansen-Taylor and Horace E. Scudder, *Life and Letters of Bayard Taylor* (Boston, 1884), 2:717; Lowell to Leslie Stephen, 15 May 1876, in Norton, *Letters of Lowell*, 2:168.

64. Norton to G. E. Woodberry, 22 May 1881, in Norton and Howe, *Letters of*

Norton, 2:120; Olmsted to Charles Loring Brace, 15 March 1887, Olmsted Papers, Library of Congress; Elizabeth Cady Stanton to Robert Livingston Stanton, 3 February 1876, in Theodore Stanton and Harriot Stanton Blatch, eds., *Elizabeth Cady Stanton: As Revealed in Her Letters, Diary and Reminiscences* (New York, 1922), 2:148; Norton to Goldwin Smith, 10 July 1902, Norton Papers.

65. Donald Fleming, *John William Draper and the Religion of Science* (Philadelphia, 1950), p. 1.

66. George T. Ladd, "The Difficulties of the Concept of God," *Bibliotheca Sacra* 34 (1877): 631. Ladd's own unusual combination of scientific and philosophic interests may have led him earlier than most toward this sort of revisionary thinking. To his role as a Congregational clergyman, he added a forty-year academic connection with Yale (1881–1921), where he championed the post-Kantian German idealists and also pioneered the scientific study of psychology, based on physiology (*Dictionary of American Biography*, s.v. "George Trumbull Ladd").

67. Frederick A. Bode, *Protestantism and the New South: North Carolina Baptists and Methodists in Political Crisis, 1894–1903* (Charlottesville, 1975), pp. 9–10; Library Registers, 1860–63 and 1867–81, Dialectic Society Records, and Library Registers, 1853–54, 1866–71, and 1875–76, Philanthropic Society Records, in the University of North Carolina Archives at the University of North Carolina Library, Chapel Hill.

Chapter 7: The Immorality of Belief

1. Journal, 26 January 1865, quoted in Frederic William Maitland, *The Life and Letters of Leslie Stephen* (London, 1906), p. 144.

2. The classic statement of this position, much admired by Victorian agnostics, was William Kingdon Clifford's "The Ethics of Belief," later the prime target of Williams James's "The Will to Believe."

3. John Weiss, *Life and Correspondence of Theodore Parker* (New York, 1864), 1:145–50.

4. W. E. B. DuBois, *The Souls of Black Folk* (1903; New York, 1982), p. 235. On the complex response of Northern intellectuals to the suffering of the Civil War, see George M. Fredrickson, *The Inner Civil War: Northern Intellectuals and the Crisis of the Union* (New York, 1965), chaps. 6–7.

5. Benny Kraut, *From Reform Judaism to Ethical Culture: The Religious Evolution of Felix Adler* (Cincinnati, 1979), pp. 33–42.

6. Tennyson's famous line comes, of course, from *In Memoriam* (1850); John Stuart Mill, "The Utility of Religion," in *Three Essays on Religion* (London, 1874), p. 112 (this essay was written in the 1850s, before the *Origin of Species* appeared). For Lyell's influence on Tennyson, see Christopher Ricks, ed., *The Poems of Tennyson* (London, 1969), p. 911n. I trust that I will not be taken as asserting that this grim picture was the only common impression of nature.

7. Ingersoll to Horace Traubel, 17 August 1893, in Eva Ingersoll Wakefield, ed., *The Letters of Robert G. Ingersoll* (New York, 1951), p. 660; Norton to Moorfield Storey, 29 August 1903, in Sara Norton and M. A. DeWolfe Howe, eds., *Letters of Charles Eliot Norton with Biographical Comment* (Boston, 1913), 2:336.

8. Oliver Wendell Holmes, Jr., "The Soldier's Faith" (1895), in *The Occasional Speeches of Justice Oliver Wendell Holmes*, ed. Mark DeWolfe Howe (Cambridge, Mass., 1962), p. 74.

9. On this comparative point, not much attended to in historical scholarship,

I have benefited in conversation from the expertise of Jane Turner Censer and Russell Blake. On the social morality of postbellum southern churchmen, see, e.g., Rufus B. Spain, *At Ease in Zion: Social History of Southern Baptists, 1865–1900* (Nashville, 1967), esp. pp. 209–13, and Hunter D. Farish, *The Circuit Rider Dismounts: A Social History of Southern Methodism, 1865–1900* (Richmond, 1938), esp. chaps. 9–10; the quotation is from p. 55.

10. Ingersoll to Mrs. J.C. Euwer, 23 November 1886, in Wakefield, *Letters of Ingersoll*, p. 273; Ingersoll, "The Gods" (1872), in *The Works of Robert G. Ingersoll* (New York, 1909), 1:70; Mill is quoted in Geoffrey Rowell, *Hell and the Victorians: A Study of the Nineteenth-Century Theological Controversies Concerning Eternal Punishment and the Future Life* (Oxford, 1974), p. 3; Stanton to Henry Stanton, 2 August 1880, in *Elizabeth Cady Stanton: As Revealed in Her Letters, Diary, and Reminiscences*, ed. Theodore Stanton and Harriot Stanton Blatch (New York, 1922), 2:171.

11. Ingersoll, "The Great Infidels" (1881), in *Works*, 3:319; Nora Barlow, ed., *The Autobiography of Charles Darwin, 1809–1882* (New York, 1958), p. 90; Donald Fleming, "Charles Darwin, the Anaesthetic Man," *Victorian Studies* 4 (1961): 219–36; Henry Adams, *The Education of Henry Adams* (1907; Boston, 1961), p. 289. Adams's sister died in 1870.

12. On this latter point—and its connections with economic change—see Mary P. Ryan, *Cradle of the Middle Class: The Family in Oneida County, New York, 1790–1865* (Cambridge, 1981). Interestingly, in the light of my following argument, the number of actual agnostics among postbellum feminists (over and above women who rejected only Christianity on feminist grounds) seems to have been disproportionately high (e.g., Elizabeth Cady Stanton and Lucy Colman).

13. Samuel P. Putnam, *My Religious Experience* (New York, n.d. [1891]), p. 48.

14. Norton to E. L. Godkin, 19 October 1866, and 4 February 1866, in Charles Eliot Norton Papers, Houghton Library, Harvard University; Ingersoll, "Individuality" (1873), in *Works*, 1:171; [Charles Eliot Norton], "Arthur Hugh Clough," *North American Review* 105 (1867): 434–77.

15. Letter from Prof. J. E. Oliver, read to Freethinkers' Convention, 1878, in *The Proceedings and Addresses at the Freethinkers' Convention Held at Watkins, N.Y., August 22d, 23d, 24th, and 25th, '78* (New York, 1878), p. 177; "Speech of T. L. Brown, M.D.," in ibid., p. 36; Ingersoll to Andrew D. White, 27 December 1888, in Wakefield, *Letters of Ingersoll*, p. 305.

16. Elizabeth Cady Stanton, 1860, quoted in Ellen DuBois, "Women's Rights and Abolition: The Nature of the Connection," in *Antislavery Reconsidered: New Perspectives on the Abolitionists*, ed. Lewis Perry and Michael Fellman (Baton Rouge, 1979), pp. 243–44.

17. Norton to E. L. Godkin, 3 May 1870, Norton Papers; Norton to Meta Gaskell, 14 July 1867, in Norton and Howe, *Letters of Norton*, 1:295–96.

18. Lucy N. Colman, *Reminiscences* (Buffalo, 1891), pp. 10–11; Putnam, *Religious Experience*, pp. 82–83.

19. [Norton], "Clough," p. 445.

20. Benjamin Franklin, *The Autobiography of Benjamin Franklin*, ed. Leonard W. Labaree et al. (New Haven, 1964), p. 150; Orestes A. Brownson, *The Convert* (1857), in *Works*, ed. Henry F. Brownson (Detroit, 1882–1907), 5:44, 46; Jane Addams, *Twenty Years at Hull-House* (New York, 1910), p. 15.

21. "Modern Culture," *Southern Review*, 13 (1873): 123.

22. Quoted in Noel Annan, "The Strands of Unbelief," in Harman Grisewood, ed., *Ideas and Beliefs of the Victorians* (New York, 1949), p. 154.

23. On differences between southern and northern conceptions of honorable

behavior, see Bertram Wyatt-Brown, *Southern Honor: Ethics and Behavior in the Old South* (New York, 1982), pp. 23–24.

24. Lowell to Stephen, 16 May 1874, in Charles Eliot Norton, ed., *Letters of James Russell Lowell* (New York, 1894), 2:125.

25. "Modern Culture," p. 123; Henry Rowland, quoted in Paul F. Boller, "The New Science and American Thought," in *The Gilded Age*, 2d ed., ed. H. Wayne Morgan (Syracuse, 1970), p. 257.

26. Andrew Dickson White, *Autobiography* (New York, 1905), 2:532.

27. Hugh Hawkins, *Pioneer: A History of the Johns Hopkins University, 1874–1889* (Ithaca, 1960), p. 115; "Speech of Brown," in *Freethinkers' Convention*, p. 28; [Norton], "Clough," p. 437.

28. I want to thank Henry Abelove of Wesleyan University for calling my attention to Bayle and pressing me to clarify this distinction.

29. Norton to E. L. Godkin, 22 October 1867, E. L. Godkin Papers, Houghton Library, Harvard University; Chauncey Wright to Francis E. Abbot, 9 July 1867, in James Bradley Thayer, ed., *Letters of Chauncey Wright, with Some Account of His Life* (Cambridge, Mass., 1878), p. 103.

30. Charles Eliot Norton, "The Church and Religion," *North American Review* 106 (1868): 383; *The Iconoclast* 1, no. 11 (1871): 2; Frances Snow Compton [Henry Adams], *Esther: A Novel* (New York, 1884), p. 299.

31. The phrase is from William James, *The Varieties of Religious Experience* (1902; New York, 1925), p. 204. James was describing the "agnostic veto on faith," with which he of course disagreed.

32. Child to Lucy Osgood, 1859, in *Letters of Lydia Maria Child* (Boston, 1883), p. 139; Norton, Journal, 6 February 1873, in Norton and Howe, *Letters of Norton*, 1:464.

33. Putnam, *Religious Experience*, p. 101; James Fitzjames Stephen et al., "A Modern 'Symposium': The Influence upon Morality of a Decline in Religious Belief," *The Nineteenth Century* 1 (1877): 539.

34. Octavius Brooks Frothingham is quoted in J. Wade Caruthers, *Octavius Brooks Frothingham: Gentle Radical* (University, Ala., 1977), p. 59.

35. See, e.g., Lyman Abbott, *The Theology of an Evolutionist* (New York, 1897), and Henry Ward Beecher, *Evolution and Religion* (New York, 1885).

36. A good example of this is *Gesta Christi; or a History of Humane Progress under Christianity* (New York, 1882) by Frederick Law Olmsted's lifelong friend, the Reverend Charles Loring Brace.

37. Brownson, *Convert*, in *Works*, 5:49.

38. Frederic Harrison, "Charles Eliot Norton," in *Among My Books: Centenaries, Reviews, Memoirs* (London, 1912), p. 322; *The Iconoclast* 1, no. 1 (1870): 1.

39. Fiske to Abby Morgan Brooks, 31 December 1863, in *The Letters of John Fiske*, ed. Ethel F. Fisk (New York, 1940), p. 118; Moody's *Science of Evil* is excerpted in *The Iconoclast* 2, no. 16 (1871): 4.

40. *The Iconoclast*, 2, no. 16 (June 1871): 4; Lester Ward, *Dynamic Sociology* (New York, 1883), 2:289, 296–97.

41. Diary of Lester Ward, 24 February 1867, in *Young Ward's Diary*, ed. Bernhard J. Stern (New York, 1935), p. 223; Mill, "Theism," in *Three Essays*, p. 204.

42. This at least seems the most plausible reading of the bizarre passage in Ward, *Dynamic Sociology*, 2:550.

43. Thomas Hitchcock, "The Functions of Unbelief," *North American Review* 125 (1877): 462–71.

44. Ward, *Dynamic Sociology*, 2:297; cf. 1:10; Ingersoll, "The Gods," in *Works*,

1:65; "Address by Mr. Toohey," in *Freethinkers' Convention*, p. 247; Wright to Francis E. Abbot, 28 October 1867, in Thayer, *Letters of Wright*, p. 134.

45. Putnam, *Religious Experience*, pp. 3–5.

46. Wright to Francis E. Abbot, 20 December 1864, in Thayer, *Letters of Wright*, p. 61.

47. Cf., e.g., Ronald C. White, Jr., and C. Howard Hopkins, *The Social Gospel: Religion and Reform in Changing America* (Philadelphia, 1976), pp. 31–33, 66–67, 132–35. This seems to have been to some extent true even of a Social Gospeler like Walter Rauschenbusch who generally assumed his audience to be committed to Christianity; see William R. Hutchison, *The Modernist Impulse in American Protestantism* (Cambridge, Mass., 1976), pp. 173–74. The relation of the Social Gospel to forces making for unbelief receives further attention in chapter 8.

48. There is no way to compile reliable statistical data to support this impression, since there is no way of plausibly guessing even the order of magnitude of the number of agnostics, much less assembling a truly representative list. But, for what it may be worth, the biographical appendix in Samuel P. Putnam, *Four Hundred Years of Freethought* (New York, 1894), lists the occupation and sometimes the father's occupation for eighty-one freethinkers. (It is impossible to say with any certainty how many were really unbelievers, how many radical theists, opinions seldom being sketched coherently.) Of these eighty-one, fourteen (17 percent) had been ministers themselves or had ministers for fathers. The other notable occupational group—aside from freethought lecturers and writers—was physicians (9 percent), presumably owing to the wider circulation of "scientific" hostility to supernatural beliefs among doctors.

49. Of the eighty-two persons in the biographical appendix to Putnam, *Four Hundred Years*, whose place of birth and upbringing are indicated, fifty-one (62 percent) came from this region. Leaving aside foreign-born, the proportion rises to 84 percent. Again, I make no claims for statistical validity; I offer these figures simply as suggestive.

50. Norton to J. B. Harrison, 19 March 1865, Norton Papers; Matthew Arnold, *Literature and Dogma* (1873), in *Dissent and Dogma*, vol. 6 of *The Complete Prose Works of Matthew Arnold*, ed. R. H. Super (Ann Arbor, 1968), p. 176; Francis Wayland, *The Elements of Moral Science* (1837), ed. Joseph L. Blau (Cambridge, Mass., 1963), p. 147.

51. Mill, "Theism," in *Three Essays*, p. 215.

52. Ethelred Philips to James J. Philips, 14 October 1864, in James J. Philips Papers, Southern Historical Collection, University of North Carolina Library, Chapel Hill.

53. Putnam, *Religious Experience*, pp. 15, 92–93.

Chapter 8: A More Excellent Way

1. Wright to Grace Norton, 29 July 1874, in James Bradley Thayer, ed., *Letters of Chauncey Wright, with Some Account of His Life* (Cambridge, Mass., 1878), p. 274; Taylor to unknown correspondent, 11 April 1870, in John Richie Schultz, ed., *The Unpublished Letters of Bayard Taylor in the Huntington Library* (San Marino, Calif., 1937), pp. 140–41.

2. Norton to John Ruskin, 8 October 1869, in Charles Eliot Norton Papers, Houghton Library, Harvard University; Norton, Journal, 12 April 1873, in Sara Norton and M. A. DeWolfe Howe, *Letters of Charles Eliot Norton with Biographical Comment* (Boston, 1913), 1:476.

3. See Lewis Perry's splendid biography, *Childhood, Marriage, and Reform: Henry Clarke Wright, 1797–1870* (Chicago, 1980). Professor Perry kindly clarified in conversation the murky issue of Wright's self-identification as a Christian.

4. My account of Harrison rests on material in the Norton Papers (see letters and box 5 of Miscellaneous Papers), with corroboration of some details from the *Year-Books of the Unitarian Congregational Churches* (Boston, 1867ff.).

5. Herbert Spencer, *First Principles of a New System of Philosophy*, 2d ed. (New York, 1870), p. 118 (a position developed at length in Spencer's *The Data of Ethics* [New York, 1879]); John Lubbock, *The Origin of Civilization and the Primitive Condition of Man: Mental and Social Condition of Savages* (London, 1870), p. 271; Harrison to Charles Eliot Norton, 1 May 1878, in Norton Papers.

6. *The Iconoclast* 1, no. 1 (1870): 2; James Fitzjames Stephen et al., "A Modern 'Symposium': The Influence upon Morality of a Decline in Religious Belief," *The Nineteenth Century* 1 (1877): 356.

7. Norton to Goldwin Smith, 14 June 1897, and to John Ruskin, 31 March 1870, and 8 October 1869, in Norton Papers; Olmsted to Charles Loring Brace, 15 March 1887, in Frederick Law Olmsted Papers, Library of Congress. In Leslie Stephen, *The Science of Ethics* (New York, 1882), see esp. pp. 32–36, 135–37, 149–55, 450–55, and 460–61.

8. Samuel P. Putnam, *My Religious Experience* (New York, n.d. [1891]), pp. 3, 81; *Iconoclast* 1, no. 10 (1870): 2.

9. Olmsted to Brace, 21 December 1873, in Olmsted Papers.

10. George Bancroft, "The Necessity, the Reality, and the Promise of the Progress of the Human Race" (1854), in *Literary and Historical Miscellanies* (New York, 1855), p. 488.

11. "Modern Culture," *Southern Review* 13 (1882): 123; John William Draper, *History of the Intellectual Development of Europe* (1863), quoted in Donald Fleming, *John William Draper and the Religion of Science* (Philadelphia, 1950), p. 84.

12. Robert G. Ingersoll, "The Gods" (1872), in *The Works of Robert G. Ingersoll* (New York, 1909), 1:22, 80; Ingersoll, "The Great Infidels" (1881), in ibid., 3:309.

13. Norton to Stephen, 2 May 1892, in Norton and Howe, *Letters of Norton*, 2:211; letter from Prof. J. E. Oliver of Cornell University to the Freethinkers' Convention, in *The Proceedings and Addresses at the Freethinkers' Convention Held at Watkins, N.Y., August 22d, 23d, 24th, and 25th, '78* (New York, 1878), p. 177; Abbot is quoted in *Iconoclast* 1, no. 1 (1870): 3.

14. *Iconoclast* 1, no. 1 (1870): 3; Norton to Mrs. [Elizabeth] Gaskell, 26 December 1859, and to G. E. Woodberry, Christmas 1881, in Norton and Howe, *Letters of Norton*, 1:202, 2:128; Lester F. Ward, *Dynamic Sociology* (New York, 1883), 2:23.

15. Norton to Leslie Stephen, 2 May 1892, in Norton and Howe, *Letters of Norton*, 2:211; Putnam, *Religious Experience*, p. 101.

16. Harrison to Charles Eliot Norton, 11 August and 1 May 1878, in Norton Papers.

17. Norton to Thomas Carlyle, 16 November 1873, to S. G. Ward, 28 November 1897, and to Goldwin Smith, 14 June 1897, in Norton and Howe, *Letters of Norton*, 2:18, 256, 248.

18. *Iconoclast* 1, no. 1 (1870): 1; 1, no. 2 (1870): 2; and 1, no. 6 (1870): 4; Ingersoll, "The Gods," p. 58.

19. *Iconoclast* 1, no. 1 (1870): 1; Ingersoll, "The Gods," pp. 81, 78, 57–58.

20. "Speech of T. L. Brown, M.D.," in *Freethinkers' Convention*, pp. 32, 41; Ward, *Dynamic Sociology*, 1:8; Ingersoll, "Orthodoxy" (1884), in *Works*, 2:410.

21. Wright to Grace Norton, 25 March 1870, in Thayer, *Letters of Wright*, p. 183.

22. Ingersoll, "The Gods," p. 89; Stanton to Robert Dale Owen, 10 April 1866, in Theodore Stanton and Harriot Stanton Blatch, eds., *Elizabeth Cady Stanton: As Revealed in Her Letters, Diary, and Reminiscences* (New York, 1922), 2:113; George Eliot to Sara Sophia Hennell, 22 November 1869, in *The George Eliot Letters,* ed. Gordon S. Haight (New Haven, 1954–78), 5:68–69; Putnam, *Religious Experience,* p. 98.

23. James to Thomas W. Ward, January 1868, in Henry James, ed., *The Letters of William James* (Boston, 1926), 1:130–31.

24. John Stuart Mill, "Theism," in *Three Essays on Religion* (London, 1874), pp. 256–57.

25. John Lubbock, *Pre-Historic Times, as Illustrated by Ancient Remains, and the Manners and Customs of Modern Savages,* 2d ed. (London, 1869), pp. 590–91.

26. Hugh Hawkins, *Pioneer: A History of the Johns Hopkins University, 1874–1889* (Ithaca, 1960), p. 303; Draper, *Intellectual Development,* quoted in Fleming, *Draper,* p. 84; Ingersoll, "The Gods," p. 86; John William Draper, *History of the Conflict between Religion and Science* (1874; New York, 1898), p. vii.

27. Norton to E. L. Godkin, 24 January 1866, in E. L. Godkin Papers, Houghton Library, Harvard University; Wright to Charles Eliot Norton, 21 March 1870, in Thayer, *Letters of Wright,* pp. 172–73.

28. Lyman Abbott, *Reminiscences* (Boston, 1915), p. 347; Rowland is quoted in Paul F. Boller, "The New Science and American Thought," in H. Wayne Morgan, ed., *The Gilded Age,* rev. ed. (Syracuse, 1970), p. 257.

29. "Modern Culture," p. 123; John Tyndall, "Science and Religion," *Popular Science Monthly* 2 (1872–73): 79–82.

30. Norton to S. G. Ward, 14 April 1901, in Norton and Howe, *Letters of Norton,* 2:305; Harrison to Norton, 1 May 1878, in Norton Papers.

31. Ingersoll, "Liberty in Literature" (1890), in *Works,* 3:251–304; John Tyndall, "Address" (1874), in George Basalla, William Coleman, and Robert H. Kargon, eds., *Victorian Science: A Self-Portrait from the Presidential Addresses of the British Association for the Advancement of Science* (Garden City, N.Y., 1970), p. 477; Norton to S. G. Ward, 28 November 1897, in Norton and Howe, *Letters of Norton,* 2:255–56. For Draper's conception of science, see Fleming, *Draper,* pp. 126–27.

32. Florence T. Griswold, "The Social Problem," *The Badger,* 13 June 1885, 201–3, quoted in Rosenberg, *No Other Gods,* p. 12. Rosenberg has very shrewd comments on this general point.

33. Lewis H. Morgan, *Ancient Society, or Researches in the Lines of Human Progress from Savagery through Barbarism to Civilization* (New York, 1877), pp. 3, 38, 554, and pt. 1 of chap. 3.

34. Thomas Hitchcock, "The Functions of Unbelief," *North American Review* 125 (1877): 462–71.

35. Putnam, *Religious Experience,* p. 84; Stephen et al., "Modern 'Symposium,'" p. 355.

36. Wright to Francis E. Abbot, 28 October 1867, in Thayer, *Letters of Wright,* p. 134; Putnam, *Religious Experience,* pp. 83–84; Norton to Goldwin Smith, 14 June 1897, 31 January 1905, in Norton Papers, and 12 July 1906, in Norton and Howe, *Letters of Norton,* 2:364.

37. J[ames]. M. Mathews, *The Bible and Men of Learning* (New York, 1859), Sixth Lecture. Although published in 1859, this book was based on lectures delivered c.1844.

38. Orestes A. Brownson, *The Convert* (1857), in *Works,* ed. Henry F. Brownson (Detroit, 1882–1907), 5:49.

39. Rosenberg, *No Other Gods*, p. 137; George S. Merriam, "Christianity and Free Thought," *Scribner's Monthly* 14 (1877): 827.

40. William R. Hutchison, "Cultural Strain and Protestant Liberalism," *American Historical Review* 76 (1971): 403.

41. Peter J. Frederick, *Knights of the Golden Rule: The Intellectual as Social Reformer in the 1890s* (Lexington, Ky., 1976), p. 212; Theodore T. Munger, *The Freedom of Faith* (Boston, 1883), chap. 1, quoted in Ronald C. White, Jr., and C. Howard Hopkins, *The Social Gospel: Religion and Reform in Changing America* (Philadelphia, 1976), p. 33; McGlynn is quoted in Aaron I. Abell, *American Catholicism and Social Action: A Search for Social Justice, 1865–1950* (New York, 1960), p. 63.

42. A. W. Coats, "Henry Carter Adams: A Case Study in the Emergence of the Social Sciences in the United States, 1850–1900," *Journal of American Studies* 2 (1968): 177–97; e.g., Chauncey Wright to Charles Eliot Norton, 18 February 1867, in Norton Papers; George Eliot to Mrs. Henry Frederick Ponsonby, 10 December 1874, in *George Eliot Letters*, 6:98.

43. Norton to S. G. Ward, 28 November 1897, in Norton and Howe, *Letters of Norton*, 2:255; letter of Oliver, in *Freethinkers' Convention*, p. 178.

Chapter 9: Sanctity without Godliness

1. Charles Eliot Norton to Jonathan Harrison, 3 June 1866, in Charles Eliot Norton Papers, Houghton Library, Harvard University.

2. "The Religion of Today," *North American Review* 129 (1879): 563; Robert G. Ingersoll, "Humboldt" (1869), in *The Works of Robert G. Ingersoll* (New York, 1909), 1:116; Benny Kraut, *From Reform Judaism to Ethical Culture: The Religious Evolution of Felix Adler* (Cincinnati, 1979).

3. Herbert Spencer, *First Principles of a New System of Philosophy*, 2d ed. (New York, 1870), p. 20; Murray G. Murphey, *The Development of Peirce's Philosophy* (Cambridge, Mass., 1961), p. 101; John Dewey, "The Significance of the Problem of Knowledge" (1897), in *The Influence of Darwin on Philosophy* (New York, 1910), p. 298.

4. Hugh Honour, *Romanticism* (New York, 1979), p. 262; John William Draper, *History of the Conflict between Religion and Science* (New York, 1874); Donald Fleming, *John William Draper and the Religion of Science* (Philadelphia, 1950), p. 129.

5. Granted, Servetus studied medicine, and the theological treatise for which he suffered also contained the first published statement that blood flows through the lungs; but even professional scientists like Draper strangely overlooked this fact. Besides, Geneva burned Servetus for his opinions about the Trinity, not pulmonary circulation.

6. Ingersoll, "Thomas Paine" (1870), in *Works*, 1:163–64.

7. Francis Ellingwood Abbot, "Modern Principles: A Synopsis of Free Religion," *Index* 2 (1871): 1, quoted in H. Burnell Pannill, *The Religious Faith of John Fiske* (Durham, N.C., 1957), p. 51; Ingersoll to S. W. Sparks, 11 December 1886, in Eva Ingersoll Wakefield, ed., *The Letters of Robert G. Ingersoll* (New York, 1951), p. 275.

8. Berenson is quoted in Ernest Samuels, *Bernard Berenson: The Making of a Connoisseur* (Cambridge, Mass., 1979), p. 283. Henry Adams's *Mont-Saint-Michel and Chartres* and "Prayer to the Virgin of Chartres" are celebrated. Less well known today is Norton's medievalist writing. Among other things, he translated Dante's *Vita Nuova* and *Divine Comedy* and wrote *Historical Studies of Church Building in the Middle Ages*.

9. William James, *The Varieties of Religious Experience* (1902; New York, 1925), pp. 91–92; Spencer, *First Principles*, p. 20.

10. Samuels, *Berenson*, p. 24; John Tomsich, *A Genteel Endeavor: American Culture and Politics in the Gilded Age* (Stanford, 1971), p. 174.

11. Frances Snow Compton [Henry Adams], *Esther: A Novel* (New York, 1884), pp. 259–60.

12. James, *Varieties*, p. 57.

13. My argument in these last three sentences derives from Fleming, *Draper*, pp. 60–63.

14. Huxley to Kingsley, 23 September 1860, in Leonard Huxley, *Life and Letters of Thomas Henry Huxley* (New York, 1900), 1:233, 235; Tyndall to Faraday, quoted in Paul L. Sawyer, "Ruskin and Tyndall: The Poetry of Matter and the Poetry of Spirit," in *Victorian Science and Victorian Values*, ed. James Paradis and Thomas Postlewait (New York, 1981), p. 230.

15. Compton [Adams], *Esther*, p. 155.

16. Henry Ward Beecher, *Norwood; or, Village Life in New England* (New York, 1868), p. 223.

17. Frederick Law Olmsted to Charles Loring Brace, 21 December 1873, in Frederick Law Olmsted Papers, Library of Congress; Wright to Francis E. Abbot, 28 October 1867, in James Bradley Thayer, ed., *Letters of Chauncey Wright, with Some Account of His Life* (Cambridge, Mass., 1878), p. 134.

18. Note, for example, the geographic and social parameters indicated in Lord Bryce's discussion of unbelief in the United States c. 1890: James Bryce, *The American Commonwealth*, 3d ed. (New York, 1894), pp. 718–19.

19. Charles Eliot Norton, "The Church and Religion," *North American Review* 106 (1868): 381–82.

Epilogue

1. Pastoral letter of the Episcopal House of Bishops, 1886, quoted in Francis P. Weisenburger, *Ordeal of Faith: The Crisis of Church-Going America, 1865–1900* (New York, 1959), p. 71; James Bryce, *The American Commonwealth*, 3d ed. (New York, 1894), p. 718; William Burnet Wright, book review in *Andover Review* 1 (1884): 341.

2. Stow Persons, "Religion and Modernity, 1865–1914," in James Ward Smith and A. Leland Jamison, eds., *Religion in American Life* (Princeton, 1961), 1:372.

3. Note, e.g., the changing concerns of college students, for whom the question of theism versus unbelief became old hat after about 1890 (Laurence R. Veysey, *The Emergence of the American University* [Chicago, 1965], pp. 227, 280–81, 343). A similar subsidence of controversy occurred about the same time in England (see Owen Chadwick, *The Secularization of the European Mind in the Nineteenth Century* [Cambridge, 1975], p. 184, and Hugh McLeod, *Class and Religion in the Late Victorian City* [Hamden, Conn., 1974], esp. chap. 8).

4. [Charles Eliot Norton], "Religious Liberty," *North American Review* 104 (1867): 588.

5. Why given individuals should choose belief or unbelief remains the most difficult question in the whole problem. The variables are numerous, hard to define, and even harder to get reliable evidence for. I have noticed two curious patterns in the upbringing of men who might be described as activist infidels—proselytizers in behalf of freethought. Among fourteen such persons with some claim to more than local importance, and about whom information regarding their fathers could

be located, five had clergymen for fathers, while seven had some clearly identifiable major difficulty with their fathers (e.g., the father died while the children were young; the father went bankrupt, leaving support of the family to the mother). There is some overlap between the two categories, so that ten of the fourteen (not twelve) had either a clerical or a deficient father or both. (This information is drawn mostly from the biographical appendix to Samuel P. Putnam, *Four Hundred Years of Freethought* [New York, 1894].) I leave the interpretation of these data to the reader's imagination, only cautioning against making too much of an exceedingly unscientific sample. Indeed, it was the difficulties of, first, defining a reliably representative sample of unbelievers and, second, obtaining a sufficient range of biographical information that dissuaded me from attempting a systematic survey of individual unbelievers.

Index

1. Have you ever personally asked Jesus to forgive you of your sins?

1. You ask, He responds.

3. Every day, pray, read scripture, and find Him working in daily situations.

4. Little by little you grow closer to the One who knew you before you were born.